Sun, Sex, and Gold

Sun, Sex, and Gold

Tourism and Sex Work in the Caribbean

edited by
Kamala Kempadoo

ROWMAN & LITTLEFIELD PUBLISHERS, INC.
Lanham • *Boulder* • *New York* • *Oxford*

ROWMAN & LITTLEFIELD PUBLISHERS, INC.

Published in the United States of America
by Rowman & Littlefield Publishers, Inc.
A wholly owned subsidary of The Rowman & Littlefield Publishing Group, Inc.
4501 Forbes Boulevard, Suite 200, Lanham, Maryland 20706
www.rowmanlittlefield.com

PO Box 317
Oxford
OX2 9RU, UK

British Library Cataloguing in Publication Information Available

Library of Congress Cataloging-in-Publication Data
Sun, sex, and gold : tourism and sex work in the Caribbean / edited by
  Kamala Kempadoo.
    p.   cm.
  Includes bibliographical references and index.
  ISBN 0-8476-9516-6 (alk. paper). — ISBN 0-8476-9517-4 (pbk. :
alk. paper)
  1. Sex tourism—Caribbean Area. I. Kempadoo, Kamala.
HQ160.A5S86 1999
306.74'09729—dc21   99-15378
                                                            CIP

ISBN 0-8476-9516-6 (alk. paper). — ISBN 0-8476-9517-4 (pbk. : alk. paper)

♾™ The paper used in this publication meets the minimum requirements of
American National Standard for Information Sciences—Permanence of Paper for
Printed Library Materials, ANSI Z39.48–1984.

Contents

Acknowledgments

Sex workers throughout the Caribbean who shared their life stories, histories, and their time are at the center of this book but unfortunately must remain anonymous. My heartfelt thanks to all. There are also many other people whose contributions were invaluable. Most important are Cynthia Mellon and Jacquie Burgess, who worked with me to coordinate the "Sex Trade in the Caribbean" project on which this book is based and who, over the project's three years, became dear sister-friends. Cynthia started with me as editor of this volume and gave feedback and assistance in the early stages of the manuscript, and her spirit and energy remained important to me during the final stage of completing this volume. Jacquie, based at CAFRA in Trinidad, was forever giving encouragement, blessings, and continual optimism, as well as sound, practical advice. I could not have wished for more responsive or caring colleagues. And while e-mail, phone, and fax were our common modes of communication, my warmest memories are of our meetings in Colombia, Trinidad, Jamaica, and Colorado, when we brainstormed, agonized, and laughed together, in our attempts to keep the project and the rest of our lives on track.

I am also grateful to Gladys Acosta Vargas and Elena Díaz for helping to conceptualize and give shape to the sex trade project. Without the first meetings and discussions we held in 1995–96 to frame the research project and to define our common interests, this book would never have materialized. Recognition must also go to the researchers for their part in the project and to the book's other contributors, all of whom were so very cooperative and patient. I only hope that the richness of their work has not been too diluted through the editing process and that their involvement in sex work studies does not end with this book.

I would also like to acknowledge a number of people who participated and contributed in different ways to the project and ultimately to this book: Yamila Azize Vargas, Puerto Rico; Francisca Ferreira and Ana Jiménez of COIN and Martha Guzmán of MODEMU, the Dominican Republic; Dusilley

Cannings, Guyana; Michelle de la Rosa of Kamaria, Puerto Rico; and Sulma Manco and Lina Franca of Cormujer, Colombia. Many thanks also to the Center for Gender and Development Studies at the University of the West Indies at Mona, Jamaica, especially to Pat Mohammed and Imani Tafari-Ama for hosting the conference at which the research results were presented.

I am very appreciative of the support given to the project coordinating team by the Women's Studies Program at the University of Colorado at Boulder, the Instituto Latinoamericano de Servicios Legales Alternativos (ILSA), and the Caribbean Association for Feminist Research and Action (CAFRA). In particular, many thanks to Nelcia Robinson and the staff at the CAFRA secretariat for their administrative input and skills. At ILSA, thanks to Ruthy de Moncayo for all her work, and to Hector Leon Moncayo and Debra Evanson for their unwavering support of the project. At the University of Colorado, Karen Lozano and Ranya Ghuma, with support from the Undergraduate Research Opportunity Program (UROP) program, assisted with research and bibliographic work. Tracee DeAntoni and Laura de Luca provided very welcome editorial assistance on the manuscript, and Anna Vayr graciously gave administrative help.

Neither the research project nor this book would have been possible without the sponsorship and kind support of the Women in Development Division of the Dutch Government, the United Nations Development Fund for Women (UNIFEM), the Mama Cash Foundation, the Tides Foundation, Interpares Foundation and the Project Counseling Service for Latin American Refugees, the Council for Research and Creative Work at the University of Colorado, and the Funding Exchange. The Dutch Embassy in Suriname and the Center for Gender and Development Studies at the University of the West Indies, Mona, Jamaica, also financially contributed to the project conference.

Many thanks to my editor, Jill Rothenberg, at Rowman and Littlefield, who, from the outset, was wonderfully in tune with the history of the project and my ideas for this book. Working together with her was a joy. Last, but not least, thanks to David Barsamian, my dearest friend and staunchest supporter.

The Caribbean Region

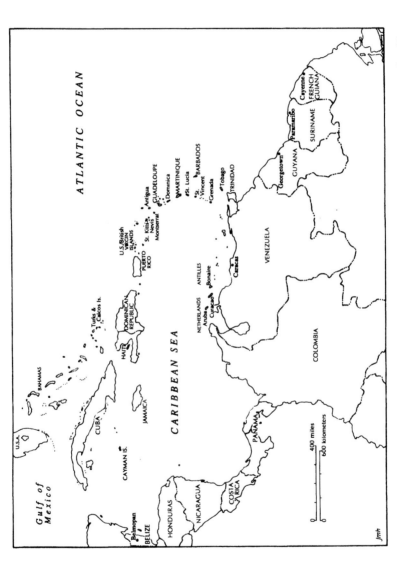

Reprinted with permission from *Globalization and Neoliberalism: The Caribbean Context*, edited by Thomas Klak. Lanham, M.D.: Rowman and Littlefield Publishers, 1998.

Part 1

Introduction

Continuities and Change

Five Centuries of Prostitution in the Caribbean

KAMALA KEMPADOO

The national bourgeoisie organizes centers of rest and relaxation and pleasure resorts to meet the wishes of the Western bourgeoisie. Such activity is given the name of tourism, and for the occasion will be built up as a national industry.... The casinos of Havana and of Mexico, the beaches of Rio, the little Brazilian and Mexican girls, the half-breed thirteen-year-olds, the ports of Acapulco and Copacabana—all these are the stigma of this depravation of the national middle class.... [This class] will have nothing better to do than to take on the role of manager of Western enterprise, and it will in practice set up its country as the brothel of Europe.

Frantz Fanon—*Wretched of the Earth*, 1961

In the early 1990s, reports of a new form of prostitution in Cuba began to appear in the U.S. media (McClintock 1992, Howell 1992, Passell 1993). Young women were shown to be selling sex to tourists in a style hitherto unknown in the country. This "new" phenomenon was attributed to the influx of large numbers of visitors, the position of Cuba as part of the exotic Third World in the Western imagination, and economic hardships in the country due to the continued trade embargo from the United States and collapse of the Soviet Union (Cooper 1995, Strout 1995, Diaz 1995). Within Cuba, it was also considered in the women's movement as an affront to society—as asocial behavior of deviant young women and men—given that Cuba was believed to have effectively eradicated organized prostitution along with the pre-revolutionary material conditions upon which it rested.[1]

This new form of prostitution in Cuba was, however, not completely novel to the wider Caribbean and, according to Frantz Fanon, was predictable in the context of international capitalism and the region's position in relationship to the industrialized, "developed" world. Reports from other islands such as Barbados and Jamaica had already signaled the emergence of similar situations around tourist resorts. Young men and women were being noted for liaisons with foreign tourists that involved sexual relations in exchange for money, luxury items, and clothes, or a ticket off the island (Matthews 1978, Press 1978, Karch and Dann 1981, Pruitt 1993).

It was also in the early 1990s that several feminist Caribbeanists began to articulate concern about the rapidity and ease with which this new form of prostitution (by then known in Southeast Asia as "sex tourism") was becoming embedded in Caribbean societies (Bolles 1992, Kempadoo 1994, Carty 1994). We realized that this new development was not isolated from a sex trade that had existed in the region for several centuries or from international racialized and gendered divisions of labor and power and a globalizing capitalist economy. In 1995 a small group of us initiated a research project to document the contemporary Caribbean sex trade.[2] Our broader aims were to encourage Caribbean feminist analyses of prostitution and to stimulate attention about the subject from the region's policy makers and activists. We hoped, in the process, to promote research that would be sensitive to the humanity of those who made a living selling sex, not pathologize or condemn working women and men for taking up prostitution, but critically examine the sex trade while cultivating respect for the actors involved.

This book includes results from both the project as well as other recent feminist-inspired analyses on prostitution in the Caribbean. We do not claim to examine here all facets of Caribbean sex work.[3] Nevertheless, central components in the organization of sexual labor in the region are identified, and parallels and similarities with other situations in the region can easily be drawn from the case studies that are presented in the following chapters. We also hope that the studies included in this book will not only provide new insights but also give rise to more of such research. Caribbean sex work, despite our efforts, remains an understudied subject and needs far more exploration and analysis.

In this chapter I provide a broader context for understanding contemporary studies of sex work in the Caribbean. I review the literature that has discussed sex work, in particular prostitution, in Caribbean history from the sixteenth century onwards. Even though it remains clear that much is still unknown about this history, the literature available to us sketches a persistent pattern about the significance not just of economic and gendered relations, but also of nationalist and racialized concerns in the formation and transformation of prostitution relations under slavery and colonialism. During the earlier part of the twentieth century the role of the colonial and postcolonial state took on greater importance in the control and regulation of prostitution, and by the late twentieth century, Caribbean sex work was well integrated into the global economy. This overview allows us to capture the complexity of the meanings and representations of sex work around the region and to detect where some of the contradictions, ambiguities, continuities and changes have occurred in Caribbean sex work.

PROSTITUTION, SLAVERY, AND EMANCIPATION

To date, no single study has been devoted to the social organization of sexual labor in Caribbean history. Nevertheless, references to sex work in studies on slavery in the region suggest that it was an integral part of the region's history (Henriques 1965, Beckles 1989, Morrissey 1989, Bush 1990, Kerr 1995, Moitt 1996, Geggus 1996). The predominant instances of sexual labor[4] that are documented are wet nursing, slave breeding, and prostitution, yet it is the latter set of arrangements—prostitution—that is of most interest to us and shall be discussed here, for it is this activity that resonates in today's societies.

Prostitution in the Caribbean is inextricably tied to the power and control exerted by European colonizers over black women since the sixteenth century. Beckles points out that slavery meant "not only the compulsory extraction of labor from the blacks but also, in theory at least, slave owners' right to total sexual access to slaves" (1989:141). White slave owners made ample use of this "right": rape and sexual abuse were commonplace, and concubinage and prostitution quickly became an institutional part of Caribbean societies.[5] "In time," writes Henriques, "no European male in the Caribbean, who could afford it, was without his colored mistress, either a freedwoman or slave" (1965: 195). Bush, Morrissey, and Henriques also point out that this power was not only exerted by the colonial elite and planter class but extended to include white men of lower classes due to the racial hegemony of white over black. Even the European bond-servant, who stood at the margins of white society in an almost comparable position to that of slave, was seen to have "augmented the process of their masters" due to the privilege that their whiteness conferred upon them, engaging in clandestine sexual affairs with slave women (Henriques 1965:201).

Assertions of this form of racialized, colonial masculine power rested in part on the ideological constructions of black slave women in the Caribbean as sexually promiscuous and immoral and on notions that they were by nature "hot constitution'd" and sensuous in an animal-like way, lacking all the qualities that defined "decent" womanhood or women of "purity of blood" (Morrissey 1989, Bush 1990, Kutzinski 1993, Reddock 1994). Henriques concludes that the planters "became adept at attributing their own promiscuity to the inherent licentiousness of the Negro," particularly stressing the "de-bauchery" of slave women (1965:195). One of the dominant images that emerges from slavery about the black woman in the Caribbean was of her as an "inferior subspecies of the female sex" (Bush 1990:15). The region came to be represented "as a land of sexual opportunity for young European males," and black women—enslaved or free—defined as the sexual prop-erty of white men (Morrissey 1989:147).

Patterns of power and dominance that configured prostitution in the Caribbean were centrally predicated upon racialized relationships, which, as can be seen in several chapters in this book, continue to be relevant in con-temporary forms of sex work in the region. The racialized dimensions of prostitution under slavery were not homogenous, however. Studies indicate that despite the generalized image of the promiscuous and sensuous black woman, the category of women "of mixed race"—the "mulatto," "mustee," or "colored" woman—was considered particularly exotic and sexually de-sirable by white men (Henriques 1965, Beckles 1989, Bush 1990). This so-cial category, which itself arose from the exercise of power over black slave women, was, however, legally and ideologically placed outside of white so-ciety, representing to Europeans racial impurity and moral, racial, and social degradation, constituting an "unnatural transgression of the rules of social propriety" (Kutzinski 1993:75). The mulatto woman (*la mulata*) thus came to be represented as erotic and sexually desirable yet was outcast and pathologized and defined as economically attractive for a slave master. The mulatto woman emerged thus during slavery as the symbol of the prosti-tute—the sexually available, socially despised, yet economically profitable body.

Within the context of slavery, prostitution was lodged at the nexus of at least two areas of women's existence: as an extension of sexual relations (forced or otherwise) with white men and of labor relations for both slave and "free colored" women. Beckles notes that slave women in Barbadian society of the early 1800s were frequently hired out by white and free col-ored families as "nannies, nurses, cooks, washerwomen, hucksters, seam-stresses," yet "the general expectation of individuals who hired female labor under whatever pretense was that sexual benefits were included" (1989:143). Concubines often served as both mistresses and housekeepers and were sometimes hired out by their owners to sexually service other men "as a convenient way of obtaining cash" (Beckles 1989:142). Further-more, in times of economic slumps on the plantations, when slaves, both men and women, were expected to provide for themselves or to bring in wages through work outside the plantation, "the number of slave women placed on the urban market as prostitutes by sugar planters would rapidly increase" and in the towns, "masters and mistresses would frequently send out female slaves as prostitutes for ships' crew" (Beckles 1989:142–143).

Reddock reports that in Trinidad "for the most part women were hired out as domestic slaves, field labourers, as concubines, to temporary male European settlers, or were made to work as petty traders or prostitutes handing over most of their earning to their masters" (1994:20). The women's manual and sexual labor was, in effect, "pimped" by the slaveholders. Geggus (1996) remarks upon the numerous cases mentioned in historical records of slave women in the French Caribbean who, besides marketing activities, were able to profit financially from selling their own or their daughters' sexual labor. Morrissey (1989) concludes that in the early nineteenth century in the British Caribbean, domestics who worked in taverns and inns in the towns also served as prostitutes. In his study of women's economic roles in nineteenth-century San Juan in Puerto Rico, Matos-Rodriguez implies that here too women's sexual labor as prostitutes or mistresses was a part of women's work as laundresses, nurses, midwives and nannies (1995:189).

Another dimension of this intersection between sex and work lay in the reproductive role that black and mulatto women were given under slavery. Rape, concubinage, and prostitution often produced children, yet in the absence of marriage and formal recognition of the child by the white father, the child followed the condition of the mother and was defined as either part of the slave population or the free colored class. Sex during slavery thus was a way in which the laboring classes and slaves were reproduced. Abraham-van der Marks points out that "concubinage gave them [Jewish men in nineteenth-century Curaçao] the benefits of a category of children which, if necessary, provided labour but could not make any legal demands and were excluded from inheritance" (1993:46). Moreover, mulattos were more highly valued in slave markets, thus a child of black slave women and white slave owners could bring in a higher income than a child of black slave parents. Beckles argues that in this respect, the prostitute was particularly valuable to the slave owner for "unlike other female slaves, she could generate three income flows: from labor, prostitution and reproduction" (1989:144).

Relations of power under slavery were not however monolithic or total, and female sexuality, besides being a basis for domination, also constituted a site for reconfigurations of power. Mulatto women sometimes made strategic use of their exoticized status through self-employment of their sexual labor.

> For the female slave to refuse the advances of her owner or his assistants led either to rape or to banishment to the rigours of work in the fields. There was, on the other hand, everything to be gained by becoming the mistress of a white man. Prestige among her fellows, preferential treatment for herself and the possibility that she might in time obtain freedom for herself and her children, were all possible goals (Henriques 1965:193).

That manumission rates for women around the region generally outnum-
bered that of men, with women of mixed descent outnumbering black
women, has led the aforementioned historians to conclude that this pattern
indicates that sexual relations with white men played a favorable role in the
process of acquiring freedom from slavery. "Sexual alliances," writes Beckles, "were one of the few devices that slave women could employ to achieve
their freedom" (1989:149). Sex was commonly used as a strategy by women
to acquire freedom from oppression, sold for money in order to purchase
their own or their children's freedom, or provided to a slave master in exchange for manumission. As Casteneda observes on the situation in Cuba,
while many domestic tasks enabled slave women to acquire their freedom,
this "could also be obtained though ordinary sexual life with a white man"
(1995:144). Studies of women's lives in towns and cities during slavery also
indicate that through sexual relations with white men, some women were
able to build up enough capital to purchase their own inns and lodging
houses and to establish independent businesses (Kerr 1995). Exoticism,
while constituting a form of control and domination over women of color,
was thus also strategically transformed through sex work to economically
and socially empower women, men, and children.

There were, however, other ways in which sexual labor was a source of
empowerment. Moitt, citing a French soldier in Saint Domingue (former
Haiti) in the 1790s, writes that there was a "particular type of prostitution associated with slave girls and women. They entered soldiers' camps shame-
lessly and exchanged sexual favours for bullets and gunpowder" (1996:245).
The weapons were intended to support slave revolts, to break the crushing
bonds of slavery for both women and men. Sexual labor in this context had
direct political implications for the entire slave community. Under conditions of slavery then, prostitution was simultaneously an enforced condition
and a way to overcome enslavement. Bush remarks that "by outwardly con-
forming to the sexual demands of the white man, [the slave woman] could
exploit the situation to the fullest and thus covertly help her own family and
kin" (1990:116). By extension, sex work by black women contributed to the
economic, social, and political well-being and survival of their communities.

This last aspect of prostitution under slavery in the Caribbean, as part of a
strategy for liberation and as a way in which relations of power were sub-
verted and reconstituted, deserves far more attention than it has received in
historical accounts of slave women's lives or in definitions of prostitution,
for it disrupts notions of prostitution as simply a relationship based on an exchange of sex and money or as a source of oppression for women.
Caribbean history suggests that sexual labor was also performed as an act of
resistance to oppressive and dehumanizing conditions of slavery, providing
women with the possibility of obtaining freedom for themselves, children,
and men from a racist institution. This specific characteristic of sex work in

Caribbean history allows us to ponder the possibility of defining Caribbean prostitution not only as a form of masculine oppression and exploitation or as a category of "naturalized" women's work that is employed as a survival strategy in time of economic hardship but also as a strategy of resistance to racialized relations of power and dominance.

The period immediately following slavery has been characterized as a time when women established autonomy of work from the plantations and where gendered relations were transformed under changing relations of production. Waged labor for women took on greater importance, with European middle-class patriarchal family ideologies gaining primacy, yet many areas of "women's work" that were established under slavery continued. Domestic service, marketing, and prostitution continued to be defined as black and "colored" women's activities. Henriques also notes that "emancipation did not fundamentally alter the patterns of sexuality which had been established under slavery. Women might no longer be bound to masters but the 'white bias' in the society still facilitated illicit sexual relations between white and coloured" (1965:203). The trend for example, that was established for the early nineteenth century in Jamaica, in which women used their sexual relations with white men to finance the purchase of a lodging house that in turn became the women's main source of livelihood, thus continued (Kerr 1995). Sex work also appears as an extension of the strategy to obtain freedom from control and domination by white men. Kerr concludes that the female lodging housekeepers in Jamaica "turned their weaknesses into strength by exploiting the white men's need for them. Their lodging houses became places 'flocked to' mainly by white males who sought them for sexual favors and more. They diversified their services so that they not only increased their incomes but eventually became women of importance" (1995:210). However, this was also a period in which prostitution by poor women in Jamaica is said to have increased, particularly in the urban areas. Henriques explains the increase in prostitution as flowing from the new economic pressures in a post-emancipation context, which pushed many ex-slaves into poverty (1965:204). Kerr also remarks on the predominance of black women in brothels. In this era in Jamaica, however, the significance of racialized hierarchies within the sex trade, the new constraints and possibilities for women in the labor markets, and the changes in demand for sex work remain unexplored.

We have no knowledge of whether European colonization of the Caribbean, the plantation system, or slavery were the beginning points for prostitution in the region, given that no studies exist on sexual labor and sexual relations among the populations that inhabited the islands in pre-Columbian eras. Henriques maintains that prostitution had origins in continents other than the Americas, influenced in particular by European, sometimes Catholic, traditions. Roberston (1996) suggests that patterns of sexual relations in the colonies, particularly premarital sexual arrangements, were also influenced by African cultural traditions. This matter is not resolved here, leaving the question of the social origins and causes of Caribbean prostitution open for future debates and research. What this reading of sex work during slavery does enable, however, is a glimpse of some of the patterns and relations of dominance and resistance that shaped prostitution in the region and that provide the historical backdrop for sex work in later centuries.

STATE CONTROL AND REGULATION

The emergence in Europe in the mid-nineteenth century of social studies, in conjunction with an increasingly rationalized medical science and a burgeoning middle-class morality, produced assumptions about the socially "evil" and "diseased" nature of prostitution, with special emphasis on the "inherent" promiscuous, immoral, and unclean character of working-class women and non-white peoples who did not, or refused to, adhere to European bourgeois family norms and ideals (Walkowitz 1980, Gibson 1986, Corbin 1986). During the following 100 years, governments were spurred to introduce measures to address this "social disease." Around the world, laws, regulations, hygiene policies, and special red-light districts were designed to control and contain prostitution.[6] The efforts were grounded in a persistent masculinist definition of the problem: that nonmarital sexual relations corrupted womanhood and turned women into "loose" and degraded beings, yet was essential for the healthy development of manhood. Through the colonial state, Caribbean countries were implicated in these dominant assumptions about prostitution and in the international attempts to contain it.

Findlay's 1997 study of the politics of prostitution in Ponce, Puerto Rico, during the 1890s shows that regulations were put in place by the local authorities to "curb" prostitution due to fears and anxieties around "unnerving social change" that was sweeping the country. Prostitutes, defined in the common imagination as *mulatas* and signified by working-class women of Afro-Puerto Rican descent, were the trope for all that disrupted emerging nationalist notions of decency and morality and hence were subjected to intense regulations. In 1894, concerns to contain unruly working-class women converged with a public-hygiene movement that identified prostitutes as the root cause for the wide spread of venereal disease in the country, producing a regulation campaign which continued until 1900. The regulations required suspected prostitutes to "register on an official list, pay a 'hygiene tax,' and submit to biweekly pelvic exams by designated hygiene physicians" (479). Prostitutes were relocated to designated prostitution zones and a special police task force was created to track down and control the women. Findlay argues that the campaign served to consolidate the category of prostitute in Ponce, through forcing "many women who had earned their living from a variety of sources, such as washing, sewing, cleaning houses, as well as the occasional sexual encounter, into a much more rigid, full-time occupation and identity" as well as heightening the stigmatization of working-class women's sexuality (1997:482). Findlay's study clearly signals the importance and relevance of the local governmental and political entities in the regulation, control, and definition of sex work. She also vividly illustrates ways in which the prostitute body became a site around which nationalist and feminist struggles were framed, as well as a basis for working-class Afro-Caribbean women to contest ruling-class hegemony.

The complexities, anxieties, and ambiguities that sex work produced in Caribbean societies, and the ways in which colonial governments sought to manage prostitution during the late nineteenth and first half of the twentieth century, are also evident elsewhere. In Jamaica, for example, during the 1930s, brothels in Montego Bay and Kingston became the focus of attention for the British Social Hygiene Council, which determined that they were hazardous to public health as concentrated sites of infection (namely syphilis and gonorrhea) and places that facilitated the trafficking of women to Central and South America (Henriques 1965). Efforts were made to stamp out the "sources" of disease and social disruption.

In the Dutch Caribbean, the founding of oil refineries in Aruba and Curaçao during the 1920s brought with it the need for a substantial labor force. Unskilled and semi-skilled male labor was recruited from primarily English-speaking Caribbean islands, and technicians were brought in from the Netherlands and the United States. Women migrated independently or were deliberately recruited to service the rapidly growing populations, particularly as domestics and nurses (Aymer 1997), continuing female labor traditions that had been established in earlier centuries. The presence of an oil industry also meant a steady stream of tankers and ships that unloaded crew members on the islands. The large single male population on the islands was quickly deemed by the local governments as a threat to the local female population and to the general morality and health of the islands. Rape and prostitution, the consequence of what at the time was considered to be the result of the natural male sexual instinct and need, were identified as social evils and the spread of venereal disease defined as a product of this situation. The problems were seen to be exacerbated in Curaçao with the arrival of Dutch and U.S. navies stationed on the island during the 1940s to protect the oil industry for the allies. In response to a situation where prostitution was being practised widely, including in the "open air," local governments in both Curaçao and Aruba adopted regulations to cater to male sexual demands, to protect local womanhood and to curb the spread of sexually transmitted diseases (Martin 1978, Kempadoo 1994).[7] Police and the government

health departments were given the authority to control and regulate prostitution, and local women were banned from working in regulated areas of
the sex industries. In 1949, the Curaçaoan colonial government opened a
central brothel—Campo Alegre—to contain prostitution even further, allowing only foreign sex workers to enter and work in the compound.[8] All sex
workers on the island were required to register with the police and government health department and to carry a certificate of good health (the "pink
card"). On Aruba during the 1950s, foreign women, from such countries as
Colombia, Venezuela, Cuba, Panama, and the Dominican Republic, were
legally permitted to work under the title "night-club hostesses" in bars and
hotels in and around the oil-refining town of St. Nicholaas (Martin 1978,
"Prostitutie op Aruba" 1978, Kalm 1985). The Aruban government was prevented from establishing a state-run brothel as in its sister-island Curaçao,
due to widespread protest among members of the Catholic Church and middle-class women's organizations (Kempadoo 1994). The local governments
in the Dutch Antilles have, however, continued to regulate sex work in their
pursuit to keep the nation "undiseased" and their womanhood "chaste" and
"pure."

Prostitution in Cuba during the twentieth century also indicates a level of
state intervention and control. While its history is still underdocumented, del
Omo (1979) notes that in the 1920s, efforts by the Minister of the Interior
were made to "solve the problem of prostitution" in the country, suggesting
that at that point in history, it was considered a flourishing business and of
concern to the state. The 1950s are also recognized as a time when the
Cuban government developed the island as a haven to which many U.S.
gamblers and gangsters flocked and where prostitution was integral to the
entertainment and tourism industries. Tourism had become the state's second largest earner of foreign currency, with around 350,000 visitors per year
in the late 1950s (Espino 1994). Richardson observes that "an estimated 270
brothels housed prostitutes, some as young as 12," with a concentration of
brothels and bars in the capital "that catered to Americans visiting Havana
on week-end excursions" (1992:91). By that time "Havana had captured its
share of North Americans who were looking for relaxation, intoxication, excitement, or thrills. Cuba's tourist industry had fashioned the image of a Latin
isle of unfettered pleasure that catered to North American tastes" and to
some tourists Cuba simply spelled "S-E-X" (Schwartz 1997:86–87, 122). Del
Omo's analysis of the four main categories of prostitutes in pre-revolutionary Cuba—"high-class" sex workers, women who worked in "appointment
houses," "mercenary women," and "prostitutes of the harvest" who worked
at the U.S. military base at Guantánamo—indicates that while some women
worked independently and were able to prosper economically, many others
were trapped in highly exploitative and oppressive conditions and worked
under the surveillance of a third party. The sex industry in 1950s Cuba rested

fundamentally upon the provision of sexual labor by black and mulatto women to predominantly white North American men, reinforcing older patterns of exoticism. Kutzinski (1993) and Schwartz (1997) both point out, however, that the exoticization of Cuban *mulatas* was not exclusive to relationships between foreign men and Cuban women but rather that male Cuban writers, artists, and poets had "enshrined the erotic image of Cuba's *mulatas*" long before the advent of tourism (Schwartz 86).

The Cuban revolution brought profound changes to prostitution—from being an activity supported by the state to one that was condemned and was to be completely eradicated (Díaz et al. 1996). The first steps taken by the new government were to conduct a census of the prostitutes and pimps and then to establish medical clinics for special health examinations, rehabilitation programs for "pimps," and reeducation programs for former sex workers (del Omo 1979). In 1961, the census counted 150,000 working women and 3,000 pimps, yet within two years the majority of both prostitutes and pimps were considered rehabilitated (del Omo 1979:36). Organized crime, including prostitution managed by third parties or pimps, was claimed by the government to have been successfully eradicated in the new society. Nevertheless, del Omo concludes that in the 1970s prostitution was not completely absent in Cuban society. Women, she states, were independently cruising the hotels of Havana, offering sex "in exchange for a pair of 'blue jeans'" (1979:38). It is this type of sex work, further accelerated by the government's promotion of tourism and generated by a tourist demand for young "exotic" bodies, in which young women and men individually and independent of a third party provide sex to acquire cash for themselves and family or to leave the country, that characterizes Cuban sex work in the latter part of the twentieth century.

NEW CONCERNS AND ISSUES IN THE LATE TWENTIETH CENTURY

Sex Tourism

Across the region, sex tourism or tourism-oriented prostitution has become an increasingly important topic of research and discussion due to the growing reliance of national governments on income generated by tourism and tourism-related activities. It was first the focus of a study in Barbados in the late 1970s. Contrary to older notions of prostitution, this study signaled men as "hustlers"—"men who receive material compensation for the social and sexual services they render to women" (Press 1978:112). Young black men combed the beaches around tourist resorts, offering companionship to visiting white female tourists for sightseeing, to participate in a water sports activity, or to enjoy the night entertainment spots. Sex was invariably involved, and the woman expected to provide some monetary or other benefits to the young man. A trip abroad was sometimes in the offing. Press established this activity as an extension of informal and formal sector activities that young Barbadian men were engaged in as a strategy to escape from low-paying and demeaning occupations and as a form of resistance to the existing social, economic, racial, and sexual order (115). Karch and Dann (1981) elaborated on these insights among "beach boys" in Barbados, drawing attention to the negotiations that took place between black Barbadian men and white women around their sexual, gendered, and racialized identities as well as the way in which the relationships were shaped by the location of Barbados as a Third World nation locked into dependency within the global economy.

Jamaica, Cuba, and the Dominican Republic have also been sites for research on tourism-related prostitution (Pruitt 1994, Pruitt and La Font 1995, Strout 1995, Fusco 1996, O'Connell Davidson 1996, Diaz et al. 1996, Brennan 1998, Cabezas 1998, de Alberquerque 1999). Within this new body of literature, heterosexual male sex work has remained an important focus as it is only in the tourism sector that it appears so prominently. Pruitt and LaFont (1994), for example, introduced the concept "romance tourism" to capture this particular form of sex work and to distinguish it from other prostitution relations. Characteristic also of sex work related to the tourism industry is the centrality of racialized fantasies and desires among the clients and the autonomy of the individual sex worker. While a wide range of arrangements exist between the tourist and sex worker, particularly noticeable are the longer term relationships that are established. These last in many instances for the period of stay of the tourist, sometimes extending into a situation where the tourist sustains the relationship through gifts, a ticket, and money after returning home, occasionally resulting in marriage. Sex tours—tours arranged by a travel agency or tour operator that deliberately promotes sex as part of the vacation package and may organize visits for the tourists to specific hotels, brothels, or nightclubs—have not surfaced in the Caribbean landscape. Instead, beaches, bars, casinos, and nightclubs within tourist hotels function as locations where tourists individually meet sex workers. Many of the studies in this book build upon these insights and analyses.

Trafficking and Migration

The rapid increase in numbers of sex workers from Third World countries in red-light districts in Western European countries since the mid-1980s is also a topic that has gained increasing attention. Cases where women—from the Dominican Republic and Colombia but also from the Philippines and Thailand—were clandestinely smuggled into Western European countries and forced to sell sex, or situations where women were provided with a visa as "dancer" yet ended up working in brothels, began to be exposed in Europe (van Ammelrooy 1989, Brussa 1989). What formerly was known as "white slavery"—the entrapment of women and coercion into prostitution by organized gangs of men—was taken up as a feminist issue under the rubric "the trafficking of women" and "sexual slavery" (Barry 1984). This topic was first addressed in the Caribbean at a regional conference held in Bonaire in 1978. However, it was the high numbers of Dominican women in the international traffic that commanded most attention, and Calvacanti et al. (1986), spurred by radical feminist analyses of prostitution, produced a first study on sexual slavery in the Dominican Republic. The authors estimated that around 25,000 women worked in the national sex industry in bars, cabarets, and brothels (see also Imbert Brugal 1991). By 1996, estimates of around 50,000 women working locally, for both tourists and Dominican men, and approximately another 50,000 working in prostitution abroad were being cited, with poverty and trafficking pinpointed as major causes for the high number of women in the international sex industries (Ferreira 1996, IOM 1996). While these figures have not been updated, the trafficking of women has continued to be a focus, particularly among women's organization and non-governmental organizations (NGOs) concerned with sexual exploitation and violence against women. In 1996 it was the subject of a region-wide research project that was part of a larger UN-sponsored initiative to document the trafficking of women and girls for prostitution, domestic work, and marriage. Research in the Caribbean identified multiple trafficking routes within the region and internationally for purposes of prostitution and domestic work, establishing that the most common forms of trafficking involved situations of indentureship. Women were contracted as workers, prostitutes, dancers, or domestics through an agent in their home country and assisted with travel to another country or region, ending up in a situation where they would have to pay off large debts for travel expenses and travel documents. Many women, it was established, were aware that they were migrating for sex work abroad but were unprepared for the slavery-like conditions that awaited them (Centro de Orientación e Investigación Integral 1994, Azize Vargas and Kempadoo 1996, Wijers and Lap-Chew 1997).

Also, as has been found elsewhere in the world, laws that criminalize sex work and the stigmas that exist around prostitution are often the cause for women to migrate and move from their own communities and homes to work elsewhere (Kane 1993, Igbinovia n.d.). The "whore stigma" (Pheterson 1996) and sense of shame forces many to practice their trade away from home—so too in the Caribbean region. This however is not a sole factor for the migration. Economic displacement—through wars and civil unrest, such as in Colombia and Suriname—the lure of payment in gold or the prospect of making a large sum of money in a relatively short period of time, a complete lack of employment possibilities in their home town or village, and abuse in the family or work setting are all cited as major factors behind the sex worker's migration. In addition to these "push" factors, we cannot overlook migratory traditions in the Caribbean. Interregional labor migrations—for example, to Panama for the building of the canal, to Curaçao and Aruba for oil refinery work, from Haiti to the Dominican Republic for work on sugar cane plantations—are well known patterns for men. Women have been documented in migrations for domestic work or as nannies and cooks to Aruba, Puerto Rico, and Cuba since the beginning of the twentieth century (Aymer 1997, Anguiera 1997, Allen 1992). More recently, informal commercial trading and "suitcase trading," where goods are bought in tax-free zones and sold elsewhere by predominantly women, are a common feature of the movements throughout the region, seen as an extension of "huckstering or "higglering" that developed around the plantations during slavery (Lagro and Plotkin 1990, Witter 1989). Freeman (1997) discusses the intersection between this new form of huckstering and pink collar work in information-processing plants in Barbados, showing the pervasive interlocking of the informal and formal sectors in the region, as well as the continued drive by Caribbean women to invent new sources of livelihood to supplement wages in jobs that pay too little. Contemporary migrations for sex work are also considered in this tradition, and trafficking and migrating practises continue to be investigated in the context of sex work and prostitution, as several of these studies in this volume illustrate.

STDs and AIDS

In the 1990s sexually transmitted diseases (STDs) once again drew attention and concern due to the HIV/AIDS epidemic, prompting several studies among the "vectors" of the disease. Prostitutes were identified as an important group. Studies were carried out, most often under the auspices of governmental health departments or the Pan American Health Organization (PAHO) in various countries, including Suriname (Terborg 1990a, 1990b, O'Carroll et al. 1994), Belize (Kane 1993, 1998), the Dominican Republic (Centro de Orientación e Investigación Integral 1994, De Moya and Garcia 1996), Curaçao (Alberts 1992), Jamaica (Ministry of Health 1996), Puerto Rico (Alegría et al. 1994a, 1994b) and Guyana (Carter 1993, Cannings and Rosenzweig 1997). Many of the studies indicate that the transmission is overwhelmingly heterosexual, with sex workers forming an integral part of complex "sexual networks" and subject to high levels of infection. Kane, however, makes a distinction based on the level of "professionalism" and self-identification among sex workers regarding the potential spread of HIV and AIDS. She claims that unsafe sex practices and consequently transmission rates are likely to be lower among women and men who recognize the professional nature of their sex work than among those engaged in "quasi" prostitution—the exchange of sex for money that "is mediated by the provisional construction of a love/friendship relation" (1993:973). This possibility, she points out, "reverses the historical and morally skewed image of prostitutes as vectors of infection" (975) and places the responsibility for spread and control of HIV and AIDS on the shoulders of the entire society.

Sex Worker Agency

The issue of female agency is one that has been taken up more recently in an attempt to theorize the contradictions and ambiguities embedded in Caribbean prostitution. In a study in Curaçao in the early 1990s, I argued that within the context of masculinist state control over the sex industry and the exoticization of Caribbean female sexual labor, many women appeared to independently organize travel to the island for sex work. Even in situations where they became indebted or indentured to a "recruiter" for the costs of traveling to Curaçao, the majority who ended up in the central brothel, Campo Alegre, were aware that they would be working as prostitutes. In this period, approximately 500 women, predominantly from the Dominican Republic and Colombia, were moving to Curaçao each year to work in the state-regulated brothel. The situation revealed a complex relationship of coercion and female autonomy, with sex work usually just one way that women "made do," in their efforts to feed, house, clothe and educate their families (Kempadoo 1994, 1996a, 1996b, 1998).

Focusing exclusively on female agency, in the absence of a structural analysis, Paul (1997), in her study of prostitution among women in Barbados, established an "entrepreneurial" spirit and strategy among working women on the island. She argued that many women "picking fares" on the island, both (im)migrants from countries such as Guyana, St. Lucia, Trinidad, Haiti, and the Dominican Republic and Barbadian women, had consciously decided to enter prostitution as a consequence of either domestic or economic troubles, the majority continuing to do so as a way to support their families. While the women defined their activities strictly as "work," Paul suggests that the prostitutes be viewed as "self-employed individuals who decide the location of business, the services to provide, the fees to charge, the hours of service provided per day, and how to avoid work-related risks" (153). Brennan (1998), on the other hand, places female agency in sex work in the tourist resort town of Sosúa as a "strategy for advancement," as a way for women "not just to solve short-term economic problems ... but to change their lives (and their families' lives) in the long term" (16). This strategy, she argues, is perceived by the woman as possible through entering into transnational relationships with foreign men and is undergirded by the location of Sosúa as a space that is represented in global and local imaginations as a place of "endless possibilities" for transgressing borders, yet which also reinforces the women's subordinated national, racialized, gendered and economic positions in global relations.

Sex worker agency in the Caribbean has also been articulated through the organized activities of sex workers themselves. The report on the first sex workers conference in the Dominican Republic, held in 1995, is one of the few publications that presents extensive analyses and testimonies by sex workers themselves, describing poor working conditions, social discrimination against them as working women, corruption of police and government officials in relation to the control of prostitution, and a lack of viable alternatives for making a living (Centro de Orientación e Investigación Integral 1996). Two autonomous sex worker organizations have been established in the region: the Maxi Linder Association in Suriname and the Movimiento de Mujeres Unidas (MODEMU) in the Dominican Republic, both of which demand respect for sex workers' rights and better working conditions and health care (Kempadoo and Doezema 1998).

Child Prostitution

Finally, the most recent topic that has been addressed on a pan-Caribbean basis is that of child prostitution, in part due to global alarm over the increasingly younger age of women and men in sex work. Research has been conducted in the Dominican Republic, Cuba, Colombia, and Guyana, describing conditions of coercion, violence, and abuse for young women and men under the age of eighteen (Silvestre et al. 1994, O'Connell Davidson and Sanchez Taylor 1996, Fundación Renacer 1997, Danns 1998). Poverty and underdevelopment are commonly understood as reasons for the increase of younger women in prostitution, although O'Connell Davidson and Sanchez Taylor also stress the importance of taking into account the role that male fantasies for sex with a "racialized other" play in the structuring of child prostitution in the tourism sector. Chapter 7 takes child prostitution as its primary concern, elaborating upon this earlier work.

SEX WORK AND GLOBALIZATION

At the end of the twentieth century, as in the past, sex work in the Caribbean cannot be viewed in isolation from the global political economy. Even though its status as an illegal or semi-legal sector means that it cannot be measured or tabulated in any quantitative way, sex work appears through the studies in this book as an integral part of the local cultures and national economies, which in turn sustain global corporate capital, First World identities, and masculine hegemony.

The link between the local and global economies for the Caribbean has had several centuries to mature. The history of the region's economy since the sixteenth century is characterized by control first by Western European and later U.S. interests, with a dependency upon foreign trade and global markets (Deere et al. 1990, Klak 1998). Sugar, and to a lesser extent coffee, cocoa, and tobacco, were created as the first staple export products for several centuries, the cultivation of which was financed by foreign firms and made possible by the use of enslaved African and indentured European and Asian labor. Oil refining, bauxite mining, banana production, fishing, and logging had entered the arena by the mid-twentieth century, also largely controlled by outside interests. Assertions of political independence and attempts to diversify the economy or delink from the global economy after the 1950s induced attempts to create economic alternatives that would allow postcolonial states independence from the dominant global economic system. However, since the 1980s with the restructuring of the global economic system, the region has been squeezed by structural adjustment programs[9] enforced by the World Bank and IMF which have heightened poverty and unemployment among working peoples and stimulated a search for new survival strategies at both the community and national levels. Strapped for alternatives, offshore banking, money laundering, drug trafficking, informal commercial trading, information processing, and export manufacturing are some of the activities that national governments have turned to or promoted to bring in foreign exchange to sustain their economies and to service their debts (Maingot 1993, Watson 1994, Safa 1995, Block and Klausner 1987). Since 1989, Cuba has also been pulled into this orbit and is not exempt from the pressures and possibilities that the rest of the region faces. Today the region's economies are dominated by multinationally owned corporations that control the majority of the hotels, airlines, offshore banks, oil and sugar refineries, mining operations, manufacturing and assembly plants, and logging companies that draw upon the labor in the region for the extraction of raw materials as well as the production of specific products. Gender implications of economic restructuring have also been widely noted and analyzed. In view of their attempts to secure a livelihood within the reality of economic hardship, Carmen Deere et al. (1990) notes that during the 1980s four main strategies had been devised by women to cope: they had entered the labor force in larger numbers; they increasingly engaged in a wide variety of activities in the informal sector; households diversified their survival strategies; and women joined and even predominated in international migration. Senior emphasized that Caribbean women's survival strategies were based on multiple "sources of livelihood." Sex, she argued, was just one of the many resources that women relied upon to "make do," concluding that "to feed their children, women will exploit any option including their bodies" (1991:134). In research in a Jamaican urban slum setting, Harrison found among women involved in "multiple and interrelated occupations" in the informal sector, such as barkeeping, ganja trading, and housekeeping, that 5 percent in her sample declared to be also involved as "sportin' gals" or prostitutes (1991:181). There is little to suggest that these strategies have changed in the 1990s but rather much to point to an intensification of this process (Green 1994, Freeman 1997, Safa 1995). Restructuring from agricultural production to export processing, light manufacturing, information processing, and tourism has entailed a search by corporations for labor that is cheap, flexible, undemanding, service-oriented, and dexterous, the qualities ascribed to Caribbean female labor. Concomitantly, restructuring has induced high levels of unemployment and underemployment, and informal sector work that allows women to continue to provide for their households, including sex work, continues to grow.

A closer look at the tourism and gold mining industries amply illustrates connections between sex work, the global economy, nationalist development strategies, hegemonic masculinity, and Western dominance. Promoted by the United Nations as a strategy to participate in the global economy since the 1960s, tourism was adopted by Caribbean governments at different times as a way to diversify their economies, to overcome economic crises that threatened to cripple the small nation-states, and to acquire foreign exchange (Crick 1989, Walvin 1992). The largest tourism markets in 1996 were North America, led by 7.2 million visitors from the U.S., and in second place, Europe—with France, the U.K., and Germany taking the lead and Sweden, Spain and Italy becoming more important (Caribbean Tourism Organization, as cited in *Caribbean Week,* February 14–27, 1998). In 1996 the industry accounted for 24.7 percent of all formal employment in the region and was predicted to be one of the fastest growing sectors in the twenty-first century. With the estimate that for every person in formal employment in tourism there is at least one other engaged in informal activities in the industry, it is assumed that tourism in the Caribbean will continue to be an important source of livelihood for its working peoples (*Travel Industry World Yearbook* 1996, Patullo 1996, *Caribbean Week,* February 14–27, 1998).

The industry hinges on the exploitation of a number of the region's resources, particularly sun, sea and sand, but also on its tropical rainforests and coral reefs as well as its music, such as reggae and calypso, its cuisine, and other cultural symbols such as carnival. It offers a variety of packages, including golf vacations, weddings and honeymoons, dive trips, and ecotours, its sole *raison d'être* to provide pleasure to the visitor. Caribbean women and men in this sector work for meager wages in jobs such as barmen, waitresses, cooks, cleaners, maids, gardeners, and entertainers. Male and female labor and energies constitute a part of the package that is paid for and consumed by the tourist during the period in which she or he seeks to relax and enjoy—in the leisure time the tourist has set aside to recuperate and restore the mind and body in order to maintain a healthy and productive working life on return home (Crick 1989, Walvin 1992, Palmer 1994, Levy and Lerch 1991, Dann 1994, Kinnaird et al. 1994). Caribbean sexuality also constitutes a critical resource within this panorama, particularly apparent in tourism promotional materials. Postcards, travel brochures, airline and hotel advertisements, all make ample use of images of brown and black women and men to market the region to the rest of the world. In these promotional materials, the women are often scantily dressed and sensually posed, inviting the viewer to "taste" the Caribbean (Bolles 1992). The promise of a vacation is also intimately entwined with notions of Caribbean women and men as the providers of service and (sexual) pleasure. Mullings points out in chapter 3 that sexual services in the tourism industry are part of a range of informal services that are solidly integrated in the tourism industry. Women and men work informally as prostitutes, escorts, nightclub hostesses, and dancers, encouraged by tourism industry operators because of the heightened attractions for the tourist and profitability for the formal sector.[10] In such tourism-oriented sex work, racialized and ethnic differences are critical. Clients are foreign by culture, language, and often race to the sex worker, with the "Otherness" of the sex workers being a source of desire for the clients. Notions of "authentic" blackness, signified by both skin color and cultural characteristics such as dreadlocked hair and dance style, dominates the imaginations of female tourists visiting the islands.

That profits from tourism are global and not confined to the local level can be seen in the way the industry is structured. Foreign investors dominate the landscape, and the majority of the tourist resorts and initiatives are controlled by large corporations that reside outside of the region (Wilkinson 1997). The development of the "all-inclusive" tourist package in which flights, airport transfers, hotel accommodations, meals, drinks, entertainment, sports facilities, excursions, et cetera, are paid in full in advance, usually in the country of origin, also means that few expenditures are made in the host country, allowing a large proportion of the income generated from such resorts to remain outside the Caribbean. In addition, Pattullo explains that around 70 percent of foreign exchange that is eventually earned in the Caribbean on tourism is used to pay for imported goods and services. In some countries this "leakage" could be as high as 90 percent (Pattullo 1996:38). The tourism product, which includes the sexual labor and bodies of young Caribbean women and men, that is consumed in the Caribbean, by and large enables the accumulation of capital by corporations in industrialized nations. Caribbean governments, both colonial, as in the case of the Dutch Antilles, or independent, as with Jamaica and the Dominican Republic, have done little more in this scenario than act as a "manager of Western enterprise" (Fanon 1961), either officially regulating sex work or informally tolerating it due to the heightened attraction it lends to the tourism industry.

For the mining industry, while gold and diamonds have long been sought in the hinterlands of Guyana and Suriname, the rise of the price of gold on the global market in the 1970s, coupled with the introduction of new mining technology and equipment, prompted a new "gold rush" in the region (Colchester 1997). Structural adjustment policies in the 1980s added fuel to the fire. In 1986, for example, the World Bank promoted private sector investment in "nontraditional exports," among them gold, diamonds, and timber, through its program for economic recovery in Guyana, encouraging multinational gold mining corporations to set up large-scale operations (Colchester 1997:39). By 1995, between 40,000 and 60,000 Guyanese "pork-nokkers" and thousands of Brazilian *garimpeiros* were involved in small-scale mining, along with several large-scale gold mining operations. Among them was the biggest in South America, which became the single largest foreign investor in Guyana—the Omai mine (Colchester 1997, Wilkinson 1995). The gold rush in Suriname took on similar proportions for similar reasons. In both countries, the industry has caused severe environmental devastation and intense disruption of Amerindian and Maroon communities in the interior.[11] Nevertheless, the profits for foreign investors and private companies remain high, with the local governments unable to enforce environmental protective measures or to secure the land rights for the hinterland inhabitants, due both to their marginal positions in the global economic order and internal pressures from local business and political elites. Gender implications of the ravaging of the rainforest have barely been discussed. However, as pointed out for other regions of the world, the introduction through mining of a cash economy in areas that were formerly subsistence economies have greatly marginalized women as food producers (Tauli-Corpuz 1997). A rise of incidences of prostitution, drug addiction, alcoholism, domestic violence, and rape are seen to accompany this process of social and economic disruption.

In the studies of Guyana and Suriname in this book, prostitution appears well integrated into the gold mining industry both as a direct profit to the "bosses" of the operations and as a way in which heterosexual masculine identity and male labor power is reproduced. Young women are employed by the mining bosses as hypersexual domestics or "temporary wives" in the homes of the miners—to ensure that the miners are fed, cared for and loved while away from home. Brazilian women are recruited and hired by the foreman of a mining operation to live for a three-month period with one miner who pays 10 percent of his total earnings to the foreman, who, in turn, pays for the woman's travel into the camp, all her lodging expenses, and a fixed salary in gold. Where women are not allowed to live in the mining camps, they are recruited or encouraged to work in the bars or to set up

camp near the mining operations to enable men to express what is culturally defined as a natural masculine instinct, i.e., to have regular sex with a
woman. The well-being of the men is at stake here—the assumption being
that sexual release for a man is necessary for his general functioning and
productivity. The profitability of the gold mining industry rests on male productivity, which is boosted by nurturing, care, and attention from women.
In the specific case of the temporary wife system, a sizable profit is also
made by the mine boss directly from the women's domestic and sexual
labor. That a part of the work carried out by women is paid for does not
change long-standing gendered divisions of labor. Sex work within the mining industry, which is both local and global, consolidates both masculinity
and femininity as, respectively, producer and reproducer of capital and
labor.

Given the history of prostitution in the region, it is difficult to confirm that
the sex trade has grown since the 1980s. Sex work in the Caribbean has existed for several centuries in the region and requires far more research and
exploration in order for us to establish whether we can speak of a growth in
absolute terms. Nevertheless, the intensified globalization and corporatiza-
tion of capitalism since the mid-1980s has had a tangible impact on the structural opportunities and possibilities for Caribbean working peoples, allowing us to conclude that due to this process, sex work has become more
important for the livelihood of Caribbean working men and women and for
the wealth of global business.

GENDER, RACE, AND SEX WORK

Caribbean history indicates that sex work, particularly prostitution, has been
profoundly shaped by both racialized and gendered processes within the
context of the wider global economy, with the black woman at the nexus.
The subordination of women is critical in the process, with prostitution often
an extension of domestic and household work or sexual relations with men.
Female sex workers are, however, marginalized and disrespected as
"whores" within local cultural logic, in a reflection of the patriarchal double
standard that dominates in most Caribbean countries around male and female sexuality (Senior 1991, Safa 1995). Many of the women interviewed in
the studies in this book spoke candidly about this stigmatization and of the
ways they are scorned because of their public appearance. The visibility of
men in heterosexual sex work in Caribbean tourist resorts, however, has
gained considerable attention, for it appears to be unlike situations elsewhere in the world, and it poses critical questions about gender relations
and prostitution. Some understandings of male sex work emerge from feminist perspectives that analyze divisions of labor as reliant upon the increasing

global economic pull of young men into labor market sectors that have been traditionally constructed as feminine, characterized by flexibility, service orientation, second-class status to male work, low wages, and reproductive over productive nature, due to the increasing search by corporate capital for cheap labor and larger profits (Mies 1989, Enloe 1989, Lim 1998). Others have addressed the issue as one that reinforces hegemonic masculine identities and power through the location and definition of male sex workers as "female" in commercial sexual acts and as the feminized subject with a feminine identity (Pheterson 1996). A third perspective argues that prostitution (by either gender) in Third World countries signifies a "libidinization" of various parts of the globe, where countries such as Thailand and the Philippines are constructed as "feminine" in relationship to Western capitalist states. The latter, it is argued, use their "masculine" power to "penetrate" local economies, turning the dominated nations into "sites of desire" and "economies of pleasure" (Tadiar 1993, Manderson and Jolly 1997). The three perspectives provide ways of viewing male sex work in the Caribbean. However, the studies in this book and elsewhere, as well as the history of the construction of prostitution in the region, suggest that taking specifically gendered forms of sex work into account allows a more complex approach.

In the first place, male sex workers in the Caribbean do not necessarily self-define in the same way as women who are in the same position. Instead of being identified by terms such as prostitute, *puta*, whore or sex worker, the men tend to be identified as "beach boy," "island boy," "player," "gigolo," "sanky panky," or "hustler," and "romance tourism" is the name given to the relationship they enter into with women tourists. While this creates a separate discursive space for male actors in Caribbean sex work and can easily be interpreted as a strategy to distance men from the stigma of prostitution or as an expression of denial by North American and Western European women about their own involvement in prostitution relations, it also points to differences in constructions of masculinity and femininity in the region. Local discourses privilege men through valuing "hyperactive virility" and male sexual prowess such as womanizing, maintaining a sexual relationship with an outside woman while married, or fathering children with different women (Lewis 1998, Senior 1991, Smith 1987, Dann 1987). In settings where young men are economically and racially marginalized, expressions of this type of heterosexuality allow them access to one of the few socially respected power bases available to them. Sex with a female tourist who holds the economic dominant position in the relationship appears not to threaten or disrupt this culturally approved expression of masculinity but rather to enable feelings of personal worth and self-confidence. Although perhaps shunned by "decent" working men and women for their hustling activities, fundamental hegemonic constructions of Caribbean masculinity are not questioned or denied to the male heterosexual sex worker. An exchange of sex for material and financial benefits with a female tourist, instead, reaffirms conceptions of "real" Caribbean manhood, creating a space for (as the study on Barbados in chapter 8 suggests), the liberation of a masculinity that, within the international context is subordinated to an economically powerful, white masculinity. This construction of the hypersexual male, in the absence of economic power, positions young black men as subjects who can provide sex on demand—as the quintessential black male stud. It is an image that is carefully cultivated and elaborated upon by the men in their relations with female tourists and highly desired and sought out by the visitors. Such constructions of black masculinity among Caribbean male sex workers stands in stark contrast to the notion of the femininized male sex worker.

Studies also show that liaisons between Caribbean men and female tourists and Caribbean women and male tourists are similar in a variety of ways. Undeniably, for both men and women who are oriented to working with tourists, an exchange of sex or romance for money, status, or material goods takes place. Phillips, in chapter 8 on male hustlers in Barbados, for example, cites men describing their encounters with tourist women as highly dependent upon the women's wealth. Martis argues in chapter 9 that the main reason for men in Curaçao to be engaged in a sexual relationship with a tourist is economic. Nothing is accidental about their choice of "romance" partners. Even Pruitt, in one of her rare interviews with a self-defined Rent-a-Dread in Jamaica, quotes him as saying: "If I am going to walk down the road with a white women then she must give me a money. If I walk, I wear off some of my shoes bottom. She must give me money to buy me a new pair of shoes" (1993:152). These economic dimensions of the relationship with female tourists are also confirmed in chapter 2 by O'Connell Davidson and Sanchez Taylor.

In addition, both male and female sex work can rest on "romancing." Kane notes of the situation in Belize that "a woman who meets a soldier in a bar or hotel enacts a sequence of verbal and gestural exchanges that are sexually stimulating and at the same time, create the aura of friendship and romance" (1993:973). This, she continues, allows the exchange of sex for money or material goods to take place in a way that is "more acceptable to the partners involved because the sex act is represented in such a way that it seems to occur 'naturally' and to be mutually desired" (973). Romancing in the Caribbean, by both male and female sex workers, can be likened to situations in Southeast Asia. There the concept of "open-ended prostitution" has been introduced to describe ambiguous relationships between male tourists and female Asian sex workers which are not strictly a short-time exchange of sex for money, but involve long-term relationships, affection, and forms of companionship as well as economic support (Cohen 1986, Phillips and Dann 1998). "Many stay with a tourist for the rest of his sojourn in

Bangkok," Cohen notes about Thai sex workers in the 1980s, "some even go abroad, as girlfriends or wives. Many continue to keep in touch by mail with their partners afterwards" (1996:257). Similarly, O'Connell Davidson (1998) writes about the "quasi-romantic" encounter in a variety of sex tourist sites: "The interaction between prostitute and client tends to proceed as if it were a flirtation rather than a business negotiation. Prostitutes flatter tourists and affect a genuine interest in them; tourists buy the prostitutes drinks, ask them to dance, sometimes even invite them to dinner.... The two parties often embark upon a fairly open-ended exchange, which may go on for one night, two nights, a week, a month ..." (77–78). Chapters 5 and 8 on the Dominican Republic and Barbados both present a similar picture. Rather than concluding that a gendered difference underlies various forms of sex work, male and female sex work can both be seen to represent the complexity of relationships that emerge between a client/economic provider and a prostitute/lover, which extend from explicit sexual-economic exchanges to more protracted liaisons, romantic attachments, or marriage.

Racialized male and female bodies in the region provide, as pointed out by various studies in this book, a stage for First World gendered performances—for European and North American men to reenact traditional masculine roles and to reassure themselves of their dominance over women, for European and North American women to experiment with, confirm, or expand their gender repertoires. Many male sex tourists, for example, expressed the view that in their home countries, women enjoy excessive power, through which traditional male authority is being undermined (see O'Connell Davidson and Sanchez Taylor, chapter 2). In the Caribbean, they are able to fully reaffirm their masculinity through the control they can exert based on their racialized/cultural economic power. Among female tourists, an experimentation with being in a position of power and control over men, while retaining a sexualized femininity, takes place. The black male sex worker is required to be the sexually aggressive and dominant partner, allowing the tourist woman to combine economic power and authority with sexual submission and subordination. Caribbean masculinity and femininity alike thus become the tableaux upon which a reshaping and retooling of Western identity occurs. Associated with this, O'Connell Davidson and Sanchez Taylor argue in chapter 2, the sexual encounter enables the tourist to attain a sense of control over her or his sexuality while reassuring him- or herself of racial and/or cultural privilege. Caribbean men and women alike are constructed in tourist imaginations as racialized-sexual subjects/objects—the hypersexual "black male stud" and the "hot" mulatta or black woman—whose main roles are to serve and please the visitor. Both women and men represent the primitive, barbarous Other to the tourist.

Further, as discussed earlier, the Caribbean serves as a playground for the richer areas of the world to explore their fantasies of the exotic and to indulge in some rest and relaxation, and the racialized-sexualized bodies and energies of Caribbean women and men are primary resources that local governments and the global tourism industry exploit and commodify to cater to, among other things, tourist desires and needs. In this respect, sex work serves as both a producer and reproducer of capital. Sexual labor and energies are inserted into the production process to fabricate the tourism package, from which profit is accumulated by the state and the tourism industry. Simultaneously, sex work is an extension of physical "care" work that enables the tourist to recuperate his or her energies, and while such activity is typically defined as "woman's work" and generally seen as an extension of female domestic work, male sex work in tourism indicates that such activities serve to reproduce labor power of the North American and Western European middle classes and elites.

Finally, male and female sex work in the tourism industry, particularly forms of hustling and *jineterismo*, represent a strategy to counter the existing social orders and hierarchies of racialized and class power and dominance. It is a strategy that allows Caribbean women and men a form of freedom from oppressive and exploitative national and global economic relations that keep them in poorly paid work or poverty and positions them to gain access to a life that takes them out of miserable social conditions and to obtain the power and freedom symbolized by the "developed" world. In practice, this struggle can rest on sex workers seeking to find caring foreigners with enough financial security to assist them to overcome economic hardship, unemployment, and a bleak future for themselves and their families; of obtaining "La Gloria" in Dominican women's words. For many, this includes leaving their home countries and migrating to live with the lover, of "going a foreign" in Jamaican Rent-a-Dread parlance (Pruitt 1993). Echoing the situations under slavery, sex work thus also represents everyday strategies to overcome unequal relations of power between nations on a global scale.

In sum, taking gender and race in Caribbean sex work into account allows us to view prostitution beyond the boundaries of reproductive domestic work, the emasculation of men, and the feminization of the Third World. It proposes that we can also view sex work in the context of international and racialized relations of power, as a (re)source for the sustenance and nurturance of the First World, which supports the refashioning of Western constructions of gender and sexuality, or as a haven for the replenishment of Western bodies and productive labor. Sex work in the region stands as an integral part of the local and global economy, as productive and also reproductive labor, and as a platform upon which the First World (re)creates its identity and power. It also continues the ambiguities and contradictions that were evident under slavery, being simultaneously a form of domination and exploitation as well as a place that enables assertions of freedom in the context of oppressive racialized economic orders.

THE STUDIES IN THIS BOOK

Sex work in this book emerges as a complex social activity that encompasses patriarchal and racialized dominations and exploitations of black and brown bodies and labor, self-empowerment by women through the strategic use of sexual labor for their own and their families' survival, and struggles by both men and women for liberation from oppressive colonial and neocolonial conditions. It is defined in these studies as an activity in which the persons providing the sexual labor do so with multiple partners, while publicly acknowledging their participation in this exchange. The studies show that it is not a simple exchange of sex for money as is commonly understood under the term prostitution but is far more extensive and complicated and, in this respect, can be seen to retain some remarkable similarities to prostitution under slavery in the region. Sex work or prostitution, for example, is represented in sex worker discourse in the following chapters as a gainful activity. It is commonly defined as an alternative to income-generating activities such as domestic work, street or beach vending, fishing, work in manufacturing factories in Free Trade Zones, security guard work, waitressing, bartending, and go-go dancing. In the majority of the cases, men and women describe sex work as more lucrative than these other jobs, and in some cases, less demanding or less hazardous to their well-being. The studies also comment upon grey areas where women and men engage in sexual-economic exchanges without ever acknowledging or referring to themselves as sex workers. Throughout the region, the "mistress" appears as one such category, represented by terms such as "outside woman," "deputy," "bijzijd," and "sweetheart," a relationship that is sometimes described by self-defined sex workers and other members of society as prostitution. The boundary between sex worker and non-sex worker is also further complicated by findings in other studies on sexual relations in the Caribbean, such as by Senior (1991), Wekker (1994), Miller (1994) and de Zalduondo (1995), in which the researchers point out that, particularly among Afro-Caribbean women and men, heterosexual relationships are constructed on the basis of explicit and conscious sexual-economic exchanges (see also chapter 3).

There are a few main sites where sex work takes place in the region. In the studies, several appear as important—hotels and guesthouses, entertainment establishments such as bars, nightclubs and go-go dance clubs, tourist resorts, small-scale gold mining camps, and docks—each representing a specific type of arrangement. Special red-light districts are unknown in the region and very few places are exclusively designated for prostitution. Campo Alegre in Curaçao is one of the few sites where non-sex working women are banned. In all the other places, clients and nonclients, sex workers and non-sex workers can mingle, dance, drink, and socialize if they so wish. In all the studies there is mention of sex work that is street-based, although this forms the focus of only one study in Cartagena, Colombia, as well as prostitution that occurs out of women's homes and through escort services.

The gendered composition of the sex-working population or the clients in these studies should not be regarded as representative for the region but more as a reflection of the focus of the particular case studies. The majority of the studies were designed around the participation of female sex workers, given the overrepresentation of women in the global sex trade as a result of the way in which female sexuality and labor has historically been controlled and organized to serve masculine and male interests. Nevertheless, all recognize that in each country men are also active in the trade. Male sex workers are, however, not always heterosexual, as the case studies in Barbados and the Netherlands Antilles describe or as represented in earlier research. They may be engaged by male clients, such as the "Sanky Pankies" in the Dominican Republic (de Moya and Garcia 1996; see also chapter 5) or as male-to-female transgender prostitutes.[12]

Also, whether the age range represented in these studies (between eleven and sixty) is typical in most Caribbean countries is subject to further research. Nevertheless, while child prostitution did not appear as a prominent feature, the involvement in sex work of teenage girls from fifteen upwards and of young women and men are remarked upon or discussed in all the studies. Mayorga and Velasquez, in particular, in their study of thirteen young sex workers in Cartagena, Colombia, also stress that even though it is important to focus on the specific vulnerabilities of minors in the sex trade, it is imperative to view sex work as one of the many perils that young people face in a region where poverty, lack of education, and work opportunities are structural features for much of the population. They argue therefore that it is critical to examine child and teenage prostitution within the context of the position of all young people in a Third World country that is dominated by neoliberal economic strategies and processes of maldevelopment.

The studies are organized into three sections. Part 2 presents various dimensions of the wider context within which sex work is configured. In the first chapter, O'Connell Davidson and Sanchez Taylor explore in greater depth hegemonic ideologies and fantasies that are embedded in the tourist demand for sex in the Caribbean. Their study draws on research with male and female tourists around the world, but in particular the Dominican Republic and Jamaica, and is easily applicable to situations elsewhere in the region. This study also highlights differences between sex worker and client perceptions of sex work in the Caribbean, showing that often men who would not necessarily solicit prostitutes at home are able to do so while on holiday abroad due to notions that what occurs in Third World countries is "not really prostitution." Mullings, in chapter 3, offers a detailed examination of the links between the Caribbean tourism industry, sex work, and the globalization of corporate capitalism, emphasizing the need for a transformation in current tourism strategies. While her chapter is illustrated with a study of Jamaica, her analysis provides a framework for understanding these linkages for the entire Caribbean. Chapter 4 on Cuba by Fernandez presents the case that dominant race and class discourses construct the *jinetera* as the working-class Afro-Cuban woman and in so doing obscure the role of elite Cuban men and women in sex work and other informal sector activities. The chapter urges us to keep in mind the variability and flexibility that permeate sex work arrangements, as well as the broader relations of power that define prostitution.

Part 3 is a selection of case studies in seven different locations, island and mainland, Spanish, English and Dutch speaking: the Dominican Republic, Jamaica, Cartagena on the Colombian Caribbean coast, Barbados, the Netherlands Antilles, Belize, and Suriname. The studies are primarily ethnographic in character and present the perceptions and definitions of sex work as described by people who sell and organize sexual labor. The specificity of each location and culture is captured in the languages of each place, accentuating the diversity and nuances in sex work as they are experienced around the region. This section in particular highlights how the category of sex worker exists at the end of the twentieth century as one that is constructed within different social and cultural settings in a number of ways, describing hierarchies among sex workers according to their work locations, level of education, age, ethnicity or nationality, and the informal and temporary character of sex work. Further, the case studies in the Spanish-speaking locations in the study, Cartagena and Sosúa in particular, point out how Catholic standards of womanhood, which stress chastity until marriage and monogamy as crucial elements of "decent" femininity, are vitally important in defining sex work. The heterogeneity and specific cultural constructions of the sex worker in the region, as presented in this section, demand our constant attention to avoid facile and stereotypical assertions and claims.

Part 4 contains chapters that propose avenues and directions for future action and policy on sex work in the Caribbean. Chapter 12 by the Guyanese Red Thread Women's Development Programme is a fine example of the way in which a Caribbean women's organization can analyze sex work in its specific context and simultaneously develop a grass-roots strategy that can empower sex workers. The chapter stresses complexities of sex work as described in the studies in Part 3 yet goes on to propose that Caribbean non-sex workers also have a role in challenging forces, ideologies, and structures that discriminate and harm sex workers. Chapter 13 discusses some of the strengths and weaknesses in international conventions, policies, and laws on sex tourism, indicating areas that can inform future Caribbean policy. In the final chapter, Mellon steers us in the direction of making links between the very concrete realities of sex work in the Caribbean and human rights concerns. This entire last section emphasizes the need for feminists, national governments, the tourism industry, and those concerned with Caribbean development, to keep the well-being, health, and humanity of Caribbean working women at the very core of future projects and plans, and offers ways of thinking about and changing sex work in the Caribbean as we move into a new century.

NOTES

1. This was the tenor of the presentations of a session on prostitution in which I participated in November 1995 at the University of Havana. Panelists speaking on the issue in Cuba included a member of the Federation of Cuban Women (FMC), a researcher who had conducted fieldwork among *jineteras,* and several other Cuban women intellectuals.

2. The project was initiated by Gladys Acosta Vargas, who at the time was attached to the Instituto Latinoamericano de Servicios Legales Alternativos (ILSA) in Bogotá; Elena Díaz, director of FLACSO-Cuba at the University of Havana; and myself, in the fall of 1995. Together we developed the concept of the project and it grew to involve other organizations such as the Caribbean Association for Feminist Research and Action (CAFRA) with its Secretariat based in Trinidad, the Instituto Mujer y Genero in Puerto Rico, the Stichting Maxi Linder Association for sex workers in Suriname, the Center for Gender and Development Studies at the University of the West Indies in Jamaica, and the Red Thread Women's Development Programme in Guyana, as well as twelve principal researchers. Cynthia Mellon of ILSA, Jacqueline Burgess of CAFRA and I formed the main coordinating team for the entire project and I served as the overall project director.

3. For the project, a team of researchers was selected, and fieldwork was conducted in eight Caribbean territories: Belize, Barbados, the Dominican Republic, Guyana, Jamaica, the Netherlands Antilles, Suriname, and the Colombian Caribbean coastal city of Cartagena. The research took place between September 1997 and June 1998, culminating in a conference, held in Kingston, Jamaica, in July 1998. In keeping with certain feminist research principles, the project was loosely constructed around an approach that would combine some forms of activism and public consciousness-raising around the subject of prostitution, as well as attempts to break down hierarchies and divides between the researcher and researched and the non-prostitute and prostitute. We sought to support studies where the researcher engaged with people in the sex trade in an egalitarian relationship through which a dialogue could take place allowing the researcher to explore various subjective meanings of sex work and to develop insights and interpretations centered on multiple experiences, perceptions, and definitions by people active in the trade. A necessary component of such an approach is the recognition by the researchers of their own positionality in relationship to the researched, the assumptions and biases they bring to the process, and relations of power involved in the research process (Wolf 1996). Taking sex workers as the main actors, as the providers of sexual labor in the trade yet whose

voices are silenced in most studies, we were emphatic from the outset of the project that the perceptions and experiences of this population in particular needed to be center stage.

We solicited research proposals and selected and sponsored eight that appeared to share the general approach, yet which contained their own specific research methods. Other important criteria during the selection procedure were the familiarity of the researcher with the country or culture where the study was proposed and her or his link to women's or grassroots organizations within the countries where the research would take place, based on both the practical element of the time that we had allocated for the project and the idea that an insider to the culture and language would have easier access than a complete outsider to such a culturally sensitive area. Given the restriction on the number of countries that could participate in the study, the site also acted as a criterion in the selection process—one study per country was to be chosen, enabling us to gather as broad a basis for comparison as possible. During the course of the project, a total of 191 sex workers were interviewed in the eight countries—of whom 170 were women and twenty-one men. In addition, twenty clients—ten male and ten female—were interviewed.

4. Truong's concept of sexual labor is particularly helpful here. She defines it as "the use of the body as an instrument to produce a service" (1990:65), where sex, as a source of life for both bodily pleasure and procreation, constitutes the material basis for this type of labor. She maintains that sexual labor does not have a universal character and meaning but rather that it can be understood in the context of social processes that incorporate it into the sphere of production and reproduction. Prostitution is just one form of sexual labor that can be identified in different histories and contexts. Truong argues that prostitution in wage-labor relations, rather than only producing use value, "creates surpluses that can be extracted by economic agents as well as by the state" (1990:197).

5. In Saint Domingue in 1789, for example, in a total population of 7,000 mulatto woman, Morrissey notes that around "5,000 ... were either prostitutes or the 'kept mistresses' of white men" (1989:146).

6. See, for example, Pivar (1981) on regulations in colonial India and the Philippines; Hershatter (1989) and Henriot (1996) on China; Grittner (1990) on the United States; Guy (1991) on Argentina; Bailey and Farber (1992) on regulations during World War II in Hawaii; Bernstein (1995) on Imperial Russia; and Caulfield (1997) on Brazil.

7. In Curaçao during the early 1940s the regulations were shaped by a commission that consisted of five men, two of whom were Roman Catholic priests. The deliberations of the commission were also supported by the director of the Public Health department and the Chief of Police. The commission's recommendations to the Governor of Curaçao stressed the need for the government to regulate prostitution. In turn this report was presented to the government council as a proposal for amendments to the legislation on contagious diseases. In 1944 the amendments were approved by the colonial government "in the name of the Queen."

8. Between 1944 and 1960, 336 Haitian women, 337 Cuban women, 662 Venezuelans, 800 Colombians, and 2,075 women from the Dominican Republic were regis-

tered with the Curaçaoan Vice and Morals police to work in Campo Alegre as prostitutes.

9. Structural adjustment in the Caribbean and other parts of the "developing" world has been widely analyzed and written about. Sparr, for example, notes that as a neoliberal process, "structural adjustment assumes an economy will be more efficient, healthy, and productive in the long run if market forces operate and products and services are not protected, subsidized, heavily regulated, or produced by the government" (1994:1). Emeagwali argues, following analyses made by Samir Amin, Peggy Antrobus, Norman Girvan, and others, that structural adjustment is "an almost deliberate scheme for the perpetuation of export dependency, maverick and unfavorable interest rates, fluctuating terms of trade, and the reproduction of existing conditions of global inequalities" (1995:5). Structural Adjustment Programs (SAPs) in the Caribbean have more often than not been put in place involuntarily as a condition for receiving new loans from foreign commercial banks and multilateral lending institutions such as the IMF and the World Bank. See also McAfee (1991).

10. This process has been analyzed in great detail for Asia. Truong notes, for example, that sexual services are part of the ongoing process of accumulation for many businesses connected to the tourism sector: "For enterprises such as bars, clubs and other entertainment establishments, disguised prostitution stimulates clients' expenditure and ensures high profits from sales.... For the international tourism conglomerates, the availability of sexual services as an exotic commodity functions as a source of tourist attraction and helps to fill airplane seats and hotel rooms. National accounts benefit from taxes on accommodation, food drinks and services" (1990:128).

11. The Omai mining disaster, in Guyana in 1995, is just one example of the kind of ecological damage that is being done to the rainforest by gold mining. The joint venture among the Montreal-based Cambior Inc. (which holds 65 percent of the shares), the Colorado-based Golden Star Resources (30 percent), and the Guyana government (5 percent) employs a technique called "cyanide leaching" to extract gold from ore. The cyanide waste is supposed to be safely stored. However, a spill that critics argue was both predictable and preventable released 3.2 billion liters of the effluent into the Essequibo River, severely polluting and contaminating the water and surrounding environment (Jodah 1995, Chatterjee 1995). The spill has raised many questions about the efficacy of such mining operations and about the unfettered ability of foreign companies to circumvent environmental protection laws. See also Forte (1993) and Colchester (1997) for further discussions of the social and environmental devastation that gold mining brings to the region.

12. Transgendered sex workers have barely been acknowledged within the Caribbean context and have not as yet been the subject of any research. Nevertheless, street-walking transgender prostitutes have been noted in Curaçao (see Kempadoo 1994) and observed during fieldwork in Georgetown, Guyana, and Paramaribo, Suriname, in the context of this project. See also chapter 11 on Suriname, where mention is made of "transvestite" sex workers.

Part 2

Tourism, Globalization, and "The Exotic"

2

Fantasy Islands

Exploring the Demand for Sex Tourism

JULIA O'CONNELL DAVIDSON AND JACQUELINE SANCHEZ TAYLOR

In a useful review of prostitution cross-culturally and historically, Laurie Shrage observes that "one thing that stands out but stands unexplained is that a large percentage of sex customers seek (or sought) sex workers whose racial, national, or class identities are (or were) different from their own" (1994:142). She goes on to suggest that the demand for African, Asian, and Latin American prostitutes by white Western men may "be explained in part by culturally produced racial fantasies regarding the sexuality of these women" and that these fantasies may be related to "socially formed perceptions regarding the sexual and moral purity of white women" (1994:48–50). Kempadoo also draws attention to the "over-representation of women of different nationalities and ethnicities, and the hierarchies of race and color within the [international sex] trade" and observes, "That sex industries today depend upon the eroticization of the ethnic and cultural Other suggests we are witnessing a contemporary form of exoticism which sustains post-colonial and post-cold war relations of power and dominance" (1995:75–6).

This chapter represents an attempt to build on such insights. Drawing on our research with both male and female Western heterosexual sex tourists in the Caribbean,[1] it argues that their sexual taste for "Others" reflects not so much a wish to engage in any specific sexual practice as a desire for an extraordinarily high degree of control over the management of self and others as sexual, racialized and engendered beings. This desire, and the Western sex tourist's power to satiate it, can only be explained through reference to power relations and popular discourses that are simultaneously gendered, racialized and economic.

WHITE WESTERN MEN'S SEX TOURISM

Empirical research on sex tourism to Southeast Asia has fairly consistently produced a portrait of Western male heterosexual sex tourists as men whose desire for the Other is the flip side of dissatisfaction with white Western women, including white Western prostitute women. Lee, for example, explores the demand for sex tourism as a quest for racially fantasized male power, arguing that this is at least in part a backlash against the women's movement in the West: "With an increasingly active global feminist movement, male-controlled sexuality (or female passivity) appears to be an increasingly scarce resource. The travel advertisements are quite explicit about what is for sale: docility and submission" (1991:90; see also Jeffreys 1997). Western sex tourists' fantasies of "docile" and "willing" Asian women are accompanied, as Kruhse-Mount Burton notes, by "a desexualization of white women ... who are deemed to be spoiled, grasping and, above all, unwilling or inferior sexual partners" (1995:196). These characteristics are also attributed to white prostitute women. The sex tourists interviewed by Seabrook compared Thai prostitutes "very favorably with the more mechanistic and functional behavior of most Western sex workers" (1996:3). Kruhse-Mount Burton states that where many Australian participants in sex holidays criticized prostitutes in Australia "for being emotionally and sexually cold and for making little effort to please, or to disguise the commercial nature of the interaction," they stressed "the warmth, affection, femininity, youth and beauty of Asian prostitutes, combined with an aptitude for disguising the mercenary aspect of the arrangement" (1995:193–4).

Our own interview work suggests that Western male heterosexual sex tourists to the Caribbean typically share these attitudes and beliefs—a finding that is unsurprising given that many have also been prostitute users in Southeast Asia, either as tourists or as members of the armed forces. They often believe that Western women enjoy excessive powers in relation to men. The following extract from an interview with an American sex tourist and an American expatriate in the Dominican Republic in 1998 illustrates just how bitter such men can be about Western women's (perceived) encroachment on men's territory and traditional authority:

> EXPATRIATE: I pay $1,100 child support a month [to his American ex-wife]... 17 percent of your gross income for one child she gets, 25 percent for two, 33 percent for three. I've no idea what happens to men who have four kids.... Women's lib in America in the United States has killed marriage in America for any man who has brains.... I wouldn't even marry a rich woman.... [In the Dominican Republic] they're raised different. Women's lib hasn't hit here....
>
> SEX TOURIST: In the States, [women] hire folks with cameras.... They go to bed with cameras. If they wake up with a bruise, they take a picture of it. Call it abuse. Possible abuse.

EXPATRIATE: In the United States, if you grab your wife like that, and you yell at her, put a little black blue mark, just a little one, she'll...

SEX TOURIST: When you've got a goddamn female announcing the NBA basketball game.... These females go into the men's locker rooms, but the males cannot go into the ladies' locker rooms. Most of these girls are dykes anyways.

Our interview work with sex tourists who are or have been domestic prostitute users also lends support to the view that their sex tourism is a means of accessing the gendered power that they feel they lack in the West:

They're not like prostitutes.... They stay with you all day.... They rub in the sun tan oil, bring us the towel, she even washes your feet. What English tart would do that?... The problem is getting rid of them. Once you've bought them, they stick to you. They even fight with each other over you. It's wicked (English sex tourist in the Dominican Republic).

[Prostitution in Europe and North America is] all businesslike. It's by the hour, like a taxi service, like they've got the meter running.... There's no feeling. If I wanted to fuck a rubber doll, I could buy one and inflate it.... A prostitute in Europe will never kiss you. In Canada, it's ridiculous. You know, if you go with a prostitute and you don't pay her, you know what? They call it rape. You can be in court on a rape charge (Canadian sex tourist in Cuba).

There is a sense in which Western men's sex tourism can be said "to constitute ... a collective behavior oriented toward the restoration of the 'generalized belief' of what it is to be male" (Kruhse-Mount Burton 1995:201). These are people who, by and large, equate true masculinity with unbridled sexuality over women more generally. Men like this experience the fact that some (though certainly not all) Western women are in a position to take legal action against men who physically abuse them as an infringement of rightful male authority. The fact that many (though again certainly not all) Western prostitutes are in a position to impose their own boundaries on the degree of physical intimacy implied by the prostitution contract (for example by refusing to kiss clients on the mouth or to engage in unprotected penetrative and/or oral sex) and are also in a position to turn down clients' requests to spend the night or a few days with them is likewise experienced as a threat to, or denial of, traditional male identity.

Though we recognize that sex tourism provides Western men with opportunities "to reaffirm, if only temporarily, the idealized version of masculine identity and mode of being," and that in this sense sex tourism provides men with opportunities to manage and control both themselves and others as engendered beings, we want to argue that there is more to the demand for sex tourism than this (Kruhse-Mount Burton 1995:202). In the remainder of this chapter we therefore interrogate sex tourists' attitudes toward prostitute use, sexuality, gender, and "race" more closely, and further complicate matters by considering white Western women's and black Western men and women's sex tourism to the Caribbean.

WESTERN SEXUALITY AND PROSTITUTE USE

Hartsock observes that there is "a surprising degree of consensus that hostility and domination, as opposed to intimacy and physical pleasure" are central to the social and historical construction of sexuality in the West (1985:157). Writers in the psychoanalytic tradition suggest that the kind of hostility that is threaded through Western sexual expression reflects an infantile rage and wish for revenge against the separateness of those upon whom we depend. It is, as Stoller puts it, "a state in which one wishes to harm an object," and the harm wished upon objects of sexual desire expresses a craving to strip them of their autonomy, control and separateness—that is, to dehumanize them, since a dehumanized sexual object does not have the power to reject, humiliate or control (1986:4).

The "love object" can be divested of autonomy and objectified in any number of ways, but clearly the prostitute woman, who is in most cultures imagined and socially constructed as an "unnatural" sexual and social Other (a status which is often enshrined in law), provides a conveniently ready-dehumanized sexual object for the client. The commercial nature of the prostitute-client exchange further promises to strip all mutuality and dependency from sexual relations. Because all obligations are discharged through the simple act of payment, there can be no real intimacy and so no terrifying specter of rejection or engulfment by another human being. In theory, then, prostitute use offers a very neat vehicle for the expression of sexual hostility and the attainment of control over self and others as sexual beings. Yet for many prostitute users, there is a fly in the ointment:

> Prostitute women may be socially constructed as Others and *fantasized* as nothing more than objectified sexuality, but in reality, of course, they are human beings. It is only if the prostitute is imagined as stripped of everything bar her sexuality that she can be *completely* controlled by the client's money/powers. But if she were dehumanized to this extent, she would cease to exist as a person.... Most clients appear to pursue a contradiction, namely to control as an object that which cannot be objectified (O'Connell Davidson 1998:161).

This contradiction is at the root of the complaints clients sometimes voice about Western prostitutes (Graaf et al. 1992, Plumridge et al. 1997). It is not always enough to buy access to touch and sexually use objectified body parts. Many clients want the prostitute to be a "lover" who makes no claims, a "whore" who has sex for pleasure not money, in short, a person (subject) who can be treated as an object. This reflects, perhaps, deeper inconsistencies in the discourses which surround prostitution and sexuality. The prostitute woman is viewed as acting in a way wholly inconsistent with her gender identity. Her perceived sexual agency degenders her (a woman who takes an impersonal, active, and instrumental approach to sex is not a "real" woman) and dishonors her (she trades in something which is constitutive of her personhood and cannot honorably be sold). The prostitute-using man, by contrast, behaves "in a fashion consistent with the attributes associated with his gender (he is active and sexually predatory, impersonal, and instrumental), and his sexual transgression is thus a minor infraction, since it does not compromise his gender identity" (O'Connell Davidson 1998:127). A paradox thus emerges:

> The more that men's prostitute use is justified and socially sanctioned through reference to the fiction of biologically determined gender roles and sexuality, the greater the contradiction implicit in prostitution. In order to satisfy their "natural" urges, men must make use of "unnatural" women (O'Connell Davidson 1998:128).

All of this helps to explain the fact that, even though their sexual interests may be powerfully shaped by a cultural emphasis on hostility and domination, prostitute use holds absolutely no appeal for many Western men.[2] Fantasies of unbridled sexual access to willingly objectified women are not necessarily fantasies of access to prostitute women. Meanwhile, those who do use prostitutes in the West imagine and manage their own prostitute use in a variety of different ways (see O'Connell Davidson 1998). At one extreme are men who are actually quite satisfied with brief and anonymous sexual use of women and teenagers whom they imagine as utterly debased and objectified "dirty whores." (For them, the idea of using a prostitute is erotic in and of itself.) At the other extreme are those who regularly visit the same prostitute woman and construct a fiction of romance or friendship around their use of her, a fiction which helps them to imagine themselves as seen, chosen, and desired, even as they pay for sex as a commodity. Between these two poles are men who indulge in a range of (often very inventive) practices and fantasies designed to create the illusion of balance between sexual hostility and sexual mutuality that they personally find sexually exciting. How does this relate to the demand for sex tourism?

Let us begin by noting that not all Western male sex tourists subjectively perceive their own sexual practices abroad as a form of prostitute use. This reflects the fact that even within any one country affected by sex tourism, prostitution is not a homogeneous phenomenon in terms of its social organization. In some countries, sex tourism has involved the maintenance and development of existing large scale, highly commoditized sex industries serving foreign military personnel (Truong 1990, Sturdevant and Stoltzfus 1992, Hall 1994). But it has also emerged in locations where no such sex industry existed, for instance, the Gambia, Cuba, and Brazil (Morris-Jara 1996, Sanchez Taylor 1997, Perio and Thierry 1996). Moreover, even in countries like Thailand and the Philippines, where tourist-related prostitution has been grafted onto an existing, formally organized brothel sector serving military demand, tourist development has *also* been associated with the emergence of an informal prostitution sector (in which prostitutes solicit in hotels, discos, bars, beaches, parks, or streets, often entering into fairly protracted and diffuse transactions with clients).

This in itself gives prostitution in sex tourist resorts a rather different character to that of prostitution in red-light districts in affluent, Western countries. The sense of difference is enhanced by the fact that, in many places, informally arranged prostitution spills over into apparently noncommercial encounters within which tourists who do not self-identify as prostitute users can draw local/migrant persons who do not self-identify as prostitutes into profoundly unequal and exploitative sexual relationships. It also means that sex tourism presents a diverse array of opportunities for sexual gratification, not all of which involve straightforward cash for sex exchanges in brothels or go-go clubs or on the streets, and so provides the sex tourist with a veritable "pic'n'mix" of ways in which to manage himself as a sexual and engendered being. He can indulge in overt forms of sexual hostility (such as selecting a numbered brothel prostitute from those on display in a bar or brothel for "short time" or buying a cheap, speedy sexual service from one of many street prostitutes), or he can indulge in fantasies of mutuality, picking up a woman/teenager in an ordinary tourist disco, wining and dining and generally simulating romance with her for a day or two and completely denying the commercial basis of the sexual interaction. Or, and many sex tourists do exactly this, he can combine both approaches.

Now it could be argued that, given the fact that Western men are socialized into a view of male sexuality as a powerful, biologically based need for sexual "outlets," the existence of multiple, cheap, and varied sexual opportunities is, in itself, enough to attract large numbers of men to a given holiday resort. However, it is important to recognize the numerous other forms of highly sexualized tourism that could satisfy a wish to indulge in various sexual fantasies and also a desire for control over the self as a sexual and engendered being. Sex tourists could, for example, choose to take part in organized holidays designed to facilitate sexual and romantic encounters between tourists (such as Club 18–30 and other singles holidays), or they could choose to take all-inclusive holidays to resorts such as Hedonism or destinations renowned for promiscuous tourist–tourist sex, such as Ibiza or Cap d'Azur. These latter offer just as many opportunities for anonymous and impersonal sex in a party atmosphere as well as for intense but ultimately brief and noncommitted sexual romances. What they do not offer is the control that comes from paying for sex or the opportunity to indulge in racialized-sexual fantasies, which helps to explain why sex tourists reject them in favor of sexual experience in what they term "Third World" countries. This brings us to questions about the relationship between the construction of "Otherness" and sex tourism.

"OTHERNESS" AND WESTERN MEN'S SEX TOURISM

For obvious reasons, sex tourists spend their time in resorts and *barrios* where tourist-related prostitution is widespread. Thus they constantly encounter what appear to them as hedonistic scenes—local "girls" and young men dancing "sensuously," draping themselves over and being fondled by Western tourists, drinking and joking with each other, and so on. Instead of seeing the relationship between these scenes and their own presence in the resort, sex tourists tend to interpret all this as empirical vindication of Western assumptions of "non-Western peoples living in idyllic pleasure, splendid innocence or Paradise-like conditions—as purely sensual, natural, simple and uncorrupted beings" (Kempadoo 1995:76). Western sex tourists (and this is true of black as well as white informants) say that sex is more "natural" in Third World countries, that prostitution is not really prostitution but a "way of life," that "They" are "at it" all of the time.

This explains how men who are not and would not dream of becoming prostitute users back home can happily practice sex tourism (the "girls" are not really like prostitutes and so they themselves are not really like clients, the prostitution contract is not like the Western prostitution contract and so does not really count as prostitution). It also explains the paranoid obsession with being cheated exhibited by some sex tourists, who comment on their belief that women in certain sex tourist resorts or particular brothels or bars are "getting too commercial" and advise each other how to avoid being "duped" and "exploited" by a "real professional," where to find "brand new girls," and so on (see O'Connell Davidson 1995, Bishop and Robinson 1998).

It also points to the complex interrelations between discourses of gender, "race" and sexuality. To begin with, the supposed naturalness of prostitution in the Third World actually reassures the Western male sex tourist of his racial or cultural superiority. Thus we find that sex tourists continue a traditional Western discourse of travel which rests on the imagined opposition between the "civilized" West and the "barbarous" Other (Grewal 1996:136, Kempadoo 1996:76; see also Brace and O'Connell Davidson 1996). In "civilized" countries, only "bad" women become prostitutes (they refuse the constraints civilization places upon "good" women in favor of earning "easy money"), but in the Third World (a corrupt and lawless place where people exist in a state of nature), "nice girls" may be driven to prostitution in order to survive ("they have to do it because they've all got kids" or "they're doing it for their families"). In the West, "nice girls" are protected and supported by their menfolk, but in the Third World, "uncivilized" Other men allow (or even demand that) their womenfolk enter prostitution. In interviews, Western male sex tourists contrast their own generosity, humanity, and chivalry against the "failings" of local men, who are imagined as feckless, faithless, wife-beaters, and pimps. Even as prostitute users, Other men are fantasized as inferior moral beings who cheat and mistreat the "girls."

In this we see that sex tourism is not only about sustaining a male identity. For white men it is also about sustaining a *white* identity. Thus, sex tourism can also be understood as a collective behavior oriented toward the restoration of a generalized belief about what it is to be white: to be truly white is to be served, revered, and envied by Others. For the black American male sex tourists we have interviewed, sex tourism appears to affirm a sense of Western-ness and so of inclusion in a privileged world. Take, for example, the following three statements from a forty-five-year-old black American sex tourist. He is a New York bus driver and ex-vice cop, a paid-up member of an American-owned sex tourist club, Travel & the Single Male, and he has used prostitutes in Thailand, Brazil, Costa Rica, and the Dominican Republic:

> There's two sides to the countries that I go to. There's the tourist side and then there's the real people, and I make a habit of going to the real people, I see how the real people live, and when I see something like that ... I tend to look at the little bit I've got at home and I appreciate it....

> I've always been proud to be an American.... I always tip in U.S. dollars when I arrive. I always keep dollars and pesos, because people tend to think differently about pesos and dollars....

> They always say at hotels they don't want you to bring the girls in; believe me, that's crap, because you know what I do? Reach in my pocket and I go anywhere I want.

Meanwhile, sexualized-racisms help the sex tourist to attain a sense of control over himself and Others as engendered and racialized sexual beings. Here it is important to recognize the subtle (or not so subtle) variations of racism employed by white Western men. The sex tourists we have interviewed in the Caribbean are not a homogeneous group in terms of their "race" politics, and this reflects differences of national identity, age, socioeconomic background, and racialized identity. One clearly identifiable subgroup comprised of white North American men aged forty and above, who,

though perhaps not actually affiliated with the Klan, espouse a white supremacist world view and consider black people their biological, social and
cultural inferiors. They use the word "nigger" and consider any challenge to
their "right" to use this term as "political correctness." As one sex tourist
complained, in the States "You can't use the N word, nigger. Always when I
was raised up, the only thing was the F word, you can't use the F word. Now
you can't say cunt, you can't say nigger."

For men like this, black women are imagined as the embodiment of all
that is low and debased, they are "inherently degraded, and thus the appropriate partners for degrading sex" (Shrage 1994:158). As unambiguous
whores by virtue of their racialized identity, they may be briefly and
anonymously used, but they are not sought out for longer term or quasi-
romantic commercial sexual relationships. Thus, the sex tourist quoted
above told us that when he and his cronies (all regular sex tourists to the
Dominican Republic) see another American sex tourist "hanging round"
with a local girl or woman who has the phenotypical characteristics they
associate with African-ness, they call out to him, "How many bananas did
it take to get her down out of the tree?" and generally deride him for
transgressing a racialized sexual boundary which should not, in their
view, be openly crossed.

The Dominican females that men like this want sexual access to are light
skinned and straight haired (this is also true in Cuba and in the Latin American countries where we have undertaken fieldwork). They are not classified as "niggers" by these white racists, but instead as "LBFMs" or "Little
Brown Fucking Machines," a catch-all category encompassing any female
Other not deemed to be either white or "African." The militaristic and impe-
rialist associations of this term (coined by American GIs stationed in Southeast Asia) simultaneously make it all the more offensive and hostile and all
the more appealing to this type of sex tourist, many of whom have served
in the armed forces (a disturbing number of whom have also been or currently are police officers in the United States) and the rest of whom are
"wanna-be vets"—men who never made it to Vietnam to live out their
racialized-sexualized fantasies of masculine glory.

Shrage and Kruhse-Mount Burton's comments on the relationship between fantasies of hypersexual Others and myths about white women's sexual purity are also relevant to understanding this kind of sex tourist's worldview. An extract from an article posted on an Internet site written by and for
sex tourists entitled "Why No White Women?" is revealing:

> Q: Is it because white women demand more (in terms of performance) from
> their men during Sex? and white men cannot deliver?
>   A: In my case, it's just that my dick is not long enough to reach them up on
> the pedestal they like to stand on.

If whiteness is imagined as dominance, and woman is imagined as subordination, then "white woman" becomes something of a contradiction. As Young notes, "For white men, white women are both self and other: they have a floating status. They can reinforce a sense of self through common racial identity or threaten and disturb that sense through their sexual Otherness" (1996:52). White supremacists *have to* place white women on a pedestal (iconize them as racially, morally and sexually pure), since whiteness and civilization are synonymous and "civilization" is constructed as the rejection of base animalism. But keeping them on their pedestal requires men to constantly deny what they imagine to be their own needs and nature and thus white women become the object of profound resentment.

Not all Western male sex tourists to the Caribbean buy into this kind of overt, denigrating racism. In fact, many of them are far more strongly influenced by what might be termed "exoticizing" racisms. Younger white Europeans and North Americans, for example, have been exposed to such racisms through the Western film, music, and fashion industries, which retain the old-school racist emphasis on blackness as physicality but repackage and commoditize this "animalism" so that black men and women become the ultimate icons of sporting prowess, "untamed" rebelliousness, "raw" musical talent, sexual power and so on (see hooks 1992, 1994; Young 1996). As a consequence, many young (and some not so young) white Westerners view blackness as a marker of something both "cool" and "hot."

In their own countries, however, their encounters with real live black people are not only few and far between, but also generally something of a disappointment to them. As one British sex tourist to Cuba told us, black people in Britain are "very stand-offish.... They stick to their own, and it's a shame, because it makes divisions." What a delight it is for men like this to holiday in the Caribbean, then, where poverty combined with the exigencies of tourist development ensure that they are constantly faced by smiling, welcoming black folk. The small black boy who wants to shine their shoes; the old black woman who cleans their hotel room; the cool, young, dreadlocked black man on the beach who is working as a promoter for some restaurant or bar; the fit, young black woman soliciting in the tourist disco—all want to "befriend" the white tourist. Finally, interviews with black American male sex tourists suggest that they too sexualize and exoticize the women they sexually exploit in the Third World ("Latin women are hot," "Latin girls love sex").

Both the sexualized racism that underpins the category LBFM and the exoticizing sexualized racism espoused by other sex tourists help to construct the Other prostitute as the embodiment of a contradiction, that is, as a "whore" who does it for pleasure as much as for money, an object with a subjectivity completely attuned to their own, in short, the embodiment of a masturbatory fantasy. Time and again Western sex tourists have assured us that the local girls really are "hot for it," that Third World prostitutes enjoy their work and that their highest ambition is to be the object of a Western man's desire. Their belief that Third World prostitutes are genuinely economically desperate rather than making a free choice to prostitute for "easy money" is clearly inconsistent with their belief that Third World prostitutes are actually acting on the basis of mutual sexual desire, but it is a contradiction that appears to resolve (at least temporarily) an anxiety they have about the relationship between sex, gender, sexuality, and "race."

The vast majority of the sex tourists we have interviewed believe that gender attributes, including sexual behavior, are determined by biological sex. They say that it is natural for women to be passive and sexually receptive as well as to be homemakers, child rearers, dependent upon and subservient toward men, which is why white Western women (prostitute and nonprostitute alike) often appear to them as unsexed. Thus the sex tourist quoted at the beginning of this chapter could only explain women's presence on traditional male terrain by imagining them as sexually "unnatural" ("Most of these girls are dykes anyways"). White women's relative economic, social and political power as well as their very whiteness makes it hard for Western male sex tourists to eroticize them as nothing more than sexual beings. Racism/ethnocentrism can collapse such tensions. If black or Latin women are naturally physical, wild, hot and sexually powerful, there need be no anxiety about enjoying them as pure sex. Equally, racism settles the anxieties some men have about the almost "manly" sexual power and agency attributed to white prostitutes. A Little Brown Fucking Machine is not unsexed by prostituting, she is "just doing what comes naturally." Since the Other woman is a "natural" prostitute, her prostitution does not make her any the less a "natural woman." All these points are also relevant to understanding the phenomenon of female sex tourism.

"OTHERNESS" AND FEMALE SEX TOURISM

Western women's sexual behavior abroad (both historically and contemporaneously) is often viewed in a rather different light compared to that of their male counterparts, and it is without doubt true that Western women who travel to Third World destinations in search of sex differ from many of the Western male sex tourists discussed above in terms of their attitudes toward prostitution and sexuality. Few of them are prostitute users back home, and few of them would choose to visit brothels while abroad or to pay street prostitutes for a quick "hand job" or any other sexual service (although it should be noted that some women do behave in these ways). But one of the author's (Sanchez Taylor) ongoing interview and survey research with female sex tourists in Jamaica and the Dominican Republic suggests that there are also similarities between the sexual behavior of Western women and men in sex tourist resorts.

The Caribbean has long been a destination that offers tourist women opportunities for sexual experience, and large numbers of women from the United States, Canada, Britain, and Germany as well as smaller numbers of women from other European countries and from Japan (i.e., the same countries that send male sex tourists) engage in sexual relationships with local men while on holiday there (Karch and Dann 1981, Pruitt and La Font 1995, Chevannes 1993). Preliminary analysis of data from Sanchez Taylor's survey of a sample of 104 single Western female tourists in Negril, Sosúa, and Boca Chica shows that almost 40 percent had entered into some form of sexual relationship with a local man.[3] The survey data further suggest that these were not chance encounters but rather that the sexually active female tourists visit the islands in order to pursue one or more sexual relationships. Only 9 percent of sexually active women were on their first trip; the rest had made numerous trips to the islands, and over 20 percent of female sex tourists reported having had two or more different local sexual partners in the course of a two- to three-week stay. Furthermore, female sex tourists, as much as male sex tourists, view their sexual experiences as integral to their holiday—"When in Jamaica you have to experience everything that's on offer," one black American woman explained, while a white woman working as a tour representative for a U.S. package operator said: "I tell my single women: come down here to love them, fuck them, and leave them, and you'll have a great time here. Don't look to get married. Don't call them."

Like male sex tourists, these women differ in terms of their age, nationality, social class, and racialized identity, including among their ranks young "spice girl" teenagers and students as well as grandmothers in their sixties, working class as well as middle class professionals, or self-employed women. They also differ in terms of the type of sexual encounters they pursue and the way in which they interpret these encounters. Some are eager to find a man as soon as they get off the plane and enter into multiple, brief, and instrumental relationships; others want to be romanced and sweet-talked by one or perhaps two men during their holiday. Around 40 percent described their relationships with local men as "purely physical" and 40 percent described them as "holiday romances." Twenty percent said that they had found "true love." Almost all the sexually active women surveyed stated that they had "helped their partner(s) out financially" by buying them meals, drinks, gifts, or by giving cash, and yet none of them perceived these relationships as commercial sexual transactions. Asked whether they had ever been approached by a gigolo/prostitute during their stay in Jamaica, 90 percent of them replied in the negative. The data collected in the Dominican Republic revealed similar patterns of denial.

The informal nature of the sexual transactions in these resorts blurs the boundaries of what constitutes prostitution for Western women just as it does for Western men, allowing them to believe that the meals, cash, and gifts they provide for their sexual partners do not represent a form of payment for services rendered but rather an expression of their own munificence. It is only when women repeatedly enter into a series of extremely brief sexual encounters that they begin to acknowledge that, as one put it, "It's all about money." Even this does not lead them to view themselves as prostitute users, however, and again it is notions of difference and Otherness that play a key role in protecting the sex tourist from the knowledge that they are paying for the sexual attentions they receive. As Others, local men are viewed as beings possessed of a powerful and indiscriminate sexuality that they cannot control, and this explains their eagerness for sex with tourist women, regardless of their age, size, or physical appearance. Again, the Other is not *selling* sex, just "doing what comes naturally."

As yet, the number of black female sex tourists in Sanchez Taylor's survey and interview sample is too small to base any generalizations upon,[4] but so far, their attitudes are remarkably consistent with those voiced by the central character in Terry Macmillan's 1996 novel *How Stella Got Her Groove*, in which a black American woman finds "love and romance" with a Jamaican boy almost half her age and with certainly less than half her economic means.[5] Stella views her own behavior in a quite different light from that of white male sex tourists—she disparages an older white male tourist as "a dirty old man who probably has to pay for all the pussy he gets" (1996:83). It is also interesting to note the ways in which Macmillan "Otherizes" local men: the Jamaican boy smells "primitive"; he is "exotic and goes with the Island"; he is "Mr Expresso in shorts" (1996:142, 154). Like white female sex tourists interviewed in the course of research, Macmillan further explains the young Jamaican man's disinterest in Jamaican women and so his sexual interest in an older American woman by Otherizing local women through the use of derogatory stereotypes. Thus, Jamaican women are assumed to be rapacious, materialistic, and sexually instrumental—they only want a man who owns a big car and house and money—and so Jamaican men long for women who do not demand these things (i.e., American women who already possess them).

Like their male counterparts, Western female sex tourists employ fantasies of Otherness not just to legitimate obtaining sexual access to the kind of young, fit, handsome bodies that would otherwise be denied to them and to obtain affirmation of their own sexual desirability (because the fact is that some female sex tourists are themselves young and fit looking and would be easily able to secure sexual access to equally appealing male bodies at home) but also to obtain a sense of power and control over themselves and others as engendered, sexual beings and to affirm their own privilege as

Westerners. Thus they continually stress their belief that people in the Caribbean "are different from Westerners." Sexual life is one of the primary arenas in which this supposed difference is manifest. More than half of the female sex tourists surveyed in Jamaica stated that Jamaicans are more relaxed about teenage sex, casual sex, and prostitution than Westerners. In response to open-ended questions, they observed that "Jamaican men are more up front about sex," that "Jamaicans are uninhibited about sex," that "Jamaicans are naturally promiscuous," and that "sex is more natural to Jamaicans." In interviews, female sex tourists also reproduced the notion of an opposition between the "civilized" West and the "primitive" Third World. One Scots grandmother in her early forties described the Dominican Republic as follows: "It's just like Britain before its industrial phase, it's just behind Britain, just exactly the same. Kids used to get beat up to go up chimneys, here they get beaten up to go polish shoes. There's no difference."

Western female sex tourists' racisms, like those of male sex tourists, are also many-layered and nuanced by differences in terms of nationality, age, and racialized identity. There are older white American female sex tourists whose beliefs about "race" and attitudes toward interracial sex are based upon an ideology that is overtly white supremacist. The black male represents for them the essence of an animalistic sexuality that both fascinates and repels. While in their own country they would not want to openly enter a sexual relationship with a black man, in a holiday resort like Negril, they can transgress the racialized and gendered codes that normally govern their sexual behavior, while maintaining their honor and reputation back home. As one Jamaican gigolo commented:

> While they are here they feel free. Free to do what they never do at home. No one looking at them. Get a Black guy who are unavailable at home. No one judge them. Get the man to make they feel good then they go home clean and pure.

This observation, and all the sexual hostility it implies, is born out by the following extract from an interview with a forty-five-year-old white American woman from Chicago, a regular sex tourist to Negril:

> [Jamaican men] are all liars and cheats.... [American women come to Negril because] they get what they don't get back home. A girl who no one looks twice at back home, she gets hit on all the time here, all these guys are paying her attention, telling her she's beautiful, and they really want her.... They're obsessed with their dicks. That's all they think of, just pussy and money and nothing else.... In Chicago, this could never happen. It's like a secret, like a fantasy and then you go home.

When asked whether she would ever take a black boyfriend home and introduce him to her friends and family, she was emphatic that she would not—"No, no, never. It's not like that. This is something else, you know, it's time out. Like a fantasy." This is more than simply a fantasy about having multiple anonymous sexual encounters without getting caught and disgraced. It is also a highly racialized fantasy about power and vengeance. Women like the sex tourist quoted above are looking for black men with good bodies, firm and muscle-clad sex machines that they can control, and this element of control should not be overlooked. It is also important to female sex tourists who reject white supremacist ideologies, and there are many of these, including white liberals and young white women who value Blackness as a "cool" commodity in the same way that many young white men do, and black American and black British female sex tourists.

These latter groups do not wish to indulge in the overtly hostile racialized sexual fantasy described by the woman quoted above, but they do want to live out other fantasies, whether they be "educating and helping the noble savage," or being the focus of "cool" black men's adoring gaze, or being the central character of a Terry Macmillan novel.[6] No matter what specific fantasy they pursue, female sex tourists use their economic power to initiate and terminate sexual relations with local men at whim, and within those relationships, they use their economic and racialized power to control these men in ways in which they could never command a Western man. These are unaccustomed powers, and even the female sex tourists who buy into exoticizing rather than hostile and denigrating racisms appear to enjoy them as such.

For white women, these powers are very clearly linked to their own whiteness as well as to their status and economic power as tourist women. Thus they contrast their own experience against that of local women (remarking on the fact that they are respected and protected and not treated like local women) *and* against their experience back home (commenting on how safe they feel in the Caribbean walking alone at night and entering bars and discos by themselves, observing that local men are far more attentive and chivalrous than Western men). Take, for example, the comments of "Judy," a white American expatriate in the Dominican Republic, a woman in her late fifties and rather overweight:

When you go to a disco, [white] men eye up a woman for her body, whatever. Dominicans don't care because they love women, they love women. It's not that they're indifferent or anything. They are very romantic, they will never be rude with you, while a white man will say something rude to you, while Dominican men are not like that at all. A white man will say to me, like, "slut" to me and I have been with a lot of Dominican men and they would never say anything like that to you. They are more respectful. Light cigarettes, open doors, they are more gentlemen. Where white men don't do that. So if you have been a neglected woman in civilization, when you come down here, of course, when you come down here they are going to wipe you off your feet.

The Dominican Republic presents women like Judy with a stage upon which to simultaneously affirm their femininity through their ability to command men and exact revenge on white men by engaging sexually with the competition, i.e., the black male. For the first time she is in a position to call the shots. Where back home white female sex tourists' racialized privilege is often obscured by their lack of gender power and economic disadvantage in relation to white men, in sex tourist resorts it is recognized as a source of personal power and power over others. Meanwhile, their beliefs about gender and sexuality prevent them from seeing themselves as sexually exploitative. Popular discourses about gender present women as naturally sexually passive and receptive, and men as naturally indiscriminate and sexually voracious. According to this essentialist model of gender and sexuality, women can never sexually exploit men in the same way that men exploit women because penetrative heterosexual intercourse requires the woman to submit to the male—she is "used" by him. No matter how great the asymmetry between female tourist and local male in terms of their age or economic, social, and racialized power, it is still assumed that the male derives benefits from sex above and beyond the purely pecuniary and so is not being exploited in the same way that a prostitute woman is exploited by a male client. This is especially the case when the man so used is socially constructed as a racialized, ethnic or cultural Other and assumed to have an uncontrollable desire to have sex with as many women as he possibly can.

CONCLUSION

The demand for sex tourism is inextricably linked to discourses that naturalize and celebrate inequalities structured along lines of class, gender, and race/Otherness; in other words, discourses that reflect and help to reproduce a profoundly hierarchical model of human sociality. Although sex tourists are a heterogeneous group in terms of their background characteristics and specific sexual interests, they share a common willingness to embrace this hierarchical model and a common pleasure in the fact that their Third World tourism allows them either to affirm their dominant position within a hierarchy of gendered, racialized, and economic power or to adjust their own position upward in that hierarchy. In the Third World, neocolonial relations of power equip Western sex tourists with an extremely high level of control over themselves and others as sexual beings and, as a result, with the power to realize the fantasy of their choosing. They can experience sexual intimacy without risking rejection; they can evade the social meanings that attach to their own age and body type; they can transgress social rules governing sexual life without consequence for their own social standing;

they can reduce other human beings to nothing more than the living embodiments of masturbatory fantasies.

In short, sex tourists can experience in real life a world very similar to that offered in fantasy to pornography users: "Sexuality and sexual activity are portrayed in pornography as profoundly distanced from the activities of daily life. The action in pornography takes place in what Griffin has termed 'pornotopia,' a world outside real time and space" (Hartsock 1983:175). To sex tourists, the resorts they visit are fantasy islands, variously peopled by Little Brown Fucking Machines, "cool" black women who love to party, "primitive smelling" black studs who only think of "pussy and money," respectful Latin gentlemen who love women. All the sex tourist has to do to attain access to this fantasy world is to reach into his or her pocket, for it is there that the sex tourist, like other individuals in capitalist societies, carries "his social power as also his connection with society" (Marx 1973:94). That the Western sex tourist's pocket can contain sufficient power to transform others into Others, mere players on a pornographic stage, is a testament to the enormity of the imbalance of economic, social, and political power between rich and poor nations. That so many Westerners *wish* to use their power in this way is a measure of the bleakness of the prevailing model of human nature and the human sociality that their societies offer them.

NOTES

1. In 1995, we were commissioned by ECPAT (End Child Prostitution in Asian Tourism) to undertake research on the identity, attitudes, and motivations of clients of child prostitutes. This involved ethnographic fieldwork in tourist areas in South Africa, India, Costa Rica, Venezuela, Cuba, and the Dominican Republic. We are currently working on an Economic and Social Research Council–funded project (Award no. R 000 23 7625), which builds on this research through a focus on prostitution and the informal tourist economy in Jamaica and the Dominican Republic. Taking these projects together, we have interviewed some 250 sex tourists and sexpatriates and over 150 people involved in tourist-related prostitution (women, children and men working as prostitutes, pimps, procurers, brothel keepers, etc.).

2. The fact that not all men are prostitute users is something that is often forgotten in radical feminist analyses of prostitution which, as Hart has noted, encourage us to view "either all men as prostitutes' clients or prostitutes' clients as somehow standing for/being symbolic of men in general" (1994:53).

3. Because the survey aims to support exploration and theory development in a previously underresearched field, purposive (nonprobability) sampling methods were employed (Arber 1993:72). Sanchez Taylor obtained a sample by approaching all single female tourists in selected locations (a particular stretch of beach, or a given bar or restaurant) and asking them to complete questionnaires.

4. Four out of eighteen single black British and American female tourists surveyed had entered into sexual relationships with local men. Sanchez Taylor also interviewed four more black female sex tourists.

5. In Negril, gigolos often refer to black American female sex tourists as "Stellas," after this fictional character.

6. Macmillan hints at the transgressive elements of a black Western female sex tourist's excitement—Stella's desire for the "primitive"-smelling younger man makes her feel "kind of slutty," but she likes the feeling.

3

Globalization, Tourism, and the International Sex Trade

BEVERLEY MULLINGS

In 1996 the Jamaican government outlined its vision for a restructured and sustainable tourism industry in a report documenting the national industrial policy (Government of Jamaica 1996). Noting that between 1980 and 1994 the sector had become by far the largest and most important contributor to GDP in the economy, the government attributed the industry's success to a number of innovations that included the concept of the all-inclusive[1] holiday and a vigorous program of marketing and promotion. In charting the future, the government stated its commitment to the pursuit of new market niches, each designed to provide flexible tourism goods and services. By the term "flexible," I am referring to a range of strategies designed to quickly respond to consumer demand at a competitive price. As Jamaican tourism policy officials continued to promote service niches such as heritage and ecotourism (Government of Jamaica 1996) another less welcomed niche service, sex tourism,[2] began to expand. Unlike ecotourism and heritage tourism, whose growth has been attributed to the success of the island's flexible tourism strategy, sex tourism is viewed as a form of harassment that threatens the viability of the tourism industry as a whole. This chapter seeks to examine the relationship between the strategies that have been used to restructure Jamaica's tourism industry and the visible growth of the international trade in sex services on the island. It argues that while the trade in sex services has not been a formal component of the restructuring of the tourism sector, its growth since the 1980s is related to the policies embodied in the strategy of flexible tourism. By examining the factors behind the demand for and supply of sex tourism, this chapter analyzes the extent to which issues of economic, trade and industry policy, business practices, race, gender, and international relations at the local and global levels are central in the development

56*Beverley Mullings*

of this industry. The chapter is divided into three parts. The first part examines the political, social, and economic context in which the Jamaican sex tourism industry has developed. Part two examines the factors behind the growth in demand and the supply of sex tourism services in Jamaica. The third part concludes by exploring the ways in which the current tourism strategies could be transformed in order to provide new income-earning opportunities for a wider cross section of the local population and the likely impact that such changes may have on the nature and character of the sex tourism sector.

THE POLITICAL ECONOMY OF JAMAICAN SEX TOURISM

Any examination of the political economy of the sex trade in Jamaica must be set in the context of a series of unequal relations that exist at a variety of spatial scales. Truong (1990) has noted in her examination of the political economy of sex tourism in Southeast Asia that the sector relies upon inequalities between First World and Third World countries, between capital and labor, men and women, and production and reproduction. These relations of power have become more intensely connected across a variety of scales of inquiry, as developments in transport and communications have brought sex tourists and sex traders into closer relations with each other. As sex tourism has grown it has highlighted the extent to which the most intimate of spatial scales, the body, has not been exempt from globalizing forces. Thus, as Pettman argues, the body has become a form of international currency creating a space where the international and the personal converge (Pettman 1997).

Sex work has been linked on a global scale to an expanding traveling public lured to the island by cheap package holidays, to the decline in Jamaica's exports and its debt obligations, and to technologies that create a virtual sex industry organized to a large extent by institutions and agents outside the country. In this respect, the growth of sex tourism in Jamaica reflects the power of increasingly globalized flows; of capital, policy directives, and information to draw places that were once "off the map" into ever-closer networks of commodified trade and exchange. On the local, national and household scales, the growth of sex tourism has been inextricably connected to the policy choices of government and the impact of those policies on the social and economic opportunities open to the population, in particular, its poorest members. Twenty years of structural adjustment have seen the liberalization, privatization, and devaluation of the Jamaican economy as well as the simultaneous loss of commodity markets, as the producers of bauxite and bananas have become the victims of falling prices or regional agreements to limit preferential markets. As tourism has become the number one foreign exchange earner, an increasing number of women, men, and children have entered this industry in search of opportunities to generate incomes at wages that more realistically reflect the current cost of living than the existing minimum wage.[3] In this regard the growth of sex tourism is also linked to the household scale as many sex workers enter the industry in order to ensure the economic survival of their households.

Sex tourism in Jamaica is particularly racialized. Like the new Third World assembly industries, the current international division of labor in the sex tourism sector primarily relies on the bodies and labor of women of color to create wealth. Such labor in both instances tends to be commodified and viewed as cheap, docile, and less politically explosive. Like women's labor in today's export-oriented manufacturing and service industries, there is much resistance to defining sex work as a form of work deserving of the type of protection afforded labor in the traditional industries. Without recognizing paid sexual labor as legitimate work, however, women and men in Jamaica's sex tourism sector are even more vulnerable to the labor and human rights abuses that many women on the assembly lines of Jamaica's export-oriented factories already face. It is important therefore that sex tourism be viewed as an export industry, with consumers who import services from local providers. Taking an industry approach to the development of sex tourism services also requires an examination of the demand and supply factors that have encouraged the sector's development and the benefits as well as costs that the current structure of the industry confers on those currently working within it.

Globalization and Tourism

While sex tourism has never been a planned or formal part of Jamaica's tourism product, it has developed hand in hand with attempts by the state and private sector to discipline the island's industries to the rules of a market-competitive, globalized world economy. The intensified speed at which economic and social networks are created (and destroyed) across national boundaries has become a hallmark feature of the globalization process (Giddens 1989, Hall 1992). This process has served not only to create a world that appears to be shrinking into a single interdependent unit, but also one where the everyday events in local communities are increasingly influenced by activities occurring in faraway places and seemingly disparate contexts. A vital catalyst behind the globalization of tourism has been the changes that have occurred in the scale and nature of demand for this service since the Second World War. The development of jet aircraft, increasing leisure time and disposable income, and the expansion of mass-produced tourism services from the 1950s to the 1970s facilitated the development of this industry. In the 1980s and 1990s the industry experienced even further growth, as the deregulation of airline routes forced many companies into virtual price wars. Tourism today has become big business. The World Tourism Trade Congress (WTTC) estimated in 1997 that the total economic value of goods and services attributable to tourism was $3.3 trillion, or 10.7 percent of gross global product, providing in the process employment for 260 million people the world over (WTTC 1997). With such numbers, more and more developing countries are seeking to develop tourism goods and services in order to provide jobs and accumulate much-needed foreign exchange. Data from the World Tourism Organization, for example, indicate that international tourism grew faster in developing countries in 1995 than in industrialized ones, reflecting the emergence of new developing-country tourism destinations.

Globalization, though often described as a shrinking process that is transforming the global economy into an interdependent and interconnected "village," in reality is a highly uneven and exclusionary process. As Hirst and Thompson (1997) have pointed out, claims of a "global village" should be regarded with skepticism given the fact that the important relationships in the international economy remain between industrialized countries, particularly among members of the Organization for Economic Co-operation and Development (OECD). Flows of international tourists are similarly highly uneven, with the majority of the world's tourists being drawn from, as well as to, the same handful of countries that constitute the OECD. Thus, despite the opportunities for revenue earnings that the global tourism industry presents, many developing countries must vigorously compete for tourists and market themselves as unique places for consumption.

The Globalization of Sex Tourism

If tourism is big business, then sex tourism is likely to be a lucrative segment of the industry. While very little is known about the size of this underground industry, writers such as Kempadoo and Doezema (1998) intimate that it is likely to be a multibillion dollar transnational industry creating employment and incomes for finders, brokers, syndicate operations, and pimp "managers." Certainly with the growth of the Internet and the explosion of information relay that has followed in its wake, it has become clear that sex tourism is just one part of a highly segmented and flexible industry providing services such as sex shops, massage parlors, escort services, cybersex, phonesex, exotic dancing, and products such as pornography and sex aids. Sex tourism is no longer associated with only Europe and East and Southeast Asia but is now an established segment of the sex and tourism industries in Latin America, Africa, and the Caribbean. As the international sex trade expands, even more complex global networks are being created as sex workers, largely from the developing world and Eastern Europe, migrate or are trafficked to large metropolitan centers to directly provide services to clients. Bindman, for example, documents that the trafficking of women, often due to debt bondage, creates complex global networks as agents transport women and girls from places as far afield as Nepal, India, and the Dominican Republic to Germany and Israel to work in the industry (Bindman 1998).

The Consumption and Production of "Far-Off" Places

The globalization of tourism, however, has not been simply the result of technological advances in transport or increased purchasing power. More recently, the nature of consumer demand has also begun to change. Particularly since the 1980s an increasing number of travelers have begun to demand travel experiences that are closely tailored to individual tastes (Poon 1989, 1990; Britton 1991; Urry 1995; Mowforth and Munt 1997). The "new middle classes," as these travelers are often described, emerged in the 1980s as new cultural intermediaries (Bourdieu 1984, Urry 1990, Featherstone 1991) initiating and transmitting new consumption patterns, including the search for "authentic" holidays in developing countries.

This growing shift in demand to more customized or unique travel experiences has been viewed by some sociologists as an expression of the tendency of the middle classes of the 1980s and 1990s to derive power and prestige from the consumption of goods and services with positional value. The consumption of positional goods and services acts as a powerful signifier of a consumer's position within a particular social hierarchy and functions as a form of cultural capital accumulation (Bourdieu 1984, Urry 1990, Featherstone 1991, Gabriel and Lang 1995, Miller 1995). Many developing countries have been drawn into the sphere of consumption of the new middle classes as destinations that are considered to be of high "cultural asset" value. Thus certain places, e.g., the Himalayas, or activities such as ecotourism have important symbolic meanings that are drawn upon by certain social classes to differentiate themselves from others, a disposition described by Bourdieu (1984) as *Habitus*.

Flexible Tourism and the Commodification of Place

A number of writers have attempted to define how the current movement toward a more consumer-oriented tourism is transforming the way that goods and services as well as places are created for consumption (Poon 1990, Conway 1993, Urry 1995, Ioannides and Dabbage 1998). Urry states that in contrast to an earlier Fordist epoch that was dominated by the mass production of standardized tourism goods and services, new forms are becoming more aestheticized and de-differentiated, transforming certain activities once considered outside of the realm of tourism, such as sport or sex services, into part of the travel experience (see Table 3.1). Poon (1989) argues that at the heart of the transformations that are occurring in the production of tourism services lies the concept of flexibility: the application of "best practice" strategies to respond quickly to consumer demand at a competitive price. Evidence of these changes can also be seen, as Table 3.1 demonstrates, in the tendency toward increased market segmentation by tourism-service providers and the shortening of the product life cycles of many destinations and services.

While some aspects of flexibility, such as attempts to widen the skills base of the average worker or the use of technologies to promote and market destinations, are to be welcomed, there is often a fine line between attempts to create a competitive product and the commodification of places and their inhabitants for profit. Mowforth and Munt (1997) argue that while the search for authenticity has become a critical feature of the consumption practices of the new middle classes, this criterion is often accompanied by an aestheticization and commodification of the places and people who form part of that travel experience. The commodification of place that often accompanies the search by travelers for a more "authentic" travel experience is an apparent contradiction that can be explained by the social and economic circumstances under which tourism-service exchanges occur. While "post-Fordist" consumers search for "real" and "honest" tourism services, they often seek to do so in societies that are compelled by financial need to create landscapes that appear to satisfy the authenticity requirement. This is not to say that all tourism spaces are contrived, but rather that as tourism has become the sole source of foreign exchange in many developing countries, so too has the importance of creating goods and services to satisfy consumer demand.

Flexible Tourism and the Restructuring of the Jamaican Economy

In Jamaica, tourism restructuring became a primary focus of the government in the 1980s, as other traditional exports such as bauxite and sugar lost their foreign exchange earning potential. Throughout the 1980s Jamaica actively diversified its tourism product by developing new market niches as well as increasing expenditure on tourism marketing and promotion. As a result of these efforts the sector has experienced rejuvenated growth since the 1980s. During this time a number of changes were also made to the structure and organization of the Jamaican tourism industry. These changes encompassed a wide range of strategies that have included privatization, market segmentation, the introduction of new technologies, and the vigorous marketing of the national tourism product. As part of the divestment package under the program of structural adjustment, for example, the government turned ownership of nationally owned hotels over to the private sector.

Table 3.1 Post-Fordist Consumption and Production in the Tourism Industry

Post-Fordist Consumption	Post-Fordist Production	Examples
• Greater volatility of consumer preferences.	• Shortening of the product life cycles.	• Increased market segmentation.
• Greater use of technologies to improve the promotion and marketing of destinations.	• Rejection of holiday camps and cheap package holidays.	• Increased attractions based on life-style research. The growth of tourism products staged around events, e.g., Reggae Sunsplash, and the rapid turnover in sites due to changing tastes.
• Increased preferences for nonmass forms of consumption, with emphasis on aestheticized forms of consumption.	• The development of many new customized products and services.	• The combining of tourism with leisure culture, sport, education, and retailing.

Adapted from Urry 1995, Table 9.2.

Between 1981 and 1990, fifteen of the thirty-four state-owned hotels were sold to private investors, the majority of whom were local. The state through the Jamaica Tourist Board (JTB) also sought to segment the tourism market by creating events such as the Jamaica Carnival and the Hot Air Balloon Festival to cater to specific consumer needs and lifestyles. Private sector market segmentation initiatives like the all-inclusive holiday were also given state support, and a number of new tourism products such as ecotourism, health tourism, and sport tourism were developed through joint public/private sector initiatives. In terms of technology, attempts have also been made to capture a larger proportion of the tourism market by linking into worldwide Computerized Reservation Systems (CRSs). In 1991, the Caribbean Hotels Association, in partnership with Cable and Wireless Plc., set up its own regional system, the Caribbean Hotels Association Reservation Management Service (CHARMS), and more recently another system, the Caribbean Reservation Centre International (CRC), was introduced by a subsidiary of the GTE multinational (Tour and Travel News 1990). The Jamaican government continues to actively promote the quality and quantity of tourism services and products, as evidenced in its recent J$1.24 billion (U.S.$33 million) promotional campaign to help create a "proper" image of the country's product (Government of Jamaica 1998).

Efforts to redefine Jamaica as a destination with something to satisfy every taste have been remarkably successful. Total visitor arrivals increased by 8 percent per year between 1980 and 1994, providing U.S.$919m in 1998, or 45 percent of the country's foreign exchange earnings. As stated in the National Industrial Policy document:

> The performance of the sector during the 1980–1994 period can be attributed to several factors. These include the success of the all-inclusive concept as an innovative market-segmentation approach, significant expenditure on marketing and promotion by government and the industry, a wide range and variety of visitor accommodation, and the strikingly diverse product (natural beauty, culture, entertainment, ambiance) which Jamaica provides for the visitor (Government of Jamaica 1996:116).

Of the initiatives to restructure the tourism industry, the all-inclusive concept has been the most successful (Poon 1990, Government of Jamaica 1996), making the largest contribution to GDP (J$1,604m or U.S.$70m) in 1992 and contributing approximately J$4,623m (U.S.$20m) in direct revenue to the Jamaican government (OAS 1994). This represented just over a fifth of the revenue received by the state from the entire tourism industry as a whole. It is therefore not surprising that the state assisted the expansion of the two locally owned resort chains, Sandals and the Superclubs Group. The hotels in these groups expanded from two in 1983, providing accommodation for 9.5

percent of the visitors to the island, to 41 in 1994,[4] accounting for 51.4 percent of all tourists to the island. Innovations such as the all-inclusive packaged holiday are viewed as post-Fordist not because of the clients that they serve (who tend to seek a fairly standardized and homogenous holiday experience) but because these thematically segmented markets are able to cater to a myriad of consumption tastes.

The restructuring of Jamaica's tourism industry, however, has not been without its critics. There is growing criticism that the success of "flexible" tourism strategies has resulted in a growing concentration of foreign exchange earnings into the hands of a few hoteliers (OAS 1994; *The Gleaner,* January 26, 1998). Others have also observed that while the tourism multiplier in the Caribbean has traditionally been small (Momsen 1994), the proliferation of the all-inclusive package holidays in particular has imposed further limits on the spread of the tourism dollar (Pattullo 1996). Small hoteliers, for example, have complained that they are being squeezed out of the industry by lack of government marketing support, which has been largely channeled toward the already successful all-inclusive hotels. Small firms also complain that the high rates of interest on loans make it difficult for them to provide a more competitive product (Gayle 1993). Other service providers, primarily those indirectly involved in the industry (taxi drivers, vendors, and local restaurant owners), also claim that opportunities to export their services to tourists have declined, as visitors to the all-inclusive hotels rarely venture outside of their hotel complexes. A 1992 assessment of the economic impact of tourism in Jamaica appeared to reinforce this claim. Comparing the financial statements of eleven all-inclusive hotels, the OAS found that while all-inclusives generated the largest amount of revenue, their impact on the economy was smaller than other hotels because they imported more and employed fewer people per dollar of revenue (OAS 1994).

While there is no doubt that Jamaica has successfully increased the foreign-exchange earning capacity of the tourism industry, the strategies used have been of little benefit to local communities. In grounding the restructuring of the tourism industry "in the market place," the government has created an industry with few multiplier effects or sectoral linkages with other parts of the economy. The impact of the narrowing of avenues for local participation in the export of tourism has been particularly hard hitting for poor rural households and micro-entrepreneurs who ordinarily would have relied upon tourists to purchase food items, crafts, and other services. Combined with the increased economic hardships that accompanied structural adjustment during the 1980s and 1990s, opportunities for income generation outside the formal hotel sector appear to be even more constrained.

In terms of creating stable tourism-related jobs at living wages, government policy since 1980 has been unsuccessful. While the industry currently employs (directly and indirectly) one in every four Jamaicans, in reality a large proportion of these jobs are low skilled and low waged, with very little security of tenure. Particularly among those in the informal sector, the financial benefits of tourism are often unreliable and, except for those in the illegal sector, less lucrative than for those in the formal hospitality sector. When one examines the reasons for the recent growth of sex tourism in Jamaica, it becomes quite clear that a major explanatory factor has been the failure of the government to provide local community members with a range of income-generation opportunities at living-wage levels. To focus, however, only on the factors shaping the supply of sex tourism services in Jamaica would be one sided. Also of importance to the sector's development have been the more general changes in the way that tourism, travel, and leisure pursuits have evolved since the 1950s.

Commodification and the Growth of Sex Tourism in Jamaica

Nowhere has the commodification of the travel experience been more clearly demonstrated than in the growth of sex tourism in Jamaica. While there is little documented information on the size and extent of the sex tourism market in Jamaica, anecdotal references suggest that this subsector has grown as the tourism sector has expanded (Pruitt and LaFont 1995; Pattullo 1996; *Gleaner*, June 16, 1997). Government representatives tend to view the growth of the trade as largely supply driven and a form of tourist harassment. Rather than viewing sex work as a form of employment that contributes to the national income, the sector is viewed largely as a threat to the prosperity of the industry as a whole, as demonstrated in the following commentary, recently published in the local newspaper:

> The pimps and the touts, the drug pushers and the sex-sellers, the hair braiders and others who see the tourists as fair game to be pestered, molested, and generally preyed upon are very effectively driving the visitors away, to the detriment of the nation as a whole (*Gleaner*, June 16, 1997).

Few representatives of the Jamaican tourism industry have been willing to acknowledge that a sex tourism industry exists on the island, and even fewer have sought to analyze the structural forces that shape the conditions under which workers trade their services. The almost visceral responses to a call in 1998 by a representative of the private sector for the formalization of sex work in Jamaica is indicative of the moralistic and condemnatory environment that sex workers must negotiate on an everyday basis (*Observer*, June 13, 1998; *Gleaner*, June 21 and 25, 1998; *Herald*, June 21, 1998).

As tourism has become the island's major foreign exchange earner and as the visibility of sex tourism has increased, so too has the criminalization of sex workers. In 1997, 55.8 percent of tourists to the island reported during a visitor satisfaction survey that they had felt harassed during their holiday (Government of Jamaica 1998). In response to these findings the government introduced an antiharassment program and made amendments to existing legislation in order to increase the severity of penalties for accused "harassers." Under the *Towns and Communities Act* and the *Tourist Board Act*, higher penalties have been introduced for individuals engaged in so-called antisocial behavior. Under these acts, behaviors considered antisocial include indecent exposure in a public place; the use of threatening, abusive, or calumnious language; loitering in a public place; and soliciting for the purpose of prostitution. Fines have been increased from J$1,000 (approximately U.S.$28) to as much as J$150,000 (U.S.$4,286) and particular areas in the capital city known to be red-light districts have been incorporated into the Act. The defining of sex work as a form of tourist harassment and a threat to the industry highlights the fact that few policy makers view this form of employment as an outcome of the narrowing of employment opportunities at living wages for all but a few of the island's population. Indeed, as the Minister of Tourism declared during his budget speech:

> The truth is that the type of harassment that has given us the reputation that we have has nothing to do with the socio-economic situation in the country—it has to do with a type of Jamaican who has no intention of earning an honest day's pay for an honest day's work but is much more comfortable preying upon others—be they visitors or Jamaicans—for a livelihood (Government of Jamaica 1998:12).

Few industry representatives have sought to examine the contribution of Jamaica's sex trade to the growth of the tourism industry, even though writers such as Truong (1990), Bishop and Robinson (1997), and Lim (1998) have argued that in Southeast Asia it is an enormously lucrative service that contributes to the wealth of businesses, state agents, and ultimately the state. Certainly, when compared to the highest revenue earners, the earnings of sex workers are likely to have a greater direct impact on local households and communities given the fact that many use their earnings to purchase items needed by other family members. The disdain that is expressed for sex workers by many in the tourism industry is all the more contradictory when the industry as a whole routinely utilizes hedonistic imagery of "sun, sand and sex" that relies heavily on racialized constructions of women as "exotic" and "wild" to market the island as a tourism destination (Hobson et al. 1994).

Structure of the Sex Tourism Sector

Part of the growth of the Jamaican sex tourism sector can be attributed to the fact that in keeping with current trends in consumer demand, it too caters to a particular segment of the tourism market. From the information that does exist, it would appear that the sex tourism sector can be divided into informal and formalized segments, accommodating both own-account and waged workers in both part-time and full-time capacities (Fig. 3.1). More formalized transactions are very similar to those found in most erotic clubs and brothels, where service providers tend to be employed in a bar or club and are paid wages by an employer. Informal service providers, on the other hand, tend to be either self-employed or regulated by a pimp. Services provided by this group often require immediate remuneration, and clients and traders rarely develop more than a transient relationship. Within this segment, however, more formalized obligations may accompany transactions, and workers might require tourists to provide hotel accommodation, meals, drinks, transport, money, and clothing in exchange for sex. Here, transactions involve more than physical exchanges, and sex workers often also play multiple roles as holiday companions and tour guides as well as sex partners. Unlike the East Asian sex tourism sector, where women appear to be the dominant sex workers, both women and men in Jamaica appear to be equally active in the supply of sex services to tourists. Pruitt and LaFont (1995) have argued that male sex workers are involved in romance rather than sex tourism, because there is often a level of emotional involvement that is not often present in sex tourism. These holiday relationships tend to be longer term, involving a much higher level of social and economic commitment on the part of both parties in the exchange. They also argue that some relationships may last for many years and result in marriage or migration. They do note, however, that the framework of romance may have contrasting meanings and confer very different kinds of benefit to each party in the relationship. Other researchers have conducted studies that challenge Pruitt and LaFont's classification. While the longer term nature of the exchanges that occur in romance-tourism encounters serve to differentiate them from other sex services, it is not at all clear that these services are largely provided by men (Codrescu 1998, Oppermann 1998; see also chapter 6). Cohen (1986) and Günther (1998), for example, both challenge this classification by arguing that men value and engage in this type of relationship too. Certainly accounts elsewhere in this book suggest that male clients are as likely to become involved in such long-term and committed relationships.

The report of the "Knowledge, Attitudes and Practices Study" among women and girls employed in the commercial sex industry in 1996, conducted by the Ministry of Health, provides some indication of the demographic profile of street-based sex workers (Ministry of Health 1996). The survey of 100 female sex workers in Kingston, Montego Bay, and Ocho Rios indicated that a substantial proportion of sex workers (23 percent) were girls and women between the ages of thirteen and nineteen years old. This sup-

Figure 3.1 Structure of the Sex Tourism Industry in Jamaica

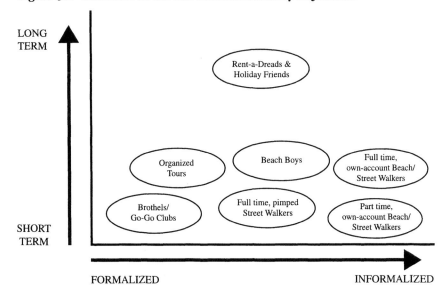

ported the findings of an earlier survey that found that 40 percent of sixty-eight sex workers interviewed had entered this form of work between the ages of fifteen and nineteen. Although 85 percent of the workers interviewed in the 1996 survey had achieved an all-age, technical, or secondary school education, the majority (86 percent) were not formally employed. While the information provided from the interviewed sample suggests that Jamaican sex workers enter the labor force at early stages in their life cycles, there are insufficient data to conclude that children constitute a substantial proportion of the industry. Unlike some parts of Asia, where as many as a third of sex workers are less than seventeen years of age[5] (Lim 1998), information provided by women in the study by Campbell et al. in this volume suggest that the Jamaican sex tourism industry is comprised of an older workforce.

Supply-Side Issues in Jamaican Sex Tourism

As Enloe (1989) points out, to succeed, sex tourism requires Third World men, women, and children to be economically desperate enough to enter into prostitution; once an individual does so, it becomes more difficult to leave. Since the 1980s Jamaicans have had to survive a long and painful process of structural adjustment that has included the massive depreciation of the value of the Jamaican dollar to less than five U.S. cents,[6] the acceleration of inflation to a peak of 80 percent in 1991, and increases in the cost of basic food and utility prices. These increases in the cost of living have taken place in an environment of business closures and reductions in public expenditure on health, social security, and education. Between 1981–82 and 1992–93, for example, real per capita expenditure in these sectors fell from J$119 to J$53, a decline of over 55 percent (PIOJ 1994). In addition to the overall economic decline, many Jamaicans have experienced diminishing opportunities for employment, as primary and secondary industries have downsized or relocated to other countries (Watson 1990, 1995). While official statistics publish unemployment rates as low as 16 percent (PIOJ 1996), many argue that this figure masks the high levels of underemployment and gender and urban/rural inequalities that exist (Massiah 1989, Deere et al. 1990).

The devastating impact of declining opportunities for income generation has been particularly hard hitting for households in rural areas. In 1992, for example, the World Bank and the Statistical Institute of Jamaica estimated that almost a third of all Jamaican households lived below the poverty line[7] and of that number 70 percent were concentrated in the rural areas (World Bank 1994:19). Given that this statistic was based on households rather than individuals, one could expect that the proportion of the population in poverty was even higher.

The loss of formal income-generation opportunities has forced many poor Jamaicans to enter the informal service sector (Bolles 1985, Deere et al. 1990, Anderson and Witter 1994, French 1994). Women are heavily represented in the informal sector that accounted for 37 percent of all women workers in 1992 (Statistical Institute of Jamaica 1993). The growth of the informal sector over the past ten years demonstrates the extent to which restructuring strategies have failed to create meaningful employment for much of the population. Anderson and Witter (1994) argue, for example, that most of the informal sector jobs that have been created are low skilled and few have the capacity to stimulate other forms of employment. The growth of informal sector employment has been particularly significant in rural areas, where the number of secondary and informal sector jobs increased by 127 percent between 1977 and 1989 (Anderson and Witter 1994:33).

In order to survive the impoverishing effects of a decade of structural adjustment, many women have turned to a number of coping strategies collectively described as "making do." Senior defines making do as

> a social phenomenon which is widely accepted: that is, it is a fundamental role of poor women to make do with what they have or better still, "make something from nothing" in order to maintain their families. At its simplest level "making do" involves "cutting and carving" or "cutting and contriving," i.e., being resourceful in using whatever is available to maximize its utility to oneself and family (1991:130–31).

While "making do" most commonly refers to strategies such as income pooling and informal commercial trading to bring extra income into households, Senior argues that for many women the practice also includes decisions regarding the kinds of relationships formed with men. It is not uncommon, she states, for women to utilize their sexual labor if necessary to manipulate and switch partners in order to meet daily domestic commitments. Massiah (1989) and Barrow (1986) make similar observations, pointing out a variety of utilitarian relations that have developed between men and women, ranging from prostitution to relationships of convenience. While women in a study by Barrow recognized the importance of sexual fidelity, they also argued that it was sometimes necessary to switch partners or become involved with another person's partner in order to get money for their own use. An article in a Jamaican newspaper recently highlighted the extent to which women from all classes in Jamaican society were making do by entering into sexual relationships with wealthy men in exchange for financial reward or security. Entitled "The Changing Face of Prostitution," the article explored the attitudes of a number of women to the material rewards gained from extramarital and temporary relationships with wealthy local businessmen. As one informant explained:

> No longer are Jamaican women willing to live with a man for a number of years and not have anything to show.... It is horrifying the number of young girls who have been used by men, who when they are tired of them put them out and go on to greener pastures.... I guess the women are demanding economic remuneration for their companionship against that background (*Flair Magazine*, November 5, 1987).

While economic hardship has forced many Jamaican women into the sex trade since the 1980s, the use of sexual labor to maintain quality of life has had a much longer precedence in the island's history. The sexual labor of women as concubines, mistresses, and domestic/sexual servants has traditionally played a role in the reproduction of Jamaican life. As a number of writers have pointed out (Richter 1989, Truong 1990, Bishop and Robinson 1997), sex tourism is just one category of sexual labor that exists along a continuum of contemporary forms. Given the traditional reliance on sexual labor to maintain livelihoods, and the narrowing of employment opportunities—particularly for women—it is not surprising that sex tourism has become a part of the tourism industry.

The tourism industry is often seen as a very lucrative route for informal service providers because transactions are often made in foreign currencies and prices are negotiated. As the number of persons entering the service sector has grown, Jamaica's tourism landscape has transformed, as increasing numbers of men, women, and children from the city as well as surrounding rural hinterlands have sought to generate incomes from the sale of cheap manufactures such as straw and wood crafts and consumer services such as food, hair braiding, sunburn massages, drugs, and sex. The expansion of the provision of these personal consumer services, however, has not been unproblematic. As tourism has become more "flexible" and consumer-oriented in the formal sector, opportunities for informal trade have become more restricted, rendering particular sites such as the beach, where tourists are most likely to be found, virtual war zones. As an earlier quote demonstrated, industry representatives have grown intolerant of the presence of informal traders in the tourism landscape and have sought to "formalize or eliminate" their presence through initiatives such as the construction of designated craft markets, the institution of beach-patrol officers, and the regulation of street vendors. Removing informal traders from the gaze of tourists, however, has served only to further minimize the benefits of tourism to the general population, because, compared to the hotel and accommodation or formal retailing sectors, both of which have high propensities to import,[8] the informal sector has a greater immediate impact on employment and society as a whole. The reality of current initiatives to eliminate informal sector traders from the tourism landscapes is that they serve to increase the alienation that local communities feel in relation to the tourism industry. As the secretary of the craft market in Ocho Rios, a major tourist center, observed, the benefits of tourism are becoming increasingly skewed toward a small and powerful group of local elites. In an article entitled "Only 'Big Man' Benefitting from Tourists' Safety," he stated:

> We are told that the high level of tourist harassment in the town was preventing us from doing good business.... Well harassment is no longer a problem and the only place I see visitors are in the in-bond plazas and all-inclusive hotels (*Gleaner*, January 26, 1998).

For young women in particular, sex tourism offers much higher income generation opportunities than most blue-collar manufacturing and other service jobs. Assembly workers in Jamaican export processing zones in 1994, for example, earned on average U.S.$1 per hour, with little or no job security, while estimates provided on Internet sites quote figures of $U.S.40–150 as the price charged for a single commercial sexual encounter. With such disparities between earning capacities, it is likely that the supply of sex workers has increased, as alternatives for income generation, particularly in the rural hinterlands, have declined.

Examining the economic impact of sex tourism on the Jamaica economy is an almost impossible task, given the extent to which much of the sector remains part of the underground economy. One estimate by a local reporter estimated the value of the industry to be J$0.5bn (U.S.$14m) per year (Riley 1994), but these figures were based on sex workers in brothels in the capital city. Such figures are unlikely to provide a realistic picture of the earnings of sex workers, given the fact, as the article itself pointed out, that brothel owners usually take a sizable portion of earnings. From the anecdotal evidence that exists, however, it would appear that the earnings of many of the women and girls who enter the trade directly benefit other household members. It is not uncommon for the earnings of sex workers to be the sole source of household income or for young girls to periodically enter the trade to supplement family financial resources. In an article that published the personal narrative of a teenage sex worker in 1996, it is clear that contrary to popular belief, young women were providing sexual services to tourists not because they enjoyed "preying upon" these visitors but rather because of the absence of alternative sources of income within their households. As Tanya, a seventeen-year-old sex worker in the North Coast tourist area, explained in the published account:

> Mi used to go to one Secondary school and mi used to be one of the brightest in the class. Boy, mi wish mi mother did have somebody fi help her cause mi know seh she nuh like weh mi a do. If ah wasn't doing this probably mi little bredda and sista dem would not be going to school.... Mi always try fi help out mi mother and mi little bredda and sista dem, A want tell you sey all right now, a just last week me go a Courts [a furniture store] go tek out one sewing machine and gi di ole lady fi start do one little dressmaking ting a di house you know. As soon as mi save up enough money mi a go tek some CXC [high school education certification] subjects and come out of dem tings yah. Mi really want to better mi life, but mi just don't want fi go siddung a my yard so. Mi have fi mek sure sey tings kinda alright wid funds yuh know (*Sunday Observer*, March 24, 1996).

Demand Side Issues in the Jamaican Sex Tourism Industry

While the Jamaican government continues to view sex tourism as a primarily supply-driven industry, a number of writers have convincingly argued that there is a significant demand-driven element to this international service (Pruitt 1995, Davidson 1996, Ware 1997, Oppermann 1998). The commodification of place that has become associated with many of the contemporary forms of tourism is often extended to the women and men who inhabit those landscapes. While many tourists travel to experience wonderful beaches, reliable sun, and the pleasure of meeting people from different cultures, some also seek the opportunity to engage in forms of hedonistic consumption that they could not have at home. As sex tourism has become globalized, so too has the demand by a certain type of traveler for the sexual services of men and women in "exotic" or "authentic" landscapes who are transformed into objects of fascination and desire. It is in this context that places like Jamaica and the rest of the Caribbean have become drawn into the global sex industry, as elements of desire, power, sexism and racism combine in the quest to consume an "authentic" Jamaican.

As a number of writers (Momsen 1994, Davidson 1996, Kempadoo 1996, Pettman 1997) have pointed out, notions of "exoticism" and racial and gender stereotypes are crucial underpinning ideologies in the growing demand for sex tourism. The exoticization of women and men of color and the corresponding desire to experience and consume their bodies is argued to be the flip side of a process of "Othering," where these so-called traits simultaneously serve to confirm their status as inferior human subjects and their suitability as commodities for consumption. As the demand for flexible tourism services has grown, so too has the global reach of the sex trade. While in the 1950s and 1960s women in Southeast and East Asia represented the ideal, erotic commodity, desired for their assumed promiscuity and passivity, by the 1980s and 1990s new, even more exotic/erotic men and women were being sought for consumption. In this regard, the relatively recent roots of Caribbean sex tourism may be quite different from that of East and Southeast Asia, which Truong (1990) argues was closely linked to the recognition by policy makers in the U.S. military and later industry and the government of the economic value of leisure time to the productivity of workers. While the importance of supply-side factors such as widening income disparities and the pauperization of many developing countries since the 1970s are important considerations, the changing geography of sex tourism appears to be corresponding to the changes taking place in the demand for tourism services, and the search for a more personalized experience. Sex tourism in the Caribbean may therefore be more closely linked to the demand for a travel experience with higher cultural capital value than other sex tourism centers like Thailand. A posting in an Australian-based Internet sex tourism travel guide indicates the extent to which the market for Asian sex services may have become saturated, resulting in a diversification in demand by a segment of the sex tourism population. As the posting boasts:

> We not only look at well-known centers of the sex industry but also inform you about those undiscovered by mass tourism. Places where girls are young, and inexpensive and the competition for them is low. Read about exotic countries like GHANA which has excellent beaches, relatively little AIDS, and beautiful girls for as little as $10 a night! (*World Nightlife Guide for Women*).

The quote points to two important factors that may be driving the current globalization of sex tourism. First, the quote suggests that the market for the more commonly known sex destinations may be saturated. Saturation appears to be related to the fact that as increasing numbers of travelers compete to consume these sex services, it renders the sexual landscapes less authentic, less real, and ultimately less desirable. Second, the posting also suggests that as well-known sex destinations are "discovered by mass tourism" they are likely to become more expensive. The appeal to join this Internet club is therefore not only geared toward the post-Fordist consumer who seeks hedonist experiences that are out-of-the-ordinary but also toward the sex tourist who would like to be distinguished as part of an even more select group within the sex travel population. Ironically, such a consumer is unlikely to be found in the all-inclusive hotels that, though post-Fordist in character, act as enclave environments where encounters between the local population and individual tourists are severely limited.[9] The type of tourist that the quote appealed to would be more likely to visit hotels where opportunities for informal encounters with local men and women were greater.

The demand for sexual services does not always come from individuals who travel solely for this experience; a considerable number of travelers do also make use of commercial sex, especially in those destinations where such services are readily available. But given the underground nature of the sex trade itself, how are consumers made aware of the services are available? Traditionally the international promotion and marketing of sex tourism would have occurred through the exchange of information between men in tourist resorts or in bars and pubs back home. Such individuals would often share accounts of their sexual exploits with like-minded travelers, supplying details of bars, brothels, and prices. Today, far more sophisticated means of information exchange exist, with media such as the Internet providing information, replete with images, to a much larger audience of prospective sex tourists (Fantasy Getaway Guide Service 1998). It is here that the inequality of the relations of power between the First World and the Third, between capital and labor and the consumers and producers of sexual services is at its highest, because it is through the transmission of information that places "off the map" become part of the global sex industry. Truong argues that the current information order is such that people in southern countries like Jamaica have virtually no control over the information that is produced about their societies. Few of the texts and images produced about Jamaica's sex tourism industry in popular holiday brochures, guide books, postcards and through media such as the Internet are actually produced within the local economy. Currently much of the sex tourism–related goods for consumption such as posters and postcards are produced in Europe and imported for sale locally. In fact, much of the more organized segments of the sex trade appear to be owned or operated by foreign interests. For example, one international conglomerate, the House of the Rising Sun, with subsidiaries in Amsterdam, Spain, the UK, and Austria, now markets its Jamaican operations through the Internet.

While state and private sector interests have not been directly involved in the creation of sex tourism in Jamaica, they cannot be excluded from the range of institutions that have indirectly supported its development. Drawing on the work of Foucault, Truong argues that advertising represents a powerful discourse that is integrated into everyday practices, even though the knowledge that it circulates is rarely viewed as ideologically constructed. She points out that the tourist market is one in which the ideological constructs mediated through advertising play a significant role in shaping the level of demand itself (Truong 1996:374). Through the discourse of advertising, state and private tourism institutions routinely provide a range of texts through which fantasy, identity, and meaning are constructed. These texts are viewed as essential and effective tools for influencing travel-destination decisions. The Jamaican government has not been blind to the importance of advertising in stimulating demand for Jamaica as a travel destination, as the recent quote from the Minister of Tourism demonstrates:

> I do not want to underestimate the importance of consumer advertising, as it is consumer advertising that usually places Jamaica in the mind of the vacationer to influence that vacationer to consider Jamaica in the first place (Government of Jamaica 1998:7).

While the government no longer has major control over the marketing of Jamaica as a tourism destination,[10] it has done little to limit the gendered and racialized stereotypes of the brown-skinned/easy and black/servile, "native" woman that continue to be routinely used to promote the island's tourism. This reluctance is somewhat hypocritical, given the fact that these dual subtexts of caring and sexual temptation are likely to play a significant role in the creation of demand for sex tourism services in Jamaica.

Through a process that hooks (1992) refers to as the "commodification of otherness," black bodies are increasingly becoming important sites of direct and indirect consumption. From sportswear to the academy, she argues, the "gendered" and "raced" body has become a signifier for certain forms of post-Fordist consumption, a fact that has not escaped the notice of companies that currently promote Jamaica's tourism industry. As demonstrated in Photo 3.1, a brochure advertising group discounts for visitors to Hedonism II,[11] not only are women's bodies used to market Jamaican holidays, but the not-so-subtle text suggests that they can easily be purchased for consumption. Other brochures advertising Hedonism II reinforce the image that this is a place for uninhibited sex, drink, food, and recreation. As one ad declares:

> If it feels good, tastes good. Is sensual, uninhibited. A little wicked, may shock your mother. Involves a trapeze, can be done in the ocean. Is healthy, fit, relaxing or requires a blender. . . . It's included (Superclubs n.d.).

Due to the enclave nature of all-inclusives like Hedonism II, tourists who visit these locations are more likely to develop sexual relationships with fellow visitors than with the local population. As the exploits of one sex tourist

**Photo 3.1 Marketing Brochure for Hedonism II, a
Superclubs Resort** (Source: Superclubs Promotional Brochure)

demonstrate, the way that resorts like Hedonism II are marketed has a powerful effect on the demand for sex tourism in Jamaica, because the dominant image that remains is that the island, by extension, is a place where the potential for a "wild," sexual adventure with the local population is easy to come by. As this sex tourist explains:

> By far the best place for sex in Jamaica is Negril. Sex is available and cheap, and for those of us who prefer black women, I can't think of anywhere that comes as close. A few weeks ago I went to Hedonism II, which, as many of you will know, is also a Mecca for free sex and swinging. If your partner is into that sort of thing, it's a great place for swinging couples from the U.S. and Canada. This time, I went alone, intending to try to score with one of the pretty young Jamaican girls who come along for the Friday and Saturday night discos (*World Sex Guide*, May 6, 1997).

The relations of power that shape the current demand for sex tourism in Jamaica should not be viewed as the preserve of any one gender or particular ethnic or racial group. As a number of recent articles have indicated, "romance tourism," the provision of male sexual services to women for financial reward, is a growing and perhaps the most visible part of the Jamaican sex trade (Pruitt and LaFont 1995, Pattullo 1996). Like men who purchase female sexual services in Jamaica, many white women also rely on racial stereotypes of the "natural," "exotic" archetypal masculine man in this kind of tourism encounter. The search by many women from Europe for an extraordinary sexual experience with an "authentic" Rastafarian man has become such a popular segment of the Jamaican sex tourism sector that the terms "Rent-a-Dread"[12] or "Rent-a-Rasta" have arisen to explain the transaction. Reflecting the influence of the international reggae counter-culture, this form of male sex work has steadily increased as Jamaican reggae has spread across the world. Pruitt and LaFont argue that unlike sex tourism, romance tourism contradicts conventional notions of male hegemony, because both partners in such relationships seek to manipulate and extend their existing gender repertoires. Many Rent-a-Dreads, for example, frequently draw on traditional models of male dominance[13] to initiate relationships as the quote below demonstrates:

> The Jamaican men swoop down upon the single women (no age requirement here), seducing them with their easy-going way and smiles of "no problem man." Most every single white girl we saw (yes, most were English nurses or an Italian tour) had a local boyfriend. Seems as we American men find Asian women a mystical creature, European women find these black hunks an irresistible delicacy (Cassirer 1997).

These displays of dominance, however, are often less than real because the economic status of the visiting female tourist automatically puts her in a position of power and control in the relationship, a position that, Pruitt and LaFont argue, tends to be reinforced when the women take their boyfriends home or decide to remain in Jamaica. Thus while these relationships do not reproduce power relations of male dominance and female subordination, they do perpetuate other power relations, namely between First World and Third World nationals and between whites and people of color.

Impact of Sex Tourism on Households and Communities

There has been little comprehensive research into the impact of sex tourism on the Jamaican population. Anecdotal accounts, however, do indicate that the island has been as affected by the negative aspects of the trade as have its other Caribbean neighbors. Like Cuba, where the rise of sex tourism is viewed as a contributing factor in the recent rise of the Human Immuno-Deficiency

Virus (HIV) and sexually transmitted diseases (*Miami Herald*, June 6, 1996), the highest incidence of AIDS in Jamaica can be found in St. James, the parish encompassing the tourist resort area of Montego Bay. The Ministry of Health reported in its survey of HIV/STD control that over the period between 1982 and 1997, the number of AIDS cases reported per 100,000 was 252.7 in St. James, an incidence level twice that of the national average. The survey also indicated that sex workers constituted a high risk group, with incidence levels in St. James estimated to be as high as 20 percent (Figueroa, et al. n.d.). Another report published by the Ministry of Health/ Hope Enterprises in 1996 also voiced concern at the fact that a quarter of sex workers, many of them teenagers, were addicted to hard drugs such as crack and cocaine.[14] These individuals constitute a very high public health risk; they are more likely than other sex workers to engage in unprotected sex. Given that 20 percent of sex workers have a main partner with whom they either live or have a visiting relationship with, the public health risks of sex tourism are quite high.

Anecdotal evidence also suggests that sex tourism is disruptive to local communities (Pruitt and LaFont 1995, Pattullo 1996). Participants in the sex trade are not only a visible reminder of the racial subordination of locals to tourists but their activities are also often a source of tension and dispute for older family members and partners with whom some continue to reside. Combined with the reported high incidence of drug use among many commercial sex workers, it would appear that the Jamaican sex tourism sector as presently constituted represents a further strain on the island's social fabric, even though the income that individuals derive may be crucial to everyday household survival.

WHAT SHOULD BE DONE?

While Jamaica has little control over the commodification of localities and cultures that has become a part of the modern travel experience and which fuels the demand for sex tourism, it does have the power to reduce the costs that are borne by workers in the industry and the population at large. To achieve such an outcome, however, will require a radical transformation in current tourism policy. As a number of Jamaicans, including government officials, have already recognized, the future of Jamaica as a popular tourism destination cannot be sustained over the long run if local communities remain excluded from the benefits of the sector. Although the sector has been relatively successful in maintaining increased visitor arrivals and revenue earnings since 1980, these levels are likely to decline if tourists are dissatisfied with the quality of their travel experience. While increased global competition is an international factor over which the island has little control, every effort is being made to improve the quality of the infrastructure that services the industry and the nature of the interactions that occur between local people and foreign visitors. Until less emphasis is placed on the maximization of foreign exchange earnings and more on the creation of sustainable sources of income generation and employment within local communities, these restructuring efforts will remain cosmetic rather than transformational.

Community tourism is increasingly viewed as a possible solution to the alienation and tension that exist between local communities and the tourism industry (Government of Jamaica 1998). By creating opportunities for local people to develop and manage tourism goods and services, it is believed that greater opportunities for regional development will occur. While "community tourism" is the current buzzword in vogue among tourism planners and policy makers, its objective seems curiously out of accord with other tourism policies that seek to regulate the presence of the local population on certain public beaches and that have the potential to label encounters between local community members and tourists as punishable forms of harassment. It seems also quite odd that a strategy designed to create greater linkages between local communities and the tourism industry should focus on the initiatives such as the local manufacture of crafts and souvenirs (Government of Jamaica 1998), when the greatest capacity for creating jobs lies in the creation of closer intersectoral linkages between agriculture and, most relevant to Jamaica, other producer and consumer services. Closer linkages between the service sector and the tourism industry, for example, could foster the growth of Jamaica's information processing, finance, social and personal services, and food and beverage sectors. These sectors have the greatest scope for bringing the benefits of tourism to local communities, many of whose members already provide these services informally.

Sex workers, like many other informal tourism service providers, would benefit immensely from an expanded definition of community tourism for a number of reasons. First, a broadened definition of community tourism would include the recognition of the contribution of sex work to the nation's tourism industry. Currently, due to the illegality of the sector, service providers are constantly exposed to unsafe working conditions, harassment, and violence on a daily basis. Recognizing the existence of sex tourism as a service provided and organized by some members of local communities would create a forum for sex workers to legitimate their occupations and in so doing claim their rights to secure working environments. Second, if formally recognized, sex workers would benefit from opportunities to develop a range of skills already utilized in sex tourism work. Many sex workers, for example, also act as tour guides and companions; these are skills that are often considered vital to the hospitality industry. Such skills could provide avenues for alternative forms of employment for those who wished to change occupations. Third, by recognizing sex work as a legitimate occupation, the truly exploitative aspects such as forced prostitution and child abuse could be more effectively policed. If part of a truly community-based tourism, sex workers would also be able to define for themselves the structures and conditions under which their services were provided.

The prospects for sex workers to define the conditions of their labor or to pursue alternative forms of income generation in Jamaica are currently weak. Religious and moral judgments continue to drive the sector into the underground economy, where the threat of violence, exploitation, social disruption, and public health epidemics are ever present. Unless there is some recognition, however, of the relationship between current tourism policy, with its preoccupation with foreign exchange earnings, and the sex trade, the creation of a truly community-based tourism service is unlikely ever to be achieved. As one commentator in the local newspaper eloquently concluded:

> Let us take a look at our loud moral and religious convictions, place this alongside the silent vices in our lives and then throw the whole mixture into the harsh economic realities that face not just those in the middle or lower middle income households but the harsher, more desperate hell facing those at the bottom.... As the economy teeters on an edge, too-long unemployed, pretty young girls, in demand for what their bodies promise have harsh decisions to make... (Wignall 1998).

NOTES

1. The all-inclusive concept pioneered by the Superclub group, has created a truly "cashless" vacation. Each resort caters to a particular segment of the tourism market (families, hedonists, heterosexual couples), and at a prepaid price, vacationers are entitled to the unlimited consumption of the hotel's goods and services.

2. In this paper I define sex tourism as any travel experience where the provision of sexual services by the host population in exchange for monetary and nonmonetary rewards makes a significant contribution to the enjoyment of the holiday itself. In this definition, sex services are not confined to heterosexual intercourse; it also includes the provision of services such as tour guidance, companionship, and fantasy voyeurism.

3. The current minimum wage of J$800 per week (U.S.$22) is just a little over a third of the poverty line estimate of J$122,114.50 per year (U.S.$3,432.10) calculated by the Planning Institute of Jamaica (PIOJ). Currently the Ministry of Health estimates that the minimum weekly cost of feeding a family of five is J$1,800 or U.S.$49, and given that food represents only about half of the cost of living basket, then in order to be able to finance other necessities such as health, education, and transportation, each of two minimum wage earners in a typical family of five would have to earn approximately J$1,650 per week (U.S.$45) to live just above the poverty line (*Gleaner*, July 6, 1998 and November 4, 1997)

4. This figure includes European Plan hotels with all-inclusive packages.

5. Lim cites a major study in Cambodia in 1995, where it was estimated that at least a third of commercial sex workers were between the ages of twelve and seventeen years of age. Researchers familiar with Cambodia thought this might be a low estimate, given the difficulty in gaining access to the very young girls in brothels.

6. The exchange rate in 1997 was J$35.58: U.S.$1.

7. In 1997 the estimate by PIOJ of the poverty line was J$122,114.50 per annum (U.S.$3,432.10). Most minimum wage earners would have a third of the estimate at their disposal (*Gleaner* 1997).

8. The 1992 OAS Study of the tourism sector found that for every $1 spent by a tourist on accommodation, approximately sixteen cents leaked out of the economy in the form of direct imports. For all-inclusives this figure was higher, with approximately twenty-seven cents being lost to imports. High propensities to import were also reflected in the shopping sector, where as much as ninety cents in every tourist dollar spent on an in-bond good was lost to direct imports.

9. Campbell, Perkins, and Mohammed (chapter 6) in their study met workers who provided services for guests at all-inclusive hotels. These workers, however, stayed at these resorts as paying guests.

10. Sandals and Superclubs, the island's two major all-inclusive resort chains, reportedly spend more money on marketing and promotion than the Jamaica Tourist Board, the official marketing agency for the entire island (Government of Jamaica 1998).

11. An adults' resort known for its highly sexual, "anything goes" policies.

12. This is a popular term used to describe the phenomenon of women visitors to the island who seek holiday relationships with men with dreadlocks, a symbol of Rastafarian identity. The Rastafarian movement, which evolved during the 1930s and 1970s, sought to create an identity that affirmed the dignity of black men through a rejection of Western standards and the search for a natural way of life. I include these relationships in discussion of sex tourism because there is often an implicit exchange of sex and romance for financial reward.

13. A number of writers have pointed out (Senior 1991, Powell 1986, Moses 1977) that despite the economic independence of Jamaican women and matrifocality of many households, men are still perceived to be the dominant of the sexes.

14. The report also stated that the majority of hard drug users started their habit after becoming sex workers.

4

Back to the Future?

Women, Race, and Tourism in Cuba

NADINE FERNANDEZ

Cuba-watchers and scholars are by now very familiar with the Cuban term *jinetera/o* used to refer to a prostitute working tourist zones. The term jinetero can be translated as "jockey" or "horseback rider," with obvious sexual and economic connotations involved in "riding" the tourist. However, who is being ridden and in what terms is a complex question. My aim here is to examine the meanings and references of this term in Cuba with two objectives: first, to explore the term itself and the diversity of types of *jineterismo* that exist; and second, more importantly, to show how constructions of race become entwined in the term when it is applied to sexual encounters between Cubans and tourists. In sum, I argue that female identities are being more strongly constructed in racial terms, with the complicated yet forceful penetrations of global capital into Cuban society.

TOURISM AND THE ECONOMIC CRISIS

The collapse of the socialist bloc in 1989 caused the Cuban economy to plummet. With a 73 percent drop in imports (in 1992) and a particularly sharp cut in Soviet oil shipments, the country was paralyzed. Cuba termed the crisis "the Special Period in Times of Peace," which called for wartime austerity in peacetime. In response, the government actively pursued the development of tourism to bring in hard currency and jump-start the economy.

Cuba is not unique in choosing tourism as a key industry as the country moves from a socialist economy to a more market-oriented one. For Cuba, like Vietnam and Hungary, tourism has a fourfold role in economic development.

It generates hard currency; provides a conduit for technology transfer (often in the form of management and marketing skills); serves as a stimulus for other sectors of the economy such as infrastructure, furniture, food, and entertainment; and finally, is able to attract foreign investment (Simon 1995, Martin de Holan and Phillips 1997, and Pérez Villanueva 1998). Foreign capital is a crucial component in developing tourism facilities as well as in other related sectors of the economy. Cuba now has more than 350 joint ventures with forty different countries in a broad range of enterprises (Paez 1999). As a result of these investments and the country's own inversions the island now boasts over 30,000 hotel rooms and is served by forty foreign airlines (Kovaleski 1999).

Many scholars (Díaz et al. 1996, Cabezas 1998) have noted the irony of a socialist country seeking economic redemption in the epitome of capitalist decadence. Tourism, of course, is not new to Cuba. Pre-1959 tourism had been Cuba's second largest industry after sugar and was characterized by gambling, drugs, organized crime (under U.S. Mafia leaders), and a flourishing prostitution trade (Díaz et al. 1996, del Olmo 1979, Schwartz 1997). In 1957, close to 350,000 tourists visited Cuba, most of whom were from the U.S. (Espino 1993). The majority of the prostitutes at this time were poor women from the countryside, with little education (del Olmo 1979). It is estimated that the total number of prostitutes on the island neared 150,000, with 3,000 pimps (of the total Cuban population of about 6 million) (del Olmo 1979).

After 1959, the materialism and consumption associated with tourism clashed with socialist ideological concerns. The dismantling of the tourism industry, which the revolution touted as one of its early successes, was fueled by these ideological contradictions (and the U.S. embargo, which curtailed the travel of Cuba's main clients). The former prostitutes along with former domestic servants were incorporated into new educational programs designed to reintegrate these women into productive society. What remained of the tourist installations came to serve the national market, and it was not until the late 1970s that tourism expanded slightly to include visitors from Latin America, Eastern Europe, and Canada. During this period some isolated incidents of prostitution appeared but it never reached the pre-revolutionary levels of becoming a widespread social concern (Díaz et al. 1996).

The return of large-scale tourism began slowly in the early 1980s, when government economic planners realized that the tourist industry worldwide was growing faster than manufacturing and other sectors. In 1982 Cuba hosted 200,000 tourists. Drawing on the country's rich natural resources, particularly its unspoiled coastline, the government began channeling materials and resources into tourism. While investments in tourism seemed wise in the early 1980s, they became a necessity by the end of the decade after the Soviet bloc collapsed. In a speech in 1989 Castro warned that with a decline in Soviet aid, tourism would be the country's leading source of foreign exchange (Schwartz 1997).

Since the start of the Special Period in 1990, tourism has grown approximately 20 percent annually (Rodríguez 1999). While about 340,000 tourists arrived in 1990, that number grew to 1.4 million in 1998. The Cuban government hopes to reach the goal of 2 million visitors by the year 2000 (Rodríguez 1999). The majority of the tourists in the late 1990s come from five countries: Italy, Canada, Spain, France, and Germany. In terms of numbers of visitors, the 1998 figures place the country as the ninth ranked tourist destination in the Caribbean (Rodríguez 1999), making Cuba's economic profile similar to those of other Caribbean islands in which tourism revenues far outpace those from traditional agricultural exports (Simon 1995). In 1998 Cuba's tourism earnings totaled $1.8 billion, displacing the traditionally dominant sugar industry as the economy's leading source of hard currency (Reuters 1999).

As in many lesser developed countries, the expansion of tourism in the midst of economic hardships has exacerbated the social differential between the foreigners and the Cubans (Harrison 1992). This has been particularly painful, given that the revolution strove for equality and equal access for all to the nation's resources. Conscious of these contradictions, Castro has declared tourism "a necessary evil," or in the words of Cuban historian Juan Antonio Blanco, "Tourism is a sort of chemotherapy. You have cancer and it's the only possible cure, but it might kill you before the cancer does" (as quoted in Pattullo 1996:91).

A NECESSARY EVIL: THE PUBLIC RESPONSE TO TOURISM IN THE SPECIAL PERIOD

The public has not been silent about being faced with the decadent, consumerist, and hedonistic character of tourism in the midst of the austerity, scarcity, and privations of the Special Period. In addition to endless commentary on the street and in Cuban homes, popular songs have appeared voicing the public's feelings about tourism. In his song "100% Cuban," the Cuban singer Pedro Luis Ferrer (1994) expresses the public's growing resentment of the tourist industry's dual dollar/peso economy and the fact that Cubans with their national currency do not have access to the best the country has to offer. Furthermore, the song plays on people's frustration with the increasing meaninglessness of the government's continued propaganda campaigns, as the song parodies the popular political slogan "100% Cuban," which blankets numerous billboards in Havana.[1] In his lyrics, Ferrer plays on the irony of this slogan in light of the growing tourism industry:

Como que mi Cuba es 100% Cubana
Manaña reservaré en el mejor hotel de la Habana
Y ir a Varadero a separar unas casas
Con este dinero mío que yo me lo gané en la zafra.

Mañana reservaré un yate allá en Barlovento
Nos pasar unas tardes capturando la langosta
Disfrutando a plenitud la riqueza de mi costa.

Cuba como un espejo
Si repartimos parejo
Cuba 100% si primero los de adentro.

[How my Cuba is 100% Cuban
Tomorrow I'll reserve a room in the best hotel in Havana
And go to Varadero to rent a house
With this money of mine that I earned in the sugar harvest.

Tomorrow I'll reserve a yacht in Barlovento
We'll pass some afternoons catching lobster
Enjoying the plentiful riches of my coast.

Cuba is like a mirror (between Cubans and tourists)
(Only) If we share equally
100% Cuban, if first for those inside (the country).]

In his song "Tropicolage," Carlos Varela (1993), another popular Cuban singer/songwriter, also expresses common critiques of the tourism industry, namely, the fact that Cubans are treated as second class citizens in tourist establishments and that tourists fail to experience the "real" Cuba as they move from one tourist installation to another.

Yo sé que la divisa hace la economía
como hace el pan al trigo.
Pero lo que no entiendo es porque el dinero
confunden la gente.
Si vas a los hoteles por no ser extranjero te tratan
diferente.

I know that hard currency makes the economy
like wheat makes bread.
But what I don't understand is how money confuses people.
If you go to the hotels you are treated differently because you're not a foreigner.

Vocal critiques have not been the Cubans' only response to tourism and the economic crisis. Resolving the endless shortages in any household has involved gaining access to dollars through one means or another, as hard currency has become increasingly essential in determining one's standard of living and social status. For many Cubans, this aid comes in from remittances sent by family in the predominantly white exile community. In 1998 an estimated U.S.$800 million in remittances entered the island. As little as U.S.$50 a month can represent a dramatic rise in a family's ability to buy essential food and household goods. However, those not receiving remittances, and particularly Afrocubans, have had to be more inventive in their search for dollars, which for many has involved some form of jineterismo.

THE FOREIGNER/CUBAN ENCOUNTER

In order to begin to unpack the complexity of the foreigner/tourist encounter, it is first necessary to examine more closely the meanings and uses of the term jinetero/a in Cuba. Secondly, I unravel here some of the racial undertones the term assumes when it refers to sexual relations between tourists and Cubans. This step requires a closer look at racial categories as they are perceived on the island.

Though often overlooked in the literature on tourism in Cuba, jineterismo is actually used to describe a broad range of activities related to tourist hustling (including selling black market cigars, rum, coral jewelry, etc.), providing private taxi services or access to "authentic" *santería* rituals, or simply serving as informal tourist guides in return for a free meal or some token gifts from the tourist. Apart from these street-level dealings, the term is also frequently applied outside of the tourism arena to refer to any dollar-generating activity or connections with foreigners. For example, intellectuals tailoring their work to gain invitations to conferences abroad or selling their writings in dollars are also said to be jineteando. When I mentioned this observation at a recent academic conference in Cuba, the room filled with the nervous laughter of the "guilty." In summary, in its most inclusive sense, jineterismo refers to any activity outside of one's salaried employment that generates hard currency or the possibility of foreign travel. In other words, it is any attempt to integrate oneself into the global market economy at whatever level and through whatever means.

Within this broad range of activities that constitute jineterismo I focus on the sexual relationships between male tourists and Cuban women. In this context it becomes most difficult to classify what types of relationships count as jineterismo. Furthermore, it is here that jineterismo is cast in the most negative light as a social problem with serious moral implications. Gender, race, and class become salient features in defining those blurry

boundaries between who is a jinetera and who is not when it comes to sexual relations with tourists.

Popular perceptions of jineteras in Cuba, and U.S. and European scholars
(Strout 1995, Davidson 1996, Fusco 1998) writing about the issue, often depict the women as predominantly Afrocuban. One recent Cuban study has
found that the majority of the jineteras are white (Díaz 1996), while another
Cuban scholar suggests that the majority are "mestizo" (mixed race)
(Domínguez 1998). Wherein lies the truth? Why such disparate views on the
racial categorization of the jineteras?

Deciding on the appropriate racial categories and enumerating the individuals that fall within them in Cuba is a supremely complex task for several
reasons. First, for many years the revolution claimed to have eliminated institutionalized racism when it rid the country of the capitalist roots of such
social ills. The last vestiges of racism were to die off with the older generations. As a result of this ideological stance, few data have been collected by
race in Cuba. In fact, the 1970 census eliminated racial categories altogether,
although they were reinstated for the most recent census conducted in 1981.
It is only in the last few years that Cuban scholars and government officials
have begun to publicly recognize that racial discrimination has continued
and have slowly started to turn their attention to the issue (Fernandez 1998).
The lack of statistical data by race is only part of the problem. Racial identification is a complicated endeavor in and of itself, making even the most
carefully calculated numbers a matter of interpretation.

Second, as in much of the Caribbean and Latin America, race in Cuba is
not defined by the bipolar, blood-based, black/white distinction common in
the U.S. The Cuban racial system is better thought of as a primarily pheno-
type-based color continuum from black to white, which recognizes a mixed-
race category of mulatto or mestizo. These mixed-race individuals are
marked by different color terms that refer to various combinations of skin
tone, facial features, and hair texture. The specific nomenclature for each
shade is not only descriptive phenotypically but simultaneously assesses the
individual's location in a value-laden racial hierarchy. The marked grada-
tions in the color spectrum from whiteness to blackness attest to the island's
history of racial mixing, which developed from the nineteenth century na-
tion-building project of "whitening" the population (Helg 1990). Racial or
color categories communicate the long-standing color scale in which light-
ness/whiteness is more desirable and more socially valued than dark-
ness/blackness. As a result, racial terminology always conveys the social
connotations of the historically constituted unequal power relations that
marked certain physical traits as meaningful signifiers.

Third, another key feature of Cuba's racial continuum is that the racial categories are somewhat fluid (although this is less the case at the very darkest
and very lightest ends of the spectrum). Color designations are often shaped
not only by phenotype but by education, class, refinement, or what Cubans

call "*nivel de cultura*" or "cultural level." As in other parts of the Caribbean and Latin America, to some degree money can whiten, and, conversely, socially sanctionable behaviors can darken. In addition, the use of racial terms is always dependent on the intention of the speaker, comparative assessments, and shifting contexts. Black, mulatto, and white are not self-evident categories as much as they are negotiable and malleable identities constructed in social interaction. The descriptions of the jineteras by race then are complicated by the multiplicities of Cuba's racial/color topology.

It is precisely the flexibility and values associated with color that shape perceptions about the race of jineteras, and furthermore cast certain tourist/Cubana encounters as jineterismo. The phenomenon of jineterismo has reinforced the historical construction of Afrocuban women as exotic, erotic, sexually available, and licentious Others (Cabezas 1998, Davidson 1996, Fusco 1998). This exoticization of Afrocuban jineteras has led some scholars (e.g., Strout 1995) to view these women as social deviants, an association astutely critiqued by Cabezas (1998). The continuing myth of the sexualized Afrocubana contributes to their appeal for foreign tourists. Fusco (1998) notes that "to engage in sex work practically means to assume a mulatta identity by association" (155), illustrating the value-laden and flexible nature of racial categories.

The strength of the association between Afrocubanas and sex has made sexual encounters between white Cubanas and tourists seem invisible, while heightening the visibility of those between Afrocubanas and foreigners. During my research in Cuba (1990–95) I observed many relationships between Cuban men and women of all shades and white tourists. Here I present just one example to illustrate the invisibility of white Cubana/tourist relations and the racialized underpinnings of jineterismo.

Loli, a 19-year-old, light-skinned white college student, was the daughter of a well positioned military officer. She and her friends had access to dollar goods and activities through their families' positions and through some of their friends of similar class and racial backgrounds that had highly lucrative jobs in tourism. This allowed Loli and her peers to enter nightclubs, shops, and restaurants restricted only to tourists (at the time of this encounter, it was still illegal for Cubans to have dollars). Through this privileged access, Loli's friend Doricel (also socially classified as white) had met a young Mexican tourist in a nightclub. A relationship developed between them during the Mexican's stay in Havana and Doricel accompanied him to tourist resorts and installations in and around the city, gaining access to places well beyond those she had through her well-placed friends. After he left, Doricel and her family pinned their hopes on his return and a possible marriage between the two.

Despite the fact that material goods and sex were exchanged, neither Doricel, her family, nor her friends perceived this relationship as a form of jineterismo even though it was a short encounter with a very uncertain future.

Loli's and Doricel's privileged access to tourist clubs and resorts served to legitimate their encounters with tourists. Their race and class position helped them blend into the tourist world. Most importantly they met the tourist within, not outside of, tourist installations. As Doricel and the tourist are perceived to be on more equal terms, the issue of jineterismo is not so clear. Their relationship is constructed instead in the discourse of romance.

By contrast, Afrocuban women with foreigners lack two of the characteristics of Doricel's encounter. First, as blacks and mulattos continue to predominate in the lower classes, it is difficult to find Afrocubans with the type of class-based connections to the tourist world that Doricel and her friends enjoy. They often meet tourists outside of the tourist installations, making their meetings much more visible and scrutinized by the public eye. Secondly, persistent negative stereotypes of Afrocubans, and particularly sexualized conceptions of Afrocubanas, make it much more difficult for Cubans to perceive of their relationships with tourists as "romance." As Fusco (1998) notes, even black Cubanas married to white men (foreign or Cuban) are often taken for jineteras. The perceived racial, economic, or educational differences between the tourist and the Afrocubanas also make the relationships less likely to be seen in the public eye as anything more than purely sexual. Furthermore, the growing identification of Afrocubans as jineteras/os has added yet another dimension to Cubans' disparaging perception of blacks. As Lancaster notes, blackness can become a "sort of semiotic sponge, absorbing the entire range of possible negative connotations" (1992:221). While these racist views are most prevalent among white Cubans, it is not uncommon to hear Afrocubans express them as well.

In Cuba, what is considered sex tourism and what Pruitt and LaFont (1995) term "romance tourism" depends on the particular intersection of race, gender, and class. The visibility of Afrocubans around tourist installations and the persistent notions of black female sexuality contribute to viewing the Afrocubana/tourist relationship as a form of sex tourism or prostitution. Despite the similarities of these encounters, the white Cubana/tourist relation is more often and more easily couched as romance. Consumption lies at the heart of tourism and also at the center of tourist/Cuban relationships (Pruitt and LaFont 1995). The myths, images, and power relations that shape that consumption are different for white Cubanas and for Afrocuban women.

CONCLUDING CONSIDERATIONS: THE NEXT DESTINATION?

As access to dollars becomes increasingly central in determining one's standard of living and social status, the limited opportunities for Afrocubans to receive dollars directly from their jobs, professional travel abroad, or family in exile become more evident. As a result, their quest for dollars, which is no more intense than that of any other Cuban, moves into the much more visible and public realm of dealings with tourists.

There are differing forms of jineterismo, and these various manifestations reflect the pervasive need for hard currency that all Cubans are experiencing. The different relationships and access to the tourist industry reproduce in a new arena Cuban society's enduring race and class divisions. In this period of crisis, social differences are heightened and jineterismo offers yet another negative element to be appended onto the pejorative popular perceptions of Afrocubans.

The phenomenon of jineterismo in Cuba must be examined within the political and economic context that has created a market for these activities. Sex work, as Cabezas (1998) insightfully observes, appears as a strategy for many women to cope with the painful economic consequences of global capitalism. In this context, the jockey image implied in the term jineterismo is, at best, illusionary, as many Cubans ride a horse far too powerful to control in a race not of their own making. We are left to see whether or not the island and its citizens will be able to find a solution that is truly "100 percent Cuban."

NOTES

1. Though void of advertising in the capitalist sense until very recently, the streets of Cuba for decades have been covered with promotions for the revolution and its virtues. These slogans and murals also aim to rouse nationalist sentiment and commitment to the revolution through hard work and sacrifice. The "100% Cuban" is one such spin effort used to evoke pride and patriotism among the struggling and often demoralized citizens.

Part 3

The Hustle and Struggle Sector

5

Women's Work Is Never Done

Sex Tourism in Sosúa, the Dominican Republic

AMALIA L. CABEZAS

Everyone in the world marginalizes us, rejects us, they mistreat us verbally and physically because they see us as parasites in society, not taking into account that there is a network in society that lives off that parasite.

Ingrid Muñoz (MODEMU 1995)

With a population of 7.8 million people, the Dominican Republic has an estimated 50,000 male and female sex workers in the national and international sex industry (Gallardo Rivas 1995, IOM 1996). Many of these young men and women meet the demands of an expanding sexual market in tourist centers in the Dominican Republic. They travel from the capital or the rural areas to provide sexual services and pleasure to both men and women, gay and heterosexual tourists. In return, they hope that their liaisons with foreigners will provide them with the possibility to travel, marry, migrate, or at least make enough money to support themselves and their families.

At the tourist beaches, restaurants, and nightclubs of the Dominican Republic, it is common to see middle-aged European men accompanied by young Dominican women and girls. North American and European men are the primary travelers to the Dominican Republic. They are the pleasure seekers who come for the sunny, warm beaches, the picturesque scenery, the food, the recreation, and "exotic" sexual experiences with women of color. With a projected two million visitors by the year 2000, this is a plot fraught with tension and contradictions for the people of the Dominican Republic, particularly its women and girls (Secretaría de Estado de Turismo 1996).

This chapter examines the political economy of sex tourism in the North Coast region of the Dominican Republic, a Caribbean nation where the development of tourism is expanding rapidly and radically altering people's lives (*Listín Diario* 1996, Manier 1996, O'Connell Davidson and Sanchez Taylor 1996). It focuses on the experiences of women sex workers—the majority of workers in the sex tourism market of Sosúa—in an effort to provide fundamental knowledge about the gender and racial practices of the industry. It describes, examines, and interprets the political economy of sex tourism within a feminist conceptual framework that addresses the formal and informal sectors of the tourism economy and women's sexual labor.

THE DOMINICAN ECONOMY

The Dominican economy traditionally depended on the production of agriculture, principally sugarcane, and the mining of nickel. After three decades of employing the import substitution structure of industrialization, in the 1960s international donor agencies urged the country to abandon this model and pursue the tourism route toward economic growth. Moving from a model of development that provided protection and subsidies to particular sectors of the economy to one whose productive structure is completely export-oriented implied radical changes in the structures of society (Silié and Colón 1994).

During the 1980s, as the nation sank into what has been termed the "lost decade of development," the International Monetary Fund recommended austerity measures to reduce the debt and financial crisis. The structural adjustment programs resulted in the end of food subsidies, the rise in prices for basic necessities, and the cutback of social programs and services, as these were privatized or eliminated (Deere et al. 1990, Silié and Colón 1994). The result was widespread violence, further declines in the standard of living for the middle class, migration, and the exacerbation of misery for the poor. Since women tend to be poorer than men, the structural adjustment programs with the accompanying rise in poverty intensified the hardships and brutality of poverty for women and children.

Moreover, the vast reductions in the price of sugar for the U.S. market propelled the development of nontraditional industries such as export-manufacturing plants. Foreign financial investments in Free Trade Zones (FTZs) targeted young women as the preferred labor force for the export-processing industries. As Safa explains, "The sharp increase in export manufacturing is directly attributable to currency devaluation mandated by the International Monetary Fund, which lowered the cost of labor and other expenses in the Dominican Republic to one of the lowest levels in the Caribbean" (1995:20). The low wages and poor working conditions in these labor-intensive industries do not alleviate poverty. In fact, Safa points out that the contributions of export manufacturing to the economy are dubious. The reduction of total household income due to men's underemployment and unemployment has generated greater financial responsibility for women. The low wages in the FTZs oblige women to supplement their income by working in the informal sector of the economy as well as in the formal sector. The rise of the super-exploitative FTZs is connected with the rise of prostitution in places where these enterprises exist, such as the United States–Mexico border and Southeast Asia (Cabezas 1998, Ong 1991).

During the 1980s, women entered the labor force and migrated at higher rates than ever before (Báez and Taulé 1993, Gallardo Rivas 1995). Despite their unprecedented participation in the paid labor force, women's poverty did not lessen. The economic changes have affected women enormously, because most are now the principal or sole economic providers for their families (Safa 1995). Yet the scarcity of appropriately paid and steady employment defines life for most women in the Dominican Republic.

Women are at the center of household production and reproduction functions. Indeed, even in families in which men are present, women tend to be the more consistent income earners. The earnings of women, whether in the Free Trade Zones or in the service economy, are geared primarily toward the maintenance of households. Studies indicate that women tend to take better care of their families than men do, contributing more of their earnings to the nutrition and education of children than men (Grasmuck and Espinal 1997).

THE TOURISM INDUSTRY IN THE DOMINICAN REPUBLIC

The idea of the international tourism industry was initially "sold" to the Dominican Republic during the 1960s as a means of developing its economic base without large outputs of manufacturing and technology. In the Dominican Republic, as in other developing nations such as Thailand, the industry was widely praised for creating jobs, bringing cultural understanding and exchange among people, and earning much-needed foreign exchange (Truong 1990, Bishop and Robinson 1998, Miolan 1994, Previda 1996). Since tourism relied on the packaging of natural assets, it was expected to support economic growth through existing resources such as sandy beaches, a warm and sunny climate, "friendly people," local arts, and music (Bishop and Robinson 1998, Taveras 1993). Through loans and development packages, the productive structure of the country was transformed and its economic strategy redirected to absorb the surplus income and foreign investments of developed nations.

The Dominican Republic began to build its tourism industry in 1967, as it emerged from years of totalitarian rule, the chaos of a United States military invasion, and rampant internal violence and unrest. These factors had slowed the development of an international tourism economy. In 1967, however, President Balaguer's regime was heavily subsidized, sanctioned, and guided by the United States, the United Nations, the World Bank, and the Organization of American States in its effort to develop an investment climate favorable for the development of international tourism (Barry, Wood, and Preusch 1984; Lladó 1996).

Tourism development sought to reduce the deficit in the balance of international payments (debts) by injecting the foreign exchange generated by tourism and accelerating the creation of jobs. The government created tax abatements and concessions to foreign investors in the hopes of producing employment, paying off the foreign debt, and generating revenues. Thirty years later, the country has seven international airports and dozens of exclusive tourist resorts alongside massive unemployment, civil unrest, a large foreign debt, and scathing reports of sex tourism and child prostitution (O'Connell Davidson and Sanchez Taylor 1996; Silvestre, Rijo, and Bogaert 1994).

Increased competition from other Caribbean destinations has resulted in continued expansion of the tourism infrastructure and superstructure. The government has provided a series of facilities and incentives for the promotion of the tourism industry. It has funneled many of its resources into building infrastructure for the tourism industry. This development approach is geared toward promoting the well-being of the country's guests, not its citizens.

The disparity in the distribution of wealth within the nation further exacerbates the inequitable conditions between hosts and guests. While 75 percent of tourism enterprises have private facilities for the supply of potable water, electric energy, and roads, constructed by the private sector with government subsidies, the population experiences daily blackouts, lack of potable water, and shortages and deficiencies in all forms of infrastructure. Tourism is now the principal industry that sustains the Dominican economy. According to an estimate in 1994, close to 150,000 persons were employed in the tourism sector, making it the largest source of employment in the Dominican Republic (ASONAHORES 1995).[1]

SEX WORK IN THE DOMINICAN REPUBLIC

The Dominican Republic has a thriving sex industry that serves both local clientele and foreign visitors. Prostitution that caters principally to heterosexual Dominican men includes sex work in brothels, bars, and massage parlors, as well as "dating" services. This part of the industry is highly hierarchical and stratified, with various categories of working women in the sex market. The growth of the other segment of the sexual services market is a direct result of the infusion of foreigners into the country. In the following paragraphs, I discuss the various categories of sex workers in the country. Since sex work with tourists is provisional and strategic, these categories are fluid and permeable. Among all categories, a sex worker's fee depends on the type of business or location where she or he works, age, looks, whether she or he works with Dominican nationals or foreign tourists, and ambition—what she or he is willing to do for the money. However, there seems to be very little mobility between women who work in the national sex trade and those who work independently with tourists. A number of factors could account for this segmentation: location of the business and the aesthetics, level of education, and fear of incarceration of the sex worker. The female body type of the national sex trade subscribes to another aesthetic, one that values voluptuousness as opposed to the slim figure preferred by international patrons. Also, street workers do not move into working with tourists. They might not have the capital, social and otherwise, to move into international circuits. Language is also a factor. The women interviewed could speak several languages to facilitate their transactions with tourists. They were not necessarily highly conversant but they knew enough to get around. Their high levels of education also helped their work.

Bar and Cabaret Workers

Pimps (*chulos* or *tigres,* as they are referred to in the Dominican Republic) could technically be the business owners who employ women in their cabarets, nightclubs, *casas de citas* (brothels) and bars to sell alcoholic drinks to clients, to dance with them, to converse with them, or to share a bed. Women who work under these kinds of arrangements usually live on the premises. Some of the cabarets provide room and board. These women are considered to be less attractive and less educated than those working with tourists; some people refer to them as *analfabetas,* illiterates. Their age range is between thirteen and forty. A study conducted by CESDEM/AIDSCAP in 1996 found that 78.8 percent of the respondents working in bars and cabarets were below thirty years of age. Of the sex workers in the area of Puerto Plata, Sosúa, and Montellano who work in bars and cabarets, 34.4 percent have less than five years of schooling, 52.5 percent have from five to eight years, and 11.9 percent have from nine to twelve (CESDEM 1996, CEPROSH 1996). Women migrate from other regions of the country to work in these businesses. They are said to come from rural areas and to work primarily with working-class Dominican men and some nationals living abroad who return to their country on vacation.[2] Foreigners rarely venture into these bars and businesses unless taxi drivers take them there or the establishments are located near the tourist enclave.

The business owner uses a *maipolo,* a man who goes out into the countryside and other regions to recruit women to work for the business establishment. These women are under the complete control of the business
owner, and they are severely penalized with fines if they "turn tricks" on the
side. The businesses give the women the security of food to eat and a roof
over their heads. However, women suffer frequent abuse from customers,
and the owners do not protect them. In fact, the owners are also very op-
probrious toward the sex workers. Some go as far as slapping and verbally
abusing them. Competition among sex workers for customers is fierce. Also,
when business is slow, the women do not make any money.

The majority of the women interviewed in this category had not worked
with a local clientele. Those that had, indicated that they much preferred to
work with foreigners because Dominican men are considered rough with
the women, mistreating them and calling them names; they are verbally and
sexually abusive, and they are always reluctant to wear condoms. Foremost,
women make a lot less money in these establishments, they cannot control
their hours, and the business owners dominate and abuse them. In comparison, foreigners pay them a lot more money, and they have the possibility of
migrating or traveling to other countries. In some businesses, women also
get a percentage of the high-priced beers that men drink. Foreign men pay
an even higher price for drinks.

Street Workers

Many Dominican and Haitian women work the streets and are in constant
risk of being arrested. They make up the lowest echelons of the sex industry. A study of sex workers in Santo Domingo states that these women have
less than an eighth-grade education, and the majority are single mothers receiving no financial assistance from the children's fathers (Ferreira 1996). A
study conducted in 1992 confirms that "the girls who work the streets are of
the lowest social status, they are less literate, poorer, less articulate, more
rustic, and less attractive" (Pareja and Rosario 1992:17). They are known as
tigras for the aggressive way in which they recruit clients. They work principally with Dominican working-class men.

Haitian women working the streets are also a highly vulnerable segment
of the sex market because they are undocumented immigrants. Their criminality as "illegals" makes them vulnerable to all kinds of abuse. Their dark
skin color and their language distinguish them. The many stereotypes of
Haitians are bound up with notions of race and black inferiority.

Street workers are very poor and cannot afford the expensive clothes, hair
styles, and makeup of the women who frequent the discos. Access to commodities becomes an issue for mobility within the different forms of prostitution. It is said that street workers earn just enough to survive. They do not have

the financial security of meals that are provided by a business establishment. These women are exposed to all kinds of abuse from clients and the police.

Some of the women working the streets are also drug addicts. This is a pattern of prostitution that is slowly beginning to emerge in the Dominican Republic; until very recently, it was more common in Western nations (Davis 1993, Høigård and Finstad 1986).

Independent Sex Workers

The women who participated in this study were working on a freelance basis in the sex trade connected to foreign tourists. At the time of the interviews, they were not working in the formal sector of the economy. They negotiate primarily with heterosexual men from Western Europe and Canada, who range between twenty and eighty years old. Their clients may be married or single, accompanied by their wives, family, and friends, or traveling alone. Dominican women solicit and recruit foreign men in the pubs, discos, beaches and restaurants. They initiate conversations with their limited knowledge of English, German, or Italian to attract the man. They approach, touch, and call out to the tourists with overt sexual overtones. These patterns of seduction deviate from the usual heterosexual relationships in the Dominican Republic. They invert the pattern of courtship whereby men aggressively pursue women.

Many of the women procure relationships with tourists that involve elements of friendship, sponsorship, and obligation. They enter into relationships with tourists that will provide them with monthly remittances long after the tourist has left his vacation haven of Sosúa. These men are called *amigos*—friends. In fact, all clients are termed amigos. Amigos generally fall into three categories—those who are committed, the transitional amigos, and the strictly short-term amigos—and these intersect and overlap. The first category is the romantic obligation, the Committed Amigo.[3] The woman or the man initiates a discussion about her financial status, usually after the amigo declares love, affection, and concern for the woman, particularly for her economic situation. He begins to send her money so that she does not have to work with tourists. These tourists contribute to the household economy by sending monthly remittances and buying gifts such as electrical appliances and clothing for her children. They return to visit, sometimes often. They might invite the woman to travel to other tourist resorts in the country. They also provide plane tickets and visas for travel to Europe, with the promise of a marriage proposal and permanent migration to Europe. These relationships share elements that approximate the general patterns and expectations of heterosexual romances. When the man seriously wants the woman as his wife, he pledges financial support in return for her promise of emotional and physical fidelity.

The second type, the Transitional Amigo, provides benefits but does not send monthly remittances or plane tickets. Sex workers can call or send them faxes when they have emergencies or their financial situation is desperate. Sometimes these amigos come to the rescue. They also send their friends to meet and visit with the sex worker, or they visit with the woman exclusively whenever they come, bringing her gifts and buying her household necessities. These men return to visit, and the relationship carries the possibility that they will become more committed in their intentions. It seems that many of them will reply to calls of compassion at first, but they tire with time and stop sending money or answering phone calls.

The majority of the women that I interviewed prefer to go to the discos to meet amigos. Some of these seductions result in sexual encounters that are short-lived liaisons by which they earn between 500 and 1,000 pesos (U.S.$36 to $72). The average tourist sexual encounter ranges anywhere between five minutes and one hour. These are the Strictly Short Term Amigos. The women are then free to procure another tourist or to go home for the night. This third category envelops all the clients that women service in the sexual marketplace. These encounters are temporary sexual transactions that do not involve more familiarity than necessary. The man's friendliness and the fact that he paid and did not mistreat the woman makes him *un amigo*, a friend.

Elements of gamble, risk, danger, and uncertainty are dynamics that women contend with in all their relationships with foreign clients. Not only must sex workers evaluate their clients carefully to determine how best to safeguard their health, safety, and well being but also how they can best benefit from the encounter.

Sanky-Pankies

The name Sanky-Pankies is both a social identity and a form of tourist-oriented prostitution in Puerto Plata. The word play is on hanky-panky. These men are the bisexual gigolos who work exclusively with foreign tourists in this region. What is now a form of established sexual behavior has developed with the high demand by tourists for recreational sex.[4] As de Moya et al. attest, "Body fitness, brown or black skin color, long bleached dreadlocks, and the company of sexy blond foreign women became their insignias" (1992:2).

Organized homosexual tours became widespread during the period from 1975 to 1985, when young men in Puerto Plata were working with homosexual men. In the late 1980s and the 1990s, the fear of AIDS, coupled with increased homophobia, decreased the homosexual sex market. Today, Sanky-Pankies work mostly with white middle-aged foreign women who seek romance and adventure during their holiday.

These male sex workers are employed primarily in the informal economy, performing various services related to the tourism and leisure markets—in fact, de Moya found that these young men were engaged in no less than six income-generating activities. Many are independent tour guides who hang around the hotels or the plaza of Puerto Plata. Some work in the formal tourism economy. A study conducted in 1996 by COVICOSIDA disclosed that 38.5 percent of the male sex workers in the area had jobs in hotels as waiters, porters, and security guards, and 36.8 percent work as *motoconchos* (motorcycle taxis operators) (CESDEM 1996). The participants in a study conducted by de Moya et al. had a median age of twenty-two years, with thirty being the disqualifying cutoff point for courting female tourists.

Most of men in the de Moya study claimed that for foreign women "black skin color is the most relevant feature" (de Moya et al. 1992:9). This was followed by "long, kinky, and trenched hair," youth, fitness, manliness, and sexiness (1992:9). The men capitalize on the demand for racialized fantasies of erotic encounters. As is true of female sex workers working with tourists, many of these men hope to migrate via marital arrangements with foreign women. As de Moya explains,

> [The foreign women] are from the USA, Canada, and Germany, who fell in love with them during their vacations and later on helped them get tourist or resident visas to travel abroad. A few others, mostly bisexual adolescents, have been legally "adopted" as sons by foreign homosexual men. Some were taken to their countries, a frequent event during the late 1970s and early 1980s, when the Dominican Republic was internationally advertised in specialized tourist magazines as a Gay Paradise (de Moya et al. 1992:5).

Sanky-Pankies exemplify the flux of sexuality and economy in this tourist setting. They move among male, female, and bisexual prostitution, and they cross the boundaries between the formal and informal economies with equal ease. Despite the separation of "respectable" jobs in the formal economy from the sex work of the informal sector, prostitution is an indissoluble connection that links the two.

Formal Tourism Workers

A form of sex work that is prevalent and yet hidden is that between formal sector tourism workers and tourists. A study conducted by CEPROSH in the Puerto Plata region highlights the common occurrence of sexual relations between hotel employees and guests. The study reveals that workers in the areas of food and beverage services, maintenance, administration, entertainment, and reception were involved in providing sex to tourists. The typical worker in the Dominican hotel industry is young: 62 percent are between the ages of seventeen and twenty-nine (CEPROSH 1997). Indeed, age, looks, and sexuality are important social characteristics in the service economy of tourism. In the study conducted in 1996, 17 percent of the employees report having sexual relations with tourists (CEPROSH 1997). The sexual transactions between them and tourists may take place within the premises of the resort, or they may occur in meetings outside the compound. Due to the low wages in the tourist resorts of the Playa Dorada complex, many of the workers live in poor and overcrowded neighborhoods where there is no access to electricity, water, sewage, or garbage pick-up. A trip abroad, gifts, and other forms of material exchange supply them with the kind of mobility and opportunity that the hotel's resort complex does not. This form of tourist-related prostitution represents an institutionalized mode of sex tourism that is taking place in the formal sector of the economy.

Casino Escorts

Finally, a new kind of sex work is developing that is connected to the casinos of tourist hotels. These are the *muchachas de su casa*—decent family girls who hang around in the casinos of the tourist resorts, gambling, drinking, and making friendly chats with foreigners. They do not have children but are attracted to the high pay of the sex tourism sector. Most are born and raised in the tourist areas or in nearby towns. Many are university students who need money to pay for their studies or technical and professional workers who do not make enough money to survive. They go out to the casinos to find tourists. They are very well dressed, can speak a few languages, and usually have high levels of education. No one suspects that they are sex workers. This phenomenon is fairly recent and is growing rapidly. De Moya et al. (1992) document this tourist-related prostitution as a development in the demand for recreational sexual services that has caused an attitudinal and behavioral change in Puerto Plata. They call these the "home-girls," single young women who live with their families and who can provide occasional, "friendly" (covertly paid) escort services to male tourists "with honest intentions," who refuse straightforward negotiation with professional sex workers (de Moya et al. 1992).

SEX WORKERS IN SOSÚA

This study was organized around interviews[5] with women sex workers who labor primarily with foreign tourists in Sosúa, the largest and oldest node of tourism development in the country, located on the north coast. The women were between twenty-one and forty-two years of age. Most were born in Santo Domingo, and the rest were from other large cities such as Santiago and Puerto Plata. Only three were born and raised in rural areas. They all came from working-class families in which both parents earned money. The educational background of the women was higher than average for the Dominican Republic (Pérez and Gómez 1997).[6] Only one woman was illiterate. The others had gone to school on and off, and most of the women had completed the eighth grade. A few had technical training in service occupations. Most of the women had been working in the sex trade for quite some time, and this was their main source of earnings even if they did this work on a part-time, on-and-off basis, migrating to the tourist resorts to make money and then doing other kinds of work when the season was slow or they were tired of the trade.

The women did other kinds of work, none of which paid as much as sex work. Most of the women interviewed had initiated their working lives as domestic workers in family homes where they took care of children and cooked, cleaned, and so forth. All the women were supporting and providing, usually solely, for their relatives and children. The majority of the women were supporting their brothers and sisters (putting them through the university) and mothers or aunts. The women relied on their mothers or other female relatives to take care of their small children. Only one woman had no children. Others had two or more children with Dominican men. Two had children with Germans with whom they had been married or were romantically involved.

Sex tourism in Sosúa offers the opportunity to engage in multiple economic activities in the tourism economy that encompasses sex work on a part-time, opportunistic basis and under more complex and permanent arrangements. In summary, I interviewed three types of sex workers—distinguished by their relationship to Sosúa and their level of professionalism—who participate in the sex tourism market of Sosúa:

1. Women who migrate from Santo Domingo and other cities to engage in sex work with tourists. These women travel back and forth doing only this kind of work while in Sosúa and in other tourist enclaves.[7] They are very focused and mercenary when it comes to sex work. They are the most professional, working full time, living in the *pensiones* and making money to send to their families. They do this to be able to go home and spend long periods of time with their children. This group of sex workers is typified by its high mobility, impermanence, and professionalism.

2. Residents born and raised in the area. A few of the women who are residents of Puerto Plata and Sosúa engage in other kinds of work in the informal sector. Sex work is something that they do if the opportunity arises, in an emergency, or just enough to survive. Constantly shifting between the various spheres of the economy, this group is marked by its fluidity and multiplicity in both work and social identities.

3. Women who migrate and stay. Unlike sex workers who move back and forth from the capital and other cities, or women who were born and raised in Puerto Plata, some women are internal migrants who went for sex work and stayed in Sosúa permanently. They work with tourists, and a few live with their children. Others have their children remain with female relatives. This category of permanent migrants captures the multifarious arrangements under which women perform sexual labor with tourists.

NETWORKS AND MECHANISMS FOR SEX TOURISM IN SOSÚA

The divisions in Sosúa between El Batey—the affluent, Europeanized, tourist zone—and Los Charamicos—the working-class area where most Dominicans live—hide from the tourist's view most signs of the variety and intensity of activities that contribute to the well-being of the tourist economy. Tourists seldom see the bustling center of Los Charamicos. The poverty and desperation caused by the low wages and unstable jobs of the tourist infrastructure remain a misery for Dominicans and a mystery for strangers.

The lives that the sex tourism economy supports in Los Charamicos constitute the antithesis of the "First World" that is El Batey. In Los Charamicos the tourism economy is incapable of guaranteeing enough jobs or integrating the wave of newcomers as part of its formally employed population. People scratch out a meager living by selling goods and services related to the tourists and tourism. Older women, children, and young men and women all work, all the time. Their contribution to the economy is bypassed by most analyses of the tourism sector, yet the relationship of dependency between the formal and the informal sector is an integral part of this economy.

The deficiency in employment and the adjustment programs of the officially recognized economy have given rise to an alternative economy in which people labor at an endless variety of human activities. Pushed into the informal economy by the contraction in income and job opportunities, women work around the clock, stretching their physical resources to the limit. In the informal sector they provide the main economic support for themselves and their families; in many cases this income is indispensable for survival. They dominate the ranks of the lower paid sector of this economy as domestic workers, washerwomen, child care providers, sex workers, food producers, and unpaid family workers.

These informal sector arrangements are clearly observable in Sosúa. They range from selling small consumer goods (gum, cigarettes, candies, handbags, pirated music cassette tapes, and watches) to a multitude of services such as cooking street meals, shining shoes, and serving as motoconchos. Street vending and other very marginal occupations are the means of survival for a significant portion of the population. Sex workers are a central component in this invisible work force. The exchange network that they comprise thrives on and compensates for deficiencies of the formal market sector. Sex workers are responsible for the flourishing of *pensiones* and *hoteles de paso* (hotels by the hour), translation services, boutiques, and beauty shops in Los Charamicos.

Everyone participates in the tourism economy, and many benefit from a sex worker's body. The circulation of sex workers in the economy brings profits to many, from the transnational hotels and airlines to the small street vendors who sell hair ornaments to be worn to the discos. Hotel managers, taxi drivers, business owners, and many other intermediaries traffic the women and usually procure a cut of their earnings. The police, the state, and local and transnational enterprises are all aware that sex has a market value and will exploit it even while they are proclaiming that prostitution is immoral and that sex workers are depraved.

Yolanda's Story

Yolanda's mother died when she was thirteen years old. A washerwoman for the rural work force, she left Yolanda and her three sisters behind. Yolanda has since been taking care of and helping her sisters and her father. At fifteen, she married a sadistic Dominican man who beat her regularly. She showed me the many scars on her face and body. Her beautiful, soft face is crisscrossed with the marks of brutal abuse. A friend told her, "Walk away—that man is going to kill you." With her friend's help, she left and came to Sosúa with her two children and two younger sisters to support on her own.

As part of the cost of doing business, she spends a small fortune on her appearance. Her permed hair, manicured nails, makeup, and store-bought dress and shoes all make her appear very glamorous. "I have not even left the house," she says, "and I've already spent a fortune." She spends another 5 pesos (U.S.$0.70) on a motoconcho who will take her to El Batey. There she has to pay the entrance to the disco and buy at least her first drink: "It looks more decent if you buy your first drink, but sometimes I don't have the money." She will be very lucky if she gets a client tonight and if she can avoid a police raid. In the week prior to our meeting, she had to pay 500 pesos (U.S.$36) when she was caught in a mass arrest of women exiting the disco. When she does get a client, a taxi takes them to a *hotel de paso* back in Los Charamicos. The hotel charges the tourist 300 pesos (U.S.$22) and later gives her only 100 pesos of that. If the client decides to stay in his hotel in El Batey, he has to bribe the security guards or the receptionist in the hotel in order to take a Dominican woman up to his room.

Any time a taxi driver, a motoconcho, or a hotel manager finds her a client, Yolanda gives him a tip. If it is the client asking about women, the tourist pays the person procuring the sex worker. The opportunity to make money from sex tourism is everywhere in Sosúa. Yolanda says that sometimes taxi drivers who are her friends will find her a tourist. She gives them a cut of her earnings. Another woman has a steady relationship with a motoconcho. He goes to the client and offers the woman as being serious, someone who does not steal:

> He [the motoconcho] tells me, "If you get 500 pesos, you can give me 200 or 150, and there is no problem." I speak English, so I tell the tourist to pay him, that he was the one to find me. The tourist gives him 300 or 400 pesos. I don't have to pay out of my pocket.

MOTIVATIONS FOR ENTRY INTO THE SEX TRADE

I asked the women what motivated them to pursue sex work. The typical response was, "*La situación económica*" (the economic situation). This choice exists on a continuum of wage work that is related to women's gender socialization. Other options are to work in the Free Trade Zones or as domestic workers. Both of these options offer much less pay and less freedom and entail more work. Working-class women have no other alternatives that pay as much as sex work.

The women interviewed were usually unemployed or employed in jobs that did not pay them sufficiently. They entered into the sex trade voluntarily, being informed and initiated by their friends as to the availability of work.

A thirty-two-year-old widow with three children, Armida felt that working with tourists was better than being exposed to the accusations and humiliations involved in domestic work.

> Q. What motivated you to start [sex work]?
> R. The economic situation. I was very needy.... I was not going to work in a family home where they would tell me, "Oh, I lost this, I lost that," so that they don't have to pay me any money.
> Q. Had that happened before?
> R. Yes.
> Q. And what other work possibilities did you have?
> R. None.

A twenty-nine-year-old mother of six who supported all her children in addition to her five sisters, Rosa had this typical response:

> Well I started to have children and life became more difficult every day because I had two children, three children, four children, and the economy was every day more expensive. The prices were very high without anyone to help me,

and that's why I have remained, not because I feel good about what I am doing, but because of the obligations.

Overall when I asked women what propelled them to start working with tourists, they tended to mention their children: "Well, necessity. My family is poor, and I am the one who helps them. I have children. One is eight years old, and the other is ten months old, and the fathers do not help with anything." The other factor involved was, of course, fathers who were absent from the household. Some were in jail, others had migrated and did not send remittances, some were unemployed, and still others had died. The women were heads of households, with their mothers and younger brothers and sisters to support in addition to their children. The mothers usually stayed home taking care of their children, while the daughters went to the tourism resorts to earn money working with foreign tourists.

Some of the women were pressured by other women to improve their economic situations, or they saw the material acquisitions and the apparently easy lifestyle of women working with tourists. Maribel's friends influenced and initiated her into sex work:

> It's that my friends, the majority of the women here, are from the capital. I am from here, and they say to me, "How is it that you, being from here, you don't get anywhere? You don't have anything. There are uglier women than you who have progressed. They have gone to Germany. They have a house, they have a car, they have everything. Because if you are from here, why don't you go?" I say, "No I don't go into that because I am embarrassed." And they say, "That is not a problem. Come and I will show you."

Women want access to the goods that they see on television and in films. Constant advertising that targets women, the spectacle of tourists loaded with Western goods, and high levels of consumerism affect and alter the culture.

When comparing sex work with domestic work, Juana thought that it was better to work with tourists, since it offered the opportunity to be able to leave the country. She saw the possibility for migration and international travel, both rare opportunities for working-class women.

> Well, sometimes one is led by seeing someone who looks pretty and arrives with so much money. Sometimes one says, let me see if this works out better than working in a house, struggling, without eating, then finding [a living] with a tourist. But that life is not good either. Although many of us have luck. Many are taken by tourists to foreign countries.

Since 10 percent of the Dominican population has left the country, it is rare to encounter someone whose family member, friend, or acquaintance has not left. The ones left behind hear the tales of houses, brand new cars, and the power of earning much more money than is possible in the Dominican Republic. Many also have known or heard of women who have married tourists. The majority of the women hope to attain what is commonly termed *La Gloria* (the glory), to enter into marriage with a foreigner who will provide them a house, a livelihood, and care and protection for their family and children. La Gloria is a fantasy that motivates some women to stay in the sex trade with the hope of meeting that one tourist who will take care of all their needs. Not all women want to marry a tourist and go overseas. But this myth regulates and structures their encounters with tourist-clients.

Rosa has been working for eleven years as a sex worker. She is now twenty-nine and has six children. Her children live with her mother and sisters in Santo Domingo. She feels very tired of the police harassment and is emotionally drained from sex work.

> And my future? Well, I want to get some money or a good tourist who is good to me and will buy me a house for my children. I want to retire from this life, because already I am exhausted physically, morally, and economically.

Yet she is holding out until she can hit La Gloria because marriage appears as a respite from so much responsibility, strife, and work. Thus sex work with tourists appears as an economic recourse that women use while young to provide for themselves and their families. Many women perceive sex work as a transitional stage to a stable relationship that will provide them with the economic means to support their families.

HOW WOMEN PERCEIVE AND DEFINE THEIR ACTIVITIES

Generally, the women interviewed had high levels of responsibility, with a fairly traditional sense of morality. Many women expressed regret about being sex workers. They expressed feelings that what they were doing was socially unacceptable. Yet they were the primary supporters of their families, and this was a heavy burden for many of them. They were also concerned about how their families viewed their situation. Twenty-five year old Dulce:

> Q. Does your family know that you work with tourists?
> R. My mama and my sisters know what I do. I do not know what the other part [of the family]—the family uncles, aunts, cousins—I do not know what they think, but I consider that no matter how badly they think, if for example, they want to have a bad thought about me, they should also not reject me. They should also know that I have too many children and I alone support them.

Patria initially went to Sosúa with a friend who told her that she could make a lot of money with tourists. She had been living in Sosúa for seven years. She traveled periodically to Santo Domingo to visit with her eight children. Every week she wired them money. Her family desperately depended on her. When she did not earn any money to send them, they called her and let her know that they were eating rice with fried eggs and that the children were going hungry. She felt very pressured.

> I know, I am conscious that it is an antisocial job. The society does not accept women who walk the streets. But also, if I live off it, how is that evil? If I abandon my children to die, or if I give them away, or if I leave them to other people, society will also point the finger at me. Then I have left it to the fate of God. God is the only one who knows. I have had a time in my life when I have felt very badly about myself. Afterwards I have reacted. I see all my children, and I say, "I am doing it for something, it is worthwhile."

According to Leonor, a young sex worker from Sosúa, her grandfather told her that

> instead of getting pregnant by one of those *tigres* [pimps] from here that only want to beat you and live off of you, that it was better for me to sleep with a *gringo* [foreigner] so that way I can support my kids.

Many of the conflicts and contradictions that sex workers face cannot be reconciled emotionally. Their adjustment seems to lie in the confidence that they are doing everything they can to provide for themselves and their families. Furthermore, in talking about her work with tourists one woman said, "You have to throw yourself at them, laugh a lot, demonstrate love and affection, act as if you like them. I don't know where so much laughter and love comes from. I don't know where. You have to find it where there is none." These responses from sex workers indicate an understanding that what they do is a "performance." Indeed, that what they labor at is not who they are.

DOMINANT IDEOLOGIES OF SEX AND GENDER

The status of Dominican women within society and the family is circumscribed by the framework of patriarchal ideology (Báez and Taulé 1993). It is expected that women will remain within the home, be submissive and dedicated to their families and husbands, and cook and perform housework (Bonetti 1983, de Moya et al. 1992). This situation varies somewhat among professional and upper-class women who have access to the domestic labor of other women (Duarte 1989). Although they may be dismissed from performing the housework duties, they are still responsible for managing the household economy, raising children, and so forth (Duarte 1989, Bonetti 1983). Working-class women bear the burden of trying to fit into the prescribed morality and survive in an economy that forces them to work in both the public and private spheres.

Men are said to be "*de la calle*" (of the street). In the center of Puerto Plata, or on the *malecón*, for example, it is common to see men hanging around, sitting on benches, talking, and playing dominos. One seldom sees women spending time on leisure activities in public. The only women in the public spaces are street vendors—working women. This cultural system serves to police and restrict women's movement and confines them to the home.

Working-class women, and sex workers in particular, routinely fuse the traditional dichotomy of public and private spaces. Consequently, they are suspect and are stigmatized as *cueros* (skins) and *putas* (prostitutes). The connotations surrounding "puta" are the worst that a woman can be, the lowest person in the society. Sex workers are also known as the *mujeres libres* (free women) or *mujeres de la calle* (women of the streets). Women who work in the sex trade are the opposite of the *Dominicanas de su casa* (Dominican women of their homes).

The hegemonic opinions about the role of men and women dictate that in sexual matters women will remain virginal and "pure" until they are married (Bonetti 1983). When it comes to sex, it is presumed that women will remain unaware and uneducated. Sexuality and the sex act are the crux of shame and dishonor except within the confines of marriage. A woman's virginity is said to be the most important carrier of her value. Sex outside of marriage taints her honor and dignity (Bonetti 1983). Many of the sex workers that I interviewed agreed with these ideas. This ideological system of honor and shame is partly the inheritance of Christian religious mores. Catholic ideologies maintain that women should be faithful, obedient, and submissive to male authority (Báez and Taulé 1993:69). Feminist scholars in the Dominican Republic assert that women are directly impacted by the discriminatory position of the Catholic Church (Báez and Taulé 1993).

The dominant ideological articulation is that women will remain ignorant of sexuality but that men will be the masters of it. It is anticipated that men will have rich and diverse sexual experiences. Sexual virility and seduction symbolize a man's worth (Bonetti 1983). The sexual social law in force calls for two constants: the repression of female sexuality and the creation of an insatiable sexual appetite in men.

The repressed sexuality of Dominican women is contradicted with a vengeance in the representations of "exotic" women lying on the pristine beaches of travel posters. The images that suggest wildly sexual Dominican women betray more than a few national anxieties. It is more profitable for the state, in conjunction with transnational corporations, to sell a tourism destination by appealing to sexual desire. Such images stimulate desire for an exotic "other" constituted in racial, sexual, and national differences. Dominican women are commodities to be sold to Western consumers.

RACE AND GENDER IN SEX TOURISM

The women that I interviewed, and other people in Puerto Plata, acknowledge that men come to Sosúa for the women, and the fact that they are women of color cannot be separated from a sex tourist's motivation to travel. The advertisements for the tourism resorts are a sexual and racial treatise on Dominican women; they are a treatise on the aesthetics of race and on the eroticism of the exotic. They tease the European male's desires for racial, sexual, and gender difference (Kempadoo 1994, McClintock 1995, O'Connell Davidson 1996, Rousseau and Porter 1990, Said 1979, Young 1995). Sexual desire for women cannot be separated from the "natural" attributes of beaches, the tropical climate, and so forth, and sexuality is a central component of the project of tourism.

The manufactured fantasy of the tropics intersects with racial/ethnic and sexual images to inform the understanding of European men about the women and the experiences they encounter (Kinnaird, Kothari, and Hall 1994). Dominican women reported that foreigners construct them, both sexually and racially, in opposition to European women. Their amigos portrayed European women as cold, indifferent to sex, and like men in the home. Dominican women, on the other hand, are said to be *más del hogar*—more of the home: they cook, clean, take care of the home and the men, and are better in bed. The discourse on Dominican women leans toward sexuality and domesticity. Dominican women are constructed in relation and in opposition to German women. White skin is devalued because it is connected to civility, or feminist discourses, and is thus less sexual. In opposition, *Dominicanas* (Dominican women) are a racial, sexual, and a traditionally feminine fetish sought out to perform racial assumptions about their sexuality. A sex worker from Santo Domingo declared:

> The men say that German women are very cold, very authoritative, that they are self-centered, and that in marriage they are two equal persons, or like two men in the house or two women. In other words, if the Dominicana lives with a German and she says I am coming home at seven, and even if she comes home at eight, she comes home. And if they go somewhere, the Dominicana will not dance with other men or she will ask permission, while the German woman gets up and dances with anyone; they get close to anyone and go with anybody, while the Dominican woman respects more. With regards to the home, the Dominicana washes, the Dominicana irons, the Dominicana cooks, the Dominicana does it all, while with a German woman, if you have wash, you wash your clothes; if you eat, you wash your plate; the man is the same as the woman, but the Dominicana is more woman in the home.

The escape to the tropics is for European men simultaneously an escape from the pressures of egalitarian work roles in the home and of feminist demands to alter relations between men and women. Indeed, sex tourism offers men the opportunity to live out certain fantasies.[8] The tourism service economy indulges and caters to all their needs. With two or three women propositioning each man, flirting and making sexual advances, tourists find it easier to establish relationships.

With European women disputing gender relations, Dominicanas appear more "womanly" to European men. A foreign country also offers the protection and comfort of anonymity to engage in paid sexual relations. Additionally, the availability of relatively inexpensive sexual offers in comparison to propositions at First World prices is an attractive feature of sex tourism (Ferreira 1996).

Foreign men tell Dominican women that they come here because of them, and the women know that even when the men bring their wives on vacation, the men will seek out the women or accept their sexual advances. The wives may be out shopping or sleeping; sometimes they are simply in the shower.

> R. They say that Dominican women are "good." They always tell me that Dominicanas, the more *morenas* [dark-skinned] they are, the better. I don't know why.
> Q. And what do they say of their countrywomen?
> R. Some say that they don't like them for their color. That they like more women of my color. Like me. There are a lot of tourists that come here that leave their woman in the hotels sleeping, and they leave them to seek women in the streets, at the discos, because they like Dominicanas. And the ones that have not been with a Dominicana want to try us women to see what it's like.

Tourism is engendering profound social and cultural changes in gender arrangements. Moreover, tourism intersects with a type of prostitution to create new modalities of racism and vice versa. The changes in the global economy, and the discourses of sexuality propagated by transnationals, are constructing Dominicanas as hypersexual workers. The desire of the white for the nonwhite continues to be contextualized within oppressive relations. Within the sector of sex tourism, such desires are structured by ideologies of race, sexuality, gender, and a Dominicana's desperate economic situation.

MIGRATION

Dominican women are also predominant in international migration (Gallardo Rivas 1995). They are one of the principal suppliers to the sex industries of Western Europe. In fact, according to the International Organization for Migration, the Dominican Republic is fourth in exporting sex workers to

Europe, after the Philippines, Thailand, and Brazil (*Listín Diario,* August 28, 1996; IOM 1996). Most of the sex workers migrate to Italy, Germany, and Austria to meet the demands of an expanding sex market. COIN, a non-governmental organization in the Dominican Republic that has studied the trafficking of women, asserts that women are traveling to places such as Baghdad, Beirut, Israel, and Athens. COIN estimates that in Greece there are more than 12,000 Dominican women in the sex trade. The Lateinamerikanische Emigrierte Frauen in Österreich (LEFÖ), a Latin American immigrant women's organization in Austria, reports that 4,000 Dominican women work there as dancers, entertainers, and illegal prostitutes (Ferreira 1996, LEFÖ 1998). Many women know that they are going to Europe to work in the sex industry. Their visas may be issued for travel as artists, dancers, and so forth, but few women are surprised that sex work is within the realm of their occupational possibilities (IOM 1996). Some of the women interviewed had willingly traveled in the Caribbean and to Western Europe to work in the sex trade. The anonymity of foreign destinations and the possibility of making more money lure women abroad.

Other mechanisms for migration abroad include marriage and domestic labor. The Swiss consulate asserts that on the average there are six marriages per week between Swiss men and Dominican women (IOM 1996). Dominican women are also a major part of the domestic worker labor force in countries such as Spain (Gallardo Rivas 1995).

The possibility of migration is one of the perks of the sex tourism trade and the desire of many women. However, this is not a proposition that women enter into without prior consultation with those in their social circle. Many women are aware of the possibility of exploitation, forced prostitution, violence, deception, and other forms of abuse against them. The women interviewed had been in the sex trade long enough to know the perils. Yet they also had heard many stories of women whose travel to Europe had brought them new clothes and jewelry, and they had seen photos of the travels and riches that their friends encountered and procured in Western countries. These are the best advertisements for travel to foreign lands.

The fear of forced prostitution circulates among the sex workers who service tourists in Sosúa. The women with whom I spoke were aware, cautious, and frightened of being trafficked for forced prostitution, since many had heard stories about this. These women are using careful judgment in familiarizing themselves with the dangers involved in international travel. They have to contend with the probability of being illicitly transported or traded for someone else's economic gain. The abuser could be an international organized crime organization or an individual looking to profit from the sexual exploitation of women. Furthermore, women also have to contend with issues of domestic violence, racism, and sexual abuse that are hazards of their interpersonal relationships. Carolina, from Santiago, said:

> Here they treat you well, and later when you go over there, they treat you badly, as has occurred with many girls. Here they treat you well, but then over there, they give you beatings, they leave you locked up, and you are not allowed to leave the house. I have seen that happen, so I think I better not go.

Notwithstanding the tales of woe in their channels of communication, many women are drawn to the possibility of traveling and finding a better future elsewhere. Fueled by their own need to feed their families and to advance economically, as well as by powerful fantasies of the "good life" abroad, the women possess strong motivation and drive. In addition, some sex workers travel to Western Europe to visit their amigos for prolonged periods of time. Minerva, who came by after the interview to show me her photo album of Germany, said:

> I went to Germany twice with two different men. I liked it there. I was at peace. The first time I lasted two months, and he gave me money for my kids and for my return. The second time, I stayed six months, and he gave me 100 marks a week. I sent money to my kids, to my sisters, 400 marks, 500 marks. In Germany I stayed home during the week, and we went out on the weekends.

It is important to differentiate between the different types of travel. For example, when women travel to Europe with the committed amigos, they are traveling on vacation to visit, to sightsee, and to meet the family and friends of their amigos. They are expected to cook and clean, but sex work with other men is not part of the deal. For some sex workers, this type of travel is a respite from hustling clients, going out to discos every night, fighting police arrests, and suffering the verbal abuse and stress in their life as sex workers.

Some women participate in trans-Caribbean migration to work in the sex industry (Kempadoo 1996). I spoke with women who had traveled to Curaçao, Panama, and Haiti to provide sexual services. However, the European sex industry is the most attractive. Foreign traffickers recruiting for the European sex trade had approached a few of the women interviewed, but only one had accepted the offer. Others were too frightened by the stories of abuse and declined.

LAW ENFORCEMENT AND ITS ABUSES

While forced prostitution and other forms of exploitation become a concern and a real threat for many women, they do not begin to compare to the daily harassment, exploitation, coercion, abuse, and incarceration that they face from the local police. All but one of the women interviewed had been arrested multiple times. The arrests take place outside the discos, on the beaches, in restaurants, on streets—in any public space where Dominican women congregate. Both the special tourism police designated to deal with the tourist population and the regular state police force are employed to regulate the labor force of the sex tourism market. Their methods include brute physical force (including rape and beatings), arrests, harassment, and bribes.

The violence against women by the state police inspires horror. All of the women interviewed denounced the treatment they receive from the police as the worst part of sex tourism. This theme prevailed through all the interviews.

Attorney Iris A. de la Soledad Valdéz (1996), reviewing the laws that govern the practice of prostitution in the Dominican Republic, states that "prostitution is not prohibited in an expressed manner by any legal text." Likewise, Arita Bergés de Farray (1983) declares that, from a legal point of view, "we could only speak of a crime of prostitution if a law prohibited such a situation; it is the crystallization of the known rule *"nulla poena sine lege* [there is no punishment without a law] (55). Indeed, prostitution operates in a grey area of the law, and therefore the police and other authorities can bend and break the rules according to their own dispositions and levels of corruption. This situation creates much of the abuse toward women, who are the ones criminalized. Certainly, the police do not arrest the women's clients or any of the other parties involved in sex tourism.

There are no laws that precisely prohibit a woman's sale of her sexual labor. The laws that speak most directly to prostitution deal with the practices of intermediaries and those who benefit from a sex worker's earnings. Articles 334, 334–1 and 335 of the penal code make criminals of those who benefit from prostitution (Ley 24–97, Señor 1989).[9] Articles 334 and 334–1 were modified in January 1997 by the government in consultation with institutions that claim to support women and families.[10] The amended articles of the legislation that address prostitution are concerned with those who aid and facilitate the practice of prostitution directly or as intermediaries and those who benefit from the earnings of a sex worker. In recognition of the transnationality of sex work the new law has a clause making it extraterritorial.

> The punishment in Article 334 and in the present article will be carried out even when the diverse acts that constitute the infraction have been carried out in different countries (Ley 24–97:23).

This law could be applied to women who travel within the sex work circuits in the Caribbean. It could also be enforced against Dominican sex workers in Europe who send remittances to their families from abroad (IOM 1996).

If the intention was to protect women against trafficking and forced prostitution, these laws disregarded the study submitted to the United Nations on this matter (see Wijers and Lap-Chew 1997). This report, as well as the work of scholars and advocates of migrant women, emphasizes that most women traveling to other Caribbean countries and to Europe realized that they would be working in the sex industry (Azize Vargas and Kempadoo 1996, Ferreira 1996).

Oblivious to the realities of women and families who are supported by the sex trade, the modified Article 334 of the penal code could potentially incriminate the mothers, children, and relatives of women in the sex trade. It accuses of a crime those that, as Article 334-1.2 states, "receive benefits from the practices of prostitution" (Ley 24-97:21). This state regulation makes sex work clandestine, driving women further into lives of shame, secrecy, and vulnerability to extortion and other forms of abuse. These laws can produce situations where women cannot access resources directly, thereby relying on procurers to serve as intermediaries between sex workers, their families, and social institutions. The law does not sanction the real pimps, those who make big money from sex workers, directly or indirectly. It is no wonder that some prostitutes rights groups have called the state the biggest pimp (Valentino and Johnson 1980).

The new laws do not address the contradiction posed by a large and widespread national sex industry. Instead, public health and sanitation laws regulate the practice of prostitution in the national sex industry. The issue is approached through the possible transmission of venereal diseases. Businesses that facilitate, tolerate, or assist in prostitution operate within the parameter of the law, as long as they do not employ minors in prostitution or violate health and safety codes (Batista 1997).

Women working in these businesses must be certified, according to the law, with a health certificate ensuring that they are free of venereal diseases (Pareja and Rosario 1992). Here again, women must bear the responsibility for public health. There is no mention of male prostitutes, and a prostitute's clients are in no way controlled. At this level of the law, however, the state recognizes, acknowledges, and sanctions the practice of prostitution. Nevertheless, this particular public health regulation is seldom enforced. Women cannot afford the costly gynecological exams, businesses are not willing to pay for them, and the state does not have sufficient health inspectors to enforce the law. De la Soledad Valdéz (1996) notes that if a woman decides "to offer her body in exchange value, no repressive government control can punish or penalize said action" (101).

The law notwithstanding, the situation for women in Sosúa is intolerable. Police arrest women on a daily basis. They do nightly "sweeps" of the discos and areas surrounding these establishments. Women are arrested *en masse*, taken to jail in Puerto Plata, and charged 500 pesos (U.S.$36.00) for "bothering" tourists. If they cannot pay the fine, they are confined, transferred to a prison, and incarcerated with a general criminal population (Batista 1997).

The majority of the women interviewed felt that police arrests and harassment of women have increased with time. One sex worker commented:

> It used to be easier, because before you went out into the street, and they, the tourists, went out, too, and they would tell you this or that, and you went with them. But not now. Now the woman cannot walk in the street. Now the tourists come out at night and during the day. But the women do not. They cannot go to the beach to seek men; they cannot go out because of the police.

Furthermore, the police have become indiscriminate in their arrests of women. Mercedes, who has been working with tourists for the past twelve years, told me:

> Now the [tourism] situation is very cold. The police are now bothering too much, too much, too much, too much! It's so bad that now there are many women, many housewives, who go out at night to eat a pizza and they are arrested. The police think that they are "of the street." This is very bad. They should know that those of us who are "in the life" look different than those who are not. Now all Dominicanas are suspect.

This quote expresses how, geographically, local women, particularly working-class women and women of color, are stigmatized and criminalized as potential sex workers. Obviously, gender, racial, and class discrimination are at the core of these arrests. Elite prostitutes who are working the casinos and driving their own cars are not likely to be subject to mass police arrests. Neither are male prostitutes.

Violations of civil laws and human rights are taking place in these mass arrests. Due process is not being served since women are not being told the reasons for their incarceration. They are arrested to regulate the number of prostitutes in the streets and discos, to exact bribes and sexual favors from sex workers, and to control the businesses that do not pay bribes to the police. The police officers and the state profit from the arrests. The treatment that the women receive at the hands of the police is brutal. This, compounded with the illegality of the arrests, represents blatant abuse of women's human rights and of the juridical process. These practices do not contribute to the creation of a democratic society, as is declared in the official rhetoric of the Dominican government.

The women's mobility is unlawfully controlled and restricted by the police. Moreover, women are violated in other ways in the process of imprisonment.

All of the women reported incidents of abuse such as verbal assault and physical violence. A young woman talked about her vulnerability to, and fear of, these aggressions:

> I have been arrested many times, not for stealing but for being in the street in El Batey. They tell me that it's for being after the gringos, and I have to pay a fine of 500 pesos and spend up to five days in jail. Sometimes up to eight days in jail. They push you and hit you and throw you in their trucks all the time, calling you names. I used to get very scared because I had never been arrested before.

Another woman discussed the disruption that the arrests cause in her life:

> The police always are arresting the women that do not steal. I have to pay them some 500 pesos I just earned, spend five days in jail, and then I end up owing the food and other expenses for being in jail. I am alone here without someone to take me a plate of food or to run my errands. So I end up in further debt. All that after being arrested.

The women are equally cognizant of the injustice perpetrated on them. One sex worker commented on police corruption and the unfairness of the justice system as follows:

> This is not an easy situation. They [the police] are now worse because the tourism police come to do arrests up to three times a week. They arrest you and then if someone calls the jail looking for you, they won't say that you are there. Recently I have been arrested three times. That's 1,500 pesos that I did not eat or drink. This is so tough that even the men are complaining. They lock you up for three days even if you are innocent. I hear the tourists saying that over there, in their countries, the police don't beat up women, the police don't arrest women. The tourist feels badly about us when they see the police arresting us. Sometimes they see that when women refuse to be arrested they get hit, because it is not easy to sleep on the floor and pay 500 pesos without doing anything. They take you and throw you like a pig, like an animal, on the bus, and the tourists see that and it makes them feel bad. Tourism is going down now, and the police say that it's because we women steal. I am conscious that some women rob and that is wrong, because to earn a living you have to struggle for it. And there are many that don't want to earn it the hard way. But the police see them stealing, and they don't do anything. They stand a little farther away, and they watch the woman stealing from the tourist. When the tourist leaves, they go find the woman, and they tell her, "Give me my cut." The police are here to defend the tourist first and to defend the Dominicans, too, but for a few pesos they also turn into criminals.

Exposure to foreigners has also brought women a comparative perspective on their situation. Tourists comment on the absurd arrests of sex workers. For sex workers, these complaints are shaping an awareness of their situation that is informed by the civil rights discourse of more developed nations. A thirty-five-year-old woman from Sosuá said:

> The women here are not being organized. They are not demanding anything. Not that here they would pay attention to that. Once they got thirty-three women, and we spent a week in jail. All that came out in the news, and they did not do anything about it. All they did was to change the chief [of police] who arrested us. They transferred him to another municipality.
>
> Q. Was he the one who was very violent with the women?
>
> R. Yes, he was that one who beat up the women without compassion in a sugarcane field in Monte Llano. The women went to channel 21, and they showed their bruised bodies. One pregnant woman even lost her baby. Nothing happened to him. They just transferred him, that's all. But it was wrong on the part of the police, because every time anyone does something wrong, they should have to pay.

It is also alleged by many in Puerto Plata that the police regulate the national sex industry, the discos, and the nightclubs through bribes. The business owners must pay their tribute or risk being shut down.

Complaints against the police exist within a social context where citizens already feel like outsiders in their own land, confined by structures that relegate them to a position of subservience to strangers. The laws serve to protect tourists, who already have many cultural, economic, and social privileges. Carolina noted that everything appears arranged to bestow tourists with preferential treatment: "Why don't they arrest the tourist women who go around without a bra on the beach, in public, as if this was their beach or their country? They should respect the people here and our customs."

The unfairness of the mistreatment that sex workers receive at the hands of the police is coupled with the lack of police protection from violence that they receive at the hands of tourists. Whether the tourist does not pay them or he abuses and tortures them, sex workers have little recourse. They tell many stories of "justice" purchased by tourists. The police are easily corrupted, and violence against sex workers—even murder—is an offense that can be ignored by paying the right price. Furthermore, because of the social stigma and hatred that sex workers face in society and at the hands of police, they are seen as already guilty and not entitled to equal protection by the law.

> The police have mistreated me. They have hit me, and one time they gave me a black eye. They hit me because I told them that there was no justice here. That there was justice for their convenience. But if you offer them money, they let you go, because he who has nothing is of no value here.

Many stories circulate of women who steal from tourists and are violent toward them. These stories take place within a context in which women sex workers have few rights to protect them against abuse by their tourist customers. Tamara clarifies this point:

> I was in jail on Thursday because I broke a bottle on a tourist's head. I gave him a massage on all of his body. Then I asked him to pay me my money, and he would not. I kept asking him to give me my money, and he did not pay attention to me. I went to speak to a police officer, and they did not pay any attention to me. So I broke a bottle on his head. The police came after me, and they asked me why I had done that. I said to them, "Because he didn't pay me my money." They took me into custody. Of course, they protect the tourist, and we Dominicans are of no consequence here.

Finally, women talked about being pressured and coerced by the police for sexual favors. Isabel was raped by a police officer who told her that he would not take her to jail if she had sex with him. She ended up pregnant and now has a six-year-old daughter from the incident. She never saw him again, but she remembers his name.

SUPPORT SERVICES FOR SEX WORKERS

In 1988 the nonprofit, non-governmental organizations Centro de Promoción y Solidaridad Humana, Inc. (CEPROSH), and Comité de Vigilancia y Control del Sida (COVICOSIDA) were established as a response to the large incidence of AIDS-related cases in the Puerto Plata region.[11] These organizations are comprised of activists, advocates, scholars, health care practitioners, and sex workers. Their primary funding comes from the United States Agency for International Development (USAID) programs, the Dominican government, and the Pan-American Health Organization (PAHO). They have conducted studies of the sex industry in the region and the practices of the formal tourism employees in the tourist resorts, and they have developed various programs for the prevention of AIDS and other sexually transmitted diseases. They are service providers for the population of sex workers, their clients, and employees of entertainment businesses such as nightclubs, brothels, and casinos. They collaborate on some of their programs with COIN, a non-governmental organization based in Santo Domingo that conducts projects and programs in the area of education and health to benefit groups, institutions, and businesses. COIN also addresses the reproductive and mental health needs of sex workers in the capital and in the surrounding beach area of Boca Chica. Both COIN and COVICOSIDA work closely with the national sex worker organization, Movimiento de Mujeres Unidas (MODEMU).

Since 1989, the educational and outreach programs conducted by COVI-COSIDA have been on the cutting edge of sexual education and disease prevention. Using a methodology that involves audience participation, street guerrilla theater, *foto novelas,* and pamphlets, they have designed a plan of action to reach the most vulnerable populations in the region of Puerto Plata. They not only target people involved in sex tourism and sex industry enterprises but also provide education and services to the impoverished Haitian sugarcane workers and the prostitutes who service this population. They employ former sex workers to conduct outreach programs through peer counseling, education, and information on sexually transmitted diseases. These *mensajeras de salud* (health messengers) are sex workers who carry the message of prevention and health care to other sex workers. Using the knowledge base of sex workers, they conduct workshops in sex industry businesses and other places where sex workers congregate. Thus, the educational programs are relevant and sensitive to the needs of sex workers. The programs start from the needs of sex workers.

Sex workers are not only exposed to a number of sexually transmitted diseases, including AIDS, but also are at high risk for other problems related to their reproductive health. In 1997, COVICOSIDA opened a medical clinic in the center of Los Charamicos to attend to the health of low-income women and specifically to that of sex workers. The clinic provides low-cost gynecological exams and counseling in birth control and HIV/AIDS prevention.

With a keen understanding of the issues and the conditions of the tourism economy, COVICOSIDA has also carried out educational programs for the networks that facilitate the mechanisms of sex tourism. They have conducted many highly successful AIDS/HIV prevention and educational workshops for hotel employees in the resorts of Puerto Plata. They have taken their guerrilla theater to the streets of Puerto Plata and to the key sites where tourist guides and motoconchos congregate.

Based in Santo Domingo, MODEMU held the first congress and published the first book about, and by, sex workers in the Dominican Republic (COIN 1995, Kempadoo 1998). The organization also publishes a newsletter, *La Nueva Historia,* and is comprised primarily of women who work in the national sex industry servicing Dominican men but also involves some women who work with foreigners. MODEMU holds workshops to raise women's consciousness about issues of equality, wages, work conditions, and health and safety. Their concept of health is broad enough to include issues of self-esteem and women's economic independence. They cooperate and work closely with business owners. Many of the workshops take place in sex industry businesses during hours (such as the early afternoon) when there are few or no customers. They are careful not to antagonize business owners even while working to create better working conditions for women.

CONCLUSION

External agents such as Western nations, multilateral agencies, and international banks continue to exercise a strong degree of control over the socioeconomic development of the Dominican Republic. The hegemony of neoliberal ideology informs the ambassadors of global capitalism to dictate programs and economic packages that continue to increase the misery of the poor and the riches of the wealthy. These financial development deals create low-paying, unstable employment for women, either in the tourism industry or in the export-processing zones. They have not alleviated the poverty of women as far as income, health care, education, housing, and child care are concerned. In fact, working-class women have more responsibilities and fewer opportunities to meet their economic needs.

Despite the prevailing inequitable arrangements, Dominicanas are using the international tourism industry to create and pursue opportunities for survival, socioeconomic mobility, and migration. In integrating themselves into a complex transnational sexual economy, they are realizing the power of their sexuality and the sexuality of power.

NOTES

1. This figure represents direct and indirect employment in the tourism industry. It does not include sex workers who work in the tourism sector informally or in other activities such as the travel and airline industry, construction, and the informal economy.

2. Although I did not work with this population, the sex workers with whom I spoke and other citizens of Puerto Plata informed me that these women come from the rural areas.

3. Some women are simultaneously involved with various men.

4. De Moya et al. state that Sanky-Panky is a "linguistic construction that placed the Spanish 's' of the article *los* (plural of 'the') as a prefix to the phrase 'Hanky-Pankies.' As such, Los Hanky-Pankies would become the Sanky-Pankies."

5. I conducted tape-recorded interviews in Sosúa with thirty-five women over the age of eighteen. The Dominican non-governmental organizations Centro de Promoción y Solidaridad Humana, Inc. (CEPROSH), and Comité de Vigilancia y Control del Sida (COVICOSIDA), and the sex worker organization Movimiento de Mujeres Unidas (MODEMU) provided me an entrée to the sex workers of Sosúa, Puerto Plata. The assistance and guidance of COVICOSIDA, CEPROSH, and MODEMU were critical to this study. A member of MODEMU contacted sex workers who were willing to be interviewed about their experiences with tourists and arranged the interview dates and times.

6. In 1991, 31.4 percent of the rural population and 10.8 percent of the urban population were illiterate.

7. Most women mentioned traveling to and from La Romana and Boca Chica, other tourism centers known for sex tourism.

8. While my information about European men is drawn from interviews with Dominican women, chapter 2 by O'Connell Davidson and Sanchez Taylor in this book draws similar conclusions from their interviews with European male tourists in the Dominican Republic and Jamaica.

9. Article 334 states, "It will be considered pimping he or she that; 1) By any means helps, assists or conceals persons, men or women, with designs towards the practice of prostitution or the recruitment of persons with designs towards sexual exploitation; 2) He or she that through the exercise [of prostitution] receives benefits from the practices of prostitution; 3) The person related to prostitution who cannot justify the sources pertaining to their way of life; 4) He or she who consents to the prostitution of their partner and obtains benefits from them; 5) He or she that contracts, coaches or supports, even with their consent, a person, man or woman even of legal age into to prostitution, the execution of prostitution, or to licentious and relaxed social customs; 6) The position of intermediary, of whatever title, among the persons (men or women) that are dedicated to the prostitution or the relaxation of the social customs or the individuals that exploit or remunerate prostitution and the relaxation of the social customs of another; 7) That by threats, prison or maneuvers or by any means disturbs the action of prevention, assistance or reeducation undertaken by qualified agencies in favor of the persons (men or women) that are dedicated to prostitution or in risk of prostitution. Pimping is punished with prison from six months to three years and a fine of fifty thousand to five hundred thousand pesos" (Ley 24-97).

10. The agencies responsible are the Dirección General de Promoción de la Mujer (DGPM), Fondo de Poblacion de Las Naciones Unidas, and the Asociación Dominicana Pro Bienestar de la Familia (PROFAMILIA).

11. The province of Puerto Plata has one of the highest rates of HIV/AIDS in the country. A study by CEPROSH estimates that between 180,000 and 222,000 Dominican adults are infected with AIDS, 80 percent through heterosexual transmission. The incidence of HIV has grown among women in Puerto Plata from 2.8 percent in 1994 to 4.0 percent in 1995. The figure of 7.9 percent for 1996 is one of the highest in the country (CEPROSH 1997, Kreniske 1997).

6

"Come to Jamaica and Feel All Right"

Tourism and the Sex Trade

SHIRLEY CAMPBELL, ALTHEA PERKINS, AND PATRICIA MOHAMMED

Sex work in Jamaica, as in most other societies, has existed in some form or fashion since "time immemorial." Its appeal as an area for in-depth social scientific research is, however, more recent. Henriques (1963) explored its manifestation in Jamaica during slavery, post-emancipation, and the early twentieth century. In all three periods he found that sex work offered women an opportunity to improve their lot through sexual liaisons with white men or because of the potential it provided during the post-emancipation period for women to earn an income in declining socioeconomic conditions.

Various sector studies such as Endoe (1994) and Ross-Frankson (1987), together with newspaper articles in 1998, have supported the view that sex work provides an alternative income in declining socioeconomic conditions. These studies also point to an idea largely unsupported by fact, that an increasing number of younger women and men are entering the trade as economic hardships increase. Nevertheless, a fast growing tourist sector and further declining economic conditions have facilitated an increase in female and male prostitution. Low wages in the formal sector of the economy coupled with the rising cost of living propels more people to informal means of earning an income, including sex work.

Sex work, because it has remained a clandestine and stigmatized "profession" and has been largely underresearched, has perpetuated a host of negative stereotypes and myths surrounding the women and men engaged in this area of work. These are about the work itself, ranging from the perception of the female sex worker as immoral and oversexed; to the occupation as being one chosen by lower class women, where women are viewed as victims in the trade; to the interpretation of this area of work as "nonwork." Previous to wide feminist concern with the condition and status of sex workers and sex work in society, the sex worker, or "prostitute," has been essentially *persona non grata* in the public view. Further in-depth study is necessary to dispel some of these myths. Research is needed to uncover the real experiences of men and women involved in this area and, hopefully, provide data that can promote informed discussions and policymaking that will ultimately be in the interest of the workers themselves.

Against this background, this study was aimed at gaining an insight into the lives and decision-making processes of those working in the sex trade and examining the issue of sex work as work.[1] Such an examination assumes critical proportions in the situation where economic choices are increasingly limited by unfavorable macroeconomic factors. Traditionally, the Jamaican economy has been marked by high unemployment, which has worsened under the Structural Adjustment Programs (SAPs)[2] initiated in 1977 under the IMF and World Bank agreements. The overall impact of these adjustments has been a dramatically worsening economic and social crisis, which has "deepened the dependency, poverty and debt" (McAfee 1991:6–29). The resulting high unemployment, the increasing number of unskilled and often unemployable, the increasing number of youths entering the job market, the closure of some factories with low status, and low-paying jobs have made a bad situation worse. Among the unemployed, women continue to dominate. Women account for 64 percent of the unemployed in Jamaica (STATIN Labor Force Survey 1996:iii).

At the national level there is a conscious decision to promote tourism as the answer to Jamaica's economic woes. The industry, which formally emerged in 1891, has now become the leading earner of foreign exchange and employs directly and indirectly one in every four Jamaicans (Tulloch 1998).[3] Taylor reinforces Minister Tulloch's point. He notes that tourism has clearly

> become the life blood of the Jamaican economy, but at enormous social cost: enclaves of privilege and ostentation that exclude the bulk of the local population, drug trafficking and prostitution, soaring prices, and environment degradation. No wonder some Jamaicans regard tourism as a new kind of sugar (Taylor 1993:flap).

The marketing of Jamaica's tourism may be said to be concentrated around the four *S*'s—sun, sand, sea and sex. When this is superimposed on the nation that at one time boasted the world's best *ganja—sensimilla* (cannabis sativa)—and internationally acclaimed reggae music, then this should create an unbeatable destination. Different packages are sold within these broad parameters, some appealing to families, singles and other groups and individuals. The Jamaica Tourist Board and other entities responsible for marketing the local product make an effort to persuade the pleasure-seeking tourist of a hedonistic holiday, thus not surprisingly attracting the client who expects to participate in the sex trade. Lastra Torres (1998), writing on the sex trade in Chile, suggests that the trade does not occur only at the level of the actual commercial relationships but is "subliminally present in the advertising disseminated by the communications media." This soft selling of sex is coupled with the growth in all-inclusives,[4] together with an increase in the informal sector.

IDEOLOGY/ATTITUDES TOWARD THE SEX TRADE

This study coincided with a campaign to clear out so-called harassers from the tourist resort areas. The exit interview of tourists conducted by the Planning and Research Department of the Jamaica Tourist Board, for example, reported that 55.8 percent of respondents said they were harassed. Minister Tulloch in his budget speech noted that the root of harassment could be only partially explained by the socioeconomic problem facing the country. He continued:

> The truth is that the type of harassment that has given us the reputation that we have has nothing to do with the socioeconomic situation in the country—it has to do with a type of Jamaican who has no intention of earning an honest day's pay for an honest day's work but is much more comfortable preying upon others—be they visitors or Jamaicans—for a livelihood.[5]

The clean-up campaign was conducted in 1998 by the government and other tourist officials and sparked a round of debates in the local newspapers. The major concern and driving force of the campaign was that harassment results in the loss of significant potential earnings, estimated at U.S.$200 million by Jamaica Chamber of Commerce (JCC) President Howard Hamilton (*Sunday Observer*, June 13, 1998). It was felt that regulating the activities of the informal sector, which grows alongside the formal tourist sector, would reduce the loss in earnings and make for a more viable tourist industry. Sex workers were conceptualized as one component of harassers, along with persons selling craft items on the streets/beach, hair braiders, and taxi drivers.

Before outlining the current views, however, it is useful to examine historical positions on the sex trade. Henriques (1963) notes that a significant number of brothels operated in Kingston as well as in the resort town of Montego Bay. Brothels tended to be conveniently located close to the docks and piers, thus facilitating easy access for crew members and other visitors who were the main clients of these establishments. The government's response through the British Hygiene Council in 1936 was framed within health concerns, as the sex trade was seen as the main means of transmitting sexually transmitted diseases (STDs). The other concern was preventing the traffic in women. Henriques (1963) states that girls from Jamaica left for work in brothels in South and Central America. In addition to regulating the activities of sex workers under various laws, discussed later in this chapter, the state has continued to respond with health interventions. In more recent times organizations like the Association for the Control of Sexually Transmitted Diseases (ACOSTRAD) have targeted and worked with sex workers, with the ultimate objective of limiting the spread of STDs.

The debate around the 1998 clean-up campaign began a year earlier when Fortsmayer, head of the Montego Bay Chamber of Commerce, announced in the print and electronic media his proposal for regulating the sex trade through the setting up of red-light districts. In 1998, Howard Hamilton, head of the JCC, also suggested that the traditional method of locking up and charging sex workers was ineffective (*Daily Observer*, June 13, 1998). It was proposed that more effective and potentially more beneficial to the sex worker and tourists would be the establishment of a red-light district, which would provide a space for both female and male sex workers to offer their services.

The proposal was met with downright rejection on the part of the church, which was guided by biblical sanctions and mores, to measured support from moralists who condemn the sex trade but recognized it as a fact of life and were prepared for discussions and possible solutions. The main concerns expressed by such parties pertained to health issues, women's safety, and the maintenance of a profitable tourism product.

Another basis for the rejection of the proposal to regulate the sector was put forward by the National Democratic Movement (NDM)[6] spokesperson on gender issues, whose suggestion, despite being framed within the moralistic argument, at least recognized a possible pragmatic motive for the sex workers' choice of occupation. She suggested that efforts should be made to ensure that, "youth... can use their intellect and creativity, instead of their bodies, to contribute to the development of their communities and themselves" (Saunders in the *Herald*, June 21, 1998).

A moralistic viewpoint was put forward by a director of the Montego Bay Chamber of Commerce, who opposed regulation of the industry, suggesting that "we do not have to resort to that.... From the moral side, I do not think that Jamaica is ready for this" (cited by Saunders in *The Gleaner*, June 16, 1998).

The Association of Women's Organization (AWOJA) joined the newspaper debate, adding new dimensions to the issues as they affected the health of both sex worker and client. AWOJA member Hermione McKenzie posited a very insightful response. She pointed out that regulating the industry was not a clear-cut and unproblematic process especially in the context of a society which is not easily regulated. She further suggested that "to regulate it will make it a social and moral issue." While another concern from AWOJA was the commodification of women through regulation (sex shops), the point was made that "since there were women who have taken on the sex trade as a 'profession,' the nation should recognize this and leave the issue open for discussion" (AWOJA 1998).

A legal position presented by attorney-at-law Hilaire Sobers suggested that in light of prostitution being a fact of life and the Constitution's guarantee of the freedom of the individual (consenting adults) to make a choice for or against sex, regulation could be aimed at providing working conditions, specifically health related, as ends in and of themselves, rather than for ensuring increased profits for the tourist industry.

In summary, one could suggest that although moral sanctions still prevailed in 1998, there appeared to be an increased pragmatism toward the issue of the sex trade. Certainly there was a more healthy recognition or acceptance of the existence of the trade. The dominant—or at least the more vocal—view within this approach clearly pointed to the profit motive as the sanitizing force behind its organization, with security and concern for the women and men involved in the trade being a secondary consideration. In debates on sex work as capitalism's commodification of the human body, the intensified interest in this area suggests it is another sphere in which capital and labor are concerned with the control and regulation of human sexuality. Nonetheless, in their response, AWOJA provided some kind of balance to this debate by articulating concerns regarding the women (and men) themselves. AWOJA further suggested that caution needed to be taken in promoting regulations that have not been clearly thought through and to which the major participants have not been invited to determine the workable solutions.

LEGISLATION

The regulation of prostitution is implemented under the Laws of Jamaica and reflects the traditional response of the law—the dominant moralistic position and social sanctions adopted by the society at large. The legislation which governs the trade is contained within the laws related to soliciting and loitering: Section 4 of the Vagrancy Act of 1902[7] (now repealed) and the Loitering Laws.[8]

The repealed Vagrancy law[9] has given space for legislative amendments to the Tourist Board Act and the Towns and Communities Act. Both Acts ensure that criminal charges can be brought against persons who are guilty of antisocial behavior such as indecent exposure and loitering in a public place, using threatening or abusive language, and soliciting for prostitution. The seriousness of the government's position is evidenced by the fact that the cabinet has already approved increased fines under the Towns and Communities Act. The increase is from J$1,000 (around U.S.$28) to an amount not exceeding J$100,000 (approximately U.S.$2,800). Repeat offenses have increased from J$1,500 to not exceeding J$150,000. Fines under the Tourist Board Act are also expected to be amended. Resort patrols in the tourist towns work with other law enforcing officials to maintain order and, importantly, ensure the visitor's safety. With respect to charges regarding the two Acts, and other cases involving tourists, and in light of insufficient time for hearing cases, night courts will soon be implemented in resort areas.

THE RESEARCH SITES

This study took place in three different tourist destinations in Jamaica: Ocho Rios, Montego Bay, and Negril. Each site is unique in the kind of attractions it offers, yet similar forms of prostitution exist in all three locations: club-work, beach boys, and Rent-a-Dreads.[10] The primary differences relate to geography, physical facilities, and socioeconomic growth patterns. Ocho Rios is the only site that consistently offers a destination for cruise ships. This provides the main area around which one category of sex workers operates. Their main clients are the crew members of these ships that are entertained during the daylight hours, unlike the other two locations, where activities are concentrated at nights. Negril with its long stretch of beach and hotels, restaurants, and nightly entertainment provides an ideal spot for picking up prospective clients, hence the phenomenon of the "beach girls." The built-up areas on the beach provide spaces in which exchanges can be made with some amount of privacy. In Montego Bay, for example, sex workers who deal exclusively with locals are concentrated on such streets as Church Street, Parade, and Howard Cooke Boulevard. Their fee averages J$500 (about U.S.$14) per five minute job. A quick job may be done in a darkened corner of the street, or a nearby room can be rented for J$300. The client must pay the cost of renting the room.

SEX WORKERS IN EACH SITE

In Ocho Rios the various categories of sex workers are: those whose main clients are crew members of the cruise ships; tourist industry employees such as entertainment coordinators and waitresses, who work as sex workers part time; persons who work in other formal sector jobs such as nursing and teaching and are engaged in the sex trade part time; high-class prostitutes; and "$20 prostitutes." Male sex workers also operate as beach boys/gigolos and Rent-a-Dreads.

Workers whose main clients are the ships' crew members tend to have special or regular clients on the ships. The exchange takes place usually in a bar or lounge, where rooms are available for rent in close proximity to the pier. During the daytime, tourists who visit the bar or lounge (sometimes introduced by taxi men) are potential clients. The average prices charged to crew and tourists in Ocho Rios are U.S.$50 for straight sex, U.S.$50 for oral sex, and U.S.$70–100 for a combination of both. Each worker who operates her business at the bar or lounge situated in close proximity to the shipping pier pays U.S.$18 for rental (per customer) of the room. On a good day sex workers see between three and five clients, but there are days, especially during the off tourist seasons, without clients. Respondents report, however, that they do save toward these periods.

Since this aspect of the trade takes place during daylight hours, these workers also visit clubs and discos (Acropolis, Shades, and Shaw Park Hotel disco in Ocho Rios) in the nights in search of potential clients, usually tourists and sometimes Jamaicans. The formal sector employees who work part time as sex workers also visit clubs and discos in the nights in search of clients. A tourist client who is picked up during the night will usually take the sex worker to his hotel room if this is convenient. If not, and as is the case with Jamaicans, a room is usually rented. On the club scene, an upscale nightclub, Jamaica Mi Crazy, provides a space for high-class sex workers to market themselves. Clients may be picked up on the same night or given business cards to use for making contact at a future date.

Another category of sex workers, the $20 prostitutes, are so called because they charge as little as J$20 (less than U.S.$1) for their service. The women employed in this category tend to be extremely poor and more often than not are addicted to hard drugs. Their clients are usually blue-collar locals such as vendors.

In Montego Bay, sex workers who deal mainly with tourists and work on the streets are concentrated on the hotel strip. Gloucester Avenue, Kent Avenue, and Bottom Road are other locations where sex workers are contacted. We cannot provide information about rates charged to tourists who make contact with sex workers who work on the streets because we did not interview that category of workers.

In the more low scale go-go dance clubs like Gold Finger and Royal Palm, also in Montego Bay, there are rooms upstairs to which a client can be taken for a fee of J$300. The client's fee ranges from J$1,500 to $3,000 and the average time for a sex job is six to twenty minutes. If the client requires more time, then they must pay for an additional period. In some of these clubs sex workers are females who may have been recruited as young as age fourteen or fifteen as go-go dancers. They then become sex workers in addition to remaining dancers. If a dancer who is performing on stage wishes to leave with a client before midnight, then the client must pay the proprietor for the dancer to leave. If a dancer leaves with a client for another location after midnight she has to pay the proprietor J$500 for loss of potential business. In the more upscale clubs such as the Flamingo, which has carpeted and air-conditioned rooms, the rate for the rooms is J$1,000, and the fee for a job ranges upward of U.S.$100. The proprietor usually has to give approval for a dancer to leave early with a client, and a fee may also be charged to the dancer for taking a client away from that location.

In some respects the situation is similar, albeit with some differences, in Negril. There, an entry fee (cover charge) is paid to gain entry into the club or discotheque where sex workers meet clients. The sex worker leaves with the client, going either to a private residence or to the hotel or guesthouse where the client may be staying. They may also secure a hotel or guestroom for the duration of the job, which averages one hour. Fees range from U.S.$150 to $300, and the clients pay for the additional cost of the room.

In the slow season, a sex worker who traditionally works the clubs and discotheques may book into an all-inclusive hotel, which usually has more guests than other locations. Karen reported that she paid U.S.$199 per night to stay in an all-inclusive hotel during the slow season. Because she has to pay for the hotel, she charges between U.S.$300 and 500 per client. Her potential problems are the security guards at the hotel and the entertainment coordinators. The hotel security may be cooperative and ignore her presence or they may want a percentage of her fees. If she refuses to cooperate they may call the police to remove her from the hotel. A fairly recent or probably more highly developed phenomenon is that of entertainment coordinators at the all-inclusives who may organize for sex workers to entertain guests in the hotel or who may themselves work as sex workers.

Beach girls work as full-time sex workers in Negril and operate exclusively from the beach. The sex workers who work in the clubs had this to say about their beach counterparts: "The beach girls are open, people say they are cheap. They will go with guys for U.S.$40, $50, anything, anything and jeopardize our business."

Beach boys, gigolos, or Rent-a-Dreads work mainly on the beaches where they may make individual contact with tourists and make private arrangements. These arrangements may involve being a constant companion to the visitor for the duration of his or her visit. It is not clear what the rates are as we were unable to interview a male sex worker currently employed in the industry. Our male participant left that profession six years ago. Male sex workers were, however, very visible at a reggae beach party that took place on a section of the seven miles of white sand beach in Negril one night as we walked the beach area. It was however not convenient to do interviews at that time as they were actively engaged in their jobs. From secondhand information it was gleaned that the female tourist may first make contact with a beach boy or Rent-a-Dread on the beach. A drug hustler may also make this arrangement for the woman or it may be someone working in an all-inclusive. Whatever the arrangement, the escort is entertained and all bills paid for the duration of the client's stay in Jamaica. A car may be rented for the escort to drive, or even bought, depending on the intensity and anticipated duration of the relationship. Some of these contacts end in marriage.

Some of the female sex workers may also develop long-term relationships with clients that end in marriage. During our field trip to Negril, a former sex worker and her husband were visiting from Italy; she had met him earlier as a client. Several of the women have visited mainland Europe and the United States. Clients with whom they had developed more than a casual relationship invited them. Visits to Europe are more frequent because it is not as difficult to obtain visas for visiting there as it is for the United States. While visiting with overseas clients, sex workers are supported financially and money is sent to relatives in Jamaica to pay their (the sex workers') bills.

High-class sex workers who may work mainly out of their homes make contact with clients in the upscale hotels through entertainment coordinators, bar workers, Jamaica Union Travelers Association (JUTA) taxi services, and others. We were unable to interview any member of this category of workers but various references were made to them in discussions with a bar attendant who worked at a couples-only all-inclusive in Montego Bay.

One interviewee informed us that the police, particularly in Negril, are themselves clients, even though they arrest people for prostitution. In addition, they may work as pimps, taking a percentage of the sex workers' earnings in order to guarantee their protection from police interference. It is also alleged that the police work as gigolos.

Encounters of sex worker and client are not limited only to one-day/night stands. In fact, each sex worker has her own clients whom she maintains as long as they visit and she is available. Relationships develop over long periods but maintain the form of sex for money. Other possible encounters involve repeat stopover tourists who maintain contact and repeatedly seek the services of a particular sex worker. In some instances, the sex worker may be employed with a particular visitor for the entire visit. In such a case the sex worker is not expected to have other clients. One respondent reported receiving J$30,000 for a period of three days. Respondents state that on some occasions they remain faithful to the contract but on others they "go rude" or "run ward" to exploit other chances of increased income. Respondents reported having spent up to three months, for instance, in Germany and Italy with previous clients. The stay usually includes living with the client in Europe with money sent home to family and friends in Jamaica to pay bills.

THE PARTICIPANTS IN THE STUDY

The six participants in Ocho Rios range in age from twenty to twenty-nine years and all have been involved in the sex trade for an average of three years. One respondent's pregnancy while in school and the need to find work to support herself and the new child coupled with the fact that she had a cousin already involved in the sex trade led her into this area of work. Another had left school and had no job and nothing to do (she has no children) and had friends who were involved. She found the idea of making a lot of money an attractive one and joined her friends. Two respondents were involved in formal job activities (working in a restaurant and go-go dancing) that provided them with opportunities for meeting tourists and ship crews, potential clients. This facilitated the occasional client for sex while still on the job, but realizing that the monetary gains from sex work far exceeded their salaries they opted to move into the sex trade full time. The other two respondents were a hair braider and a domestic helper. For both, the incomes earned from these jobs were inadequate to support themselves and their families, so they—again through introduction by friends—opted for work in the sex trade. Self-employment as a sex worker ultimately provides independence, which is preferred to working for someone.

In Montego Bay and Negril nine females and one male participated in the study; their ages ranged from seventeen to forty-two years. All had attended primary, secondary, or high school,[11] and, with the exception of one female, could read and write. Three had attended and graduated from primary school, five had attended high school, and the remaining two had attended secondary schools. Of the seven who attended high or secondary school, four had dropped out because of unplanned and unwanted pregnancies and one had graduated. Of the remaining two, one dropped out because she suffered a mental relapse at examination time. She attributed this to the psychological trauma of being sexually abused by her stepfather. The other reported that her mother couldn't afford to keep her in school and her father, who could, did not believe in supporting his children beyond feeding them.

Of the four students who became pregnant in school, two had been thirteen and two seventeen years old. One of the thirteen-year-olds was impregnated by a "big man" who was a family friend. The seventeen-year-olds were impregnated by fellow students. One was raped, the other consented. The other two sex workers who reported early pregnancies were seventeen and eighteen years at the time of their pregnancies. By that time both had stopped attending school. Their families were upset and one reported having to sleep outside on the verandah "all night until daylight" with her baby. The other's child was supported by her grandmother while she ran away from home to find work.

The occupational background of the sex workers' parents included farming, public service, voluntary social services, housewife, businessman, and preaching (*Modda*).[12] The number of siblings ranged from two to fourteen. Four of the sex workers reported having to run away from home because of hostile relationships with stepparents; one reported being overworked, having to "carry wood, water and look after" her siblings; and another reported being sexually abused by her stepfather, with her mother's knowledge.

The sex workers interviewed had worked in the industry for between three weeks and twenty years. The youngest started when she was fourteen and a half years old, the oldest at thirty-seven. Between them they have accumulated sixty-nine and one-half years in the industry. They came from various occupational backgrounds: for 20 percent it was their first job; others had previously worked in such jobs as domestic helper, waitress, bar attendant, farmer, among others.

In almost all cases the main reason given for entering the sex trade was encouragement by friends or family members who worked in the profession. These friends or family members provided support for potential recruits who were unemployed or were earning low wages in other low-status occupations. What is significant here is that what appears to determine entry into the sex trade is the support network which is available to potential entrants. In other words, if a friend or family member who was a higgler, a domestic helper, or a newspaper vendor had provided support, it is likely that the individual being helped would also have engaged in similar economic activities. Specific individual reasons for entering the sex trade provide insights into the social situation at the micro level. At the macro level, the increasing economic pressures have resulted in fewer and fewer jobs being available to an increasing number of youths entering the job market. Very often they are lacking basic numeric and literacy skills and are sometimes unemployable. Some of these girls and boys migrate between parishes seeking jobs in the tourist resort areas. One police officer described the situation as being similar to seeking a visa to visit the United States. As in the stories about America, he said they hear that the streets of the tourist resort areas are paved with gold. They come and they find out it is not true. As indicated earlier, in explaining the connection between tourism and the sex trade, there is a particularly unsubtle way of marketing Jamaican tourism and a strong suggestion that sex is readily available in Jamaica. Both the potential clients and the Jamaican population are clearly targets of the marketing strategies promoted by the tourist board and other agencies who situate Jamaica and Jamaican culture on the world map.

A quick glance at what the workers reported as the difference between the wages they earned in low skilled jobs as opposed to sex work will indicate why there may be a preference for employment as sex workers. A domestic worker makes on average J$1,000 per week, a Free Zone worker between J$850 and J$2,000, and a waitress around J$850. In contrast sex workers earn anywhere from J$3,000 per week on the street to around U.S.$1,400 if they work freelance. It is significant to note that sex workers' earnings peak during specific periods. For those who work mainly with local clients, the best nights are Fridays and public holidays; for those in Montego Bay who work the clubs, Friday nights are slow; in Negril Saturdays (day time) are their slow days, while Wednesdays and Saturdays (discotheque night) are peak periods for working the clubs.

Sex workers also report that there are some nights when they do not have any clients. Those who work exclusively or mainly with tourists earn most of their money during the tourist season, December 15 to April 15, and Spring Break (March), when students from the U.S. visit during their spring vacation. In the off season they live off the savings they made during the peak earning periods. Some return home or migrate to other locations.

Sex workers in the clubs at Montego Bay reported a poor Spring Break season and in Negril a poor "Italian Season"—a time when the majority of visitors to Negril are Italians. When we visited at the end of May, the sex workers said that there were very few Italians around. In Montego Bay the view was expressed that it was the complete packages being offered by the all-inclusives which prevented the Spring Breakers from visiting the clubs more frequently. The offer of a complete package means that all the tourists' needs are organized and provided for by the hotel and they do not have to leave the premises to get anything. If and when they do leave it may be to attend an event organized by the all-inclusives. In Negril the view was expressed that the Italians had gone to Cuba where prices were lower than in Jamaica.

Apart from the seasonal work, one other factor impacting sex workers earning potential is their age. The capacity to attract clients is influenced by their attractiveness as well as their age. The amount of money spent on clothes, hairstyles, and makeup also impacts the clients they may attract. Consequently, older workers reported that they supplemented their incomes with domestic work, sidewalk vending, or working as Informal Commercial Importers (ICIs) and often worked only on weekends. As they grow older, sex workers' earning capacity is also reduced by a change in clientele. The younger women have a tendency to deal mainly with tourists and the older ones with locals; tourists are charged more than locals.

Another factor influencing the potential earnings of the sex worker is menstruation. Almost all reported not working during their periods, which averaged five days per month. One reported taking the pill continuously to delay the arrival of the period; another, of drinking gin and stuffing her vagina with toilet paper in order to continue working. Yet another reported that if she started working the day following the fifth day of her period she would begin bleeding again and that this was inconvenient to her, reducing her earnings.

Sex work was not always the sole form of economic support; others were manifested mainly in two ways—the throwing of partners[13] and sharing monetary and other resources when "times were hard." These activities are similar to those used by other women in the wider society.

MANAGEMENT OF HEALTH AND OTHER RISKS

Sex workers were asked to comment on how they protected themselves: whether they used condoms, whether clients requested the nonuse of condoms, and what their reactions were in such situations. In addition, they were asked to comment on what their understanding was of HIV/AIDS; in what situations, if any, they may be tempted to have unprotected sex; how often they had medical checkups done; and when the time of their last checkup was. The issue of personal security is considered in this study because of the potential risk which the sex worker faces in her/his job.

All except two sex workers reported having had a medical checkup within one to five months of the time the interviews were conducted. Medical checks included blood tests for HIV and other STDs, pap smears, and routine checks such as for hypertension. One sex worker who reported not having had a recent checkup had her last one in 1996 when the peer counseling clinic closed in Montego Bay; the other did not say whether or not she had a recent checkup. All reported using two or more condoms at once. Sixty percent of the participants in Montego Bay and Negril and one in Ocho Rios said they would never do a "blow-job" (oral sex) because of the possibility of contracting infections. Those who said they did said they used condoms. In fact respondents showed an avid knowledge of the various types and strengths of condoms. For instance the condoms provided free of cost by clinics were considered weak and useful only when performing oral sex. For this reason sex workers preferred to purchase brands that they felt more secure using. They all insisted that they would never go without a condom and "no one could offer them enough money to do so." Those who may have sex without using condoms were identified by our participant Phyllis as those

who tek the drugs and [have] careless sex. Most prostitutes you meet upon the first thing they offer you is a condom; the sensible ones they say, "Here is a condom" or "You have a condom?" On our corner you have girls who are on drugs and don't care. The drugs can carry you in a far way. You realize seh that person want to have sex with you but the way it have you you not conscious enough to mek sure seh him use a condom. You want to tell him to use it but at the same time the something [drug] hold you. But when you finish... you come back to you normal self, you say, "Shit you mean I go without condom?!"

Phyllis had been on cocaine for ten years; she stopped four years earlier when one of her friends nearly died after four of them had binged on a *eights* (a dealer's portion) of coke for two days. Her friend had collapsed, foamed at the mouth, and her body started swelling. Phyllis was the one who took her to the hospital, while the others ran away. She had not used coke since.

Returning to the subject of those who may be compromising the health of sex workers, themselves, and their partners she continued:

> You still have men coming out, big responsible man, drive some big fancy, flashy car, waan have sex wid you. You say use a condom and dem say, "Mi naah use condom, mi have mi wife a mi yard and mi wife clean and me clean." And you say, "But I am a whore suppose mi have AIDS." "You look good you can't have AIDS." I mean you still have whole heap a big, intelligent, responsible men who do not accept. All some a dem say to you say,... "If AIDS fi kill mi mek it kill mi."

> On my little corner, my girls dem well educated pon sex. We do not do blow job because teeth can eat off the condom pon di penis and give you some kine of disease. But you have some big responsible man dem wife and kids and they will try to bring the money higher and higher to entice you. But it is up to you. From you are educated enough to know to refuse it ... because if that person was safe he wouldn't take that risk with you not knowing the condition of your health. When dem say prostitute spread AIDS I am not saying prostitutes don't spread AIDS but not to how dem wouda really think. Because prostitutes always have dem condom. A di men dem who come a road and will not use the condom.

Another sex worker who worked at a go-go dance club noted that she uses her condoms "All di time.... Mi wouldn't mind if mi couda use di whole box," which she buys at the clinic, 100 for J$100. Sometimes she uses three at once. We met a few days before she was scheduled to go for her health check. In a troubled voice she said, "Mi deh yah a fret pon di blood test; mi fraid it yu nuh. Mi dweet [do it] but mi fraid a it. But anyway mi tell meself seh Father di deh an nuttin do mi."

We asked, "When was the last time you did one?" She responded: "Mi do three fi last year. Three fi last year an mi do one a di hospital; x-rays also." She returns to the discussion about condoms:

> Sometime the condom bruck all inna mi.... Mi fine it all three day lata. The top one eva a burst, but because mi use all two, three and mi eva notice seh di sperm inna dat. Mi tek it off mi self because mi waan check it every time.

She ponders why her condom may be bursting all the time and concludes "Mi passage maybe too small so dem mus buss." She feels pain during intercourse, which she attributes to the smallness of her passage. In addition, the condom she purchases from the clinic gives her a rash sometimes, yet she is reluctant to use the Kiss of Mint, which is recommended by her doctor. When she uses it, the other sex workers accuse her of having oral sex, which is generally regarded as taboo in public spaces in Jamaica.

She looks much younger than her thirty-four years and lowers her voice when she explains that she had just given all the cash she had to her sister for paying her youngest child's school fee and did not know where the next money would come from to buy condoms, which she had run out of. She had been having her period over the last four days and had done no business. She reported that the Spring Break had been disappointing. I reminded her that at the end of our discussion she would be getting U.S.$25 for her trouble. She expressed gratitude and said she was going to the clinic to purchase condoms immediately after our talk was finished.

Other health precautionary measures being taken by sex workers were identified as:

- Douching regularly, because the lubrication on the condom leaves "stuff." Karen said "You let that stay there believe me you gonna get stink after awhile. And even that may cause infection too."
- Regular checkups with the local doctor. "If we don't have money or feel like going to the doctor we have friends. We can go to the pharmacy because they know our job and will give us what we need."
- Showering with two rags, one for the vagina and the other for the rest of the body.
- After urinating, wiping the vagina from the front towards the back (anus) to avoid getting bacterial infection.
- Not wearing tights, because they trap the heat and encourage bacterial growth.
- Washing your underwear and drying them in the sun, not the bathroom.

Simone noted that now she goes to the doctor only every five months because she knows how to take care of her vagina: "I do not get infections any more." As the discussion was brought back to the health issue, the researcher queried: "How often do you do the health checks? One participant responded, "As often as possible." Another said, "I do it like every end of month. It costs on average J$500 for the visit and between J$750 and $1,000, for a prescription."

PERSONAL SECURITY

The nature of sex work exposes the worker to certain potential dangers. Unless she or he works with a regular client, the worker is likely to be with new persons on different occasions. They must therefore face each new client on trust because they never know whether a client may be dangerous. In that regard, we asked sex workers to outline for us what were their best and worst experiences. Best experiences were consistently when a client was generous and paid without an argument, but, better yet, when they simply paid without asking for sex. An encounter, which ends in love and marriage, is also significant. Jobs such as giving a "Golden Shower"—urinating all over the person's body—walking on them with high heels on, or letting him smell the sex worker's underwear are considered fairly good if not entertaining jobs. Worst experiences ranged from a client attacking a worker with a machete because of dissatisfaction with the job, to agreeing to have sex with a client who then turned up with six men in a hotel room. One woman had to fight her way out of the room and mashed up all the hotel furniture in the process. Lorraine told us of having journeyed to Kingston during the slow season. She went with a client who tried to rape her; she jumped from the moving vehicle. She pointed to the resulting scars, which she will carry with her for life.

Regarding risk of abuse by clients, participants in Ocho Rios reported that the bar or lounge from which they operate provides a means of protection. They suggest that they are less likely to be attacked because the rooms where they conduct business are located on the premises. Problems, however, do arise from time to time and are more likely during their nighttime activities. One respondent explained that she has been robbed twice when she fell asleep after sex. Another was able to recover her money and more when, on returning from the bathroom, she discovered that her money was not in her bag. She attacked the client, who gave way, and she retrieved her money plus all the cash he had.

CONFRONTATION WITH THE LAW

In Ocho Rios, confrontations with the police are at a minimum in comparison to two years ago. According to the respondents and police, locking up streetwalkers was rampant in the past because the sex workers used to solicit on the road. However, their move to the bar and lounge areas which are more secluded, has meant that police can turn a "blind eye" to the illegal activity, as it does not encroach too much on public (respectable) space. The police, however, seem to occasionally make their presence known. One respondent explains that since this change, she has been stopped once by the police, who asked what she was doing on the street and how she earned a living. She responded that her baby's father abroad sent money for her. That was the end of the exchange.

While there appears to be a culture of acceptance of sex workers on the part of the police in Ocho Rios, workers in Montego Bay and Negril are consistently faced with confrontations. This is a direct result of the fact that sex workers operate in more public areas, such as the streets and beaches in Montego Bay and Negril, while in Ocho Rios they are in the bars and lounges.

Sex workers who work in clubs, discotheques, hotels, and their private residences reported occasional hostile encounters with the police. Those who worked on the streets and on the beaches recounted several incidents of police harassment. Two participants reported incidents in which they were satisfied with police behavior. Generally the police were accused of unnecessary physical and verbal abuse; of discriminating against female sex workers, while in some instances ignoring male sex workers; of being involved in the industry as pimps and gigolos; and of taking bribes from both tourists and locals.

A sex worker who works on the street in Montego Bay describes the situation:

> Sometimes they want to have sex with you for free (like you working wid the government). When you refuse dem call you Old Dog, Old John Crow, and run you down and stone yuh and lick [beat] you. Box you and kick you and then you cannot go and make a complaint.... Why?, why?, why? You cannot go and make a complaint against them.

There is nowhere for you to make a complaint, she lamented, "Because if you go up to the station to make a complaint they tell you [you] are a whore [and] you are not to come back again."

She tells of an incident in which a jeep full of soldiers once apprehended her and one demanded, "Come suck mi cock." Refusing, she responded, "You can't disrespect the girl so.... You need to be setting an example." They struggled, she bawled murder and members of the surrounding community began to stone the soldiers. She also speaks of a police officer who, when he was a vendor in the market and later a security guard, was her client but that as soon as he became a police officer he started to attack her. "There are those," she says, "who will want to beat you... then go around the corner, park the car, and them beckon you to come and have sex with them." She says that is the reason she refuses to deal with security guards or police officers:

> I will not have sex with them because if you have sex with them one time and they come back the next time and they don't have any money and you no decide fi do what dem waan you cannot stand up deh so in peace. They send the rest a police dem pon [upon] yuh.

She notes that the senior police officers are more respectful of them than junior officers:

When the big police dem a pass they say, "Girls, don't you see you are not making any business why don't you go home?" They don't give you a problem... but
the likkle [little] one dem weh just come inna di [into the] force dem teck [take]
stick and run yuh dung right round the town a night time.

She concludes by saying, "I mean what we are doing is not right but it is our
livelihood.... We naah really molest nobody because if you neva have man
out deh buyin' you wouldn't have women out deh sellin."

In Negril, the sex workers stay in the clubs rather than go to the beach
where the majority of tourists are, "especially in the slow season, because as
soon as you go on the beach you go to jail. But the police do not go into the
club and harass us." One group member points out that the police are prej-
udiced, as they favor certain girls. One group member interrupts quickly:
"No, they don't really. If they are not fucking you they don't like you. And I
don't fuck cops." Yet another notes: "You have to be giving them a percentage of your money or you have to be sexing them or giving them blow jobs
for which they do not pay sometimes in order for them to leave you alone."

One of our participants alleged that some sex workers who work on the
beaches escape this harassment because they have insider cops who inform
them when there is going to be a raid on the beach, at which time they stay
away. Those who are not so lucky face possible jail time:

Two weeks in jail before they even get bail. Most times they are allowed bail
within twenty-four hours on self security [surety]. They pay a fine in court and
the judge may tell them they ... gotta leave Negril as if Jamaica is not a free
country.

The gigolos, beach boys, or Rent-a-Dreads lead better lives, our participants
advise us. "On the whole ... they are not harassed by the police. By nobody,
not even by security guards."

An interview with Detective Frater of the Montego Bay Criminal Investigation Branch, which is responsible for patrolling the streets and arresting
sex workers, confirms that many more females than male sex workers are
arrested. He says that whereas it is obvious by their loud and aggressive behavior that the females are harassing the potential client, it is nearly impossible to tell when the men are working. Their mainly female companions
identify them as friends and the nature of the relationship is different in that
the male companion often acts as an escort for the duration of the visitor's
stay. He pointed out that it was not generally a one-hour or one-night
arrangement as with the majority of female sex workers. One participant in
Negril describes the situation:

I have know dis place from 1976. It's not easy. One time you could walk, talk
to people, no problem. Now, yu don't have to do nothing. I see the police bruk

up youth just fi talking to the tourist... bruk dem hand, bruk dem foot, den charge dem.

He accuses some police in Negril of being corrupt:

> They drive on the beach [if] they catch a tourist with ganja they tek money U.S.$300 an let dem go. And dat no right. If you are taken to jail two time you become their regular customer. Some of di people in prison just walking on di beach and they lock dem up. What gonna happen in di next year or two? You won't have any tourist coming here either. I think they gonna go to Cuba so all these big hotels only black people gwaan live in dem. Yeah, because the tourist dem no too like police and dem don't like fi se police a brutalize a next one.

FAMILY RELATIONS

The participants in Ocho Rios stated that at least some family members were aware of what they do for a living. The most painful situation in this regard has been ensuring that their children never find out what they do. One respondent related how on one occasion she heard her child telling others that her mother worked on the ship. She has nightmares of teachers at the child's school finding out and punishing the child as a result. She therefore consistently fabricates stories of what she does for a living in order to protect the child and hopes that she will never find out before she gets a chance to leave the sex trade, which she intends to do in the very near future.

Four of our ten participants in Montego Bay and Negril agreed to be interviewed on condition that they could be guaranteed anonymity. Their families did not know about their occupation. In Montego Bay some literally ran away when we approached, saying they had family in other parishes and abroad and they could not let them know what their jobs were. One participant in Negril said, "We tell our parents that we are waitresses, bartenders and stuff like that but we never say, 'I am a prostitute,' because we think that the parents will hate us."

Gwen, who works as a go-go dancer and sex worker when she feels like it, has told her grandmother, with whom she lives, that she works as a bar attendant. Apparently her family does not believe her; they are a Christian family and refuse to spend the money when she brings it home. She uses her money to support herself and her daughter.

When family members visit, coworkers give support by pretending that their main occupation is nonsex work. A Negril participant supports her three younger siblings by paying their school fees. "I am trying to give them an opportunity I never had," she says.

Lorraine says, "Yes, my mother knows and her response is that I should be careful. Come out of it soon. Go back to school and do something."

"How did she find out?" we ask. "Well, I tell her. I don't hide anything from her." What was her reaction? "Well, I can't study my Mom [cannot figure out what she is thinking]. I can't, I can't.... She didn't fight or nothing she was just cool."

In Phyllis's case her older son knows about her profession but not the younger one does not.

> I have been doing it from he was a little baby boy. And what really happen him grow up with it and get used to it. When I had him I went back to my mother's house and I couldn't really afford it so them used to treat me and hangle me. Sometime me and him out a door siddung pon di verandah fi di whole night till day light. So him really understand and sometime a out pon di street him haffi come deh wid mi and standup and mi go look a money fi him buy a box a food. Me go look a man and get the food and a drink mek him eat it and mi say gwaan up. I was on drugs that time but... no matter he was always my major interest no care how mi get carried away mi remba mi likkle boy. Him just grow up with me alone, he know seh mi doin it and him know mi nuh waan dweet but him just see the cause and know. Because me and him... a big man taller than me now... yeah... much taller than mi.... He reminds me of the time we slept in a bush in an old car.... Sometimes we sit down and we make much of life and laugh.

In Petunia's case her fourteen-year-old daughter who attends a high school says, "Mummy, a time yuh stop go pon di street now." Petunia responds, "How will your school fee be paid?" Nadine, looking at a picture of her oldest child, said he has no idea what she does for a living. They have a good relationship and they talk a lot, but "I haven't told him," she emphasized.

We were told that younger and younger girls are choosing to drop out of school and work as sex workers, with knowledge of their parents. Simone tells us:

> Young girls of twelve, thirteen, have friends that are prostitutes, and for some their parents have difficulty sending them to school and they just get out there. I think these parents in Negril are neglecting their kids. When I was fifteen my Mom was strict on me. In Negril parents stop looking at them when they are twelve. They let them go anywhere they want to so that's why they start going out so early. For one night they may earn U.S.$200 from a tourist and for a twelve-year-old that's a lot of money so they continue. When the parents find out she gives the parents the money, and the parents are so glad fi di money they allow the child to continue. They get tired at nights and soon stop going to school all together. That is the route by which they are being introduced to drugs as well. Often some client's rooms are full with drugs. They offer X amount of money to the sex worker to participate, and because the money is big they do it and they like it and they keep doing it and then one day they are hooked.

SUPPORT NETWORK

There does not exist in Jamaica any membership organization or support organization exclusive to sex workers. Rather, there are health related organizations. The sex workers interviewed indicated that they used the public health sector clinics and hospitals as well as private practitioners.

Members of the health sector told us that in Montego Bay, the STD clinic at the Type V Health Center on 5th Street is open to the public, including sex workers. It is open Monday through Thursday from 8:30 A.M. to 5:00 P.M. and Fridays from 8:30 A.M. to 4:00 P.M. They felt, however, that only "one or two" sex workers actually use the clinic, usually those who have had previous contact with the nurses through the now defunct peer counseling clinic. The women may drop in once a month for condoms or when they have a particular health problem. Health workers believed that the women who attended the Women's Health Intervention Project, which closed in August 1996 after being in operation for two years, may now be going to private practitioners. The project closed because the international funding came to an end and local resources have not been mobilized to reactivate it. While it operated (between 6:00 and 8:00 P.M. on Mondays), the drop-in clinic had over 200 new (to the health clinic) sex workers registered. Attempts are being made to restart this program, which was evaluated as being very successful. The main weakness, which many hope will be corrected in any future program, was its failure to target the higher-income sex workers (the focus was mainly on sex workers who worked on the streets) and male sex workers.

There are also churches that have been operating health clinics to which sex workers have access. Two examples are the Blessed Sacrament Roman Catholic Church, near the city center, which operates a daily clinic, and St. John's Methodist Church on the corner of Duke Street and Humber Avenue, which operates a clinic on Tuesdays and Thursdays from 3:00 to 5:00 P.M. and Saturdays from 9:00 A.M. to 12:00 noon. Several other churches in the area are setting up health clinics.

In Savanna-la-Mar, the capital of Westmoreland, and other surrounding communities such as Negril, Grange Hill, Darleston, and George's Plane, Contact Investigators visit sex workers in the clubs and give them individual counseling. Workers may then volunteer for testing, which is done mainly for HIV and syphilis. Counseling services are also offered at the health clinic to contacts brought in by health workers or those who come in voluntarily for testing. Sex workers also have access to the regular STD clinics, which operate similarly to the one in Montego Bay. In addition, there is an active peer educators program in Savanna-la-Mar. Along with Contact Investigators and health workers, the peer educators conduct health discussions in the bus park. On Thursdays buses plying various routes drop off potential recruits to go-go dance clubs. Club owners visit the park and recruit the dancers there. The health educators show videos, distribute literature and provide counseling, with the result that people volunteer for testing. The objective here is to make contact with these workers as soon as they arrive in the parish. The health team also visits schools, church groups, and other community groups to facilitate programs.

In Ocho Rios and Montego Bay, a Jamaica AIDS Support (JAS) Center, which has been in operation for four years, gives assistance to both male and female sex workers. They are provided with free condoms (subsidized by the Ministry of Health) and testing for HIV and syphilis. Counseling and referrals for medical care are also available where necessary and a doctor visits once per week. A donation is requested for seeing the doctor and for testing, but if the client cannot afford it she or he is not denied attention. JAS has recently started a program of selling condoms—"the condom social market"—which sells condoms such as Stamp, Erotic, and Midnight. Contact is made by officers who visit the female sex workers on location at night, engage them in discussions, and encourage them to visit the JAS Center. Contact is made with the male sex worker through a project called the "Beach Boy Project." This name was selected to destigmatize the concept of the male sex worker. The center, funded by the Dutch government, has offered these services to males for the last two years and to the females for one year. Support for the Beach Boy Project has fallen off as a result of personnel changes followed by reduced contact with persons such as lifeguards, boatmen, and gigolos.

The center has been unable to establish a support group for either group but counsels the female sex workers individually. Center representatives visit the beach once a week to talk individually with male sex workers. A closed support group of gay men, however, does exist. According to the director of JAS, community support for the center is good, although more material support is needed. Donations such as food, paint, and other hardware materials are provided; the doctor also gives her services free. Sex workers also obtain significant support from private practitioners and pharmacists who understand the nature of the workers' business.

Family members mainly undertake child care: grandparents, sisters, grandfathers, and family friends take care of children. Money is sent home every two weeks for support of the children. This ranges from J$1,000 to J$5,000. The amount of money sent home is dependent on the season, which impacts the earning capacity of the sex workers. "Child shifting"[14] also takes place when mothers feel that their children are being neglected. This is done on a regular basis until the mother is convinced that suitable accommodation has been found.

PSYCHOLOGICAL NEEDS FULFILLMENT

The job of a sex worker can be taxing. One participant describes the job as "full of fear because you don't know what can happen. You always have some fear because you don't know who bad and who good." Sex workers use various coping strategies to overcome the fear of working on the streets. For example in Montego Bay they have a quick response system to potential danger. Phyllis tells how her corner is organized. She is the leader and checks to make sure her girls have condoms. She sometimes distributes free condoms that she has bought with cash because the other sex workers assume she has obtained them for free at the government clinic. To avoid an argument she simply gives some away. She also carries an ice-pick; if one of the ladies has a client who proves to be difficult, she may need to reach for it. For example, several sex workers will rush to a person's assistance if a client wants to take back his money, expressing dissatisfaction with a job.

Sex workers may utilize the JAS individual counseling service or the peer educators and counseling clinics at the Savanna-la-Mar Health Department. The women in Negril, however, rely on one another for counseling support. One remarked, "Like me, Simone and Lorraine we counsel each other. We are there [to assist with] each other's problems."

Their doctors also are an important source of psychological support. Simone says sometimes she imagines that she is plagued by many kinds of illnesses. Her doctor constantly reassures her, often by humoring her, taking time to examine her, then giving her two antibiotics for relieving her anxiety. She usually feels better by the next day.

While participants do provide financial and social support for each other, there also is competition for clients and for "looking good." Simone also tells us that Negril is the first place she has heard about so much obeah[15]: "The girls they obeah each other to make each other don't make any money." Karen chimes in, "They go all over the island [to visit obeah men]. They don't want to see you prosper. If they see a way you can get out before them they 'fuck' you up. Even if they can't do it with obeah they do it with their mouths." Simone continued, "I rely on this lady. She reads the cards and she is enough for me. I like to know what's happening." Karen reaffirms her point by attesting to the capability of this woman, who she said had read her correctly each time for three weeks, and the devil card had come under her name. This was just before she was jailed for four weeks for stabbing another sex worker during a fight. She is out on J$10,000 bail and is scheduled to return to court in June. She has a lawyer. "He represents the prostitutes; he is highly recommended," said Simone.

Being new to the job is another psychological barrier that sex workers have to overcome. When Karen started working, she found it difficult to deal with the situation of being new, because the older workers fought her; but when she was with a veteran they didn't argue with her. Simone provided support for her. She tells us, however, that when she was new:

> I had nobody to go out with because I don't talk and the few friends that I had I didn't talk to them much. So I had a real hard time, I had to fight my way through. For six months I spent practically every night fighting the "bitches" because they would wanna fight with me because I was new. And then after six months I got my respect. They think "she is old now, she is tough." And then I started enjoying it.

HOW SEX WORKERS PERCEIVE AND DEFINE THEIR ACTIVITIES

The response varies. Phyllis said that when she started out twenty years ago she enjoyed it. It was a quick way of making money. Simone says, "I like my job for the money but not for the sex." Almost all participants reflected this view. While admitting that it paid comparatively good money, that it provided the opportunity for travel and sometimes marriage, some seemed psychologically traumatized by the moral conflict reflected in the wider society. This is what a few of them had to say about the issue:

> We kinda like the job.... It helps me to live, take care of my daughter. It makes me strong and independent, I don't have to live on men. We love the job for the money.... I hate it for the sex... but other than that, if I had [other] ways and means of getting this money I wouldn't do it.

> Well, it's O.K. so far but it tedious because weh we a do mash we up... because every man have a different size wood... and that alone is not good enough fi you womb.

> To tell you the truth [she says slowly], it's hard, it's not something good. I think it is not something I should be doing because some people come and they say anything to you and you say, "If I were at home this wouldn't be happening to me," but I don't plan to stay in this thing for long, not for long. If my family knew, especially my mother, it would be [a] problem for me.

> The other day I was lying in the room crying and praying. Talking to God and saying, "Please God don't let me do this for long, don't let anybody find out." And I say, "Why, why things have to be so hard, why I have to do this?" Just lying down there crying and nobody know why I was crying.... For some people it is sweet.

> Being out on the street is just like everybody shun you, no care who. Because you is a whore you no worth nothing. That is what I feel. You nuh worth noth-

ing to nobody. I may be sitting here talking to you nicely and intelligently. And somebody may come in and say to you, "Do you know that is a prostitute." Maybe your attitude toward me change yuh know, simply because of the work. I have been with people who show me nuff respect not because of what I do but people who just know me for what I am, and there are others who shun me, don't even want talk to me or ride inna di same taxi wid mi.

You have a lot of people out there love us. In Negril people don't really disrespect prostitutes; dem get more respect even more than the office girl. The way they deal with prostitutes in the bank, telephone company, business places... because they know we have money.... Negril is all about money and they think that prostitutes have money so....

DRUG AND RELATED ACTIVITIES

In Ocho Rios the sex workers interviewed reported that they did not use drugs. In Negril, ganja is used by respondents and seems to serve the purpose of dulling the more painful aspects of this kind of employment. For instance, respondents reported that they would smoke ganja before going to work, as this allowed them to go through the motions of their work with more ease. When asked about hard drugs they explained that some sex workers used such drugs, some of whom would have been exposed to them through a client who requested shared drug use. When asked by clients to engage in such activities, respondents reported that they would pretend to be using the drugs to ensure that the job was successful and they earned their money.

However in Ocho Rios there is a group of sex workers situated around the market who are drug users. This dependence results in a more desperate need for money and a willingness to engage in more dangerous liaisons, largely with locals but also with the occasional tourist.

In Negril a symbiotic relationship exists between drug hustlers and sex workers. One drug hustler we interviewed described the relationship, explaining that as a hustler he meets tourists and locates clients for sex workers. After the exchange he gets a part of the receipts. Similarly, sex workers on the job will help in locating clients for his trade.

MIGRATION AND TRAFFICKING

Internal migration is significant, as workers move from one resort location to another, depending on the season and the potential for earning in those areas. The three resort areas studied attract workers from rural parishes such as Manchester, Clarendon, St. Ann, rural Westmoreland, and Hanover. Workers also travel from the city of Kingston, Jamaica's capital. Sex workers move frequently between these locations and travel to other tourist areas on the east coast, such as Port Antonio, and on the south coast, such as Black River. For those sex workers who are not permanent residents of a location, the average stay is between three to six months. The reasons they give for moving around is that it is important not to get stale—that is, not to become too much of a familiar face in one location.

Emigration is mainly to Europe, with the United States a distant second. During our interviews, the possibility of sex workers traveling to Cuba was raised as one way of responding to the competition Cuba poses as a tourist destination. This development would be in keeping with the traditional approach of the Jamaican woman, who devises strategies to cope with macroeconomic developments that restrict her earnings. Her response to a shortage of imports in the 1970s was to become an Informal Commercial Importer, plying Venezuela, Panama, and Curaçao and bringing into Jamaica imports that had become scarce due to the shortage of foreign exchange. She continued the tradition of the woman who will "make do" with anything to make a living. The migrations to North America during the 1970s and 1980s are a good example of this phenomenon.

RACE RELATIONS

The issue of race relations was raised during a group interview. The psychological trauma resulting from black women and men working with a white clientele was considered. Because the tourist industry caters mainly to white Europeans and North Americans in a society where over 90 percent of the population is black with a history of slavery and colonialism, it is not surprising that the contradictions of race, class, and color discrimination still plague the industry. These are manifested mainly at the psychological level, for open hostility among different races is not cited as a problem in the industry or in the wider society.

One participant outlined for us the contradictory feelings generated by working with a white clientele:

> I love my job but I hate it for the sex. We are talking to a guy, he makes me feel sick but he is paying the price. You have sex with him. It really hurts. It makes your heart get sick too, you know.... He is real ugly, he is real white, he is so soft and you just want to scream.

Sometimes they drink tequila and get stoned on ganja so that "we can't see the person we are going with. Our eyes are real closed so that we don't have to see that."

Some of our Negril participants who deal exclusively with foreigners had interesting comments to make. Asked where she expected to be five years from now, Karmen said, "I am just sitting here waiting for my white guy.... I am just waiting for that ring." Simone cuts in:

One advantage of the job is that we get to travel often. If a European guy really likes us he can buy a ticket within a week. But we don't want to marry them. After three months [in Europe] you come home. Three months with him felt like eternity.

Karen's rebuttal is quick. "Well, some girls want it." She reiterates that in five years she hopes to be in America "married to mi white man an a live life." They are convinced, however, of how important it is to get help to leave the profession. They speak of women they knew who were trying to leave the profession for ten or fifteen years and were unable to do so. Their decision to get help appears frighteningly practical in the hot afternoon sun as we sit in the circle and exchange ideas.

Another of our participants said her clients were mainly Japanese because "them nice." She further explained that they treated her gently and caringly and said that they have sisters just like her.

The perception of the black Jamaican male as being strong and always ready to cater to the needs of the white female tourist plays a significant part in attracting clients to the Rent-a-Dreads and beach boys. Carolyn Cooper, in *Noises in the Blood,* reminds us:

The Jamaican male, whatever his class, enjoys a common instinct for handling pussy. Of the ever-ready white American female tourists and their apparently deficient counterparts at home Hilton contemptuously muses in the spirit of mass Nattie that: "the man dem up there confuse, not sure what dem supposed to do. Then the women dem run down here and want to kill off the male population wid pussy. But we up to the task man, more than up to it" (Cooper 1993:113).

Another compelling issue is the impact of the tourist/sex worker relationship on regular relationships with local Jamaican men. Simone, who told us earlier of the psychological difficulties she experienced having to work with white clients, also reminds us what drives some women into the profession:

I think men are what brought most of us here. They abuse us and we start hating black men because we come to Negril and see white guys; they treat us like princesses and we appreciate that. That's what drove us away from black men and now we hate them and we just wanna treat them like shit. I wanna do that.

CONCLUSION

The most revealing insight of this small-scale research project with sex workers is that sex work, in some ways, must be viewed as another form of employment undertaken by men and women. In many cases it is a means of earning necessary additional money or it may be the only source of income. Nonetheless, sex work also differs in a fundamental way from other kinds of employment.

The first difference is that the work has been appropriated by the state in the same way that it is used by the public at large. For instance, sexual labor is used to regenerate members of the formal working sector, a prime example being military personnel or concentrated groups of male workers employed in isolated industries such as mining.

The second fundamental difference is based on the fact that "work" has been understood generally as the use of mental or manual faculties of head, hands, feet. Sex work, instead, employs the sexual organs and draws on the capacity of the individual to stimulate and satisfy sexual desire—a process that clearly involves both mind and body. This kind of labor and employment requires that sex workers become engaged with members of the public in expressions of intimacy not expected in other areas of employment. That there is a critical element of risk taking in this mode of employment must be recognized—the use of drugs by clients, the use of drugs and alcohol by sex workers themselves to endure the physical act, the danger of work at night on the streets, the risk of contracting STDs from clients, and so on.

A third difference is that this area of work is considered, by and large, to be an immoral means of earning an income. The issue of immorality with regard to sex work is skewed. Sex workers are deemed to be immoral, while those who seek the services of sex workers are deemed pleasure seekers and not necessarily tainted with this immoral brush.

The underlying feature that emerged from this study is the idea that countries such as Jamaica represent a scarce resource of sun, sand, and sea for holiday makers. Either implicitly or explicitly, the package of sun, sand, and sea is gift wrapped with the promise of sex. Yet there is a simultaneous narrative constantly unfolding—that tourists are being harassed by sex workers and that this in turn is affecting the tourist trade. The state's response at the level of legislation (at present) is to employ more strenuous measures against harassment, thus implicating the sex workers as perpetrators. Intervention at the macrolevel of the economy and polity, especially by those involved in the tourist industry, is made in recognition of the inescapable contribution of sex workers to the attraction of tourist sites. But at the same time, they condemn the harassment that, it is argued (with supporting statistics), cuts down on repeat visits of tourists and therefore on potential tourism earnings. Regulations have been considered, which, in some form, will serve to curb harassment and secure the rights of tourists. From our interviews with sex workers themselves, however, very little attention is paid to the fact that their own right to protection continues to be secondary. The kind of regulations being debated in Jamaican society at present, especially emerging from spokespersons and business representatives from the tourist sector, promotes the setting up of red-light districts in resort areas. The advantages and disadvantages of formalizing this virtually informal area—which is at the same time implicitly organized around rules and regulations created by the actors themselves—must be thoroughly investigated. For instance, what are qualifications for entry into the red-light district? How will the sex workers be recruited? How will payment itself be determined? What other forms of support, such as health centers, need to be in place? Are clients going to be screened in any way? The questions are many.

Undertaking sex work, we have found, is a conscious choice made by the majority of workers in this field. They argue that it allows them the autonomy of self-employment and the flexibility to schedule work and time for their private lives as necessary. The choice of sex work as an occupation is dependent, by and large, on one major and fundamental factor. The individual sex worker must be prepared to undertake the demands of this kind of work, which requires no formal qualification but does involve the creative use of one's own body as the commodity being sold and resold. We found that the majority of sex workers feel disreputable about their engagement in this kind of work. They are influenced by the ideologies of morality expounded in their society and have internalized feelings of guilt, secrecy, and unworthiness surrounding their occupation. Nonetheless, the sex trade provides relatively higher incomes than other low-paid, low-status jobs, which come with their own problems. Some opportunities exist for meeting potential partners or for getting an income that allows the sex workers to meet the needs of their families; these positive aspects of the trade ensure sex workers' continued involvement in the trade. Finally, as is typical of many relationships, sex workers enjoy an ostensibly contradictory relationship. Despite the antagonisms that are the result of a competitive trade, they have developed close, supportive networks with each other. They "hang" together, enjoying each others' company, while, at the same time, providing security in numbers in a business that attracts high levels of personal risk.

ACKNOWLEDGMENTS

We express our gratitude to the sex workers who opened their hearts and lives to us. Without the sharing of their experiences, the writing of this chapter would not have been possible. Our thanks also to the friends who provided us with shelter, transportation, and a listening and sympathetic ear during our fieldwork. The workers in the public health, security, tourism, and non-governmental sectors also deserve our thanks for their cooperation; they often interrupted their busy schedules at short notice to answer our questions. To our families and loved ones who gracefully released us from the guilt of separations: we cannot thank you enough. Last but by no means least, we want to thank the Caribbean Association for Feminist Research and Action (CAFRA); Women's Studies Program, University of Colorado; Instituto Latinoamericano de Servicios Legales Alternatives (ILSA); and the Mona Unit, Centre for Gender and Development Studies, University of the West Indies, Kingston, Jamaica, for providing the monetary and administrative support that made this study possible.

NOTES

1. The data for this study are drawn from in-depth life histories from sex workers: three female and one retired male in Negril, six females in Montego Bay and six females in Ocho Rios. The clandestine nature of the trade made for a qualitative rather than a quantitative method of investigation. A feminist qualitative approach (life histories) was considered the best method of gathering this information, as it invites the acceptance of women's and men's experiences as legitimate data. It allows for deeper insights and allows the researcher to probe beyond the limits imposed by most quantitative research methods. The sensitive nature of the subject is better explored by asking open-ended questions and allowing the participants to explain their feelings and experiences. This approach brought researchers closer to the participants' realities, not only making them more visible but privileging their voices. It also allows for analyzing their choices in the context of the social circumstances in which they were born and have grown up.

2. Structural adjustment refers "to the process by which many developing nations are reshaping their economies to be more free-market oriented. They are acting upon the premise that less government intervention in the economy is better. More specifically, structural adjustment assumes an economy will be most efficient, healthy, and productive in the long run if market forces operate and products and services are not protected, subsidized, heavily regulated or produced by the government" (Sparr 1994:1).

3. Minister of Tourism Francis Tulloch's contribution to the 1998/99 Budget Debate, May 5, 1998. See also chapter 3 by Beverley Mullings for further details on the tourism industry in Jamaica.

4. All-inclusives offer a total package. Tourists do not have to leave the premises, and if and when they do, the trip is usually organized by the establishment.

5. 12.8 percent of the incidents of harassment is attributed to prostitutes (Jamaica Tourist Board, Planning and Research Department).

6. The most recently formed national political party in Jamaica, which offers itself as an alternative to the two main political parties, the People's National Party and the Jamaica Labor Party.

7. This act makes soliciting a criminal offense. The prostitute can be picked up for wandering in a public place or annoying persons by soliciting them. The offense is a misdemeanor, punishable by imprisonment not exceeding two months. The law also applies to men, who can be punished with imprisonment not exceeding twelve months under the Offences against the Person Act (OAPA). While this section of the law has been repealed, it informs practices and attitudes to prostitution in the last few decades, and its legacy continues today.

8. Loitering—*Laws of Jamaica*, Volume 17, states in the Town and Communities Act, Section 3, paragraph 3, that any person who shall loiter and solicit for the purposes of prostitution is guilty of an offense and can be fined. Encouraging women to become prostitutes—is prohibited by Section 58 of the OAPA and is a misdemeanor punishable by imprisonment for a term not exceeding three years. Living on the earnings of a prostitute—applies primarily to men who, if convicted of living either partially or wholly on the earnings of a prostitute, can face imprisonment of up to twelve months under Section 63 of the OAPA. Keeping, managing or assisting in the management of a brothel—is also a crime against the law. Landlords can be charged under Section 66 of the OAPA and may be fined and/or imprisoned if convicted.

9. An attorney-at-law interviewed for this research project proposed that the Vagrancy Law was repealed in a climate where the economic conditions and people's chances for survival rested heavily on their ability to hustle. It thus became necessary for the government, unable to create opportunities in the formal sector of the economy, to repeal the laws, which would then decriminalize the kinds of activities involved in hustling.

10. "Forms of prostitution" refers to persons who select their clients from nightclubs and to beach boys who select their clients on the beach and may work full time as lifeguards, in water sports or similar activities. "Rent-a-Dreads" refers to men who wear dreadlocks and provide companion or escort services, mainly to women, for the duration of their visit.

11. Students usually attend the primary (public) school system at age seven and sit the common entrance examination, which may get them a place in high school (usually dedicated to the teaching of liberal arts and sciences). Those students who are unable to secure a place in high school may be placed in the secondary school system, which focuses on vocational training.

12. A *Modda* is a spiritual and physical healer who relies heavily on visions from the Almighty to inform her work.

13. "Partners" is a form of saving in which people pool their money on a daily, weekly, or monthly basis for a predetermined period and an individual gets a draw (the total pool) at the end of that day, week, or month. Each contribution is called a "hand" and the person in charge of collecting the money is called the "banker."

14. Child shifting refers to the arrangements made between women to ensure that alternative parenting arrangements are made if the caregiver or parents are not able to carry out the parenting role. It may imply shifting the child temporarily to an aunt,

grandmother, sibling, or family friend while the caregiver goes to work. Financial support is given for this arrangement.

15. Obeah is a set or system of secret beliefs in the use of supernatural forces to attain or defend against evil ends; it is African in origin and varies greatly from the simple, such as the use of items like oils, herbs, bones, grave-dirt, and fresh animal blood, to the criminal (although rare) such as taking a child's life. It is carried on by practitioners in order to gain for their clients success, protection, or cures for mysterious illnesses, as well as to cause trouble for, or the death of, an enemy. (Source: *Dictionary of Caribbean English Usage*, edited by Richard Allsop, Oxford University Press, 1996)

7

Bleak Pasts, Bleak Futures

Life Paths of Thirteen Young Prostitutes in Cartagena, Colombia

LAURA MAYORGA AND PILAR VELÁSQUEZ

I feel like I am already lost.... The only thing that I ask God is for me to be able to get... from this lifestyle... a house where I can drop dead, that is the only thing that I ask.... I am not going to be like this the rest all my life, with men looking for me... because I am a girl, perhaps now I am doing well but later I won't be.

A sixteen-year-old interviewee

Recent trends in the global economy have led to major changes in many countries (Garay 1997). Since 1990, Colombia, like most of Latin America, has pursued a neoliberal economic strategy.[1] Theoretically, this implies a reduced role for the state in the management of the economy and an increasing "internationalization" of the economy, based on free market principles.

One of the principal criticisms of the project has been its authoritarian-like implementation and the insulation of economic decision-makers (the president and his cabinet) from societal pressures. In other words, the sectors most adversely affected by the changes (such as urban labor and participants in the rural economy), have been the least able to participate in decision making. Domestic technocrats, often working in alliance with international financial institutions such as the World Bank and the International Monetary Fund, have imposed economic reforms upon weak and suffering populations. The poorest have most often paid the costs of structural adjustment.

These complaints have wide resonance in Colombia, where the project is commonly referred to as the *apertura económica*, or economic opening. Of Colombia's forty million habitants, nearly 53 percent were defined as poor in 1995 (Ramírez 1998). Fourteen million of them earned U.S.$1 or less per day, according to a national survey conducted by the DANE (Departamento Administrativo Nacional de Estadística) in 1997. The country has one of the continent's (and the world's) most unequal distributions of income, and the problem has become more pronounced since 1990 (CEPAL 1997). The inequalities in education and health care within the national population limit work opportunities and social mobility for the majority. Furthermore, rural violence in Colombia is the most multifaceted and extensive in Latin America today. These conditions have traditionally worked against underprivileged members of society, such as poor women and children. At present, there are an estimated 1.5 million people displaced by violence (Padilla and Varela 1997), of which more than 50 percent are children (Conferencia Episcopal de Colombia 1995, Departamento Nacional de Planeación 1997). The economic dislocations engendered by the neoliberal reforms have, in many cases, accentuated these people's misery, and they are frequently left with few alternatives other than to migrate from war-torn areas to intermediate and large cities where they are ill-prepared to meet the challenges of urban life. Given the massive migration due to the violence and the high levels of unemployment associated with neoliberalism (at least, during its initial stages), some of these women and children may enter prostitution (among other options) as a means of overcoming temporary economic hardship.

Many advocates of neoliberalism cite the internationalization of the economy as a benefit to all countries. Tourism is an industry many countries wish to promote, and the impulse has become particularly strong since the neoliberal wave of the 1980s and 1990s throughout the developing world. Colombia, despite its tremendous violence and insecurity, has attempted to encourage tourism, particularly in the historically rich, coastal city of Cartagena de Indias.[2] Tourists arrive not only to enjoy its beaches and architecture but also its women.

This chapter provides an analysis of adolescent prostitution in a particular area of Cartagena.[3] It identifies circumstances that set the stage for participants' engagement in and continued practice of prostitution, comments on the degree to which interviewees saw themselves as having no option but to engage in prostitution when they were girls, and documents the choices—aside from prostitution—available to young prostitutes for survival. It argues that individual development is best understood by paying attention to socioeconomic and political phenomena that influence people's lives. The study is also contexualized within the wider phenomenon of adolescent Third World prostitution.

THE HISTORY OF CARTAGENA AND ITS TOURISM INDUSTRY

During the sixteenth century, Cartagena became the principal port of the country. In the seventeenth and eighteenth centuries, it acquired great importance as a military and trade center, becoming as well one of the most significant posts for the traffic of black slaves (Hernández 1997). In the nineteenth century, the struggle for independence from Spain resulted in a variety of national economic problems, and Cartagena's importance as a port declined (Bell 1991). It was not until the 1950s that it reactivated its port activities, as the country developed a petrochemical industry. During the 1960s, an incipient tourist industry began to take shape, which in the 1980s and 1990s, grew with greater speed as a result of narcotraffic money and the economic apertura (Streicker 1993). At present, the tourist industry is more important than the petrochemical industry as a direct, indirect, and informal employer (Banco de la República 1992).

Historically, armed conflict in the interior of Colombia has drawn many migrants toward the Caribbean coast (Hernández 1997). During the early part of the century, Cartagena had 8,000 residents. In the 1980s, the city grew to 500,000 and, at present, more than one million people live there (Streicker 1993).[4] Although the increase in tourism has brought more money to the city (which is located in the Department of Bolívar), it has not necessarily led to an improvement in the living conditions for the majority of its poorest residents.[5] More than 40 percent of the population lacks basic public services such as potable water, sewage systems, and electricity (Departamento Administrativo de Planeación, Departamento de Bolívar 1995).

According to a tourist promotion organization, between 1994 and 1996, 686,832 foreigners and 1,451,275 Colombians visited Cartagena (Empresa Promotora de Turismo 1997). The majority of foreign tourists come from Spain, Italy, Canada, and the United States. The tourist zone is located in the old center of Cartagena and the nearby peninsula of Bocagrande. These two areas host the majority of hotels, casinos, bars, and discotheques, and perhaps for this reason, the majority of prostitutes are also found there.[6]

It has been suggested that politicians and promoters of the tourist industry work very hard to sell the image of friendly, servile, black Cartagena (Streicker 1997). Streicker describes Colombia as a country plagued by the effects of narcotraffic and political violence. By making Cartagena part of the Caribbean, and not part of Colombia per se, tourist promoters can persuade tourists that it as safe as other Caribbean destinations. He cites a representative of the tourism industry who stated that "the tourist image of Colombia abroad should be totally Caribbean" (from *El Universal* 1989, cited in Streicker 1997). Another representative, Pedro Mogollón, said to the *New York Times* in 1994 that "we are promoting the Caribbean without mentioning Colombia" (cited in Streicker 1997). In this analysis, the fact that Cartagena is predominantly Afro-Colombian (while the historically war-torn interior is *mestizo*) allows tourism promoters to persuade tourists, at least psychologically, that Cartagena is not really Colombia.[7]

THE PRACTICE OF PROSTITUTION

The adolescents and two of the young women who participated in this study live in motels that are located in an ill-reputed part of Cartagena. There, they walk the downtown streets and recruit customers. Only local men and occasional backpacking foreigners venture into this part of the city. Backpacking men are reportedly uninterested in becoming customers for local prostitutes. The young prostitutes who were interviewed work independently, since their services are not procured through a pimp or brothel.

The majority of Cartagena's discotheques and luxury hotels are located in the peninsula of Bocagrande, which is isolated physically and socially from downtown Cartagena. The area hosts a police station and a naval base, which offers tourists "security" and isolation from the rest of the city. Since it caters to the needs of both vacationing families and single people seeking adventure, Bocagrande appears to shift its image between daytime and nighttime. Daytime fun for parents and children includes going to the beach, water sports, and shopping. At night, however, the image of the area changes as discotheques play loud music and young women stand on street corners and at club entrances to cater to male tourists' desire for companionship and sex.

At the time of our fieldwork, the authorities had established a timespan (between midnight and 5:00 A.M.) during which it was permissible to practice prostitution. They also required that all prostitutes register with the police. Most of our interview participants were minors and therefore were not eligible to register with the police. Only one of the three adult women whom we interviewed had registered with the authorities.

Most of the young prostitutes we talked to worked both with local men and with tourists. Downtown, local men pay an average of 8,000 pesos (U.S.$5.50) to have a sexual encounter with a young prostitute. Research participants reported that the money that local men pay varies depending on a variety of factors, including the age of the prostitute. Most claim that they used to make more money when they were younger and that younger prostitutes make a little more money than older ones. They added that being pregnant makes it difficult to earn money, since most local men are reluctant to have sex with pregnant women.

Sexual encounters with local men usually consist of one-on-one sex with a minimal amount of touching. If clients want anything "extra," like being allowed to touch the young woman's breasts, they have to pay more. Interviewees said that sometimes they refuse to have sex with men who request sexual interactions that they do not want to engage in. The prostitute discusses the price of the sex and the kind of sex that will take place before she goes into a room with a man. Sometimes, the interaction will go no further than the street if a girl or young woman does not agree to engage in a particular sexual activity. Other times, the young women feel economic pressure to agree to a sexual encounter with which they are not comfortable.

Stories about harassment or dangerous interactions with clients did not predominate. It is clear, however, that young women in prostitution risk being subjugated to the desires or humiliation of clients. Clarita, a twenty-two-year-old who became a prostitute when she was fifteen related this situation:

> There are people who harass us a lot, men who... for example, I have even had to fight with men.... I tell them, "Don't you have a family? Don't you have sisters?" and they say, "No, but my sister would not be capable of getting into this." And I told him, this is something that can happen to anyone.... Sometimes they hit you, they maltreat you, they call you ugly names, and I have even had to fight in the motel room.... There are men who are drugged; there are men who are very drunk; there are men who have a bad odor; there are men who are... the worst.

On the average, the young women we talked to make 30,000 pesos per day (approximately U.S.$24). The younger ones make a little more, especially with tourists. This amount barely covers basic needs, since most interviewees presently support a child and some also support a boyfriend (at least partially). As a result, the research participants have to work virtually every day.

Having sex with tourists, especially foreign ones, is more lucrative than working the downtown streets. They charge, on the average, 40,000 pesos (U.S.$32) to have a sexual encounter with one tourist—though the price can go up to 70,000 pesos (U.S.$56) or more depending on the appearance of the man (i.e., how wealthy he looks), on the characteristics of the prostitute, and on the kind of sexual encounter that he desires.

The young women we interviewed reported that when they work with tourists they can go "home" after having one or two sexual encounters, whereas when they work downtown they must have sex with four or five men to meet a day's basic needs. During one of the focus groups that we conducted we asked research participants to tell us about their experiences with tourists, especially foreign ones. Some girls responded by saying that most tourists were pretty nice. They expressed preferences for tourists from European or North American countries and, with a burst of laughter, some made fun of the physical appearance of local men. They insinuated that they find foreign men more physically attractive.

Surprisingly, however, most prefer to have sex with local men in the downtown area than with tourists. These opinions came up in the private interviews and not as much in the focus groups. Interviewees reported that when they work with tourists they usually have to stay out all night, often drinking and perhaps taking drugs as they accompany their clients. In contrast, sex with local men happens predominantly during the day—sometime in the afternoon or early evening.

They characterized sex with local men as being brief and "to the point." That is, copulation and orgasm may occur with very little touching or kissing. Requests for more contact are negotiated and refused if men do not have enough money or if the prostitute feels uneasy. Tourists, however, have more money to offer and sometimes ask for sexual acts that a prostitute may engage in, due to economic need, despite feeling uncomfortable. Discomfort with specific sexual acts was one of the issues that challenged interviewees in their engagement with tourists.

Patricia, a sixteen-year-old who is full of scars and looks prepubescent, told us about her encounter with two tourists from Spain the night before. They hired her and another girl to have sex with each other in front of them. She felt very awkward but needed the money badly. She asked the other girl just to go along and pretend to enjoy herself. A fight broke out between the two girls because the other girl complained that Patricia was not really having sex with her. Patricia says that subsequently "I almost got my face all cut up" by the other girl. As a result of the struggle, one of the tourists asked for his money back. Patricia relays her response to him:

> So then I told the man that I wanted to earn the money the right way, and the man said, "No," because he was married. And I told him, "Just wear a condom and we will not have any problems." In the end, the man put on two condoms, and he was with me and I earned my money....

Patricia made 80,000 pesos (U.S.$64) in the above sexual encounter. This illustrates tourists' ability to ask for sexual performance that a young woman may be reluctant to engage in. The local practice of allowing prostitutes in the Bocagrande tourist area only in the late hours of the night was another reason why sex with tourists was unattractive to some research participants. A sixteen-year-old reported that she outright refuses to have sex with tourists because she likes to be in bed by 10:00 P.M. Others feel similarly about staying out all night and say that staying out late makes them sleepy; this makes it difficult to work the tourist area.

Our interviews and focus groups yielded at least two stories about the dangers of Cartagena nightlife, which may further elucidate reluctance to work at night (i.e., with tourists). One girl described the murder of her boyfriend's sixteen-year-old ex-girlfriend (also a prostitute). She was seen getting into a car with some men at night and was later found strangled to death. The background of the murderer (i.e., whether a tourist or not) is unknown. A prostitute in her forties, who participated in one of our focus groups, also recounted a nighttime incident on the beach that she thinks could have resulted in her own murder. Furthermore, some interviewees described local men who stand in the tourist area at night and mug prostitutes or attempt to collect "protection" money from them (though unsuccessfully, according to one account).

The above descriptions about the context of engagement in prostitution by the young women who were interviewed for this study suggests a few interesting aspects that must be underscored. First of all, it is hard to conclude from the interviews which group of clients the young women derive most of their income from—tourists or local men. Though encounters with local men seem to be more frequent, tourists pay more money per sexual encounter, so it is difficult to tell which type of customer contributes a greater amount to a prostitute's income. It would be fair to estimate that the young women we interviewed derive half their income from locals and half from tourists. Continued engagement with local men probably ensures that they have customers throughout the year, including when the tourist season is low.

A second point worth underscoring is that engaging in sex with tourists is not seen as inherently "worse" than sex with local men. It is seen as high risk primarily due to "external" factors such as the fact that it takes place primarily at night, a time when criminal activity tends to be higher. Though they seem to feel uneasy with some of the sexual activity that they engage in with tourists, there also seems to be some room to negotiate what kind of sex will take place. Some girls may feel uncomfortable with this process and may shy away from sex with tourists or may agree to engage in what appears to be an economically attractive offer, despite feeling uneasy.

ENTRY INTO PROSTITUTION

The Socioeconomic Background of the Family of Origin

The Atlantic (or Caribbean) coast, where Cartagena is located, is one of the poorest regions of Colombia. In recent years, of the seven departments that comprise the Atlantic region, six were classified as the poorest of the country. Seventy percent of the residents of the Atlantic coast are unable to satisfy their basic human needs, while the figure is only 45 percent for the country as a whole. The rate of malnourishment for children is 10.4 percent, the highest in Colombia (López and Abello 1998). The illiteracy rate is 24 percent on the coast, whereas the rate is only 12 percent for the rest of the country (Departamento Administrativo de Planeación, Departamento de Bolívar 1995), and only 68.1 percent of the inhabitants obtain an elementary education, while 87.7 percent do so in the rest of the country (Vélez 1995). On the coast, one of every five children between six and twelve years old does not attend school.

Ten of the young women we interviewed were born and raised on Colombia's Caribbean coast and three came from poor areas of the department of Antioquia (adjacent to the western portion of the Caribbean coast, directly south of Panama). On average, they had studied up to grades three or four. All reported having grown up in poverty. Their childhood homes were unfinished (i.e., exposed to the elements) and lacked one or more public services (e.g., running water, electricity, telephone). Two were originally from rural areas where their fathers farmed or fished and reported having grown up with plenty of food. Most of those who grew up in urban areas, however, reported having suffered food shortages during childhood. Five of them reported hunger to be an immediate factor that motivated them to have sex for money for the first time.

Marisa, who entered prostitution when she was thirteen, tells a story of being hungry growing up. Her parents and siblings used to work and eat outside the home during the day so there was no lunch available to her. She said the following about the first time she had sex for money:

> I was really down and hungry that day, and I said, "Wait a second... I am going to go out." And I got the idea to do that, to come here [downtown]. I sat over there to the side, and I got good money there. Then, the next day, I got a lot also, and then I wanted to come here every day!

Angela is fifteen and became engaged in prostitution at thirteen. Her mother died when she was born. A series of family members took care of her while she was growing up, but they seemed resentful of the responsibility:

> My aunt used to tell me: "Get your own food... Go, go beg for it."... And I said "But, auntie, why do you humiliate me?"... Days used to go by, and I used to put up with being very hungry... and they used to tell me to just leave... and I turned 13 and I could not take it anymore. Living with hunger is very tough....

Angela's words demonstrate how hunger can move a person to become engaged in prostitution at an early age. In addition to the lack of food, however, her statements, and Marisa's, show a pattern that was common in most cases where hunger was a precipitating factor. Specifically, it was not just the lack of food but the caregiver's attitude about providing food for the child (i.e., whether they were neglectful or rejecting) that appears to have made the girl feel rejected and willing to leave home for the life of the streets.

Psychological Environment of the Family of Origin

Four out of the five young women who reported that hunger had precipitated their immediate decision to exchange sex for money also expressed that problems at home were important precipitants for their decision to run away from home and later start engaging in prostitution. In addition to these four, another four provided accounts of difficult relationships at home as important factors in their decision to leave home and eventually sell sex for money. In virtually all these cases, family difficulties were related to the separation of the young woman's biological parents and the subsequent union of the custodial parent with a new partner. A pattern (which we saw in four cases) was that a girl's mother started a new relationship with a man who made sexual advances toward the girl, including two cases of attempted rape. Almost uniformly, they reported telling their mothers about the incident and their mothers refusing to believe them. In some cases, the situation worsened because the mother beat up the girl or threw her out of the house. Alternatively, the girl felt rejected by the mother's disbelief about her story and simply chose to leave.

Only one young woman was a mother already when she became a prostitute. She recalls the situation at home as one of hunger and economic need. Her work in prostitution supports not only her children but her siblings and parents as well. This was also the only case in which a girl came from a family of origin where she had suffered hunger but had not felt neglected.

Beatriz, who was sixteen years old at the time of the interview, says that she became a *gamina* (a female street child) when she was twelve years old. She returned home briefly and decided to leave again after her stepfather made sexual advances toward her:

> [My stepfather] got into the bed where I slept... One day I felt that I had my panties down and that he was sucking me... Yes, he was in my parts... And then I talked to my mom and she did not believe me... so then she used to throw my clothes in the streets, hit me. I have marks on my legs....

The stepfather's sexual advances culminated as he started to demand that she "pay him back" for the food and shelter that he provided for her by, as Beatriz put it, "making love to him." This harassment culminated after he gave her a gold chain—which she subsequently sold—and then put a gun to her head to force himself on her. Beatriz fled to her grandfather's house and later ran away with her aunt. She says that her aunt induced both her and her little sister into prostitution. One of the ways that the aunt was able to do this was by introducing Beatriz to addictive drugs such as *bazuco* (similar to crack cocaine). This was the only case in which a girl reported having been induced into prostitution by an adult.

Relationships with Men

Seven young women reported that they first left their family home and eventually became involved in prostitution after having fallen in love with a man. There appear to be two divergent patterns with respect to the backgrounds of those who listed falling in love with a man as an event that contributed to engagement in prostitution. The first pattern was described by three interviewees who became engaged in prostitution between nine and eleven years of age (the earliest ages reported in this study). They came from some of the most neglectful households depicted in the interviews. Specifically, they were not fed or cared for consistently at home. These girls "fell in love" with men before they had reached puberty. The men (aged twenty-five to thirty years) were described as caring in the sense that they provided food, temporary shelter, or marihuana (in one case). The participant who reported becoming a prostitute when she was nine also said that the man she was in love with raped her one day, which led to her being put in the hospital and subsequently becoming employed as a domestic worker.

The second pattern that emerged, regarding falling in love with a man and becoming engaged in prostitution, consisted of four adolescents (aged fourteen and fifteen) who fell in love with young men (in their late teens to late twenties) who then left them for a variety of reasons. The four girls who left home under these circumstances came from poor homes where they were relatively well cared for. They left home knowing or fearing that their boyfriend would not have been accepted by the family. Once the relationships turned sour, they found it difficult to return home. This group of young women who fell in love, but who came from homes where they had been well cared for, seemed to have better relationships with their family of origin at the time of the interview than the girls who started in prostitution at ages nine to eleven years (i.e., those who had been neglected). Though they had not returned home for good, they had gone back occasionally. Though they had no children, nor were they pregnant when they ran away, most of these girls eventually did give birth and their babies are now being taken care of in their families of origin.

FACTORS THAT KEEP YOUNG WOMEN INVOLVED IN PROSTITUTION

Loss of Virginity

Colombia is a predominantly Catholic country, where female virginity is revered. Culturally, it is also a country where appearances matter such that if a young woman of marrying age is not a virgin she must at least "act" like one. By being young and publicly no longer virgins, adolescent prostitutes are an affront to "proper" Colombian society. The biggest issue is probably not the loss of their virginity but the fact that they are public about it. On the Caribbean coast, female virginity at the time of marriage is a source of pride for the family. The family hopes that unmarried daughters do not "screw up" by becoming pregnant before marriage so that they will "make the Virgin [Mary] weep" (Mosquera 1994:101). Local terms referring to the status of virginity, and to the loss thereof, are revealing about these social values.

Interviewees were asked explicitly about their first sexual encounter for money and whether they were virgins at the time. In response to this question, girls used a term that confused the interviewer at first. They said, again and again, that they had been "harmed" by someone other than their first customer. We discovered that the local term used to refer to a girl's first vaginal penetration is to "harm" (in Spanish, *perjudicar*). This term is broadly used in the Colombian Caribbean coast and seems to reveal an attitude about the consequence of having sex for the first time.

One of those interviewed illustrates this phenomenon well. Angelina was given away by her mother to an extremely religious woman when she was two years old. Preferring to be with her biological mother—whom she knew—she went back to her eight years later. The neglect was fierce; her mother routinely "forgot" to feed or care for her. Angelina had sex with a customer when she was ten years old. When asked why she did not go back to live with her adoptive mother, she replied:

> I asked [my adoptive mother] to let me live there again, and she said "No," and that I had already been damaged [*dañada*].... [Men] had already had sex with me [*ya me habían comido*] and she said that she could no longer accept me that way because then I was going to set a bad example for her daughter.

Another term the girls used to refer to a virgin was *señorita* (a young lady). Angelina, for example, mourned that if she had stayed with her adoptive mother, she might still be a señorita today. Another illustrates the importance of virginity in her account. She had become engaged in prostitution—working in "striptease" bars and having sex for money—when she was nine years old. A woman "rescued" her by hiring her as a domestic worker in her house. One day, a fight broke out between the girl and her employer about the fact that the woman had not paid her in two years. The woman beat the girl up and the girl responded:

> You think that because I came to work here when I was ten years old I am going to let myself be hit by you? No, *m'ija* go hit your own daughter.... Even if I have worked in bars your daughter can be worse than I am and maybe she is not even a señorita, that's what I told her....

Writings about female sexuality on Colombia's Caribbean coast assert that the local belief is that the purity of a woman's genitals defines her (Mosquera

1994). As the stories above illustrate, the research participants recognize the social value of virginity. Indeed, they have been abandoned or attacked, to a great extent, due to their non-virgin status. In coy, good humor, participants laughed—during a focus group—about the fact that they were still *señoritas por el chiquito* (young ladies in the little one—i.e., the anus). When asked to elaborate, they explained that refusing to have anal sex is one of the definite limits that they set with their clients. Though not asked to elaborate further, preserving anal virginity could be inferred to be a struggle to preserve a sense of decency.

Motherhood

Though generalizations cannot be made based on these interviews (due to the very small sample size), a regional difference seems to have emerged regarding girls' decisions to enact traditional family-formation patterns. Eight of the ten young women who were raised in the Caribbean coast had boyfriends—whom they called "husbands"—and seven had their own children or were pregnant. In comparison, only one of the three adolescents who came from the department of Antioquia had a temporary boyfriend, and none had children. We cannot conclude, however, that these observed patterns represent cultural differences, since we may actually have observed "selection" effects. That is, young prostitutes who are mothers and reside in Antioquia may simply be reluctant to move to the Caribbean coast with children unless they have no other choice. Most interviewees who had babies became pregnant at about sixteen or seventeen years of age, around three to four years after having become engaged in prostitution.

Though abortions are illegal in Colombia, we heard two spontaneous reports of girls who had what appear to be induced abortions. Therefore, though not asked explicitly about decision-making regarding motherhood, it is safe to assume that motherhood was chosen or at least accepted by those who became mothers. Once the young women became mothers, it was clear that they felt a strong commitment to care for their children financially. Clarita, a twenty-two-year-old who became engaged in the sex trade when she was fifteen, describes the need to continue her engagement in prostitution in order to provide for her child:

> I really do not want to be doing this. Sometimes I lock myself up here, disappointed in the way men treat me. They have tried to kill me twice.... Sometimes I regret it and I go back to my [parents'] house for two months or a month or so. I would like not to come back here, right?... But then, necessity makes me. My children don't have a piece of bread and sometimes they ask me, "Mommy, give me money for some bread," and I don't have it, and that is what forces me to come here.

Even those who had not had children at the time of the interview seem to view motherhood as an important, redeeming state. For example, when Carmen, who is from Antioquia and became involved in prostitution when she was nine years old, was asked how she felt about it, she answered:

> I feel like I am so bad.... I know that when I die God is not going to forgive what I am doing.... He would forgive me if I had children, but since I don't have children.... I started doing this when I was very young, so then for sure he will not forgive me....

Most of the participants, with the exception of three, considered motherhood to be an important part of life—whether they themselves had become mothers or not. Thus, in an important way, girls uphold traditional religious and cultural values of the region.

Love Relationships

At the time of the interview, nine of the respondents were involved with men. These relationships were usually portrayed as stormy and, in fact, most expressed a desire to leave the man they were involved with. Often, they reported that their boyfriends beat them up. In fact, during the week that these interviews took place, two research participants were beaten up by their boyfriends for not bringing enough money home. One of them was a very thin sixteen-year-old who was not getting any clients because she was pregnant and showing. She said the following about her relationship:

> He is just very jealous; he gets jealous a lot regarding me. So then he stabbed me here, twice, in the back, and once here in the head, because I was taunting him....

This adolescent had suffered two different stabbing episodes. Tumultuous, physically violent relationships occurred, most often, in live-in relationships. About half of the respondents were currently or had recently come out of a live-in relationship. These relationships occurred most often in cases when a young woman had a small child that needed care and she felt that her family of origin was not available to help. Their boyfriend became their "husband"—as interviewees referred to their partners—and a father to their child. Biological fatherhood did not appear to be a requirement for this type of family formation.

Not all interviewees seemed to be willing to be primary breadwinners. One of the girls from Antioquia says that she has seen too many of her friends supporting a man—buying him clothes, paying for his room and food. She was once in a similar position:

> A guy wanted to come live with me and I said OK. So then he came and he did not go to work... and I said, like, "Why didn't you go to work?" and he would say, "No, my love, I was very tired, I have a headache." The next day: "Why didn't you go again?"... I used to pay for the room... and I was, like, "Are you still sick?" "Ah no, honey! Go home so that they take care of you and then you come back to me."... I don't support men, that is why I don't like to have a boyfriend.

Aside from living off a young woman's earnings, the boyfriends that were described supplement this with a variety of illicit activities. All the girls' partners, except one, were involved in illegal money-making schemes. The most common money-making activities were stealing and dealing drugs. One was a paid assassin. The adolescent who was dating him narrated her relationship landscape this way:

> I live alone. I have my clothes, I live in a room over there. There is a guy that I like around but he like also wants to come live with me, but I am scared of that because he is a man who kills [a paid assassin], and then if I give myself to him, perhaps he will become addicted to my pussy and perhaps he could beat me up and then it is better to live alone....

A profile of the young women's romantic partner emerges as someone who is economically dependent and involved in activities that may potentially land him in jail. The fact that interview respondents are involved with men who are socially regarded as "delinquent" speaks to the status that young prostitutes probably apply to themselves. That is, it is likely that young prostitutes, by living on the fringes of the law, see themselves (and are likely to be seen by others) as dragged into a life of criminal activity. Furthermore, as young women who are publicly non-virgins, it is likely that they are not regarded as good candidates for marriage—one of the ways that young women in similar socioeconomic or family conditions may manage to stay out of prostitution.

JOB OPPORTUNITIES

Work opportunities have been limited for young women on the Atlantic coast because of recent economic difficulties in general. The national unemployment rate has been hovering around 15 percent. In addition, schooling is available to only a minority of residents in the area. According to the Planning Department of Bolívar, only 40 percent of residents of the department receive elementary and secondary education.

Research about black populations in Colombia (Wade 1997)—including that about Cartagena (Streicker 1992, 1993, 1997) and Bogotá (Mosquera 1998)—suggests that in Colombia, as in much of Latin America, there is a wide economic gap between blacks and mestizos. This discrimination is lived by the blacks who migrate to Bogotá from the Pacific region of Colombia. For example, in the capital, many black women work as domestic workers, although some have completed secondary education (Mosquera 1998).[8]

The economic, educational, and race-related conditions described above set the stage for a life in which girls have only the choices to get married, work as servants—usually as household workers or janitors—or work in prostitution. Indeed, 16.7 percent of the employed female population in Cartagena is engaged in domestic service and nearly all are black. The number of local women practicing prostitution is unknown, though it is tentatively estimated to be 25,000–30,000 (Vélez 1997).

Outside of prostitution, the only other job that interviewees had performed was that of domestic worker. One girl had also worked scaling fish in the market and selling plastic bags on the street, but these were temporary and did not pay as well as prostitution. Of these jobs, informal sector activities (i.e., selling bags on the street) are seen as being the least economically advantageous because they pay very little (compared to prostitution) and do not even provide shelter (as is the case with domestic work).

Most of the young women we interviewed had been employed as domestic workers at some point in their lives—sometimes before they ever practiced prostitution, sometimes afterwards. Stories about household work reveal lives trapped by broken promises and economic blackmail. They described having worked, largely, in exchange for food and lodging. It was common to be paid very little, at most 90,000 pesos (about U.S.$72) per month, but usually about half of that, if anything at all.

Cristina's story provides a good example of life as a domestic worker. She had run away with a man when she was fourteen years old. When she arrived in Cartagena she worked in prostitution briefly but says she really hated it, so she tried work as a live-in domestic worker again. She recounted the working conditions of a place where she got paid 90,000 pesos per month but was given only one meal per day:

> So then I went to work [as a domestic worker]. I lasted a few days, but then I did not like it because...it was a starvation diet, and then I could not live with that.... I am not used to living on just lunch, without dinner or breakfast. But that is the way the job was....

The only place where Cristina had been given three meals per day as a domestic worker was a place where she got paid 35,000 pesos (about U.S.$25) per month. Cristina soon found herself working as a prostitute again, an activity that allowed her to eat regularly and to have some independence.

In many domestic work situations, a young woman may agree to work solely in exchange for food and lodging. Interviewees depicted a common pattern of employers' promises of shoes, clothing, or money, but these went unfulfilled. Some agreed to work for a seemingly decent salary but then got fired on payday, empty handed. In addition, these and other interviews with Colombian women who have worked as domestic workers show that it is not uncommon for girls to be beaten up or sexually abused by their employers (Mayorga 1998). Furthermore, those who are hired as domestic workers are occasionally accused of stealing—accusations that may or may not be accurate.

Marcela had been working as a maid since she was seven years old. When she was twelve, some friends of her sister came to visit her at the home where she worked. She left the girls behind to go shop for food and returned to find out that they had left, having stolen some things that belonged to her employer:

> When I arrived, I did not find [the girls].... I went up to the bedroom of my *patrona* [boss] and there were some things missing. And there I was, I, I was a little girl because I was...thirteen years old...I was just about to turn thirteen, so I hurried and grabbed my things and I left....

The employer sent the police after Marcela. She fled, having been accused, and soon thereafter she became engaged in prostitution. Though most did not report that they left household work because they had been accused of stealing, employers' mistrust about the safety of possessions is a common characteristic of this type of employer–employee relationship.

Another characteristic that must be pointed out about domestic work is that it is extremely rare for live-in domestic workers to be able to have their children with them in the house where they work. This means that a young woman who has children must usually opt to leave them to be cared for by family members and that children may get to see their mother only two or three times per month. This would be an unattractive prospect for many women. If a woman does not have an ongoing relationship with family members—as was the case for several research participants—working as a domestic worker may simply not be an option.

LEGAL CONCEPTIONS AND THE REGULATION OF PROSTITUTION

Since 1991, the Constitutional Court has become Colombia's most important judicial institution. Its role is similar to that of the Supreme Court in the United States. That is, the Court is the guardian of the Constitution, and its decisions are derived from its interpretation of that document. The Court also reminds the public authorities of their responsibilities and jurisdictions (Orozco and Gómez 1997).

In 1995 and 1997, the Constitutional Court signaled that prostitution is a phenomenon common to the development of all civilizations. It is the product of economic, cultural and social factors, which makes its full eradication impossible. Therefore, the state only has the capacity to control its radius of action through the creation of zones of tolerance to prevent geographic expansion of the activity. In this way, prostitution is *"una conducta no ejemplar ni deseable que es preferible tolerar y controlar a que se esparza dañando a la niñez y a la juventud"* (a non-exemplary and undesirable conduct that is better tolerated and controlled lest it spread, damaging children and youth) (Corte Constitucional 1995:683).

On the other hand, the Constitutional Court argues that, in agreement with the free development of personality, people can opt for prostitution as a lifestyle, but prostitution cannot violate the rights of children or damage family stability. Although prostitution can be a chosen lifestyle, that does not mean it can be a form of work. It is argued that prostitution cannot fall under the protections of "work" (e.g., insurance, pension) because it is unethical, it does not perfect people, and it produces no goods (Corte Constitucional 1995:364). The Court has also stated that, although the law does not penalize those involved in prostitution, it demands that public authorities use the means available to them in order to prevent prostitution and to facilitate the rehabilitation of those dedicated to it (Corte Constitucional 1997:31).

Furthermore, the police code states that prostitution is a minor offense, which is tolerated but recognized as harmful (article 178). Therefore, the mere act of prostitution is not punishable (article 179), although the departmental and municipal authorities can regulate it (article 180). The authorities can request information from the prostitutes themselves for the purpose of finding better means of rehabilitating them (article 183).

The ambiguity in the position established by the Constitutional Court fails to make explicit either the legalization or the decriminalization of prostitution in Colombia, considering that decriminalization "entails only the removal of criminal penalties for sexual commerce" and legalization implies the "normalization" and "regulation" of the sex trade (Chapkis 1997:155–56). This has led to an increased vulnerability and social stigmatization on the part of prostitutes, who are exposed to the whims of the police and other authorities as well as clients and pimps. Furthermore, the judicial decisions have left the control of prostitution in the hands of local authorities, thus allowing the latter to violate prostitutes' human rights and to ignore their opinions when making decisions about the regulation of prostitution. An example is found in the fact that police still demand that prostitutes carry a health certificate, although national legislation has annulled such a requirement. This is due primarily to the lack of adequate enforcement mechanisms to ensure compliance among the local authorities.

At the same time, prostitutes are not well informed regarding their rights nor are they sufficiently organized to promote them.

On the other hand, child and juvenile prostitution is illegal, despite the fact that 21,000 sexually exploited children exist in Colombia (Consejería Presidencial de la Política Social, Departamento Nacional de Planeación 1996). Law 360 of 1997 increases the penalities for a range of illegal activities. These include pimping, having sex with children under fourteen years of age, forcing minors into prostitution, and allowing minors to "work" in strip clubs and brothels. Since 1996, the Instituto de Bienestar Familiar has waged a national campaign to combat prostitution as well as creating an interinstitutional committee against the traffic of women and children, with the participation of different governmental organizations.

THE ROLE OF THE POLICE

The National Police has joined forces with Colombia's state-supported child welfare agency *(Instituto Colombiano de Bienestar Familiar*, ICBF, also known as *Bienestar)*, the People's Ombudsman's Office *(Defensoría del Pueblo)*, the Attorney General's Office *(Fiscalía)*, and the Prosecutor General's Office *(Procuraduría)*, to promote a national campaign to prevent child prostitution. Its motto is "Colombia without child prostitution" and its objective is to conduct activities for the management and protection of minors who are involved in prostitution (Policia Nacional 1996a). During July, August, and September, 1996, this institution conducted raids of some establishments in Cartagena. These operations found more than twenty minors working in bars, who were turned in to the ICBF. Four people were arrested (Policia Nacional 1996b).

The police believe that there is a strong link between commercialization of drugs and prostitution. This belief has been sustained by the aforementioned raids. On the other hand, according to the subcommander of this institution, the work of the police is to support the actions that the ICBF conducts to prevent child prostitution (Acevedo 1997, Villamizar 1997).

Despite claims that it works to promote children's rights, however, the police are not seen by the prostitutes as a source of support or protection. In fact, reports by the minors that we interviewed present an image of the police as threatening and corrupt. They described a series of police round-ups where physical force was used. Two different prostitutes independently reported an incident where the police kicked the belly of a prostitute who was pregnant. She subsequently miscarried.

Manuela, a seventeen-year-old who started prostituting herself when she was twelve, explains how she was battered and framed by the police. When she was sixteen, she was taken in a round-up. Men and women were asked to get naked so that the police could search them for drugs. Though most adult women were being searched by a female police officer, as her turn came she realized that a male policeman was going to search her. According to her, the search included the probing of bodily orifices. She recounts her words to the policeman:

> You do not have to treat us this way just because we are whores.... So they started, like, "What is this little girl thinking?"...[She replied,] "It's the truth; if you want to be respected then you respect *us* also."...[A female police officer] grabbed a stick and...she hit me here.... I don't know if I have the scar still, a little scar [on the side of her face].... I had been drinking...I bled a lot, from that little wound.... I bled a lot...so then I started insulting her.... The next day....I washed my face, they had hidden the stick...and I said that I was going to report them.... [The police] told us that they had found me with seven envelopes of *bazuco* [similar to crack]...and I said, "Where did they get that?" I don't do that, I don't sell that.

Manuela alleges that the police planted the drugs to accuse her. Then, although she was a minor, the sergeant sent her to the adult women's jail, claiming that she was nineteen years old. She cried a lot and a few days later the Renacer Foundation came and took her to their rehabilitation center. She ran away from there and ended up back in jail, accused of drug-dealing again. She remained in the adult women's jail for three months.

PROGRAMS FOR PROSTITUTES

Studies about women and juveniles who practice prostitution have shown that they are highly vulnerable to becoming infected with sexually transmitted diseases (De Zalduondo 1991, Vanwesenbeeck 1994). The result is that a majority of activities by prostitutes' organizations are directed at the prevention of sexual transmission of diseases, including AIDS. For related reasons, the Colombian government has tried to exert direct or indirect control over prostitution.

The young women we talked to seemed reticent to speak about sexually transmitted diseases that they may have contracted. They reported that the most common health problem they suffered as a result of their practice of prostitution was an obstruction of their urethra. They believed that this came from having contact with condom latex and self-prescribed a medication for it, although one woman reported that this medication once induced in her an unwanted abortion. We asked if they wore a condom in their work with clients and all responded that they did. Most seemed uncomfortable with this question and one mentioned that she was well acquainted with all the men with whom she had sex. This leads to the suspicion that they may have used condoms less frequently than they reported, especially with "regular" customers.

In the 1970s, the city of Cartagena created an ambulatory clinic (*Centro de Antivenereas*) that helps adult sex-workers prevent and treat sexually transmitted diseases. An average of 400 women visit this center each month. If a sex worker has no disease or is in treatment, she is given a certificate attesting to her health, although this practice has been legally abolished at the national level. Nonetheless, the Cartagena police, who routinely visit the bars and strip clubs of the city, continue to require the certificate. The vast majority of prostitutes who use the clinic's services (90 percent) are from other parts of the country (such as Medellín, Cali, Montería, Bogotá, and Barranquilla) and their ages most often range from twenty to twenty-five years (Vélez 1997). According to the center's director, the most common STD treated is chlamydia.

Despite the existence of this center, the prostitutes we spoke with find themselves in an unsafe situation regarding health matters and the prevention of STDs. The clinic caters to adults, eighteen and over, exclusively. No services or certificates of good health are given to minors. The only way for minors to get treatment there is to be brought in by a member of a local "rehab" program for child prostitutes, known as Renacer. Therefore, a juvenile who has not decided to give up prostitution cannot access the clinic's health services. Of the three adult prostitutes we interviewed, only one had acquired the health certificate. Although the other two had received attention in other health centers, they claimed that they had no legal identification and were thus unable to acquire the certificate.

The Instituto Colombiano de Bienestar Familiar is the primary national institution that establishes programs and policies to improve the nutritional and health conditions of Colombian children. According to a representative of ICBF, sexual abuse and child prostitution have become two of its major concerns. As a result, ICBF has taken part in the aforementioned national campaigns (Narváez 1997). During the operations of 1996, ICBF was entrusted with the identified children and placed them in foster homes. At the same time, they hired Renacer to perform a diagnostic study about child prostitution in the city. Later, ICBF contracted them to organize a rehabilitation program similar to the already existing one in Bogotá (Narváez 1997).

Bienestar's actions follow two lines. First, with the cooperation of other state organizations such as the police, they seek out brothels and strip clubs where children are involved in prostitution. Second, they attempt to treat the children through protection and rehabilitation programs financed by nongovernmental organizations (NGOs). In the majority of cases, the programs attempt to teach the children a trade, such as sewing or hairstyling. Nonetheless, these activities do not necessarily correspond to the socioeconomic context with which the children have become familiar nor do they meet the children's perceived needs and expectations.

The Renacer Foundation is the only institution that works with child prostitutes in Cartagena, although there are other NGOs, such as Funsarep (the Santa Rita Association for Education and Promotion of the People) and Children International, which work with underprivileged children. Renacer was founded in 1986 (Velandia 1996), and in 1990 it began its first rehabilitation program in Bogotá. In recent years, it has intensified its work in other cities. Its program in Cartagena is called Rehabilitation and Social Reinsertion Directed toward Minors Involved in Prostitution. Its principal objective is to accompany the prostitutes in the "voluntary processes of human dignification, recuperation of themselves and personal fulfillment" by offering technical, educational, therapeutic, and human resources that allow them to "rebuild their lives" (Renacer 1997). To achieve these goals, they carry out four activities: 1. establishing contact with child prostitutes on the street or in establishments; 2. attempting to capture the interest of the children through hairstyling and health activities in Renacer's "temporary home"; 3. rehabilitation through psychotherapy and workshops about sexuality and self-esteem in the "permanent home"; 4. after "reinsertion," the offering of crafts training and elementary schooling. The permanent home has space for twenty children for a period of a few months.

Most of the prostitutes that we interviewed had participated in some phases of Renacer's rehabilitation program. Some had turned to the temporary home to receive food and to take advantage of the activities, although none had plans to get completely involved in the program. Renacer representatives realize that many of the girls are not interested in staying in the program but believe that they will participate in the future (Rodríguez 1997, Valiente 1997). One girl explained that she had been in jail for carrying drugs and was later put under Renacer's supervision, but she escaped from the permanent home. Others had been in the permanent home for a short time, and they left because of the fights among residents. In the words of one, "I thought it was fine there, but, ah, no! There are a lot of fights there with the other [young prostitutes]." Another criticized what she perceived as the lack of trust on behalf of the employees:

> You go there to ask for a favor [e.g., money to buy food], and they say no. They don't do it, because the first thing they tell us is that we're going to do drugs. Why do they have to tell us that? When they give me an appointment, I don't go. If they wanted to do us a favor, they would do it without caring what we're going to do, isn't that right?

FINAL DISCUSSION

Efforts to eradicate child prostitution have become most salient since the development of the United Nations' 1989 Convention on the Rights of the Child. This convention, which has been ratified by the majority of countries in the world, seeks to promote the protection of minors (i.e., those under eighteen years of age) regarding a variety of issues affecting youth, including health, education, child labor, involvement in armed conflict, and sexual exploitation.

The UN Convention has led to the mobilization of efforts throughout the world to institute programs for the eradication of child trafficking and prostitution. During the summer of 1996, the former First Lady of Sweden and child advocacy agencies organized the World Congress against the Sexual Exploitation of Children in Stockholm. This Congress gathered experts from throughout the world and released a variety of reports (World Congress against the Sexual Exploitation of Children 1996). Since the Congress took place, isolated efforts to combat child prostitution have propagated. For example, ECPAT (formerly known as End Child Prostitution in Asian Tourism) recently expanded beyond its regional coverage of Asia and is currently working to create additional programs throughout Latin America and Africa under a new name: End Child Prostitution and Trafficking.

A note of caution must be made, however, about organizations that fight to abolish child prostitution. Abolitionist perspectives have tended to focus on the elimination of prostitution, often ignoring infrastructural and socioeconomic factors that contribute to its prevalence. Observers of the phenomenon may be persuaded to believe that a minor's engagement in prostitution is intrinsically more evil than any other socioeconomic, sociopolitical, or family-level circumstances that he or she could be in. The illusion is that if only prostitution were eradicated, children would be safe. Yet, in a country as full of perils for children as Colombia—where more than one-half million children have been displaced through political violence, where children have been recruited to fight in guerrilla and paramilitary groups, where economic scarcity pervades in the lives of more than half of its population, where youths have limited access to educational and work opportunities— it is difficult to argue that prostitution is more intrinsically evil than other difficult situations that children face. In fact, for most participants in our study, some of the experiences that predated their engagement in prostitution appeared no less traumatic or challenging than their current lives. Prostitution is just one more manifestation of a very painful life path that is both created and perpetuated by socioeconomic forces.

A review of the reported stories shows that all the research participants came from economically deprived homes. Some were hungry the first time that they decided to engage in prostitution. The majority came from areas of the country that have been affected by armed conflict (though this was not a salient aspect of interview accounts). In addition, at least half of them suffered sexual abuse or neglect and found no safe haven other than life on the street. All these conditions predisposed girls to engage in prostitution for the first time.

The main alternative money-making activity that the young women engaged in, aside from prostitution, was live-in domestic work. This type of work did not provide enough earnings to ensure them a modicum of economic independence. In fact, most reports of early household work reveal stories about mistreatment, distrust, nonpayment, and even hunger. A young woman who has children and no family or social support ties cannot raise her children on the salary of a domestic worker. Furthermore, unless she has these extended support networks, she would not be able to raise her children at all as a live-in domestic worker, because most work sites do not allow children to live in the household.

The young prostitutes we talked to had little access to other work or education. Being black and poor limited their opportunities even further. Being publicly *perjudicada* (i.e., no longer a virgin) reduced the opportunities that they may have had to marry a man who would support them (and their children). The only men they were able to attract were those in similar socioeconomic conditions and who have been lured into illicit money-making activities. Association with these men potentially reinforces a young woman's self-concept as "low" or "delinquent," increasing the probability that she will not find a way out of prostitution.

Evidently, young women get trapped in a variety of socioeconomic and cultural circumstances that perpetuate their engagement in prostitution. Consequently, long-term efforts to eradicate child and adolescent prostitution should be directed at the creation of infrastructures that provide options for young people and their families: education, job opportunities, programs for families at risk of neglecting and abusing children, hotlines, and placement programs for runaway youths. This requires economic restructuring and political will. Organizations that work to abolish child and adolescent prostitution would be most helpful if they channeled a significant portion of their long-term efforts in this direction.

In the short term, a heartfelt desire to eradicate child and adolescent prostitution should not prevent advocates from being open to asking about the different ways that minors may experience prostitution. The discourse of abolitionist organizations that automatically equates prostitution by minors with "sexual exploitation" tends to obscure aspects of its practice that must be taken into consideration in the development of programs to help child and adolescent prostitutes. Black (1995) argues that important variables, such as age and degree of volition/coercion, may become negligible in the language of exploitation. A ten-year-old girl who is chained to a bed and made to have sex with ten different men each day is violated in different ways than a sixteen-year-old who runs away from home and works the streets independently. The trauma experienced by people who are directly coerced into prostitution (e.g., kidnapped/sold, deceived into indentured sexual servitude) is different from the trauma of being indirectly coerced into prostitution through socioeconomic stress. Though both forms of engagement in prostitution constitute violations of human rights, the first type is more blatant. Adult women who choose prostitution over a variety of other money-making activities that are available to them and who charge high prices to have sex with people that they carefully select operate at the lowest level of coercion.

The issue of age is also important to keep in mind in developing programs and intervention concerning prostitution. Younger children are generally more vulnerable than older ones and are potentially more harmed by engaging in prostitution (given the same conditions of coercion). Black suggests, and we agree, that it is important to consider "age of consent" as an important point of reference. In many countries, an adolescent is considered capable of deciding to engage in sexual activity at about thirteen years of age. Though it is not desirable for thirteen-year-olds to practice prostitution, all things being equal, children who are younger than the age of consent need more urgent protection than older ones who have reached the age of consent. Ideally, however, protection and options would be available to all minors engaged in prostitution. In fact, protection and options should be available to prostitutes irrespective of age.

Finally, it is important to consider how young prostitutes view themselves. The "sexual exploitation" view of prostitution defines young prostitutes as victims. Yet, the extent to which a minor would characterize himself or herself as a victim is a matter to be explored with each child or adolescent. This does not mean that one should abandon a protective stance regarding minors who are engaged in prostitution. However, the interviews that were collected in this study showed a variety of mixed feelings about engaging in prostitution. On the one hand, young women told stories of economic and psychological hardship that culminated in their engagement in prostitution. On the other, they described feeling happy about making enough money to support themselves and their children well. The young women who still had strong family ties had plans to start small businesses and go back to their childhood home. The young women who had left home under conditions of neglect or abuse may remain stuck in the practice of prostitution, a practice that will yield fewer and fewer gains as they become older.

Though young women involved in prostitution may feel victimized, it is important also to question to what extent they also feel and act as agents. This study's participants all currently work independently, and there is evidence that they turn down sexual encounters with which they do not feel comfortable—unless the price persuades them. To some degree, they practice prostitution on their own terms. Programs that philosophically view child and adolescent prostitutes only as victims may miss out on some of the independence and strengths that young women develop along the way to cope with their very difficult situations. We believe that organizations that protect young people involved in prostitution must acknowledge the pain and trauma of engaging in prostitution without negating the strengths that young people rely on. Building on these survival mechanisms is most helpful, given that there are few means for Colombian government and non-governmental organizations to be helpful to young prostitutes in the long term.

Another reason why it is important to listen to prostitutes' own accounts of their lives and of their engagement in prostitution is that different life histories call for different types of intervention programs. A minor who became a prostitute as an adolescent and still has potentially strong ties to her family of origin might benefit most from individual or family counseling that would help her make the transition back home. Educational and career programs also could help her to contribute economically in her home. In contrast, a girl who has left a very difficult family situation that she is unwilling or unable to return to probably needs provision for her basic needs and help in becoming economically self-sufficient.

ACKNOWLEDGMENTS

The authors are grateful to the prostitutes in Cartagena, who willingly answered our questions and told us their life stories. Additional thanks go to the public officials, NGO representatives, and academics in Cartagena and Bogotá who took time out from their busy schedules to speak with us. Sulma Manco and Lina Franco, from Cormujer, shared their experiences with us and were indispensable in establishing contacts in Cartagena. James Mensing and Jason Thor Hagen provided technical support, helpful criticism, and intellectual stimulation. Only the authors, however, are responsible for the article's content.

NOTES

1. Two of the best discussions of the politics of neoliberalism in Colombia are found in Ahumada (1996) and Cepeda (1994).

2. Tourism accounted for 2.17 percent of the Colombian GNP in 1997 (Boletín Informativo Cotelco, May 1998). In Cartagena, the most important "tourist" city in the country, the percentage of income derived from tourism is much higher, although figures were not made available to the researchers.

3. We decided to make our first contact with research participants through a research assistant who had been a sex worker locally. We recruited this assistant through Cormujer, a Colombian sex workers' organization. Thirteen young women agreed to participate in the study. Ten were aged fifteen to seventeen years and three were between the ages of nineteen and twenty. They were currently working as prostitutes in the downtown area of Cartagena, where they had sex mostly with local men. Most of them supplemented their earnings by working with Colombian and foreign tourists in the beach hotel area a few times a week. All of them had first entered into prostitution between the ages of nine and fifteen years. Nine of the research participants appeared to have an Afro-Colombian ancestry and four seemed to be *mestizas* (a mix of indigenous and Spanish heritage). We did not ask any of them to identify their racial or ethnic background, however. A Life Course perspective (Elder et al. 1993, Elder 1998) was adopted for data gathering and analysis.

4. According to the Planning Department of Bolívar, 54 percent of the department's population resides in Cartagena.

5. In 1989, in all of Colombia, 14.2 percent of employed women worked as domestic workers (Flórez and Cano 1993).

6. Of the thirteen prostitutes we interviewed, eleven work in Bocagrande because they earn more there than they would in another part of the city. One of them told us that in Bocagrande, prostitutes of all ages work, as well as children and transvestites.

7. However, since Streicker did his field research, the number of people displaced by violence nationwide has increased, and, in particular, those from the coastal departments have settled in Cartagena. Hence, it is now more difficult to sell Cartagena as more Caribbean than Colombian, because the city attracts those fleeing violence in neighboring (coastal) regions.

8. The phenomenon is not unique to Colombia. According to a recent study in Brazil, a country widely noted for its racial heterogeneity, blacks earn half as much as whites (Esnal 1998). The study cited is George Reid Andrews, *Blacks and Whites in São Paulo, Brazil, 1888-1988*, Madison: University of Wisconsin Press, 1991.

8

Tourist-Oriented Prostitution in Barbados

The Case of the Beach Boy and the White Female Tourist

This ethnographic study focuses on the relatively recent phenomenon of male tourist-oriented prostitution in Barbados. It explores issues of gender identification and negotiation between the white female tourist and the black, often dreadlocked "beach boy." Predominantly qualitative research methods were employed in order to gain an emic (insider) view of the phenomenon and discover how these actors conceptualized their situation.[1] The study argues that male tourist-oriented prostitution is based on a quest for the sexual Other. This quest is structured along racial and gendered lines, where the white emancipated Western female goes in search of the quintessential hypersexual black male in the center of the Other.

PROSTITUTION IN BARBADOS

Prostitution in Barbados, although deemed illegal by common law and more recently in the Sexual Offences Acts of 1992 and 1998, has had a long, informal yet covert subculture in Barbados. The predominant attitude of the state toward prostitution is based on the view that prostitution as an activity is detrimental to the moral fabric of society. With laws against loitering, brothel keeping, and soliciting, the Barbados government has made its stance quite clear. For example, the Minor Offences Act of 1998 states: "Any person who

183

loiters in any street or highway and importunes passengers for the purpose of prostitution... commits an offence and is liable on conviction before a magistrate to a penalty of B$2,500 or to imprisonment for 2 years or both."

However, that is not to say that prostitution is not a culturally accepted practice. The few studies that have focused on the issue of prostitution have looked at female prostitution and pointed to Barbados's colonial legacy in playing a part in its development (Kempadoo 1996). Beckles, focusing on the pre-emancipation period, 1650–1834, in Barbados argues that "slavery in some ways corrupted the sexual values of the inhabitants" (1989:141). He points to the fact that in Bridgetown organized prostitution and the keeping of resident mistresses was very much the norm. This practice was further facilitated by liberal urban values. The geopolitical significance of Barbados as an important seaport provided a steady demand for sex. Levy argues that "black prostitution during slavery was an occupation which was more common at Bridgetown than in any other city in the British West Indies" (1980:30).

This subculture of prostitution was part and parcel of an informal domestic service sector that provided for not only the white planter class but also its maritime counterparts (Beckles 1989). Owners leased out slave women as a convenient way of earning money, and prostitution was considered more lucrative than the breeding of slaves. The sex market was very much linked to the more structured legitimate formal market, with the hiring out of female labor providing dual functions to individuals.

According to Beckles (1989) the more developed institutional patterns of prostitution were located in the Bridgetown area and linked to the leisure and entertainment facilities such as taverns, bars, and inns. It is within this context that the construction of different categories of womanhood along racial lines can be viewed where "white elite males possessed a sexual typology in which white women were valued for domestic formality and respectability, 'coloured women' for exciting socio-sexual companionship, and black women for irresponsible, covert sexual adventurism" (Beckles 1989:146).

Prostitution, in its traditional role, provided a means of support for not only black or colored women but also the white owners. After emancipation in 1834 the practice was continued, indicating its entrenchment within Barbadian culture, with the role of prostitute/mistress providing a steady income for those who worked either in a brothel or from home. Black men in this arena are given little attention. However, evidence suggests that their role within this subculture was very marginal, significant only in terms of offering "stud" services to the black females on the plantation, formally or otherwise. Hence, coming out of postemancipation society a typology of sexuality developed based on race and ethnicity, where the black woman was viewed as whore, the white woman as the Madonna, and the colored woman falling somewhere in between. The black man's role continued to be defined as marginal, except in terms of his sexuality, which came to be viewed as a defining characteristic.

Currently, although prostitution is an illegal activity, female prostitution is tolerated within the confines of established districts of Bridgetown, such as the historical red-light area of Nelson Street. It is deemed a female activity catering more to local demand, with the majority of prostitutes being street-walkers and club workers. Little, if any, attention has been placed on male prostitutes as playing a significant role in prostitution in Barbados. The focus of this research is to fill part of this void.

MALE TOURIST-ORIENTED PROSTITUTION IN THE CARIBBEAN

Contemporary studies on tourist-oriented prostitution in the Caribbean have maintained that the phenomenon is based on racial stereotypes and sexual fantasy. Theorists focusing on Barbados have argued that "beach hustling" is based on the acting out of sexual racial fantasies about the natives (Press 1978, Karch and Dann 1981). In the case of male prostitution, an adherence to this approach would maintain that "hustling" should be viewed within a framework of continued First World exploitation of the Third World. However, to some extent, Press moves away from the view held by anthropologists and adopts a more plural framework, arguing that "although Barbadians tend to stress the sexual nature of tourist-hustler relationships,... the hustlers usually emphasize the material gain" (1978:114).

Considering sex tourism in Jamaica, Pruitt and LaFont (1995) contend that gender becomes a significant variable in analyzing these relationships between "Rent-a-Dreads" and the female tourists. There is "playing off of traditional gender repertoires" between the actors with regard to masculinity and femininity. They offer the term "romance tourism" to distinguish their views from those of anthropologists who deemed these relations as exploitative. They define romance tourism as a relationship "where the actors place emphasis on courtship rather than the exchange for money and sex. These liaisons are constructed through a discourse of romance and long-term relationship, an emotional involvement usually not present in sex tourism" (1995:423).[2]

O'Connell Davidson's 1996 study on sex tourism in Cuba, although presenting the obverse with regard to gendered actors, provides us with an insightful analysis about motivation and typologies of tourists involved in the phenomenon. Although this study adopts the more traditional approach of early feminist writings, the conceptualizations cannot be ignored, especially considering sex tourists.

The above studies provide us with a conceptual and theoretical base in which any work on tourist-oriented prostitution or sex tourism can be carried out. This study attempts a more eclectic theoretical framework in viewing male tourist-oriented prostitution in Barbados. Its special emphasis is on the definitions of the phenomenon by both actors, utilizing both traditional and contemporary approaches.

BEACH HUSTLERS IN BARBADOS

Beach hustling falls under the broader category of hustling as defined by Pryce (1979) and Brathwaite (1983) as an alternate means of earning a living. In their sexual behavior, beach hustlers can be defined in terms of "gigolos"—men who receive material compensation for the social or sexual services they render to women" (Press 1978). In the case of Barbados, hustling can be viewed as the exploitation of white female tourists by young black Barbadian males. Beach hustlers are young, underemployed black men who provide sexual services and act as escorts to white female tourists of varying age in exchange for economic goods and services, which range from brand name clothes to airline tickets. Although these liaisons might start off as "sex for money" in the one extreme, if continued, emotional attachments are formed and the relationship is extended over a period of time, sometimes resulting in marriage.

The beach hustler, beach boy, or beach bum, as he is sometimes referred to in Barbados, is usually between eighteen and thirty-five years old and from a low socioeconomic background. He is not educated beyond the secondary level and has few qualifications, hence his subsequent inability to procure much in the way of jobs, except unskilled or semiskilled manual work, i.e., odd-jobbing, fishing, or painting. He might have started off as an odd-jobber working on the beach and procured more formal employment by assisting with the handling of jet skis or catamarans, or have a more entrepreneurial activity such as selling coconuts, coral, or aloes. As a respondent states, "I got into it as soon as I left school, 'cause I couldn't find no job, so I do something that could support me, but as time goes on you pick up different things. You pick up different ideas on how to do things...." Or as a key informant describes another beach hustler, "Terry know a lot of white people. Terry does paint and do different things, while doing these things you meet people...." Hustling is not his only means of support, as a key informant articulates: "The hustlers are those who work with the water/ski/wind surfing and water sports. Most hustlers does work 'cause if you ain't got no money you does got to get yourself an income to buy yourself a drink."

This demographic profile of Barbadian beach boys parallels that given by Pruitt and LaFont of Jamaican Rent-a-Dreads, whom they describe as "a group of rural young people with little education and few social and economic prospects" (1995:428). Take, for example, twenty-one-year-old Carl,[3] who attended one of the newer secondary schools and left with no certificates. He usually supports himself by doing odd jobs such as carpentry and just used to "lime"[4] with the fellas on the beach, where he met Beth, a French European woman. She supports him when she is in Barbados, and he survives on remittances and odd jobs when she returns to her country of origin. Physically, he is well built, with well-defined muscles. He is very dark, obviously from his days in the sun, and sports short "natties" (short dread locks) which are bleached by the sun—a hairstyle that he is sure to tell you is "easy to manage, and the tourist women like it so."

Pruitt and LaFont make the same assessment with regard to hairstyle where "those men with dreadlocks who are assumed to be Rastafari receive substantially more attention from foreign women than do other Jamaican men" (1995:430). Although the Barbadian hustlers do not adhere to the Rastafarian characteristics, as their counterparts do in Jamaica, they do recognize the appeal of the hairstyle. As a beach hustler explains:

> You know why some of the girls like the knot-up hair? When some girls send photos and stuff up to England, you don't be seeing clean-cut men. They send a picture of Rastas. So when a girl come down here they think a Rasta is a real Caribbean man, so that is why they go for a Rasta man. Some girls like nature, so they say a Rasta like peas and vegetables. But some of them does fool themselves, 'cause they don't get a Rasta, they get an impostor. That's how they judge the Caribbean by the Rasta, and the thing is now when they come they can't go to Harbor Lights,[5] a Rasta can't go to Harbor Lights...."

However, the point must be made that in Barbados, the natties have become a trademark of the marginalized youth, which, it can be argued, parallel the Rastafarian appeal of the 1960s, so the wearing of the natties is a combination of a marketing strategy and a show of brotherhood.

The beach boy's attire is usually brand-name beach shorts worn in a manner to show off his well-endowed proportions. His appearance, an obvious marketing strategy, is based on the Western female's notion of the quintessential hypersexual black male—skin darkened almost blue-black to acclaim his pride in his African ancestry and to suggest an untamed, primitive nature and an exotic appeal. To the Western female he becomes the archetype of black masculinity (Pruitt and LaFont 1995).

The beach hustler tends to emphasize his masculinity, a point that reinforces the racial stereotypes of blacks, one of the exotic Other, in order to give the female tourist what she is expecting. The exotic Other has been constructed as more passionate, more emotional, more natural, and more tempting than his white counterpart (Pruitt and LaFont 1995). For example, when he goes to a club, immediately he will begin showing his "natural rhythm," gyrating to the latest calypso and reggae tunes, sometimes showing his "natural" athletic ability with a few seemingly improbable flips and splits. When the music changes to a slower beat, he will hold "his woman" and sing in her ear showing his "natural" ability to sing and demonstrating that he is "passionate" about her. Unlike his counterpart in Jamaica, he does not construct a "staged authenticity" (MacCannell 1989) but these are simply traits of his constructed masculinity of reputation (Wilson 1969). He is the black man that the white female imagines in this constructed paradise. The beach boy also has a large repertoire, including the ability to speak a sprinkling of a few European languages. Being able to communicate with his woman effectively is important in order to impress upon her the fact that he cares enough to try to learn her language. Pruitt and LaFont also note that in Jamaica, "learning to speak a little German or developing an expertise for guessing what types of experiences the specific tourists are seeking" also occurred (1995:431). Not only is the hustler skilled in languages, but his ability to speak in the accent of any tourist that he encounters is exceptional. Further he has quite a cosmopolitan lifestyle, spending a few weeks a year in Germany or Sweden with "a friend."

The young male is quick to deny that his liaisons with white female tourists are hustling or prostitution, as it is known in the Barbadian context. He points to the fact that "hustlers don't work and workers don't hustle for white women." Rather he seeks to make the clear demarcation between his "situational liaisons" and what he calls the "gigolos," "them guys who go around fucking and harassing the tourists for money." The interviewer, however, could not identify this category in the course of the research. For the hustlers, situational liaisons might start off as any other between male and female: "Yah meet a girl on the beach or at a disco, and she start smiling at you, and you start smiling at she, and you'll get to dancing...." As Carl asserts:

> The beach ain't no prostitution thing like that, it's a work and during yah working you get involved with people from all over the world and some like you 'cause they friendly and to compare wid the people that from your country they more nicer, they more friendlier, they even help you more than you own, so yah get kinda close to them and all kinda scenes play.

Yet at the same time, these situational encounters are selected on the basis of one primary prerequisite, i.e., wealth. Tim, for example, asserts: "I like to get involved with executive ladies, with women with class, women with cash. Technically speaking I love women who have money. I can tell the ones who got money...." His partner also iterates:

> As a matter of interests if you meet someone, and they say they like you they will return shortly, like next week. That's how you find out if they have a lot of zeros behind the point. Not many people can do that if you save for the vacation....

They even speak of sometimes being fooled by the female tourists, who pretend to have money in order to gain their attention: "Some of them girls does come down here and don't got nothing but credit cards and fool the boys. You got more than them. You see a girl at a bar with a credit card down and you think that she got money...."

Economics more than romance seems to be the mitigating factor in these situational relations on the part of the beach boy. They too, however, refer to the beach boy or beach bum at times unthinkingly to denote the relationship between young black males and female tourists, like themselves. For example:

> All the guys working in the bank hustling tourist women too because they see the fellas getting ahead, progressing quick, so they let me get in on this action. When I go to the Boat Yard[6] checking the women, a lot of businessmen in there. Is not only on the beach, you know....

Tim admits that to some extent that he defines himself as such:

> You know that I is a beach bum, because when I go down to Speightstown every day of the week I walk with two or three grand in my pocket, and a lot people can't get that and I working legal. So, like to be a beach bum. I ain't inferior, I ain't dirty. They got land bums too you know; a lot of girls is land bums, go bum a man. See men with heavy with big gold, and see him and say boy I have to get to know him....

THE WHITE FEMALE TOURIST

The literature on gender and tourism articulates that "travel has become part of the gendering activity of women as they seek to expand their gender repertoires to incorporate practices traditionally reserved for men and thereby integrate the conventionally masculine with the feminine" (Pruitt and LaFont 1995:425). Travel for the emancipated Western woman becomes an arena to test out new notions of a liberated femininity that goes in quest of the sexual Other, an Other who is endowed with a primitive masculinity that can no longer be found in the West.

The female tourist in this study is between twenty-five and fifty years old. She is usually from Europe, maybe Belgium, France or England, but may also come from the United States or Canada (see also CTO 1996, Press 1978, Karch and Dann 1981). She would probably have saved for this trip to Barbados. She is a secretary or nurse or holds some other job that puts her in a middle to lower income. She would tell you that she heard about Barbados through friends or acquaintances, generally female. Her first trip to the island would be with another female friend. Typologies of the white female tourists can be applied with regard to their liaisons with the beach boys. These are: the situationer, the repeat situationer, and the one nighter.

The Situationer

In this category, the tourist does not apply the label of hustling or prostitution to her encounters with beach boys. She emphasizes the romance element of the relationship. These relationships are situational encounters paralleling the typology of the situational sexual tourist of O'Connell Davidson's studies in Cuba and Thailand (1996). In this context she is defined as a female tourist who travels not with the intention of having sex with the locals but who enters into these relationships as soon as the opportunity presents itself.

An example involves Beth, who came with some friends, met George on the beach, and spoke to him a few times. They encountered each other in one of the many tourist spots, started dancing, and things developed from there. Beth bears the economic burden of the relationship, since George does not have a full-time job. When asked about his job status, the researcher was told: "I am not working right now, but I do this and that.... Right now I just showing my lady here a good time." She, like her male counterpart in Cuba, denies the instrumental nature of her encounters, being quick to tell you that she is "not like those other girls who just come down here to have sex with a black man." But Beth like so many of the situationers tends to support her guy, and he stays with her in a guest house for the duration of her stay. The situation still remains very much sex in exchange for money and services, a situation that Beth seeks to ignore.

The Repeat Situationer

Another variation is the female tourist in her early to late forties who returns about two or three times a year. She is a well-known figure on a particular beach, which is near her guest house or hotel. She would have had a number of "boyfriends" over the years and have alternated between having them visit her country and traveling herself to Barbados. She tells you that eventually she wants to settle here as soon as she has enough money, because "everything here is so nice, and the people are so friendly." She too denies the remunerative nature of her relationships.

A case in point is Paula, who has been coming to Barbados since 1990 and has had three boyfriends, one of whom she has a child with. Paula speaks to me as she clings possessively onto the arm of her boyfriend. Responding to a query on why Barbados, she said, "This is a very beautiful place and I found what I was looking for. He is everything to me." Her current boyfriend is around twenty years old, and he too has no full-time employment status;

rather, he helps out the guys on the beach. Paula "helps him out" by buying him clothes and anything he wants, as well as sending him money to tide him over until she returns.

The One Nighters

Although the researchers were unable to access this group, its existence was quite apparent in the details provided by male and female key informers. These girls are usually British, "come down here to say they fuck a black man." The one nighters are usually in their twenties who are "here for fun. You will see them with one guy tonight and tomorrow night you see them with another. The next day you see them with another hustler...." These women behave similarly to the macho lads of Cuba, seemingly content with anonymous sexual encounters (O'Connell Davidson 1996).

THE DILEMMA OF ROMANCE, SEX, AND MONEY

The usual setting for encounters between tourist and hustler is the beach. This provides the backdrop for chance meetings, overtures, and sexual encounters and is the locale for this informal sector. As maintained by one key informant, "The beach is a place where you have all kinds of hustling...." Clubs catering toward entertaining tourists also provide a backdrop for these encounters. These are the two settings where the beach boy can affect his "cool pose" and his "hustle."[7] The successful encounters are usually consummated on the sand.

The encounters are usually based on a mixture of racialized sexual fantasy, economics and emotion. Although, the researchers contend that the liaisons might start off as a combination of sex and economic services, they can be easily fitted under the umbrella of prostitution. The relationships may be extended, resulting in repeat visits to the island, visits to the tourist's place of origin, or by the migration of one of the actors involved. However, the motivation on the part of the beach boy usually is of the former variety, and their involvement in a steady romantic relationship becomes an indirect result of prolonged encounters, while the white female tourists define these liaisons in terms of situational romances and racialized sexual fantasies.

A conceptualization can be made, with reference to the hustler and the white female tourists, that is a mixture of motivation and circumstances:

1. Racialized fantasies—racial stereotypes of sexuality between the actors
2. Arrangement—economic exchange with some degree of staged emotional involvement on the part of the male

3. Mixed—both economic exchange and some degree of emotional attachment
4. Emotional—emotional involvement or "love"

The researcher wishes to articulate that these categories are not mutually exclusive, but merely an attempt to conceptualize the relationship between the actors.

Racialized Sexual Fantasies: The Black Stud and the Easy White Woman

Liaisons between the hustler and the female tourist are based on mutual racial stereotypes of sexual fantasy. These are usually of the one night stand variety or, if extended, last no more than two or three days. These encounters are based on such stereotypes as "black men can go all night" and "white women are easy, and give you head, no problem." Both actors mutually realize some racial stereotypes. Take the case of Jake, who maintains that "most women if you meet them at the club, you can get a one night stand."

George also makes his position abundantly clear:

Bajan women can't fuck, and they doan even wanta suck you. You got to beg she to do it, and still she might not do it, and if she do it she acting like if she doin you a favor. Now a white woman, you gotta beg she to stop!

Arthur makes a similar claim:

Bajan women is too much trouble, you gotta feed she carr' she out, and buy things for she to eat and drink, but a white girl you just gotta tell she ooh you look brown today, and she would gi' you it just like that.

For others:

Bajan women got too much pride, you would find that a Bajan woman come to the beach to swim, they have nice bodies, they have a nice bikini on, and still they go in the sea with a long dress, why is that? What are you hiding? You don't want to attract the boys, that means that you either gay, or you like girls. But you don't want the boys to see your body. You buy expensive swimwear you go to the beach right, you look good in it, but still you got a tee shirt covering it up. But you find a tourist woman as old as eighty years old, looking terrible with a big belly, no ass and still showing her body.... I think that fellas just getting fed up, trying to ask a woman out, and just walking with her face in the air. Tourist women are not like that....

Female tourists also adopt similar attitudes. For example, Judy maintains:

It's an entirely different situation. Black men like fucking, black men enjoy the sex act, they don't make love. Some white men make love. Black men in my experience don't make love, they fuck, and it's all of this brag stuff. How good the act was, and how good they are, and it's all of this brag stuff....

One beach boy, in explaining the attraction by white female tourists to beach boys, speaks about the white male's inability to sexually satisfy his female counterpart:

They ain't up to the mark, so when them women come to Barbados and see that we black boys healthy and look good and thing. They [white women] want to try something new. You can't beat that. I have seen women divorce their husbands, get divorce, you know what I mean....

Another speaks about the fantasy element:

White woman come from overseas come to live out a fantasy and walk away; a man might take advantage of that situation.... Some women maybe telling themselves you see me for right now I like these jungle pictures, all of these big, strong men. I want to go down there and get fuck in the bush and thing, all kinda fantasies....

Actors adopt the racial stereotype of the Other. The Western female embodies the "free sexuality" and adventurism of the North in contrast to the "respectability" of the Caribbean woman (Wilson 1969), where open sexuality is frowned upon. The Barbadian male embodies the primitive, aggressive nature of the black man, having an animal-like quality, which is constructed as opposite to the white man, the gentleman. This is the type of man who "would fuck you in the sand and wouldn't think anything the matter with it."

The Arrangement

This type of relationship usually lasts the duration of the tourist's visit. The woman is approached on the beach while sunbathing or at a nightclub, and conversation is initiated about her visit, her impressions of Barbados. The hustler might then give himself the role of guide and promise to show her "the true Barbados." The woman usually becomes enamored by such attention, which is further reinforced by his propensity for "sweet talk" (Abrahams 1983, Wilson 1969) and agrees to the hidden layers of the "contract." The

194   *Joan L. Phillips*

arrangement is usually sex and money or goods in exchange for such services as tour guides and escort to clubs and restaurants.

In the arrangement, the hustlers emphasize the economic aspect of the relationship. Peter points out:

> Tourists carry you to dinners. When I was on the sand [beach] I used to eat food at Sandy Lane,[8] and all today, I still eating food there me and my girl at Sandy Lane. I don't spend anything. I don't get to spend a cent. They invite me out, they going to treat you nice....

Ted makes the claim that "Bajan women always looking for somebody to support them. I looking for somebody to support me too, what is wrong with that? I happy." One key informant puts it more clearly: "I like to get involved with executive ladies.... My women are lawyers, own their own companies, are executives of other companies.... Technically speaking I love ladies who love money." In fact, most of those who were interviewed had their own cars, were renting apartments, and owned or had part ownership in beach sporting equipment. All had been funded or given start-up capital by their girlfriends.

Female tourists within this arrangement classify themselves as victims of love, seemingly unable to see this relationship as an arrangement instead of a romance. However, at the end of the vacation, they recognize the reality. Susan, now living in Barbados, examines the plight of the female tourists:

> They get here and all of a sudden they are on a beach wearing next to nothing, and up and down the beach parading are all of these gorgeous men like peacocks coming up to you saying, "You are so beautiful, you are so gorgeous. Can I take you out tonight, can I do this, can I do that." Before you know it the girls are intoxicated.... The usual scenario is this: she spends her money on him, she pays for the taxi, she buys the clothes. She mistakes sex for love....

James explains why they are mistakenly caught up:

> They does get into us and do everything with us, everything. We does carry them places, island tours, sailing and so on. We does be with them showing them everything, giving them a good time, making sure they enjoy their holiday. So they are going to devote time with us, they ain't going to look for another person....

Pruitt and LaFont (1995) also found that in the Jamaican context where the woman is caught in a relationship, its nature was not initially defined in this context.

Mixed/Romance Relationships

Mixed relationships might start off as arrangements, owing to continued contact between the two actors. The nature of the relationship begins to develop along romantic lines, although the economic aspects still play a significant part. The hustler finds it more lucrative to stay with this particular woman, and on his part begins to develop feelings for her. This type of relationship closely parallels the romance tourism framework of Pruitt and La-Font (1995), where the courtship element in the relationship begins to play a more significant role. It is in this case that the hustling element of the relationship is usually threatened and the cool pose begins to crumble. Like Aldrick the Dragon Man in Lovelace's novel (Lewis 1998), it calls for a redefinition of masculine identity "to be more himself than the pose [or the hustle] could ever be" (1998:172). According to Mark:

> At first, we weren't in anything, you know; she used to come down here and I would show she a good time, then she start staying longer and longer.... Now I only got she one, and I does go up and she does come down.

James also holds a similar view. He blames it, however, on sex: "People fall in love despite not wanting to. Sex is a powerful thing. You start off, you want a fucking, before you know it there is feeling there.... Maybe it's the pussy, maybe it's the lady...."

The women also develop deep feelings toward the young men. Beth, a Belgian who has had a relationship with Rick for two years, maintains that "after a while, I started to love him, I started to think about him constantly, and I would call him, and when I came back he also had feelings for me."

Emotional

Usually if the mixed relationships endure, they continue to the next level, where marriage can result. One of two things can happen. Either the hustler emigrates to the woman's country of origin or the woman moves to Barbados. In the North, the marriage often ends, since the constructed world cannot be maintained in the reality of living day to day in the female's country of origin (Wagner 1977). Hustlers usually complain about the weather or the fact that they felt constrained: "She didn't want me go nowhere, only wid she...." Female tourists on their part are surprised when their new husbands continue along the lines of the stereotype of the black man, for example, indulging in promiscuous behavior, obviously not realizing that this is part of the beach boy's masculine identity. As Paula maintains: "He had a huge addiction to chasing pussy...."

Those marriages that survive do so when the female decides to live in Barbados. An example is the marriage of Meg and Dave. Meg works as a tour rep, while Dave works at a windsurfing club; they just had a baby. Both declare that they are quite happy together; Meg even speaks with a quasi-Barbadian accent. Meg confesses that she still has some problems with her adjustment to Dave's family and to Barbadian women in general, who are highly suspicious of her. But for the most part, the couple still has a lot of friends, mainly their co-workers. The relationships that develop between the hustler and the female tourist tend to foster along the periphery of the tourist culture. Seldom do they actually enter the local culture.

NEGOTIATING GENDER IDENTITIES

Barbadian working-class young men are products of a colonial legacy, which has fostered the marginality of the male, both socially and economically, in society. Caribbean writings have articulated the complexities of Caribbean peoples' inability to adopt Western European gender roles within the context of poverty and deprivation (Clarke 1957, Massiah 1986). The result has been the dominance of Caribbean women in the family and in the marketplace, while Caribbean working-class men have been denied equitable access to competition in the market place by virtue of institutional racism and have continued to be unemployed and underemployed in the face of economic recession.

Black masculinity is constructed as a response to the colonial framework of the white hegemonic masculinity. It is a form of resistance and an active redeployment of white masculinity (Cornwall and Lindisfarne 1994). It is measured in terms of male virility, which is manifested through sexual conquest and the fathering of many children—poor man's riches—and established by other behaviors, such as boasting in the public domain and exaggerated complementing or "sweet talk" (Wilson 1969:106).

Beach hustling in this context represents an attempt by young black males to construct a type of masculinity whose prosaic symbols are achievable within Caribbean society. Tourism has facilitated development of an informal sector in which "he is his own man," not working for anybody and answering "yes sir, no sir." In fact, this entrepreneurial activity allows him to affirm his masculine role among his peers. Beach hustling provides the forum for the young black male to successfully test the limits of a cultural masculinity. He uses cultural constructions to his economic advantage in his liaisons with female tourists.

The white female, with her foreign income power, adventurism, and race, assumes a hegemonic gender power in Barbadian society denied to the local Barbadian woman. Her encounters with the beach hustlers represent an opportunity to test out this hegemonic dominance under balmy skies in the center of the Other, with the Other, who, she maintains, is "so different from the men at home...so aggressive" (aggressive in his "come on" tactics and his general demeanor). She adopts the role of economic provider within his cultural context. She understands that "her guy is from the ghetto.... He doesn't have any fucking money..." and that is all right by her, because he shows her a good time, becoming her passport to Barbadian culture. She feels guilty about her comparative economic wealth and overcompensates by not only paying for him to go places but also buy him clothes and anything that he may need: "She does what she can for this poor guy living in the ghetto."

Unlike his Jamaican counterpart, the Barbadian hustler has no problems dealing with the economic dominance of his white partner, since this role is not new to him in the context of the local culture. The status and recognition given to him by his peers subsume any contradictory feelings that he may have (Press 1978). His status is augmented by the material gains of the relationship, not only by owning jet skis or brand-name clothing but by the propensity of the woman to provide him with opportunities denied to him by his race. As one key informant maintains:

> A woman would send for me from here to go overseas with a return ticket. I can travel from here any part of the world. I can make a phone call and say I want to leave Barbados they would say, "Come, the ticket on the way." I don't have to ask twice you understand....

The white woman does not threaten his masculinity by demanding symbols not constructed as part of his cultural masculine role, e.g., money—demands that are so much part of his relationships with local women. In the context of a Caribbean culture, it is expected within a relationship that the man will give money to the woman (Pruitt 1992). As one informant asserts, "Bajan women want too much material.... Big man with big car.... White woman don't check for nothing so...."

Further, these encounters provide opportunities for the black male to affirm and reinforce his cultural masculine role of sexual prowess, and his other "expressive" traits like sweet talk. He is also able to demonstrate his "skills of strength and knowledge" (Wilson 1969:106) in his role of tour guide and escort. She also allows him to be "a man" and to adopt a dominant role in the relationship, which is usually denied in encounters with local women. According to George: "You gotta to be tough when you dealing with these women. Not fight with nobody or nothing, but you gotta know what's going on around you, if you versatile with the language you pull women easy...." Another key informant maintains, "Them done know that we are kings. We are kings, creatures of the earth you understand. De white boys are more laid back and take de orders, de black boys now does give them de orders...."

In a postcolonial society where race, color, class, and status are very much intertwined, and with society having a predilection to accord status based on color, being seen with a white automatically accords her black companion some status within the local society (Lowenthal 1967, O'Connell Davidson 1996). If the analysis of Karch and Dann (1981) is accepted, these relationships give the black male an opportunity to act out his own fantasy of being a white man and having the power that whiteness brings. It echoes Fanon's analysis:

> Out of the blackest part of my soul, across the zebra striping of my mind, surges this desire to be suddenly white. I wish to be acknowledged not as black but as white.... Who but a white woman can do this for me? By loving me she proves that I am worthy of white love. I am loved like a white man. I am a white man (Fanon 1970:63).

Arguably this can be conceived as being true in this context, since many of the beach boys interviewed no longer have relations with local black women. The interracial encounters provide a context for the liberation of masculinities denied to them in encounters with Barbadian women. However, the point is noted that Barbadian women also refuse to have relations with those men who are labeled as hustlers. The hustlers also speak of Bajan women as having too much "pride," too much "attitude." The impression given is that in their new role, Bajan women are viewed as lacking in some respects when compared to the white female tourists who are viewed as more sexy, more adventurous, friendlier; a view that is in keeping with this still very racist postcolonial society.

The hustler's companion, in her hegemonic feminine role and her quest of the exotic Other, is not unlike her male counterpart and is able to construct a gender identity denied to her in her own country. She adopts the masculine role of economic provider yet also explores the traditional feminine role thrown off by the feminist movement. It allows her to explore these gender contradictions, playing both man and woman, in the center of the Other. She seeks out the quintessential male with his attributes of primitive sexuality and sexual prowess that is denied in the construction of the Western male, and in her new hegemonic role she has the power to do so in paradise—the stuff of romantic novels. As one informant argues, "It's a combination. It's the island. It's being away from England. It's the air, the warm blanket around you, the feeling of the balmy air on your skin and them coming along telling you how gorgeous you are...." In essence, these encounters present an arena where the Western female, although adopting some degree of the masculine role and hence having some measure of power, can enjoy the traditional role of femininity.

THE ROLE OF MIGRATION

Migration has been given very little focus in tourist-oriented prostitution in the Caribbean, with the exception of Press (1978) and Pruitt and LaFont (1994), where it was found that tourist-oriented prostitution allows the local "prostitute," by virtue of forming extended liaisons with the tourists, to emigrate to the "Center." Historically the Center has been perceived by the Other, in colonial and postcolonial ideology, to be "El Dorado"—a place of endless opportunities. These interracial encounters allow the beach hustler to fulfill this dream of endless opportunities in the context of limited available options within the host culture. Indeed, as articulated by Pruitt (1993:147), in the context of Jamaica, "hooking up" with a white woman becomes the passport to a better life. In Barbados a similar situation arises, where many of the beach hustlers speak of "the boys who get thru"—who have gone on to a better life—since "Barbados ain't got nothing to offer you." This becomes the ultimate goal for many, and those who are successful are admired by their peers.

A case in point is Trevor, who appears as the prime example to other beach hustlers. Trevor met a rich woman from Germany, whose family is in the construction business. Now he divides his time between Barbados and Germany and when he returns exhibits all the antics and symbols of a rich man, including a white Mercedes. Indeed, many of the guys interviewed spoke of spending a few weeks in the United States or Europe. They explain that "sometimes a guy might meet a woman who has got money, he can go up there and see what he can do to get an opportunity, because a guy wants a break."

CONCLUSION

Beach hustling in the Barbadian context is a social and economic activity that provides an opportunity for marginal young black men to "achieve some notoriety, if not self-esteem, in their home communities and male peer groups" (Press 1978:116). It provides the young black man with a forum in which his cultural definitions of masculinity are affirmed. It allows for successful negotiations of gender between himself and the female tourist. He is able to achieve status, material goods, and independence through a legitimate but wholly unconventional set of means in the context of the wider society. In fact he is quite adamant about the significant role he plays in the tourism industry and views beach hustling as "playing his part," sometimes more effectively than many others. The beach hustler embodies all the racial sexual stereotypes that the white emancipated woman has come in search of. Tourism allows the consummation, realization, and affirmation of these two gender identities within this paradise.

NOTES

1. The research was carried out over a period of six months in the latter part of 1997 and early parts of 1998 by the researcher and an assistant. The main techniques of investigation were observation, informal in-depth interviews, and focus groups. Observation was carried out at the main "pick-up sites," namely popular West Coast beaches and main tourist clubs. Respondents were selected on the basis of consent and were asked for the names of additional potential informants. Interviews were conducted with twenty beach boys and ten female tourists, the latter proving quite difficult to access. Three focus-group sessions were also conducted. Additional interviews were conducted with individuals who, though not engaged in tourist-oriented prostitution, could provide useful perspectives for understanding the phenomenon, e.g., hair braiders, security guards, and hotel workers.

The researchers recognize the existence of other types of prostitution, of which hustling of female tourists by young black males is just one type. Observation suggests that female club prostitutes as well as streetwalkers cater to male tourists as well as the local clientele. Further, female beach hustling, very much like its male counterpart, is also noted as specifically catering to white male tourists. The researchers also observed male homosexual hustling of male tourists. However, the focus of this study was intended to be the liaisons between black male Barbadians and white female tourists, thus male–male relationships were not subject to further examination.

2. To the extent that there are "transformed gendered" identities and contradictions of "conventional notions of male hegemony" on the part of the Jamaican males speaks to the ethnocentric bias held by the researchers with regard to theorizing of masculinity. Their tendency is to assume that the Western notion of hegemonic masculinity is the same in the context of working-class Jamaica. However, even with these limitations, the study does provide a useful frame of analysis from which to view other studies on male tourist-oriented prostitution in the region.

3. Any names mentioned in the text are pseudonyms owing to the guarantee of anonymity.

4. Barbadian term for a social gathering or for hanging out.

5. An exclusive nightclub in Barbados known somewhat for its racist policies.

6. A popular tourist club in Barbados.

7. Hustling or "cool pose" are responses to the young black man's alienation from the confining trappings of traditional masculinity (Pryce 1979, Majors 1986). The evidence suggests that hustling itself can connote any type of informal job activity, illegal or otherwise. Taken in this context, hustling and cool pose are cultural constructions of black masculinity, responses that concomitantly rise in direct relation to unemployment and economic hardship.

8. A very exclusive hotel on the west coast of the island.

9

Tourism and the Sex Trade in St. Maarten and Curaçao, the Netherlands Antilles

JACQUELINE MARTIS

The Netherlands Antilles consists of five islands with a total population of about 208,000. The islands are geographically separated into two groups: the windward islands of Saba, St. Eustatius, and St. Maarten, and the leeward islands of Bonaire and Curaçao. The distance between the windward and leeward islands is about 900 km. This chapter concerns research in two of the islands: Curaçao and St. Maarten.[1]

The majority of the populations in Curaçao and St. Maarten are of African descent with a mixed upper class consisting of descendants of European Protestants, Jews, Portuguese, and Africans. The Dutch colonized Curaçao in 1634 and the southern part of St. Maarten in 1648. In 1954 the Antilles became an autonomous member of the Kingdom of the Netherlands, whereby the group of islands in the Caribbean retain internal self-rule, and military and foreign affairs fall under authority of the Dutch government in the Netherlands. Due to this colonial relationship most of the laws and regulations governing the five islands are based on Dutch laws and regulations. Laws concerning prostitution are a reflection of the Dutch laws. In the Netherlands Antilles the act of prostitution is not illegal. Men and women sex workers are not prosecuted for practicing prostitution, but, instead, pimping, procuring, and other related third-party involvements are punishable by law.

CURAÇAO

Curaçao is the largest of the five islands of the Netherlands Antilles and is situated just off the coast of Venezuela. The total population of the island is around 152,700. The main pillars of the economy are the offshore companies, the oil refinery, and tourism. While tourism is not the main source of income for Curaçao, the island government has made it top priority, and it is seen in some sectors as the panacea for all the economic problems. The stay-over tourists for 1997 numbered around 208,900 and cruise tourists around 221,500.[2] The number of stay-over tourists has been steadily declining. Tourists who visit the island are mainly Europeans and Americans (1.5:1 ratio) and, to a lesser extent, Latin Americans and Caribbean nationals.[3]

Curaçao houses the largest legal brothel in the Netherlands Antilles: Campo Alegre (Happy Camp), or Le Mirage, as it is now called. This state-controlled sex house has rooms for about 100 sex workers. It is an enclosed complex situated on the outskirts of town close to the airport, consisting of an entertainment center—Le Mirage Gentleman's Club—a casino (a few slot machines), some bars, a kitchen, and restaurants. The brothel operates under a hotel licence as Campo Alegre (*Beurs-en Nieuwsberichten*, April 1998).

Several smaller hotels and pensions also profit from prostitution. They often rent rooms on either a long-term or short-term basis to prostitutes. Other smaller establishments also operate as illegal brothels or facilitate prostitution. Many of these function as dance clubs and "snacks" (little roadside eateries with beer licences) and smaller restaurants with bars. These snacks and bar-restaurants are spread all over the island, sometimes tucked away from view. They can be so well hidden or camouflaged that only those that belong to certain circles might know of them. Some provide sleeping areas for the workers, usually striptease dancers, while still others have shacks in the back where sexual exchanges can take place.

ST. MAARTEN

This island has the second largest population of the Dutch Antilles, numbering around 38,000, and is situated very close to the Dominican Republic. The French and the Dutch share the island. The main airport is situated on the Dutch side; consequently most tourists have to travel through the Dutch side of the island to get to the French side. There are no clear boundaries, and tourists and locals travel from one side to the other without restrictions. In St. Maarten, contrary to the situation in Curaçao, tourism is the number-one economic product. The total number of stay-over tourists and cruise-ship visitors was estimated at respectively 439,234 and 885,956 in 1997.[4] Tourists are predominantly from the United States and Canada, France, and other European countries, with a far smaller number originating from the Caribbean and Latin America.

St. Maarten is home to the second largest brothel in the Netherlands Antilles, the Seaman's Club. This club was established to service Japanese fishermen and sailors who arrived on the island in the 1960s to work in the fishing industry, hence it became known as the "Japanese Club." As the story goes, in the 1960s there were only a few thousand people living in St. Maarten when the fishing industry was first established. After the arrival of the Japanese fishermen on the island, babies soon were being born with "slanted" eyes. The community became worried and took action to protect women and girls from the fishermen (interview with the manager of the Seaman's Club). Apart from this club, several others operate legally as nightclubs and hotels and illegally as brothels. Prostitution is tolerated and accepted as necessary for tourism.

DOMINANT IDEOLOGIES ON PROSTITUTION

The government-controlled brothel Campo Alegre was established in 1949 in Curaçao as a way to control prostitution. Before its establishment, prostitution was seen to be taking place openly all over town and in other public places (Martins 1984). Many bars and brothels were operating in town as a result of Curaçao's position as a trading and transshipment port and the many visiting single male sailors and ships' crew members. Before 1949, measures had already been taken to regulate prostitution, such as mandatory registration of prostitutes, but these were considered to be insufficient. Prostitution, the government and the church believed, had to be centralized and controlled. It was considered a necessary step in order to protect the public (women and children) against the "physical and psychological consequences of an evil" (Kempadoo 1994:163). Prostitution was and still is considered a necessary evil.

When owners of bars and brothels, and men in general, are asked why prostitution is necessary, the first answer that is usually given is that men need sex. Institutionalizing prostitution was (is) tolerated because of the perception that it protects St. Maarten and Curaçaoan womanhood. According to several public officials, the dominant idea is that local women should be protected from being harassed or raped, having affairs, getting diseases or getting pregnant, and having babies with sailors, tourists, military personnel, and other (local) men. To protect local women and girls from men who need to relieve their "natural" sexual urges, foreign women are brought in by the club owners to work as prostitutes. Furthermore, it is argued by some that it also protects the family because the local man who visits a prostitute does so infrequently and does not form a steady relationship with her, as he could with an "outside" local woman.

In St. Maarten, a government representative voiced his support for the existence of facilities (brothels) for (foreign) men. He too was convinced that this was to protect local women and girls. He also argued that prostitution needed to be controlled and monitored because it was a breeding ground for disease. Representatives of both island governments indicated that the problem of prostitution has the attention of the government and they are making plans and policies to deal with this issue. In Curaçao, most recently, there have been several demands to the Lieutenant Governor to assist in moving prostitution off the streets in order to protect public morals and decency. The demands were for more regulation and control and not necessarily for complete elimination of prostitution (interviews with police officials).

Some of the male respondents in this study viewed prostitution as a necessary evil. For them, prostitution provides physical release and has nothing to do with love, emotions, or commitment. Regulated prostitution, according to their view, means less disease, but they also admitted that in 1998, nonregulated prostitution was in greater demand.

The view held by men contrasts with that held by many women. In 1996 a seminar called "Prostitution Seen through the Eyes of Dutch Antillian Women" was held in St. Maarten. During the conference the St. Maarten Women's Steering Committee emphatically denounced prostitution and asked for more control to be taken on the issues and stricter immigration laws implemented. According to the steering committee, "St. Maarten has been invaded by prostitution from foreign lands such as Santo Domingo, Colombia, Haiti, Jamaica, Guyana, Trinidad..." and this needed to be halted.[5] The general sentiment at the seminar was one of concern for the decaying morality, spread of disease, and loss of family life because of prostitution.

SOME SPECIFIC GOVERNMENT LAWS
AND REGULATIONS FOR PROSTITUTION

Prostitution is regulated and institutionalized in the Netherlands Antilles. This system permits prostitution to take place within government-controlled institutions and allows registered sex workers to work as prostitutes in other areas. Local women, for example, may not work in Campo Alegre as prostitutes; thus they are allowed to practice their profession in their homes, hotels, bars, and other sites outside of the government-controlled areas. Foreign registered prostitutes can obtain a work permit for up to three months and must undergo weekly medical checkups to ensure that they are disease free (interviews with medical doctors).

There are designated areas where prostitution can take place openly—government-controlled brothels—as well as hotels (*pensions*), where organized or individual acts of prostitution take place. Any person, male or female, caught prostituting can be picked up by the police and not released until they are registered as a prostitute with the Vice and Morals Police Department and are medically checked for sexually transmitted diseases. A consequence of this process is that they are issued a pink card which acts simultaneously as a working licence and health record. From that point on they have to be regularly checked by a government-appointed doctor and are defined in public records as a prostitute (interviews with KZP officers).

Due to a shortage of police manpower, however, and the fact that a person caught publicly prostituting does not go to jail, there exists a permissive attitude among the police toward streetwalking and other forms of prostitution. The police will pick up persons prostituting if they think that they are on the island illegally but not necessarily because they were prostituting (*Ultimo Noticia*, October 20, 1998). No one has been prosecuted in the last forty-odd years for pimping or procuring in the Netherlands Antilles. It seems to be very difficult to prove that bars, striptease clubs and snacks are operating as brothels. For example, in Curaçao there is a well-known lower-class hotel and nightclub in town where prostitution takes place openly. Ironically, the police cannot arrest the owners of the hotel and nightclub and charge them with pimping because it cannot be proven that they are facilitating prostitution. The nightclub functions as the pickup site, and rooms can be rented at the hotel next door. The women usually stay at several hotels and pensions in the vicinity and charge their clients the rent of the rooms. The owners of this nightclub claim that the women operate on their own and that they do not know what goes on behind closed doors (interview with a police officer).

THE ORGANIZATION OF PROSTITUTION

The Streets

In Curaçao, streetwalking is predominantly done by nonlicenced sex workers. Most of the streetwalkers observed were drug addicts who lived out on the streets or in *chollhouses*[6] or those who had homes but went out to prostitute occasionally when the need arose. Streetwalking is also very common among young girls who prostitute and homosexuals. There are specific areas where young female and male prostitutes hang out and pick up customers. Also known to work the streets, especially in town, are undocumented Haitian and Dominican women.

In St. Maarten, not much streetwalking was observed, although it is also practiced there. With the increasing number of drug addicts who live out in the streets or in drughouses, it is generally expected that the number of streetwalkers will increase.

"Snacks"

Snacks on both islands employ predominantly Dominican women. These establishments are little food tents, usually situated along the roads, that sell snacks rather than entire meals and have beer licences. They are not allowed to sell hard liquor, although many of them do. In Curaçao, snacks are licenced to stay open until 11:00 P.M., but many stay open later. Snacks are a cultural phenomenon, where during the day anyone (men and women) stop to get refreshments or something light to eat. It is another story at night. After work and at night these snacks are invaded by men who go to relax, have a beer, and maybe play dominoes before going home. Lately, however, dancing the *Bachata*[7] has become an added attraction at the snacks. During the weekends, for example, you can hear the sound of Bachata and Merengue and see men dancing with the women who work in the snacks. The women who work in these snacks are usually very scantily or provocatively dressed to attract attention from the men. As one man put it, "The women are the reason we go to snacks. If I was to be served by a man I wouldn't want to go there."

At most snacks it seems that sex work is voluntary. The women might not be forced to prostitute, but both the owners and clients expect it. Some of these snacks are actually illegal brothels fronting as snacks. They might have little shacks in the back where the women live and work. Some snacks advertise explicitly for "Nice-looking Latin women. Antillian women need not apply." There are numerous legal and illegal snacks on both islands.

Bars/Dancing Halls/*Hofis*[8]

Women who work in the bars that function as dancing halls are hostesses who have to entertain the clients. Their work includes dancing with the clients, enticing them to buy drinks, generally showing them a good time and making them spend money. Several respondents indicated that some of the women might be forced also to have sex with the clients, depending on the owner and the job conditions. In one instance, five Colombian women took the owner of the club where they worked to court because he was forcing them to prostitute themselves. In the majority of the bars—as in the snacks—prostitution might not be forced on the women directly, but they know that if they want to make money they will have to sleep with the clients of the establishments.

Some of the women working in these locations are married to Antillian men, some are on the island illegally, and still others might be legal residents. The wages in most of these bars are very low, and thus women feel compelled to solicit clients in order to earn a decent living.

Strip Clubs

The latest trend on both Curaçao and St. Maarten is the striptease club, which is permitted to provide night entertainment. The permit allows the owners to import a certain number of international dancers to give shows. In Curaçao there are four or five such striptease clubs where dancers are brought in from different countries to work. A few of the clubs work exclusively with women from one country, such as the Dominican Republic or Colombia. Still others like to vary what they offer their clients. A newly established club (a bar without a permit to bring in dancers) has arranged for women from countries such as Venezuela and the Netherlands to travel to the island to give shows at the club. A major difference between clubs in St. Maarten and Curaçao seems to be the fact that in St. Maarten black Caribbean women from countries like Guyana, Jamaica, and Trinidad are also in favor, whereas in Curaçao light-skinned Latin women are preferred.

Brothels

The two government-controlled brothels are family owned and managed. Women must apply and go through a selection procedure to be admitted to these brothels. The women usually know that they will be doing sex work but are not always aware of the conditions under which they will be working (interviews with sex workers; see also Kempadoo 1998). Campo Alegre in Curaçao has, however, been steadily declining over the years. By 1997, the compound had deteriorated to such an extent that the living conditions for the women were below standard and the clients preferred to visit places where the women were better cared for and had more class. According to police informants, both clients and sex workers protested against the situation. The men started looking elsewhere for entertainment in nicer surroundings. Foreign men also complained that the women who worked there were not as nice as they used to be and demanded some variety. Forced by competition and the government, Campo Alegre was undergoing some major changes in 1998. The area was being cleaned up, the rooms renovated, and air-conditioning added. Italian ceramic tiles and other amenities were being added to some rooms. These new rooms would cost more than the old rooms, and it was suggested that they would be reserved for a better class of women, possibly from Brazil and the Netherlands (interview with male worker/"guide" at Campo Alegre). Another way of attracting clients has become the "live shows." During these shows women strip and use sex toys and other objects—including whiskey bottles (interview with a client). Men are invited or challenged to have sex with the women on stage, in front of the audience. If a man plucks up the courage and performs, he is rewarded with cash (interviews with several clients). The women, on the other hand, are offered free lodging for a specific time for their participation in the live sex shows.

The Seaman's Club in St. Maarten houses up to eighteen women at a time. In comparison Campo Alegre has room for about 100 women. The atmosphere at the Seaman's Club seems, however, less formal and warmer. At this brothel, professional dancers are often contracted, as striptease shows are part of the whole appeal. Recently, brothels and strip clubs in St. Maarten have been placing ads with explicit photographs in newspapers and entertainment bulletins, in which they invite men to visit and enjoy the "For Men Only" shows.

Other Arrangements

Apart from the prostitution activities described earlier, other forms of prostitution exist. For example, in St. Maarten there is an escort service that employs young males and females who will date and let their clients have a good time while on the island for fees ranging from U.S.$150 an hour to U.S.$500 for the whole evening. This escort service, run by a European man, seems well organized and advertises in newspapers and other places. Another form of prostitution is "sponsoring." This involves local women and girls who have relationships with usually older men who pay for their company. Most of these women and girls would not consider what they are doing prostitution. A pervasive attitude exists on the islands, particularly among young people, that sex is not a big deal and that it can and should be used to get what one needs, such as nice clothes and shoes for a party, or drugs. There are numerous pickup sites for these types of liaisons, such as parties and discos. Finally, there is the *kas di biaha,* a privately owned house or apartment where the sex worker (male or female) or the client can rent a room.

TOURISM AND PROSTITUTION

The relationship between tourism and prostitution is clearly visible on both Curaçao and St. Maarten, although in Curaçao, prostitution depends mostly on local men. Tourism is the most important economic product for St. Maarten. Most of the island revenues are from tourism and related services (CBS 1997). Attracting tourists to the island and catering to their needs is, of course, of utmost importance if the island is to survive economically.

Several categories of tourist visit St. Maarten regularly: those who arrive on private yachts and boats as well as their crews; cruise-ship tourists and crews; the crew of U.S. and Dutch Navy ships; stay-over tourists, who average around ten days stay on the island; suitcase traders (St. Maarten is a duty-free port); visiting nationals—St. Maarteners and other Antillians; businessmen; and Dutch technical assistants. All these categories, except the suitcase traders, represent the client base for the sex trade in St. Maarten. The suitcase traders make up a special category because most are women and it is known that some of them also engage in prostitution while in St. Maarten.

In 1996 St. Maarten became the homeport for a U.S. Navy ship that docks at the port every three months and stays for about a week. The crew of this ship consists of between 4,000 and 5,000 men (and some women). It is accepted and expected that the sailors need entertainment and release of their physical needs, and the brothels and bars overflow with customers. The demand for sex workers is so great that more women are flown in during the week the ship stays in port. One sex worker interviewed in St. Maarten explained that since she was new she had not previously known about the navy ship. Other women had told her that the time to make money was when the ship was in port, and she was planning to return to St. Maarten to work whenever the ship came back to St. Maarten.

There are somewhat mixed feelings about the economic impact of this navy ship. One striptease club owner said that he did not make that much money from the sailors: "They have no money and bring their own alcohol, so I don't make that much from them." The women on the other hand claim to make money and to have quite a few more clients than usual. Still another brothel owner said that he made three times the amount of money he normally makes at the bar. The Commissioner of Tourism calculates that the navy personnel spend around U.S.$1,000,000 on each visit.

For a small island, St. Maarten has an impressive number of bars, snacks, and striptease nightclubs. Officially there are around forty snacks and thirty-two bars, not counting bar-restaurants. The number of official striptease nightclubs was, at the time of the study, five. These strip clubs and brothels operate under a hotel permit and are allowed to rent rooms to women who come to the island to work in the sex trade. According to the St. Maarten Women's Steering Committee (at a conference about prostitution held in St. Maarten in 1996), "They [prostitutes] have sprung up like mushrooms in all areas and are not controlled. You will find some in apartments, in bars, guest houses, and clubs...."

Authorities tolerate much of the prostituting or the so-called entertainment activities that take place illegally. They feel that something must be done but do not really know what. It is considered that tourists need and expect entertainment and should be given, whenever possible, what they want. One government official readily admits that St. Maarten has a good reputation among sex workers—they want to travel to the island to work because they make "good money." According to the St. Maarten Tourism Office and the Commissioner of Tourism, sex tourism is not organized or promoted in St. Maarten, but they acknowledge that it does exist. The Commissioner of Health, Women's, and Social Affairs also credits male migrant workers for the high demand for prostitutes. The boom in construction brought men from all over the Caribbean to St. Maarten to work. The men did not migrate with their families and, according to the commissioner, this created a need that was filled by prostitutes.

On Curaçao, tourism is widely seen as the activity that will save the economy—it is considered essential and very desirable. Consequently, a lot of economic resources are allocated to the development of the tourist industry. The same categories of tourists that serve as the client base in St. Maarten for prostitution are also present in Curaçao. There are however some differences worth mentioning. As was stated earlier, the tourists that visit St. Maarten far outnumber those that visit Curaçao, but Curaçao has some additional client categories. There are men who are attached to the tanking and transshipment industry located in the vicinity of the deep-water harbor. Curaçao also possesses a dry-dock, which is a significant source of revenue for the island; numerous ships with their crews go to the island for repairs. The Venezuelan boats that serve the floating market selling fruit and vegetables also provide a group of clients. As in St. Maarten, suitcase traders—predominantly women—travel to the island to shop at the Free Zone, some of whom engage in sex work to complement their income or use suitcase trading as a cover for sex work (interview with a police official; see also Kempadoo 1994).

SPECIFIC CONDITIONS

Any man or woman who works as a prostitute on the islands must be registered with the authorities and undergo regular medical checkups. Formerly, both foreign and local women were registered as prostitutes. According to a police officer, very few locals were being registered in 1998. Most worked clandestinely, primarily in nightclubs or on the streets. It would seem that most of the locals involved in the sex trade work individually or in small groups. The most noticeable group of locals is comprised of drug addicts who walk the street and homosexual prostitutes. Others are more discreet. They might work the nightspots, clubs, and bars, or hook up with a short-stay tourist. However, these forms are not very visible. What is noticeable are the women who become involved with technical assistants and consultants from the Netherlands who are on the islands for a designated period. It appears that the local person involved in this kind of sex work does not consider the activity as prostitution and would not admit to prostituting. Also, local prostitution seems to be geared toward longer term "relationships of convenience."

The number of bars and clubs outside the legal brothels that bring female dancers to entertain male clients is growing steadily on both the islands. Apart from these establishments, many snacks and bar-restaurants employ hostesses whose job it is to entertain clients; part of the entertainment is to dance with them. The music of choice in the snacks and bars is Bachata, in which (according to one informant) any sexual message can be insinuated. The Merengue and other Latin music can also be heard, but it was the Bachata that was the rage in 1998.

The situation is different at the striptease clubs. The music depends on where the dancers are from and whatever is considered highly sensual. In one club in Curaçao, for example, the women were from the Dominican Republic and danced and lip-synced to Latin music. In St. Maarten there is more diversity in the type of women that they employ as dancers. The women come from several of the English-speaking Caribbean countries and cover a range of skin colors, hair types, and body shapes. Each of the five bar-clubs in St. Maarten that have permits can bring in up to ten women at a time for up to a month. The bar-club owners have to apply for the women's work permits and pay NAf.800 (U.S.$420) per dancer. There has been a lot of protest on the part of the stripclub owners against the fee.

MAIN REASONS WOMEN, MEN, BOYS, AND GIRLS ENTER SEX WORK

The women interviewed were all the caretakers of their families, which could include ailing parents, children, and sometimes husbands. Some were very well educated but could not get a decent paying job in their countries. They had heard about the money they could make in St. Maarten or Curaçao and decided to give it a try. In a lot of cases they turned to prostitution as a last resort. They needed to take care of their families, and although the families did not know what they were doing, they were willing to risk it.[9]

The reasons the men gave for starting in this line of work were also economic, but whereas the women were willing to sacrifice for their families, the men did not mention this factor. They said that they wanted to get ahead in life, hoping they could hook up with a woman who would take care of them and take them away from the island.

These heterosexual men wanted to think of themselves as having a romantic liaison, not as prostituting. One man, however, did acknowledge that what he was doing was prostituting and referred to himself and other males like himself, as "players." They may accept cash, depending on how professional they are. Hotel workers, for example, who come into contact with tourists may develop a relationship in the hotel; they may fix the tourist up with another person, or they function as guides and sometimes get involved with the tourists in that way. They do not necessarily receive cash but are taken to restaurants, clubs, and other places and are given clothes and other gifts. The professional players expect and are given cash in addition to the other gifts. The men on St. Maarten want to get ahead in life and view North American women tourists as a ticket to their "American dream." In Curaçao, the tendency is for the men to pick up Dutch women.

COERCION AND TRAFFICKING

Most of the women working openly in the sex trade in Curaçao and St. Maarten are foreigners, women who are in many cases desperate about their economic situation and have to leave their countries to try to better their situation. Some of these women knowingly enter the sex trade in the Netherlands Antilles, others are coerced. Coercion takes on different forms. There have been reports of women who marry Antillians and are then forced into the sex trade by their husbands. Others are enticed to come to the Netherlands Antilles with offers of well-paying jobs in the hotel industry or offers of domestics jobs. Very few cases of coercion have come to light in Curaçao but, in 1996, in what can be seen as a landmark case, five Colombian women took their employer to court and won.[10]

The five Colombian women were recruited in Colombia by a woman to go to Curaçao to work in the hotel industry as waitresses. The women declared in court that they were misled and ended up working in a nightclub as waitresses, having to entertain clients against their will. They lodged a number of complaints:

a) They were promised U.S.$700, but got considerably less than this from the club owners.
b) They were forced to hand over their passports (a common and illegal practise on both the islands).
c) They were paid NAf.200 (U.S.$110) per month, from which their airfare to Curaçao would be discounted (NAf.446/U.S.$246).
d) They were given no days off because they did not have to work in the mornings. Working hours were: Monday through Friday from 3:00 P.M. to 11:00 P.M., Saturdays and Sundays 11:00 A.M. to 12:00 midnight. Some nights they worked until 1:00 or 2:00 in the morning.
e) They had the right to only one meal a day, and if they wanted more would have to ask their clients for food.

f) The way they could get more money was to drink with the nightclub clients and to have sex with the men, using the condoms that the owners sold to them.

g) They had to dress provocatively and sexily and had to permit the men to touch and fondle them.

h) They would have to become friends with the men and ask these so-called friends to pay for their ticket back home.

i) They were not allowed access to a phone to either make or receive calls from their families.

The case went to court and the women won back payment of their salaries. Interestingly, no case was made against the employer for coercion or anything else having to do with prostitution.

Although one other case has been filed against an owner of a strip club for mistreatment, several of the conditions listed above are experienced by women working in many of the other better brothels, bars, and clubs. The most common is that their passports are taken away from them upon arrival on the islands, and the women do not know that they have to pay for their tickets and, in many cases, for their dancing permits if they are on the island illegally (interviews with bar owners and sex workers). The women are sometimes also harassed by bar owners and their friends and clients (interview with various informants). They may be subjected to rape and other acts of violence and cannot escape or leave because they do not have their passports or any money. Some women have been able to get away through becoming friends with a client, who then becomes their "protector." In general, the owners of bars and brothels hold a lot of power over the women, and interviews with the women and clients give the impression that the women are treated badly by their employers. In some instances the employer is the one who becomes their protector (interview with the manager of the Seaman's Club).

Another situation is that it appears that many of the women recruited as dancers think that they only have to dance in skimpy outfits or to take off their bras. However, deduction of money for not taking off all their clothes while dancing or for not having sex with clients is not uncommon (according to a frequent club visitor). Some also must pay a penalty from $35 to $200, for leaving the premises at night with clients.

CONCLUSION

The sex trade in the Netherlands Antilles is characterized as permissive and it is seen on the one hand as a necessary evil and on the other as a way to make a living. Both men and women are active in the sex trade, in hetero-sexual and homosexual liaisons. No proof could be found of lesbian prosti-tution, although it was rumored to be occurring more frequently. The link between tourism and the sex trade could clearly be seen on both islands, al-though prostitution takes different forms according to whether it was regu-lated or not.

In St. Maarten it was evident that most, if not all, the female and most of the male sex workers were foreigners. The women were on the island with or without a permit, while the men usually worked in the hotel sector. The women went for work in order to send money home to take care of their families, and most worked in a brothel, bar, or other spot frequented by men. The men were usually younger and worked independently, although they also would set up other players and women they knew with clients.

Both islands permit, and even invite, sex workers to work. The islands have good reputations as places where women can earn money as prosti-tutes or can get married and move on to other places such as the United States or Europe. These women and men are willing to risk being caught and deported.

The government indirectly profits from prostitution in various ways, among them from the revenue generated from the permits for dancers, taxes on hotels, and sales tax on clothing and other goods purchased by sex workers. Although there are many similarities between the two islands, St. Maarten has a more open attitude toward prostitution and also embraces di-versity among sex workers.

NOTES

1. To gather information for this study, interviews were held with key informants and sex workers; observation at dance clubs, snacks, and other sites was conducted; and a review of available literature was made. Around sixty interviews were held on both the islands with people who were directly or indirectly involved in the sex trade; people who had contact with persons involved in the sex trade such as brothel/danceclub owners, clients, and professionals who came in contact with sex workers because of their jobs, i.e., doctors, nurses, taxi drivers and the police; and members of the general public who had an opinion on the subject. A lot of time was dedicated to visiting (night) spots where trade in sex took place. These included snacks where women worked, dance (strip) clubs, brothels, discos and bars where (especially) male sex workers worked. Difficulties encountered were mostly related to the fact that the subject is not easily broached and that certain aspects of the trade are illicit. Sex workers were usually foreign women and men who were on the is-lands in an undocumented status or had a permit to stay but worked illegally. An-other constraint was the fact that there was the threat of physical violence against the women sex workers if they were thought by the brothel keepers to be divulging too

much information. This severely limited the number of female sex workers I could, in all good conscience, interview.

2. Figures from the Central Bureau for Statistics (CBS) for 1997.

3. According to the CBS for 1996.

4. CBS statistics for 1997. These figures, while showing an increase in numbers of stay-over tourists since 1996, are still well below the figures from 1994. In 1995 Hurricane Luis crippled the tourism industry on the island, destroying many of the larger hotels.

5. From a paper presented at the St. Maarten Women's Steering Committee conference, 1996.

6. An abandoned house used by drug addicts.

7. A type of popular, highly sensual, erotic music, originating from the rural areas of the Dominican Republic.

8. Open-air, fenced spaces, usually with a bar, that can be found scattered around the island outside the city limits, where parties, dances, and other social gatherings are held.

9. This situation appears to exist for women involved in the sex trade in various places in the world. See, for example, Wijers and Lap Chew (1997).

10. From the original court proceedings.

10

The *Muchachas* of Orange Walk Town, Belize

A. KATHLEEN RAGSDALE AND JESSICA TOMIKO ANDERS

Belize, located on the Caribbean coast of Central America, is a country of many ethnicities, languages, and cultural norms and practices, which sometimes fuse, sometimes exist with little tension, and sometimes seem to be in direct conflict (Klein 1986, Moberg 1997, Shoman 1994). Shoman writes that these frictions are "a creative force of conflict that gradually creates a new, hybrid reality." Belize Creole culture was born out of the interaction and accommodation between the British and African cultural traditions: "The British had the institutional power and were able, to some extent, to use it to impose their worldview, but they could not determine the nature of popular cultural expressions" (Shoman 1994:142). Even after colonialism's end, Belize continues to struggle with identity formation as an agent of empowerment for racial, ethnic, and national identity that can offer an alternative to the predictions of global homogenization (Macklin 1993:171). This is important for several reasons.

With an estimated population of 200,000 persons, Belize is a small country when compared to its neighbors, Mexico and Guatemala. Belize continues to have a long-standing national border conflict with Guatemala. It achieved political independence from Great Britain in 1981 and has prioritized the ongoing process of creating a unifying sense of nationhood since that time. Finally, the country is negotiating Belizean identity while being bombarded with North American cultural media and commodities, primarily in the form of television programs and fashion, as well as a growing population of Mestizo and Mayan economic migrants and political refugees, which increase ethnic and cultural tension (Hegstrom and Mohan 1998). Belize is a nation of mixed ethnicity with strong Afro-Caribbean, Central American, European, Garifuna, and East Indian influences. While the official language is

English, most inhabitants primarily use Belizean Creole and/or Spanish in their daily lives. Dialects of Garifuna, Mayan, East Indian, and Chinese are also spoken and mirror the country's rich cultural diversity.[1]

Reflecting the global trend, Latin American and Caribbean female international migration is on the rise, as the historical pattern of male-led migration is being replaced by female-led family chain migration (Campani 1995, Simmons and Guengant 1992). Many Central American women who migrate to Belize in the hope of improving their economic condition become temporary sex workers to make ends meet and send remittances home (see also Kempadoo 1996 and 1998, Margolis 1994).

Little research has been done in Belize on sex workers and their lives until quite recently. A Department of Women's Affairs publication, *From Girls to Women: Growing Up Healthy in Belize* (1997), gives only three short paragraphs to health issues linked with sex work. What is known about sex work in Belize is primarily confined to Kane's research in Belize in 1990 on the British military and their AIDS intervention programs (Kane 1993 and 1998). Our research supports Kane's findings that both undocumented immigrant women from neighboring countries and Belizean women were involved in sex work when the British military was a strong presence in the country. We were, however, informed that almost all participating Belizean women left the sex trade when the British military left the country.

Through qualitative data collection, we explore here the conditions confronted by women in Belizean society who are affected as sex workers. The research includes but is not limited to issues of sexual violence, social stigmatization, and condom usage among participants in our study. The importance of these issues in developing a better understanding of the situation of sex workers in Belize is clear. Whether women are involved in "elite" forms of sex work, such as escort services (Plachy and Ridgeway 1996), or in the "survival sex" (Raffaelli et al. 1993) of street sex work, they tend to share some characteristics. These include becoming involved in sex work in their teens, having little knowledge of their legal rights, a tendency toward economic marginalization, exposure to physical violence, the risk of increased exposure to the AIDS virus through sex partners' insistence on unsafe sex practices, and heightened social marginalization due to their mode of earning a living. In addition, women whom we interviewed in Belize are, by and large, participating in sex work as a short-term adaptation to conditions of economic need and the lack of adequate employment in their own country.

Unsafe sex practices and sex work are often considered to be strongly connected. The transmission rate of the AIDS virus from infected men to a female partner is estimated at one in three sexual contacts. The estimated female-to-male transmission rate is one in fifty contacts (Sacks 1996:61). Yet it is women—and especially sex workers—who have historically been stereo-typed and penalized as disease vectors for male "victims" who fall prey to "un-natural" women's sexual appetites (Hunt 1996, Kane 1998, Kutzinski 1993, Sacks 1996). A major concern of governmental and non-governmental organ-izations who develop and administer health policies is the so-called "complic-ity" of sex workers in the spread of AIDS (Gil et al. 1996, Kane 1993, Maticka-Tyndale et al. 1997, Sacks 1996), although the occupational hazards to health that female sex workers face are of less concern in the public consciousness.

In addition to increased exposure to STDs, sex work has other occupa-tional hazards that are unique to the intimacy of the transaction. While sex workers desire the use of condoms within the client relationship, they can be at a social and economic disadvantage to insist on compliance with safer sex practices (Kane 1993, Plachy and Ridgeway 1996, Sacks 1996). Health and personal safety risks are also heightened because sex workers are asked to perform "deviant" sexual acts, i.e., acts that their clients' wives and girl-friends will not perform, such as oral or anal sex and acts of bondage (Plachy and Ridgeway 1996, Wolf 1997). Yet the health risks posed to sex workers are often ignored by governmental and non-governmental organi-zations designing STD-intervention programs (Kane 1993, Sacks 1996). Other occupational hazards for sex workers include sexual and economic exploitation by another (including clients, procurers, brothel owners, and governmental officials) as well as increased risk of sexual violence (Kane 1998). A heightened awareness of violence against women is increasingly important in the Belizean national consciousness and has positively im-pacted social policy toward domestic violence (Government of Belize 1995, McClaurin 1996, SPEAR 1993). But our research finds that the legal and so-cial protections afforded women who are identified as sex workers within Belizean culture are quite limited.

Despite the emerging importance of the tourism industry in Belize, there is little research to suggest that Belize has experienced a rise in sex work in conjunction with increased tourism. This contradicts the available literature on the links between the promotion of tourism within a country and an in-crease in sex tourism. It suggests that sex work is either invisible or not as pervasive within Belize as other research on global tourism and the sex trade have indicated.

ORANGE WALK TOWN: "GIRLS DEM SUGA"

The town of Orange Walk is located in Orange Walk District, sixty-six miles from Belize City on the Northern Highway, which runs through the heart of this large town. It is one of the largest communities in Belize, with a population of approximately 10,000 inhabitants. Originally settled by refugees from the Yucatan Caste Wars in the late 1800s, Orange Walk retains a strong Mestizo cultural heritage. Spanish language and culture predominate in the area, augmented by a constant infusion of economic immigrants from the surrounding countries of Guatemala, Honduras, and El Salvador.

The agricultural sector leads the country in employment, production, and export. Sugar, citrus, and bananas are the primary crops. Sugar production contributes almost 50 percent to Belize's agricultural sector, followed by citrus and banana production, and agriculture provides an estimated 40 percent of employment (Neal 1993). Unlike many of the highly concentrated sugar-production systems found in Latin America and the Caribbean, the Belizean system consists of about 5,000 small farm holdings that produce the entire sugar crop. Farmers raise and cut the sugarcane, which is loaded onto the trucks of independent haulers and taken to the Belize Sugar Industries processing plant, located on the Northern Highway between Belize City and Orange Walk. According to the participants in our study, it is these haulers who are the primary clients for commercial sex in Orange Walk.

We interviewed thirty-five *muchachas* (female sex workers) during the month we lived in Orange Walk Town.[2] With the exception of one, all the women we spoke with were immigrant women from Guatemala, Honduras, or El Salvador. We interviewed only one Belizean who worked in a bar in Orange Walk. She was adamant that she was not a sex worker but only served drinks to customers visiting the bar.

While Mestizos predominate in Orange Walk, there is a sizable population of Creoles who live in the town and surrounding countryside. On the streets of the town and in the central plaza, the blonde-haired, blue-eyed Mennonites who maintain farms near Orange Walk are also numerous. By choice, Mennonites are only partially integrated into Belizean society and live in their relatively isolated large farming communities in the countryside surrounding Orange Walk. The striking phenotypic differences between most residents of the town and the Mennonites are reinforced by language usage, dress code, and mannerisms.

Though Mennonite men usually speak some Creole and/or Spanish in addition to the archaic German dialect of their community founders, the women are more socially isolated due to a lack of Spanish or Creole language skills. Mennonite farming communities specialize in dairy, poultry, and egg production. At the same time that they are economically integrated into Belizean culture, they remain distinctly separate in most ways, and social interaction with non-Mennonites is kept at a minimum. Nevertheless, many of the sex workers interviewed in Orange Walk report that they are solicited for sex by Mennonite men who come to the local bars.

THE MUCHACHAS

Paola, a muchacha[3] at the Hibiscus Bar, is small and plump. Her straight, glossy black hair falls to her shoulders around a beautiful face. She gives her age as eighteen years, though she looks much younger despite the heavy application of mascara and deep red lipstick. Born and raised in El Salvador, Paola was a sex worker in Guatemala before coming to Orange Walk Town nine months ago to reap the greater financial benefits of the Belizean economy. She plans to return "to get married in Salvador" in a year and thinks she'd like to start a family in two years. Paola is very relaxed and friendly as she sits and chats with us and Mr. Romero, a Ministry of Health worker. Already showered and ready for the day, she is wearing a chartreuse-green stretch top printed with a design of large white hearts and a short skirt of royal blue with white stripes that zips up the front. Her flat, black patent leather sandals are decorated with shiny white daisies. It is about 10:00 A.M. and we are seated at a small table in the now-empty bar. The Hibiscus, a large room that is approximately thirty-by-fifty feet and painted pale blue, will open for customers at 11:00 A.M. Smudge marks of grime mar the walls, giving the bar a patina of disrepair. There is a nice stage of varnished wood set against the far wall. Its acoustics are fashioned from egg cartons painted in blocks of neon orange, blue, pink, and black and arranged in a checkerboard pattern on the back wall.

The Hibiscus has twelve tables, each covered with a blue plastic tablecloth. The chairs are varnished wood, sturdy and well made. A small bar is at the far end of the room, opposite the double doors that open into the large room. On the wall behind the bar is a typical assortment of liquors, including the local rums. There are also small displays of canned snacks for the customers. Long strips of white plastic fringe line the front of each shelf and flutter in the small breeze from the open windows. Two other muchachas sit at the bar's counter on high stools. One young woman is absorbed in doing a book of children's crossword puzzles while the other listens to a Spanish-language *telenovela* that blares from the TV above the bar. As other young women pass the bar on their way to and from the shower room (located outside in a separate building) they stop to watch a bit of the drama and romance unfolding on the TV screen overhead. Paola, too, occasionally glances up at the telenovela as she talks with us, but her attention becomes focused when we begin to talk about her use of alcohol. We ask Paola if her clients want her to drink with them and she responds, "Yes, but it is hard on my body to drink so much." While many of the women we interviewed report that they rarely drink on the job, Paola thinks that she might have a drinking problem related to her work. She uses alcohol to make her feel better about doing sex work because, as she says, "I feel in my heart that it is not right." Paola does not use drugs recreationally but acknowledges that alcohol is becoming a problem for her because, "When I drink I feel fine about my work, but when I don't it is not so good."

Like most of the young women performing sex work in Orange Walk Town, it is very important to Paola to keep her occupation unknown to her family and friends, because sex work is highly stigmatized within her social group. In the *La Sala* project with sex workers in Costa Rica, researchers Van Wijk and Barboza find that sex workers "share a constant fear of being discovered, which creates very stressful situations when they run into an acquaintance or a family member near or in their place of work" (1997:106). That sex workers internalize the negative ideology of society toward sex work seemed to be supported by many of the comments made by the women performing this labor in Orange Walk. Paola tells us that her family does not know how she earns her income. She says, "Only my brother knows, because when he was in Guatemala he saw me [at the bar where she worked] when he was going out and figured it out." Paola believes that if her family knew the source of the remittances she sends home to support her mother and younger sister they would not accept them. Further, she feels that if her male friends found out about her occupation, "They would lose respect for me and harass me and want free sex from me," which she says as she pantomimes reaching out as if to touch someone's buttocks.

ATTITUDES TOWARD SEXUALITY

Another finding in the La Sala project is that female sex workers are negatively stereotyped as "indecent, over-sexed, foul-mouthed drug addicts, husband-stealers and bad mothers, who are unable to be friends and who transmit venereal diseases and AIDS" (Van Wijk and Barboza 1997:105), stereotypes reiterated in the work of Tannahill (1992) and discussed and even challenged by other scholars (see Chapkis 1997, Hunt 1996, Kutzinski 1993, Plachy and Ridgeway 1996, Wolf 1997). The internalization of negative sex-worker stereotypes can leave little room for job satisfaction and the self-esteem boost that usually comes from being able to financially support oneself and family members.

Our research uncovered an indicator that suggests that the sex workers of Orange Walk Town, like the women who participated in the La Sala project, have internalized negative social ideology regarding sex work. When asked the question, "How do you feel about this work?" every one of our thirty-five respondents voiced a negative reaction to participating in sex work. Lupe's answer to our question is a typical one. She is a twenty-three-year-old from Guatemala and a mother of three children who are being cared for by relatives in her country of origin. Lupe has been a sex worker for about one year and uses her earnings to support her children. Lupe states, "I am not so contented with this kind of work. I would like to drink only [participate in the *ficha* system] and get money that way. I don't like to go to the room, but do it because of my need." Ficha is the term used to describe how a muchacha earns commissions on the drinks that a client buys for her. Essentially, the woman generates income for the bar and herself by only socializing with bar patrons in lieu of having sexual relations with them. Among our participants, ficha is universally preferred over having sex with a client. In reality, however, ficha does not generate enough income and so eventually most of the women perform sex work to support themselves and their families.

STD PREVENTION

Since 1995, when the walk-in clinic for STDs was discontinued, Mr. Romero and other Ministry of Health officials have attended to the health needs of sex workers by visiting their places of residence. According to Mr. Romero, part of official health outreach includes STD-prevention workshops, which are held each month or so at alternating bars in Orange Walk Town. We were invited to attend one such workshop during our stay in Orange Walk. At this two-hour workshop, we were surprised at the shyness and reticence of the muchachas to discuss sexual matters, since the majority of the women have been sex workers for at least one year. When the meeting began at 10:30 A.M. there were nineteen sex workers present as well as two bar owners. Three Ministry of Health personnel attended, including Mr. Romero, who was also the primary speaker. As the workshop began another five muchachas arrived, for a total of twenty-four participants. The last to arrive were two muchachas from the Iridescent Bar, who looked far more like children than adults. Other muchachas at the workshop told us that these little girls had been "kidnapped" from Guatemala and were believed to be only twelve or thirteen years old.[4]

A Ministry of Health source told us that in the economic boom years of the early 1990s there were an estimated 150 muchachas in Orange Walk. By 1998 that figure had shrunk to an estimated count of fifty sex workers who lived at bars in Orange Walk. Just under half of the women were assembled together at the workshop. The women wore a wide variety of outfits, from jeans and T-shirts with sneakers to more dressy clothes such as a bank clerk might wear on Casual Day at the office. Some muchachas wore casual clothes and modest makeup no different from that seen on many woman in Belize. Others wore body-hugging lycra tops and dresses or sexy midriff-baring tops paired with short skirts, outfits that are also not uncommon in everyday Belizean life.

Workshop discussion topics included advice on douching, the normalcy of female odor after sexual relations, and STD/HIV prevention. Using a dildo as a prop, a Ministry of Health official gave a hands-on demonstration of condom usage and the proper way to remove and dispose of a used condom. When the dildo was brought out the entire room burst into giggles. Many of the participants raised their hands to their mouths in a gesture of embarrassment. Near the end of the presentation, two women volunteered from the audience to demonstrate how to place a condom on the dildo yet were unable to do so correctly despite the fact that each had been a sex worker for over a year. Since many women asserted that they used condoms regularly with their clients, perhaps it is the clients who are held responsible for putting on condoms.

SEXUAL ACTIVITY

Rather than the common stereotype of sex workers as nymphomaniacs, Orange Walk muchachas seem to be trying to follow the idealized model of Latina female behaviors encapsulated in the concept of *marianismo* (Gil and Vazquez 1996). Drawing on a study by Lagarde, Gil and Vazquez state, "Although we might assume a *puta's* life is one erotic thrill after another, just the opposite is true: Lovemaking is their job, and the aim of it—not unlike the job of the marianismo wife/mother—is to give pleasure to others, not to themselves" (1996:136–7). The muchachas echo these findings in their expressed desire to avoid sexual activity and even reported that they often turn away willing customers. Yet we must point out that transactions between muchachas and their clients—though obviously of an economic nature—cannot be reduced to as simplistic an analysis as Gil and Vazquez suggest.

Muchachas usually seek from one to a maximum of three clients per night. They voice little enjoyment of the sex act and are not interested in experimenting with different sexual positions. They state that they only participate in what is known as *sexo normal* or *sexo regular*—meaning sexual intercourse in the "missionary" position. A typical sexual encounter lasts approximately fifteen to twenty-five minutes (though the client has thirty minutes of time in the room) and costs between Bz$25 and Bz$35 (Bz$2 = U.S.$1). The women tell us that the popularity of the bar and the beauty and friendliness of the woman have a direct influence on her ability to negotiate a larger than usual fee. Some women of the *Pajaro Verde*, which has the reputation of being one of the best bars in town, report charging Bz$40 for a thirty-minute session. A woman at the *La Luna*, which is the most rundown of any bar we visited, reports that she only charged Bz$15 for sexual intercourse. While most women charge another Bz$10 if the client does not have an orgasm in the allotted thirty minutes, some do not. The motivations for this difference seems to vary according to the woman. Perhaps some muchachas are too intimidated to ask the man for more money, while others feel that the client has paid for a service and, therefore, is entitled to an orgasm no matter how long it takes.

Isabel is diminutive and looks to be about fifteen years old, though she gives her age as eighteen years. She is very pretty and has huge black eyes fringed with startling long lashes. Her straight black hair is cropped at the chin and she wears vivid red lipstick, lots of black mascara, and heavy black eyebrow coloring. She tells us that her friends in Guatemala got her into drugs when she was in high school, "doing cocaine and stuff, and then I started having sex, then doing sex on the streets." She has worked at three other bars in Orange Walk Town before coming to the Hibiscus.

Isabel likes to have one or two clients a night but never more than three. When we asked her how long an average session lasted, the question made Isabel giggle. "It depends," she laughed. "Usually fifteen to thirty minutes." For her services, a client will pay her Bz$30 to Bz$40 if they stay in the bar complex and go to her room. The bar owner gets Bz$5 of this fee and the remainder is Isabel's. If a client would like to take her out and leave the bar during the week she charges a fee of Bz$120, of which Bz$10 goes to the bar owner. On the weekends, this fee goes up to Bz$140 and the bar owner's cut is Bz$20.

VIOLENCE AS AN OCCUPATIONAL HAZARD

Many of the muchachas of Orange Walk tell us they have experienced physical violence in their workplace. None reported violence from a bar owner, but a number of women have been exposed to violence or the threat of violence from drunk and/or disgruntled clients. While the La Sala project findings say that generally speaking "clients think that women who work in prostitution are worthless and must do whatever they say because they are paying" (Van Wijk and Barboza 1997:106), the muchachas of Orange Walk report a different type of dynamic between themselves and their clients. Our participants overwhelmingly state that they demand to be treated respectfully by the men visiting the bars. They are adamant that they will not allow a client to "behave wickedly" and can *and will* refuse a client who is verbally disrespectful or attempts to touch them intimately in public.

Yet violence does occur in the workplace of these muchachas. When this happens, the women first turn to their girlfriends at the bar to help them with a violent client. But if a client gets really rough they will call the bar owner for help. None of the bars had security personnel, but the women told us that bar customers were also active in preventing violence against the muchachas. For example, if a woman screamed for help, it might be a client who was closer to her bedroom and would therefore come to her aid before the bar owner. Unfortunately, sometimes the aid is not quick enough to prevent a woman from being hurt or having her savings stolen by a client. While some women report that they have never encountered a violent client, others have been attacked when they would not perform a sexual service such as oral sex or after they asked the client for more money if he failed to achieve orgasm within the agreed-upon time. Others have been attacked and robbed after the client had sexual relations with them.

Marlena's experiences as a sex worker have encompassed all these forms of violence. She tells us, "One time a client asked me to suck him and I said 'No!' because that wasn't the arrangement. Because of that he became very violent. When we got to the room he said, 'Now give me a blow job!' I said 'No' and he said, 'Do it, because I'm a cop!' He got very angry at me. I'd only been doing this a week and I told him I don't do that." Marlena also says that she "has suffered at the hands of a thief" who broke into her room and stole a couple hundred dollars she had hidden under her mattress. This was a terrible financial blow, since her earnings support her three children. Now she deposits her savings in a bank and sends Bz$200 home monthly through a trusted friend.

WORKING CONDITIONS IN ORANGE WALK BARS

The lodging house–brothel model of habitation-workplace described by Tannahill (1992) as existing in London, New York, San Francisco, and Amsterdam at the turn of the century seems to be in operation in Orange Walk today. We visited eleven bars that had sex workers working there. The bars vary remarkably in terms of size, cleanliness, type of clientele, fees for sexual services, and the overall atmosphere of the establishment. La Luna is the most extreme example of a bar with filthy working conditions and a lack of basic sanitary amenities.

La Luna is very tiny and has only four tables. Outside, the colors on the hand-painted logo are faded and chipping. Grime covers the walls inside, which look dreary despite a coat of deep yellow paint. We conduct the interviews at La Luna in the open courtyard at the rear of the bar. We arrive at La Luna at about 9:00 A.M. and are greeted by the intense odor of rotting food that emanates from a large pan on the ground filled with tan-colored liquid in which pieces of old tortillas and vegetables float. Occasionally, a chicken will hop into the pan to peck at a tortilla then step out and shake herself dry in the morning sun. The only cheerful spots of color at La Luna are the brightly colored bedspreads and sheets hanging from a clothesline in the courtyard. A double-sided sink stands in the yard and serves for cooking, laundry, and showers. To bathe, the women fill a bucket with unheated water and pour it over themselves in a secluded spot in the yard. The bar is run-down looking and the muchachas are dressed in clothes that are shabby in comparison to the clothing of the women from other bars. The women at La Luna are very quiet and docile and seem intimidated rather than jovial and talkative like muchachas at other bars.

The bar *El Sapo Guapo* is a dramatic contrast to La Luna. This bar is very clean and pretty. The paint is bright and the wall murals look fresh. El Sapo Guapo has eight tables and a small bar at the back of the one large room. The second floor contains the living quarters of the servers as well as the bar owner and his family. The muchachas at this bar speak openly and confidently with us. They dress in nice clothes that look clean and well maintained. The owner of El Sapo Guapo, a Mestizo man who looks to be in his early fifties, tells us that at his bar clients are not allowed to touch the muchachas in any manner unless that is what the women want. "People that come here might have a problem at home and want to come here to relax. They are free to drink. A client here can drink strong if he wants, but the girls drink a very light drink and the clients know she is not wanting to get drunk, but is just keeping him company." The bar owner acknowledges that alcohol abuse can be an occupational hazard with sex workers and tells us that there are muchachas working at El Sapo Guapo who want to drink too much "and some clients will say, 'I'm paying to get the girl drunk!' He says that he tells those types of bar patrons, "Go to another bar if you want to do that! I won't allow my girls to do that."

SEX WORK AND THE POTENTIAL FOR EXPLOITATION

The often clandestine nature of sex work can lend itself to exploitative practices among those who are in positions of power in relation to the workers. In addition, many sex workers are economic immigrants who are undocumented and are in the country illegally, which also puts them at risk for exploitation. In Orange Walk Town, those in positions of potential power in comparison to the muchachas include bar owners, immigration and police officers, and health care providers.

As has been documented in other research on sex work (Kempadoo and Doezema 1998), some of the muchachas of Orange Walk indicated they had been misled as to the nature of the work they would be doing in Belize. Women had been told that they would be servers in a restaurant or bar but later came to find out that they were also expected to engage in sex work. Josefina, a seventeen-year-old from Guatemala tells us that when she decided to come to Belize she thought she'd work in a private home as a domestic, but the man who brought her to Belize "pushed me to work in a bar." This is her first experience with sex work and she says, "I cried for a whole month because of the shame of being here. The *dueña* let me ficha for a while—but in order to pay my food and all that I had to go to the room."[5] Josefina's financial predicament is an example of the inability to support oneself by ficha alone. It reinforces the importance of being able— and willing—to keep an accurate record of one's earnings. Yet many muchachas turn this responsibility over to another, usually the bar owner.

"GOING TO THE ROOM" AND KEEPING TRACK OF EARNINGS

The transaction known as "going to the room" usually follows a general pattern that begins by informal socializing among the muchachas and the clients who mingle at the bar. This socializing creates a comfortable atmosphere for the customers and encourages them to drink, thus generating more income for the bar owner. After a client selects a companion he will ask her to "go to the room." If she is willing to have sex with him they negotiate a fee for the service he desires. The standard time she will be sexually available to him is one-half hour. They leave the bar together for her room and—assuming the sex worker is one who collects her payment up front—money will change hands in her bedroom at this time. The bar owner will make a note of the transaction and time when the couple leave the bar for the room. The muchacha will be expected to give the bar owner the house portion of the fee after each transaction, regardless of whether she is able to collect the fee from the client. Once in the room, the woman will inspect the man's genitals for signs of disease. If he passes this inspection, she will wash his genital area with an alcohol solution and they will proceed with the sex act. The bar owner keeps track of the time for the muchacha and will knock on the door when the client's time has expired. The couple may negotiate overtime if the client desires, and the muchacha will collect the extra fee at this time, of which the house will also get a portion.

From interviews with the muchachas and bar owners, we gathered that bar owners vary widely in their adherence to fair bookkeeping practices. We went away with the impression that, when given the responsibility of keeping track of the wages earned by the women who work in their establishments, some bar owners took advantage of their positions of power. After our first day of conducting interviews, we realized there was a marked disparity in muchachas' knowledge of how to document their financial earnings. For the women who did not know how to keep track of their earning from ficha and "going to the room," we made it a routine part of the interview to explain how to create a simple bookkeeping system using a notebook to tally the woman's earnings.

Still, some women did not seem to want the responsibility and autonomy of keeping their own financial records. As Lydia, a twenty-year-old Guatemalan who has worked at El Sapo Guapo for just over a year, explains resignedly,

"I got here and they told me I would work as a server. I didn't know for another week that I was also going to have to sleep with men. But I accepted it because I had been looking and there was no other work." Economic need was an important impetus for Lydia's entry into this work. She goes on to tell us, "I don't want to learn how to use a notebook because then I will be preoccupied with how much I'm earning." There could be other factors that influence her reluctance to keep track of her earnings. Perhaps Lydia is illiterate, a fact that she might have wished to keep private during our interview. Another possibility could be that Lydia may not want to know the actual breakdown of her expenditures and earnings from sex work. A cost/benefit analysis might show that sex work is not producing the earnings that Lydia might desire. Alternatively, if Lydia has emotional conflict about performing sex work, this may compel her to distance herself from tabulating her earnings.

CONDOM USAGE AND OTHER HEALTH ISSUES

Juanita is from Guatemala and has worked at La Luna for one and a half years. Her face is unique among the muchachas of Orange Walk because she has the most pronounced Mayan features of any of the women with whom we talked. She is very petite and, though she is only six months pregnant, looks almost dwarfed by the ripeness of her first pregnancy. When questioned about condom usage, Juanita tells us that she doesn't ask her clients to use one because, "If they don't want it, they don't want it," even though she acknowledges, "I'm afraid of [contracting] AIDS." She lives and works at the most rundown bar we visited in Orange Walk and makes some of the lowest wages we recorded. While Juanita does not feel that she can demand that a client use a condom, this is not a universal among the women whom we interviewed. Some muchachas, such as Conchita, tell us that they are able to get client compliance with regard to condom use.

Conchita is a twenty-year-old from Guatemala and has been a sex worker at *Pajaro Verde* for one year. She has a three-year-old who is being cared for by her mother in Guatemala. She first began to do sex work in Corozal after her marriage dissolved and she needed to support her child. Conchita seems to be one of the most proactive and financially successful of the workers. She tells us that she sees only "Latino businessmen" and has "a special type of client: he must be nice looking and an older guy. I don't like youngsters." She earns Bz$2 per ficha but does not allow herself to get drunk with her clients because once she "was drunk with a client and he stole Bz$600."

She buys her own condoms from the pharmacy and pays Bz$2.50 for a box of three. She tells us that she will not have sex without using a condom—except with her boyfriend. Conchita usually goes home every fifteen days or once a month. She takes Bz$500 to her mother every two weeks or Bz$1,000 on her monthly trips. She tells us that once an Immigration official in the town "tried to abuse me by having sex without paying. He tried to force me to go [to the room] without paying. He said he wouldn't stamp my passport next time. But I gave my passport to the bar owner and he got it stamped."

Yet other women are more like Juanita in their attitude toward male compliance with condom use. Such is the case with Delilah, a twenty-nine-year-old from Guatemala. She has supported her two children and her mother through sex work for one year and plans to stay in this occupation at least another year, "if police and Immigration don't bother me," due to her lack of legal immigration status. While some muchachas, like Conchita, told of sexual harassment and sexual coercion by police and immigration officials in Orange Walk, the majority of sex workers had not experienced their negative impacts. Delilah's sense of self-empowerment is markedly different from that of Conchita. Delilah tells us that she charges a client "after [a session of sex], so sometimes men won't pay."

Our Ministry of Health–appointed translator, Mr. Romero, advises Delilah to charge before a session of sex to insure that she gets paid by her clients. He tells her, "You should not allow men to abuse you and disrespect you because you are a sex worker. You deserve to be paid for your work." The need to collect her fee becomes even more important, because Delilah tells us that even if the client refuses to pay her after having sex, the "bar owner will not intervene with the client for me to make sure I get paid, but I still have to give him Bz$5 anyway."

Delilah seems very sad and unhappy to be working at the bar and tells us, "I don't feel comfortable here. It is not nice being in a place like this but there's no way out. I get bored here." Boredom is something that other muchachas mention. Unlike Conchita, Delilah also seems very fatalistic about safeguarding her health. She conveys that she gives her clients all the control in the choice of whether to use a condom. She tells us, "If a client wants to use a condom I don't do anything [to clean the penis] but if he doesn't I will wash it with [rubbing] alcohol." Delilah says that not all men will use condoms, "I ask but some don't want to. If he won't use a condom I will check him out [for diseases] and wash him [with rubbing alcohol]." This alcohol wash is used by many of the muchachas as a prevention against STDs, despite information presented during the workshop we attended that this is an invalid preventative measure. Delilah says she constantly worries about getting AIDS but despite this doesn't charge more for unprotected sex because, as she tells us, "If I try to charge more he won't pay and then I won't make money and my children will go hungry." She is aware of the risk of getting STDs and tells us, "If a man has a sore [on his penis] I will refuse sex. If he is dirty and smelly I still will serve him. If he has a sore on his mouth I'd serve him." She tells us that her last AIDS test was fifteen days ago and she tested negative.

Many of the sex workers in Orange Walk sport one or more tattoos on their bodies. Some look homemade while others seem to have been applied by a professional tattoo artist. For example, one muchacha has an impressive display of body art, including an iron cross on her inner thigh, a heart design that reads "*Te Amo*" on her upper left arm, an elaborate tattoo of a saint that extends from her wrist to her elbow, and a cannabis leaf on her upper right arm. Ministry of Health officers and other health care officials in Belize have pinpointed tattooing as a major potential source for the spread of HIV/AIDS due to the lack of enforced regulations and unsanitary conditions. Informants in Belize City state that the reuse and sharing of tattooing needles was common—even at tattoo parlors.

FREELANCE SEX WORKERS IN ORANGE WALK TOWN

Mr. Romero had been told by an unnamed source that there were freelance Belizean sex workers in Orange Walk. Since this was a community that he wanted to target for safer sex counseling, he agreed to try to bring us together for a meeting with two local women from the Orange Walk area. One of the women is in her early thirties and has a child who lives at home with her and her father. The other freelancer is the seventeen-year-old cousin of the older woman. She now lives with her older cousin and uncle because her mother physically abused her.

During the interview, the younger woman seemed to have a very nonchalant attitude about her occupation, though she preferred to talk privately with Mr. Romero. The older woman had a strong rapport with one of the authors (Anders), and she and I talked for almost an hour until the woman's father came home for lunch. She was very open about her past sexual experiences, which included a marriage to an American man, several lesbian affairs, and having sex in exchange for drugs. She said that she had calmed down her lifestyle considerably since her child was old enough to understand.

Mr. Romero and the two freelancers told us that freelancers most often operate from their homes or the central plaza downtown. During lunchtime women sit on benches alone as men pass through the plaza. If a man is interested, he will sit down and begin talking with a woman. If they can agree on a time, place, and price they leave the park separately and meet at the designated location. According to Mr. Romero, freelance work is not well known in Orange Walk Town, even by local people. Mr. Romero, who has been working with the muchachas and STD prevention for several years, tells us that he has been unable to make solid contacts with freelancers in the town. This may be due, in part, to the fact that freelancers in this area tend to have a job, and sex work is a supplementary way to augment their income.

PREFERRED CLIENTS

While "exoticism"—often played out as the importance of the sex worker's race/ethnicity to the client—has been explored across many social disciplines (Bolles 1992, O'Connell Davidson and Sanchez Taylor 1996, Hooks 1992, Kempadoo and Doezema 1998), the importance of the client's ethnicity to the sex worker has yet to be explored to the same degree. The vast majority of the muchachas whom we interviewed state frankly that they make decisions about whom they have sexual relationships with based on the skin color and ethnicity of the potential client. We found that the muchachas voice a clear preference for light-skinned Mestizo men rather than dark-skinned Creole men. The literature on the importance of ethnicity as social markers in many Caribbean countries can offer some insight into this finding.

In the Caribbean, skin color is both a phenotypic characteristic and a social category whose "referential use shift[s] with observers and context" (Segal 1993:90). This theoretical construct describes part of the relationship between the muchachas and the men of Orange Walk. The word that muchachas use to describe Creole men is *moreno*, which literally means dark skinned as opposed to *criollo*, which translates as "Creole" or "mixed." If it is true that "persons of color... seek to downplay the significance of 'shade' between themselves and relatively 'lighter' persons and to emphasize the difference between themselves and relatively darker persons" (Segal 1993:91), this may help to explain the reluctance of muchachas to have sexual relations with morenos. The social marginalization of the muchachas is a fact of which they are well aware. They are recognized by others in the community as *prostitutas* or *mujeres malas* and report that although most inhabitants of Orange Walk Town are friendly, the muchachas still feel a stigma attached to being known as a sex worker. By associating with only Mestizo or Mennonite men, who are of higher social status than the muchachas, they bolster their position in society.

We found that the vast majority of sex workers we interviewed in Orange Walk report that they do not have sex with the Creole men of the town. They say they will only have sexual relations with the Mestizo men of the town. As Marlena says, "If they're Latin, I go with anybody—there's no difference." She has not been with a tourist, though others reported that tourist men occasionally visit the bars. These men are usually Latin American, though sometimes European men solicit their services, as well as Mennonites and

Chinese. Yet Isabel, for example, accepts "any group, any kind [of men as clients], Negroes, *Indios*." These interviews illustrate some of the complexities of race/ethnicity and class issues that affect sex workers in unique ways.

WAITING FOR PRINCE CHARMING?

The La Sala project states that "women have been taught to dream of 'Prince Charming' and wait to be rescued" from sex work (Van Wijk and Barboza 1997:106). This is a complex statement that, we believe, fails to fully recognize the importance that many women place on having a committed and fulfilling partnership with another person. The women of Orange Walk did not seem to seek a Prince Charming in the sense that someone would "save them" from their current situation. Yet they generally did hope to meet someone nice someday to live with, have children with, and build a life together. This is not a dream any different from that of many women. Our participants view sex work as a very short-term occupation to meet specific financial goals and establish savings.

Since the muchachas consider sex work as transient, we asked them what types of job they envision themselves having after they return to their home countries. For the most part, the women have no specific career goals, but their plans for the future include being economically stable and having a family. Some muchachas, however, do have specific goals in mind. When asked if she has dreams for her future, Paola responds, "Yes, to be a nurse." Naming a specific trade or vocation was unusual for the muchachas that we interviewed. Most feel that they will be unable to acquire academic or professional skills, as they have very little formal education, but see themselves as becoming trained as a beautician or seamstress or opening a small *bodega* or other shop.

SAFE SEX IN A MACHO WORLD

The muchachas of Orange Walk cannot be easily categorized into a homogenous group. Yet they all seem to struggle with being *una mujer buena* in a society that would deny them self-worth. One of the areas of contestation is between being seen as *femenina* and the need to be assertive with clients. For a muchacha, self-assertiveness means getting paid when a client has sex with her, getting a client to use a condom to protect her from STDs, and keeping track of earnings and expenditures so that she is not taken advantage of by the unscrupulous. All the women we interviewed describe themselves as being self-employed. They feel they have autonomy to move from bar to bar in Orange Walk, and many women had worked at more than one bar in the town. Yet the deep-seated beliefs and norms that give "sexual rights and decision-making to the man [and] demands submissive behavior of women" (Gil and Vazquez 1996:145) can put them at an economic disadvantage and needlessly increase their exposure to potentially catastrophic health risks in *la epoca del SIDA.*

The muchachas stated that they anticipated returning to their home countries with their earnings to begin some form of entrepreneurial enterprise and get married. Sex work is seen as a marginalized and highly stigmatized profession within their social group, and the women work hard to keep the source of their earning a secret from family members and friends in their own country. They see their hard-won earnings as a nest egg that will help propel their children into improved economic conditions and gain them a better education.

CONCLUSION

While this pilot study has added to the knowledge of some aspects of the nature of sex work in Belize, there is more to be done. What sex work is in Belize is still contested. We feel that Kane's "quasi-prostitution" (1993) model is an etic and inadequate one to explain freelancing, the behavior of those who participate in sex work on an occasional basis, or the consensual sociosexual unions known as "sweethearting" within the context of Belizean culture, gender relationships, and economic conditions. In another vein, gaining access to sex workers in the tourism industry (for example in Ambergris Caye) could also be enlightening as to the nature of sex work in Belize. It would also be interesting to compare the living conditions of sex workers in various parts of Belize.

Finally, we feel that there is a critical lack of outreach to the sex workers of Orange Walk to supply information regarding the prevention of STDs. As we observed during the STD workshop in Orange Walk Town we attended, the two women who volunteered to place a condom on a dildo were unable to do so correctly, despite each having performed sexual labor for over a year. In terms of AIDS/STD prevention for sex workers, this is perhaps one of the most important findings of this study and one which we hope will receive more attention and concentrated effort.[6]

NOTES

1. Belizean racial/ethnic categories are complex. This is due, in part, to the recognition that many Belizeans and immigrants to the country identify themselves as belonging to multiple categories. These categories are based on various factors, such

as ethnic descent, skin color, language(s) spoken, place of birth, and an individual's choice to identify with a particular group. It is also important to note that we are not only looking at Belizean categories of race and ethnicity, but also at those expressed by muchachas whom we interviewed, who are immigrants from Guatemala, El Salvador, and Honduras. This means that not only are we dealing with the already complex ethnic terminologies specific to Belize but are also integrating the categories imposed on the Belizean community by migrant women. To clarify the terms used in this paper, based on our interviews with the muchachas of Orange Walk and on research into Belizean ethnicity and racial categorization (see Macklin 1993, J. Palacio 1992, M. Palacio 1990), we define the categories as follows:

* Creole—term used by Belizeans to describe dark-skinned people of Afro-Belizean descent, for whom English and/or Belizean Creole are primary languages. For example, 60 percent of the inhabitants of Belize City are considered to be Creole.
* Mestizo—term used by some muchachas and some Belizeans to describe themselves and others as Spanish speaking and light-skinned, who can often trace their ancestry to the indigenous peoples of Central America.
* Latina/o—term used by some muchachas to describe themselves and their preferred clients as Mestizo.

2. We are deeply grateful to the muchachas with whom we spoke for their generosity in participating in this project and their exceptional openness with outsiders such as ourselves. We also recognize that the obligatory presence of the Ministry of Health official at our meetings with the muchachas and bar owners influenced the data collection process. Perhaps had our stay in Orange Walk been longer and uninterrupted by illness, the Ministry of Health official would have allowed us certain luxuries of interviewing we were unable to access under the circumstances. We would have liked to carry out repeated interviews with muchachas at a more in-depth level and leisurely pace than that set by our "chaperone," especially with particularly articulate informants. Repeat visits to certain bars where we had initially established rapport with bar owners during our first visit could have facilitated this process. We feel that the bar owners would have become more comfortable with our presence over time and would have been more willing to talk more openly with us. This would have allowed us a more intimate knowledge of the bar-brothel system from the perspectives of both the muchachas and the bar owners.

3. The women interviewed in Orange Walk most often refer to themselves and each other as "muchachas." Less often, they describe themselves as *"meseras"* or waitresses. They do not use the term "prostituta," which they are familiar with, to describe their occupation. A Ministry of Health official who works closely with the women said that this term has strong negative associations for them, which might explain why it is avoided. The women are, by and large, unfamiliar with the term *trabajadora del sexo*, though they did not seem to negatively associate its use to describe their occupation. We have chosen to use muchacha, server, and sex worker as descriptive terms. These terms are chosen because they are terms with which our participants identify, though we acknowledge that the term "sex worker" is contested. The names of the women, the bar owners, and the bars, and the health officials who have participated in this research have been changed to protect their anonymity.

4. We were unable to confirm the girls' ages because we were denied permission by the owner of the Iridescent Bar to interview anyone who worked at his establishment. A Ministry of Health worker told us that the matter would be investigated further by that department.

5. The phrase "to go to the room" is used by muchachas to refer to having sex with a client.

6. In December of 1998, the Orange Walk District Sex Workers STD Clinic began operations. It is staffed by Public Health nurses, the District Medical Officer (a physician specializing in obstetrics and gynecology) and Public Health Inspectors (who assist in discourse with the local bar owners). This clinic provides testing, counseling, and treatments for STDs, including HIV, for sex workers in the Orange Walk area.

11

Gold and Commercial Sex

Exploring the Link between Small-scale Gold Mining and Commercial Sex in the Rainforest of Suriname

CHRISTEL C. F. ANTONIUS-SMITS, WITH JUANITA ALTENBERG, TEERSA BURLESON, TANIA TAITT-CODRINGTON, MURIEL VAN RUSSEL, DIANA VAN DER LEENDE, DEBORAH HORDIJK, AND RUBEN F. DEL PRADO

Suriname is a country fairly large by Caribbean standards—163,820 square kilometers with a population of approximately 414,000.[1] In the last two decades, many internal as well as external factors have negatively influenced the Surinamese economy. The reduction of income from bauxite exports by as much as 31 percent (1980–1983) and the unilateral cancellation of Dutch aid after the execution of fifteen leading politicians, trade unionists, lawyers and journalists in 1982 during military rule (1980–1987) were major factors in this decline. Some other influences were a massive brain drain since independence in 1975, a decade of internal political strife, a flourishing "black market" resulting from a shortage of foreign exchange, a lack of investment in all sectors, and an antigovernment guerrilla war in the rainforested interior of the country, which lasted from 1986 to 1992.

The decline of the Surinamese economy resulted in a relentless inflation and depreciation of the Surinamese guilder and a drop in the standard of living. Large segments of the population now have less access to basic needs and social security. Many people combine a job in the formal sector with jobs in the informal sector, selling goods and offering services. There are mainly women in this informal "hustle-and-struggle" sector. Unfortunately, hustle work does not strengthen the position of already economically vulnerable women. It provides no social security, no steady regular income, no medical benefits, and no pension. Increasing unemployment in a climate of spiraling poverty clearly puts women in a vulnerable position, often without a steady partner on which they may rely for support and care of children. Therefore, more and more are being pushed into the informal labor market, including sex work, to gain additional income (Antonius-Smits et al. 1994).

This study was conducted among female commercial sex workers and their clients operating in small-scale gold-mining areas in the eastern part of the rainforested interior of Suriname. The interior, south of the coastal belt, comprises about 80 percent of the total land area. Approximately 40,000 people, 10 percent of the total population, live there. Traditionally, these are descendants of runaway slaves, Maroons (75 percent of the population), and indigenous peoples, Amerindians (25 percent). During the military rule in the 1980s, Suriname experienced an insurgency in the interior that started in July 1986, whereby most of the infrastructure of the easternmost district Marowijne, including houses, schools and clinics, was completely destroyed. As a result of this antigovernment guerrilla war, 8,000 people took refuge in French Guiana, where they were detained in refugee camps. Others moved to different parts of the interior, while about 13,000 migrated to Paramaribo. The war came to an end in 1992, after which the affected areas began slowly recovering from the damage. Most refugees, after having been displaced for six to seven years, have now returned to the interior, while many still remain in Paramaribo or in French Guiana (Antonius-Smits et al. 1994).

For Maroons, as well as many economically deprived men in Paramaribo, small-scale gold mining offers a way of making money. Apart from a state-owned company and several foreign companies, an estimated 20,000 small-scale gold miners are operational in different gold-mining areas in the east of the interior. The majority of these small-scale gold-mining activities take place illegally, meaning unauthorized (*De Ware Tijd*, March 14, 1998). With the recent gold rush, migrant workers, locals, urbanites, and foreigners, including several thousand Brazilians, have entered this territory. These so-called *porknokkers* and *garimpeiros* work under harsh conditions, often in remote and unpopulated areas with no representation of government authorities or police. Gunfights, abuse, robberies, and other criminal acts that occur in the camps are frequently reported in the media.

Migrant work, such as gold mining, often creates conditions that contribute to the development of sex work. Informal information about a thriving sex business in the gold-mining areas has reached Paramaribo. Research was conducted to validate these rumors by assessing the association between gold and sex work in the eastern part of the interior of Suriname and by documenting conditions under which sex work takes place in the gold-mining camps.

SEX WORK IN SURINAME—AN OVERVIEW

According to the Surinamese Penal Code, which dates back to the colonial era and has never been changed since that time, prostitution by itself is not a criminal offense. It is "the promotion of female indecent behavior with obvious sexual provocation" which is prohibited by law. This implies that street- and club-based commercial sex are, in fact, prohibited. In reality, the law is seldom enforced and leaves plenty of opportunity for commercial sex.

The sex business, and the women working in it, is not an untouched research area in Suriname. The groundwork, by Julia Terborg (1990) among club workers and by Claris O'Carroll-Barahona and Juanita Altenberg (1994) among street workers and on the issue of trafficking, has provided us with some basic information on commercial sex work in Suriname. Demographic profiles of female sex workers, working conditions (both club-based and in the streets), sexual practices, basic needs and problem areas, condom use, safer sex practices, knowledge of sexually transmitted diseases (STDs) and risk assessment, birth control methods, and HIV[2] prevalence were the main issues studied. The Stichting Maxi Linder Associatie (SMLA)[3] has been working extensively since 1994 with self-identifying club- and street-based female sex workers in the capital of Suriname, Paramaribo.

There are about forty registered and licenced nightclubs in Paramaribo that employ mainly foreign female sex workers. This group, primarily from Brazil, Colombia, and the Dominican Republic, is very mobile and has a high turnover rate. Foreign sex workers usually stay in Suriname between three and six months and work in clubs, hotels, and bars. It is therefore difficult to estimate actual numbers. The most popular nightclub has around eighty women working there. For some of them, Suriname is the springboard for the traffic in women to Holland. The government tries to control the club activities by regulating the licences for running a club (brothel). These licences are provided under two conditions. First, foreign women must register at the national public STD clinic and with the immigration authorities. Second, all women working at the clubs have to undergo biweekly checkups at the STD clinic. Informal agreements are in place between club owners and the national clinic for these mandatory, biweekly STD checkups, which do not include testing for HIV. Club workers diagnosed with an STD are reported to the club owner, who makes sure the woman does not work until she is adequately treated. Whenever a male patient is diagnosed with an STD at the clinic and claims to have picked it up from a club worker but is not able to identify which woman, the clinic is authorized to close the entire club in order to screen all the women working there and take necessary precautions for treatment. If club owners do not concur with these agreements, the STD clinic has the authority to call in the Military Police, who will shut down the club.

For nonregistered sex workers, no official policy or any form of regulation is in place, making their numbers even more difficult to assess. The sex workers are mainly street-based Surinamese or Guyanese women, the latter mostly illegal residents. Out of fear of deportation, these sex workers avoid all contact with official authorities, including health services. A 1994 National AIDS Program Needs Assessment among sixty-seven street workers, aged fifteen to sixty-four, showed that 84 percent did commercial sex work to support their children. Out of fear of stigmatization, they did not go for STD checkups. Forty-four percent had never heard about HIV, AIDS, or other STDs. Condom use was low and irregular. They reported that men offered two to three times more money for unprotected sex. They presented a general feeling of hopelessness and low self-esteem.

In 1998, 246 street workers were registered with the SMLA. This number is only a fraction of the real number of women working the streets. Apart from the above-mentioned two categories of sex workers, other groups also remain invisible, unreachable, and therefore unstudied, such as juvenile and teenage sex workers, illegal residents, and male sex workers. According to information gained from outreach work, pimps do not allow "their" sex workers to participate in the activities of the SMLA center, so this group too has remained unstudied, together with women working at home as well as those who sell sex regularly but infrequently in order to meet extra expenses and who do not identify themselves as sex workers. During outreach work in the streets of Paramaribo, female peer educators come across teenage boys and transvestites picking up male clients. No further information is available since no research has been conducted in this obscure area.

Suriname is experiencing an increase in the number of HIV infections, and the country ranks among the highest in the Americas in this respect.[4] In the face of this epidemic, the Ministry of Health of the Republic of Suriname established a National AIDS Program (NAP) in 1988 for national HIV/AIDS program development and design, implementation of surveillance activities, and HIV/AIDS education. From January 1989 through December 1997, a total of 783 cumulative cases of HIV infection have been reported.[5] Available epidemiological data suggest that heterosexual transmission has, until now, been the predominant mode of spread of HIV infection in Suriname. Of those infected, two-thirds are within the lower socioeconomic classes, supporting the general perception that AIDS is a disease of the underprivileged. A 1996 HIV seroprevalence study among 189 street-based female commercial sex workers in Paramaribo showed a point prevalence of 22 percent positive for HIV.[6]

THE SEX WORKERS' ORGANIZATION

The Stichting Maxi Linder Associatie was founded in October 1994 as a result of the Needs Assessment study discussed earlier. The overall goal of the foundation is to optimize the social, economic, mental and physical health and well-being of female commercial sex workers in Suriname. This goal is pursued by empowerment through providing education, information, and skills training; support and advice on social, legal, and health matters; raising social awareness and encouraging a positive self-image and solidarity; and offering protection against violence and abuse. It also provides alternative job training and schooling activities for those who want to leave the sex business as well as a safe haven—a drop-in center. Apart from being an advocacy organization, it also distributes condoms free of charge.

The SMLA defines sex as a human desire and need, and sex work is considered to be informal unregulated labor (Wijers and Lap-Chew 1997:32–33). One of the main issues of its work is the destigmatization and regulation of sex work in order to reduce the vulnerability and lack of rights of women working in this sector and to ensure access to health care, social services, and insurance.

The Stichting Maxi Linder Associatie was named after Suriname's most celebrated sex worker, Maxi Linder, who was born on May 23, 1902, the daughter of a freed slave.

She started sex work as young as thirteen years old after she was raped for an orange. She continued to do sex work until she retired at the age of sixty-eight. She then became a Madam, running a call-girl business that catered to the needs of "big shots" in Surinamese society.

She never married and all her life worked independently. She owned a house in a respectable neighborhood of Paramaribo, where she lived with her fifty-one dogs.

She was known for her social work and her generosity toward anyone who came to her for help. She supported several men financially and helped them to get an education.

She was, and still is, famous in Suriname and far beyond the borders as the "Queen of Paramaribo," astonishingly beautiful and always dressed according to the latest fashion. She was very open about her profession and in spite of regular emotional and physical abuse from society and clients, she remained proud of herself and her work.

She died on January 14, 1981, and was buried in the presence of 250 of her admirers, of whom the majority were women.

(Source: SMLA/NAP 1994)

THE STUDY

This research endeavor was a joint effort of the Anton de Kom University of Suriname and the Stichting Maxi Linder Associatie. The overall goal of the study was to integrate newly found information on the Surinamese sex business with existing strategies of the SMLA for empowerment of female sex workers. The main objectives were to assess the association between gold and sex work in the eastern part of the interior and to identify and document different forms of sex work in the gold-mining areas. Additionally, the study sought to research the main reasons for women to participate in the sex business, the women's perceptions and views of their activities, and safer sex practices among sex workers in the gold camps. Finally, the study aimed to document views of male clients—gold miners—on the issue of sex work and sex workers and to identify the most urgent problems and needs of sex workers and their clients.

Data were collected among female sex workers and their clients operating in the eastern part of the interior of Suriname. Semistructured in-depth interviews were carried out with fifty women and men in the following four categories: adult Surinamese and Guyanese female commercial sex workers (twenty respondents), Brazilian (ex-) club workers (ten respondents), teenage sex workers (ten respondents), and male clients operating in the gold-mining areas (ten respondents). The interviews were conducted in the native language of the respondents, namely Dutch, Sranan Tongo,[7] English, Portuguese, or one of the Maroon languages. Interviewers were asked to keep a fieldwork diary to record their own personal remarks, observations, and experiences. These observational notes were included in the analysis of the data. Finally, additional information was obtained from a three-day observational field trip to a gold-mining camp.

The average age of the women interviewed was 29.3 years with the youngest sex worker being eleven years old and the oldest sixty years. The majority of the women were single and had an average of 2.3 children. Women of mixed and Creole ethnicity made up 72.5 percent of the population. Sex workers of three different nationalities were included in the study: Surinamese (52.5 percent), Guyanese (22.5 percent), and Brazilian (25 percent). All women were Christian, with the exception of one Hindu. Four of the respondents had no formal education, twenty-three women had completed primary school, nine sex workers had a junior high school diploma, and four of the teenage respondents were still in junior high school. The average number of years in the sex business was 6.2. One of the respondents had thirty years of experience (see Table 11.1).

Table 11.1 Demographics of the Female Commercial Sex Workers Interviewed

	Adult Sur/Guy sex workers (N=20)	Brazilian (ex)club (N=10)	Teenage sex workers (N=10)	TOTAL (N=40)
Average age (years)	36.4	27.9	17.5	29.3
Single	10	8	9	27
Common-law union	9	1	1	11
Married	1	—	—	1
Divorced	—	1	—	1
Average # of children	3.6	1.8	0.3	2.3
Creole	11	—	2	13
Maroon	3	—	5	8
Amerindian	1	—	1	2
Mixed	4	10	2	16
East Indian	1	—	—	1
Surinamese	12	—	9	21
Guyanese	8	—	1	9
Brazilian	—	10	—	10
Christian	19	10	10	39
Hindu	1	—	—	1
No education	3	1	—	4
Primary school	9	9	5	23
Junior High	8	—	5	13
Still in school	—	—	4	4
Average number of years active in sex business	10.5	1.3	1.7	6.2

SEX WORK IN THE INTERIOR

The conditions of sex work in the interior were found to be diverse for the different groups of sex workers. Five distinguished categories of sex work were identified by this research: that which took place in a club setting; a "temporary wife" system that involved "sex-on-credit"; freelance sex work based in women's camps; occasional sex work done by saleswomen and cooks; and, finally, sex work based in Maroon villages.

The Club Setting (5 respondents)

These respondents—four Brazilians and one Surinamese—indicated that they were working in a club in the interior. The club provided bar, restaurant, and hotel services. The women rented a room on a weekly basis for five grams of gold, including food and drinks. Their clients were mostly Brazilian and Surinamese gold miners and local Maroons. The working conditions were reasonably good with all sanitary facilities available, such as running water, electricity, bathrooms, and toilets. The Brazilian respondents had previously worked in clubs in Paramaribo and had come to look for "big money" in the interior. They had heard about the place from girlfriends or clients in town. The Surinamese woman had been taken to the interior by a client, a gold miner. She explained how she had ended up in the club:

> He was very much in love with me. He had taken me to the interior as his wife. He was taking care of me so I quit the sex business. But then I became very ill and he could no longer afford to pay the hospital bills. Finally, he kicked me out and I was forced to take up sex work again in order to survive. I knew about the club in the interior and that's where I went.

The women charged five grams of gold (U.S.$50) for a "short time" (thirty minutes) and ten grams of gold (U.S.$100) for "sleeping." For these prices all sexual practices were allowed ("all in"). They considered themselves to be sex workers, but none felt good about what they were doing. The four Brazilian respondents that were interviewed in this category had the intention to quit the sex business in the very near future and return home. They planned to live a "normal" life again, and since they assumed that nobody knew what they had been doing in Suriname, believed it would all work out fine.

The "Sex-on-Credit" System (5 respondents)

The women interviewed in this category consisted of club workers and street workers who were recruited in Brazil by Brazilian foremen. The women were hired for a period of three months and were contracted to cook, perform household tasks, and provide sexual services to the local gold miners, who worked for the same foreman or "boss." The foremen invested in the women by paying their airfare from Brazil to Paramaribo and by providing transportation to, and accommodation in, the gold-mining camp. By the end of the three months, each woman was paid a fixed salary of 100 grams of gold. For the sexual services of a woman, the boss automatically deducted 10 percent of the gold miner's total earnings at the end of his contract. It is noteworthy to remark here that three gold miners working together can easily find between 500 and 4,000 grams of gold per week.

By paying the women a fixed salary of 100 grams of gold, and by encouraging them to have plenty of sex with the gold miners, who paid 10 percent for each woman they have sex with, the bosses assured themselves of a profitable investment. The women were also required to perform striptease shows in the camp in order to excite the gold miners and stimulate sexual activity. Because the women were always available in the camp, this system provided the gold miners with the opportunity of sex on credit. Whenever the gold business hit a slow week, the men could continue to have sex on credit, because they only had to pay for the sexual services at the end of their contract. The miners, in fact, were offered the possibility of hiring themselves one or more temporary wives.

The Women's Camps (15 respondents)

The majority of sex workers in this category were street workers from Paramaribo. They had been attracted by stories of colleagues about gold and big money in the gold-mining areas. Because most gold-mining camps do not allow women inside, the sex workers took the initiative to set up special women's camps in the neighborhood. When the gold-mining camp was located near a village, the sex worker rented a hut for two or three grams of gold per week. In the camps, working conditions were harsh. Some of the sex workers' camps had nothing more than a barracks to tie a hammock in, with no sanitary facilities. The most common complaint from the women working in these conditions was the lack of safety. They felt extremely vulnerable to robbery, violence, and abuse from clients as well as colleagues. There was virtually no protection from authorities, since in such remote areas, no police are present. Nevertheless, according to the respondents, the gold was worth taking the risks. According to the respondents, they made more than twice as much in the goldfields as in town: "The earnings are better in the interior. The hustle is tougher, but it pays off."

The sex workers charged five grams of gold for a short time and ten grams for sleeping. Whenever the client wanted something other than straight vaginal sex, the price went up by two grams of gold. The respondents claimed that in some areas they had received as much as twenty grams of gold for a short time and thirty grams for sleeping. According to the women, the gold miners were willing to pay an extra two or three grams of gold to any sex worker who was new in the area. For these women, sex work was their only form of income and the only way to survive. In general, they felt that they were forced into the sex business because society had offered them few or no chances. Others indicated that they were proud to be independent, self-reliant working women who were able to take care of themselves and their children. When asked about their future plans, most indicated that they would prefer to leave the sex business and lead a normal life.

Some of the women fantasized about finding the right man who would support them and their children and would save them from their current unfortunate life.

Saleswomen and Cooks (9 respondents)

In this category of sex work, two groups of women could be identified. The first group consisted of women who traveled within the three Guyanas to sell goods in the villages along the rivers and in the gold-mining areas. To earn some extra money, they sell sex whenever the opportunity presents itself. The respondents indicated that the high demand for sexual services among the gold miners, in combination with the scarceness of women in the mining areas, created ideal conditions for them to make a lot of extra money. They either stayed in a women's camp or, whenever women were allowed in the camp, rented a hut for two or three grams of gold per week. The second group consisted of women who initially were invited by a gold miner to cook and perform household tasks in the camp. Once they arrived, they were asked or, in some cases, forced to perform sex work. The respondents in this category explained that in the beginning they had felt bad about the whole situation, but the extra money had quickly soothed the unpleasant feelings.

Although both of these groups sold sex on a regular basis, they did not describe themselves as "real" sex workers. One respondent used the term "opportunity sex worker." The main reason for this attitude was the fact that they did not rely solely on sex work to survive. Selling goods or performing household tasks in the gold-mining camps was the job that allowed them to pay the bills. Sex work merely provided a means to supplement their incomes so they could afford anything they wanted and be totally self-reliant and independent. Depending on the area they worked in, they charged between three and five grams of gold for a short time and between ten and thirteen grams of gold for sleeping.

Local Maroon Women (6 respondents)

This category was made up of local Maroon women and teenage girls who lived in villages surrounding gold-mining areas. The respondents were all single mothers with little or no formal education and no job skills, for whom job opportunities in the interior were limited. Most of the areas where the women used to carry out small-scale agricultural activities had been invaded by gold miners. Goods in the interior, being imported from town, were increasingly expensive. The presence of groups of single gold miners with a sexual appetite had made the option available for them and their daughters to engage in the sex business to generate income.

Both adult women and teenagers viewed sex work as normal, considering their situation. For the survival of their children, they were prepared to make this sacrifice. They said that it was widely accepted in the interior because "everyone does it." Sex work in order to survive was justified, contrary to sex work for "extras," which was considered bad. The majority of the respondents defined a sex worker as: "A woman who is forced to sell sex because she is very poor and has to support herself and her children."

The local women charged less than the other sex workers. They entertained the gold miners in their huts and performed short-time sex for two to three grams of gold with one gram extra for a "special time" or sleeping. The teenagers who were forced into the business by their mothers explained that they had performed sex for small amounts of money, two grams of gold, or as little as a bag of rice.

Relationship between the Different Categories

The women in this study tend to work within one specific category. A street worker who decides for herself to go to the interior will most probably stay in a women's camp. Or, a gold miner can make her an offer to work in a specific camp, in which case she might end up in the sex-on-credit system. The decision when and where to work is primarily based on the opportunities that are being presented to her.

The majority of sex workers in the women's camps were street workers from Paramaribo, both Surinamese and Guyanese. The saleswomen also worked in these camps and some of the Maroon teenagers who had moved from their villages in the interior and continued to perform sex work also preferred to visit the women's camps. In the sex-on-credit system, which was designed by Brazilian miners, the women stay in the gold-mining camps. The women working in this system were therefore primarily, but not exclusively, Brazilian. Occasionally, the foremen also recruited among club and street workers in Paramaribo. The Brazilian women in this study either worked in this system or in the club setting.

MOTIVATION FOR SEX WORK

In reference to motivation, three groups were identified: women who were driven by poverty, those who were forced by third parties, and those who acted on their own free will.

Seventy-five percent of the adult Surinamese/Guyanese sex workers indicated that poverty had been the main reason that they took up sex work. These women seemed to find themselves in a vicious circle with no way out. Their low educational level and the lack of other job qualifications left them with few options on the job market: "I had domestic and money problems; the only way out was through sex work." Some respondents indicated that they had a daytime job but were not earning enough to make ends meet. Being single mothers, in most cases, they were forced by economic necessity to go to the streets in an effort to supplement their income: "I worked for the government for over seventeen years. But the salary was not enough. Now I hustle and can provide for myself and my children." They all expressed the need to find "the right man" who would support them and enable them to quit the sex business. In their search for this man, they had drifted into several relationships with favorite clients, with whom they had unprotected sex and often a child, in an attempt to establish some form of security. Unfortunately, these attempts had repeatedly left them with just another mouth to feed.

Among the Brazilian women, 20 percent listed poverty as their motivation for sex work. One respondent had been in Suriname for several years and had also performed sex work in Brazil. She explained: "Sex work is the only job I know and it has kept me alive all these years." The other respondent said:

I have had bad luck. My intention was to come to Suriname for a short period of time and make enough money to return to Brazil to start my own business. Unfortunately, I became very ill and was completely destroyed financially. I was then forced to postpone my original plan indefinitely, and with my lack of any education, sex work was the only way to earn enough money to pay off my debts and save something for the future.

The second group of women had been forced into the sex business by a third party. Three of these were teenage sex workers who had been introduced to sex work by their mothers in order to supplement the family income, one at the early age of eight. These girls had sex for money but also for basic foodstuffs such as rice and other products that were not available in the interior. Most of the women in the category of "cooks" had been misled by their boyfriends, gold miners, who had brought them to the camps to perform household tasks. Once they arrived, they found out that sex work was part of the deal.

For the third group of respondents, sex work was performed of their own free will and was considered a quick way to make extra money. Sex work was performed in times of need, in order to pay for extra or unexpected expenses such as school necessities at the beginning of the school year, clothing, or hospital bills. Most of these women did not identify themselves as sex workers because sex work was not their primary income. They could probably have survived without the sex business. They decided for themselves when, where, and with whom they had sex for money or goods.

Seven of the ten teenagers explained that they engaged in sex work for the purchase of luxurious commodities such as name-brand sneakers and designer jeans or simply because they loved gold. Eight of the ten Brazilian women had gone to Suriname with the explicit purpose of earning a lot of money in a short time through sex work. They had left Brazil and their families with a clear vision of what they wanted to establish in the near future. Their plans were to return to Brazil and realize whatever goals they had set for themselves. For them, sex work was a temporary choice, not a way of living.

SAFER SEX PRACTICES

Unprotected vaginal and oral sex was most often performed by the respondents. Because of the pain factor, requests for anal sex and *back poen*[8] were refused by most sex workers. The Brazilian women hardly refused any sexual request from a client, since their prices were "all-in." As one Brazilian respondent said: "I perform anything they ask for and I pretend that I enjoy it. That's how I make them come back to me every time." Group sex, one man with more women, was mostly performed by teenage sex workers. "I always go with girlfriends, not with strange women, because I don't trust them. The men pay more gold for group sex."

STD knowledge was very low among all respondents. Six women reported having contracted an STD previously. Apart from the popular local names, the women knew little to nothing about the conventional STD. More women knew about HIV/AIDS, but many misconceptions regarding efficient safer sex practices were present. The most important misconceptions were:

"You can smell the disease."
"You can always detect from the appearance whether someone is infected or not."
"Rinsing the vagina after sex clears away all disease."
"Drinking herbal potions makes you pee out the disease."
"Withdrawal is a good method to prevent STD."
"With regular clients it is not necessary to use condoms."

Three teenage sex workers—7.5 percent of all respondents—reported that they never used condoms. Around 78 percent indicated that with clients they used one sometimes, but never with husbands, boyfriends, or favorite men (regular clients). This finding, again, confirms the common practice among sex workers in Suriname, not to use condoms with their favorite men or boyfriends. The remaining 15 percent claimed to use condoms consistently, with all their sex partners, including boyfriends. In most cases, the women brought their condoms from Paramaribo because they were not available in most parts of the interior. Wherever condoms could be obtained they were three to four times more expensive.

All respondents preferred to put the condom on the men, just to be sure that it was being used. They had the experience that many men did not know how to use a condom correctly or that they would try to pull it off. When asked how they protected themselves against potential STD/HIV infection, the following methods were given:

"I rinse my vagina after sex with water or a disinfectant" (25 respondents).
"I check the penis of the client for sores or pus" (23 respondents).
"I use condoms" (17 respondents).
"I screen my clients on their appearance" (13 respondents).
"I was tested for HIV" (11 respondents).
"I regularly take antibiotics" (9 respondents).
"I only have a vast pool of regular clients" (4 respondents).
"I refuse anal sex" (3 respondents).
"I refuse back poen" (3 respondents).
"I regularly go for STD checkups" (3 respondents).
"I take herbal potions" (2 respondents).
"I trust in God" (1 respondent).
"I don't do anything to protect myself" (4 teenage respondents).

Since drug and alcohol use are often cofactors in the transmission of STD, the respondents were queried on this subject. Nine respondents (22.5 percent) reported marihuana use and thirty-three (82.5 percent) used alcohol on a regular basis. IV-drug use was not reported by the respondents. One interviewer, however, wrote in her diary that during one interview, she had the feeling that the interviewee was high on drugs and had clearly visible needle marks on her arms. Based on this personal observation, the use of hard drugs among the population was probably much higher than what was found in this research.

Another form of unsafe sex was sex during menstruation. Four sex workers indicated that they continued working while menstruating, stuffing the vagina with cotton. One of them explained: "There is nothing else for me to do in the camps, so I am not going to sit around and do nothing. I just stuff it, and continue to work."

WORKING CONDITIONS AND PROBLEMS

In general, the working conditions for sex workers in the interior are worse than in Paramaribo. Traveling to and within the interior is not always easy and safe. The respondents indicated that a bus drive of up to four hours, followed by a boat trip of another few hours, or an airplane flight of one to two hours with a subsequent boat trip, were the only ways to reach the gold-mining areas. They also reported that they did not like to travel alone. They preferred to go into the interior in the company of girlfriends or gold miners because of the many robberies they had already experienced on their trips.

Particularly for those working in the women's camps, the hardship was not over once they arrived at their destination. Electricity and sanitary facilities were very poor and in many places completely nonexistent. The river had to be used for personal hygiene, washing clothes and dishes, to drink from, and to urinate and defecate in. Most women just kept a bucket with river water to clean themselves between clients.

One of their major concerns was malaria. Eleven of the forty respondents had, at least once, contracted the disease while working in the interior. They were forced to quit the job and return to Paramaribo for treatment. Minor health problems were treated with medication they had brought from town: "We are our own doctors. We bring painkillers and antibiotics from the city." They also used bush medicine whenever available or consulted a health post of the Medical Mission[9] where possible. Those with children felt very concerned about having to leave them alone while they were working in the interior. For some of them, the only option was to put the eldest child in charge. Women who were not ostracized by their family, because of their sex work, could sometimes rely on a grandmother. One had her children taken away from her by her own mother. Other sex workers indicated that out of fear of this happening, they were doing everything thinkable to hide their lifestyle from their family.

When asked about common problems in the camps, a list was presented that clearly illustrated the harsh conditions in which the sex workers operate:

- "Clients often refuse to use condoms. Many of them still want to pay more for unsafe sex" (23 respondents). This situation continues to exist and is identified by the Stichting Maxi Linder Associatie as one of the major obstacles in STD/HIV prevention efforts among sex workers. For the respondents, it posed serious dilemmas. The majority indicated that the intention to use condoms with a client was always there, but in reality, today's needs almost always won out over tomorrow's potential problems. In other words: "When you are hustling in order to feed yourself and your children, the extra money that a man offers for unsafe sex lets you take the chance and forget about any disease." The six women who reported consistent condom use explained that they worked by the principle "no condom, no pussy." Even though it was not always easy, they tried to negotiate condom use with each and every client. "If all sex workers would abide by this rule, the clients would not have a choice and everyone would benefit from it."

- "The hostile ambience among sex workers" (19 respondents). The atmosphere among sex workers was described as "bitchy" and vindictive. There was a lot of distrust, jealousy, and competition. They explained that they had been robbed several times and even physically abused by fellow sex workers and therefore did not trust anyone anymore. Actions of solidarity and looking out for each other occurred only among good friends. "If you are not fast enough, you don't eat. They snatch away the client by offering him a lower price, and you stay behind with nothing."
- "Clients often refuse to pay" (15 respondents). Newcomers in particular faced this problem. The more experienced sex workers settled the payment up front. "Sometimes the client does not want to pay. Nobody talks about it, and because some of the men are violent, I just let them go and keep my mouth shut." Some women indicated that, apart from defaulters, they also had met with clients who had deceived them with fake gold. "I was deceived a few times, but not anymore. I now ask for cash because there is no way to check the metal. Only when you are back in town, you find out."
- "Colleagues who work below the going price" (14 respondents). According to the respondents, the junkies among sex workers were spoiling the market for everyone because their addiction forced them to accept anything in return for sex. "If you try to use condoms and the client doesn't want to, he will always find one of those junkies who will give him unprotected sex. They will go with anyone, do anything for almost nothing."
- "Police harassment" (12 respondents). The respondents reported that police harassment in the neighboring country of French Guiana was common. Some of them had been arrested several times by the French police. They mentioned that they had been stripped of their money and gold by arresting officers.
- "Abuse from clients/boyfriends" (12 respondents). Apart from the violent working environment with robberies and gunfights, sex workers also had to face abuse from clients and boyfriends. Eight sex workers mentioned having experienced emotional abuse, such as insults and threats, or physical abuse. One sex worker had been stabbed with a knife, others were beaten up. With the exception of one sex worker who had received help from gold miners who had disciplined the offender, most of them expressed feelings of complete helplessness. There was nowhere to go and no one to turn to. "When it happens, there is not much you can do. Most of the time you just leave it and try to forget."
- "Clients who are drunk and junkies" (3 respondents). These clients were described as the worst kind: "They are aggressive, smelly, don't want to use condoms, don't want to pay; in short, they always mean trouble."

When asked about urgent needs, the majority of the women indicated that education was their number-one priority, specifically in the areas of malaria, STD/HIV, general hygiene and women's health issues. Secondly, the need for a national condom distribution network was mentioned, in order to increase condom availability everywhere in Suriname. Finally, the issue of regulation of the gold sector, including police protection throughout the interior, was raised.

MALE GOLD MINERS WHO VISIT
SEX WORKERS IN THE GOLD-MINING AREAS

Against expectations, recruiting male clients of sex workers for participation in the study required little effort. Coming from the eastern part of the country, they arrive in Paramaribo by ferry, crossing the Suriname River. For most of them, the bars and pubs close to the ferry are the first place to visit, making it easy to locate them. The interviewer for this group of respondents hung out at these bars, and she approached any man who was spending large amounts of money, bragging about his wealth, and flirting with women. She confirmed with him whether he had been working in the gold mines and had visited sex workers. After he gave his permission to participate in the study, he was interviewed at the SMLA center. The first respondents then recruited participants for the study among their friends and colleagues. This sampling method resulted in ten completed interviews within two weeks. The main focus areas of the face-to-face interviews were: demographics; motivation to visit sex workers; familiarity with sex work; sexual practices, preferences, and prices; general problems in the camps; safer sex practices; and specific needs.

Demographics

The profile of the male gold miners in this study can be described as follows: single, Surinamese or Brazilian man; average age of 38.8 years; of Creole or mixed ethnicity; Christian; finished primary school; lived in Paramaribo; and worked in the gold business in the eastern part of the interior of Suriname. The majority lived in Paramaribo but worked full time in the gold business in the interior. They usually stayed three to four months each time and then returned to the city for supplies, family visits, relaxation, and to spend their money. They liked to brag about their gold and money and spent it generously on sex workers in the interior as well as in Paramaribo. The men either worked independently or under a boss. The average time they had been working in the gold business was 1.4 years, with a variation of two months to six years.

Motivation to Visit Sex Workers

The primary motivation of the respondents to visit a sex worker in the gold-mining camps was to satisfy sexual needs. One respondent mentioned that the lack of other entertainment made him visit the women. All men defined sex as a natural desire and something that is "good" and "sweet." Seven men perceived sex work as a profession, one man looked at it as an emergency solution, and, finally, two men disapproved of it. For most men, sex workers were a necessary evil:

> They do a good job. It's easy and convenient for us; we don't have to wait until we're in town to have sex.

> Because I need to satisfy my sexual desires, I make use of the offer. There is no other way; I can't bring my wife to the camp.

> All that these women think of is money, money, money. They are dirty and don't care about nothing. The only thing they want is to take money out of our pockets.

The fact that everyone did it seemed to make it less wrong, but the feeling of doing something bad regularly came into mind: "Everybody does it, everybody knows about it, nobody judges. We're all in the same boat."

According to the respondents, visiting sex workers was completely accepted among themselves. At home, however, among relatives, it created problems, especially with girlfriends and wives when they found out about the sexual practices in the camp. Nine men indicated never to have had problems with sex workers in the interior. They said they knew who the troublemakers were and preferred to avoid them. One man reported to have been beaten by a jealous sex worker because he had gone with another one.

Familiarity with Sex Work

The respondents were familiar with three forms of sex work in the interior. The Brazilians who worked under a boss, on a contractual basis, talked about the sex-on-credit system. Most Brazilians indicated that they remained with the same woman throughout their stay in the camp. They had agreed to pay the boss 10 percent of their earnings for each woman they had sex with: "The boss takes care of all the necessary equipment and supplies, including women who cook and provide pleasure to us."

The Surinamese miners worked more independently and talked about the women's camps and the local sex workers. They did not allow women in the gold-mining camp. For sexual services, they went to the women's camp or they visited local Maroon women in the villages.

Sexual Practices, Preferences, and Prices

Both Surinamese and Brazilian men preferred women of their own nation-ality, mainly because of the language barrier. Whenever they wanted some-thing "wild," Surinamese men visited Brazilian women. They explained: "The Brazilian women are known to give you a special and good time, everything is allowed, they don't refuse anything. They know how to please a man." For cheap sex, they frequented the local Maroon women.

With an average of three to four visits a week, the spending on sexual pleasure added up to thirty to forty grams of gold, which equals about U.S.$300 to $400 per week. The Surinamese respondents reported plain, vaginal sex, "straight sex," as the most performed sexual practice. Whenever they wanted any variety, such as back poen, oral or anal sex, they went to a Spanish- or Portuguese-speaking sex worker, because their prices were "all-in." Surinamese or Guyanese sex workers, although oftentimes reluctant, charged four to ten grams more for any extras. The price also depended on the amount of time spent with the sex worker. As one miner said: "The longer the sex, the more gold you lose."

In general, all men preferred sex with a different woman each time, but in reality there was not always the freedom to choose, so they took whoever came along, even when she was not their type. As some men put it:

> If you take the same woman all the time, she becomes expensive. She will always try to get more money or gold out of you. That's why it is better to take another one every time. Those who give you more than just straight sex are popular.

> Sex with more than one woman at the time is almost impossible. Women are scarce in the camp; there is always someone who awaits his turn.

> I personally prefer big, black Surinamese women. In Paramaribo I only go with this type, but in the interior I take what is available at the time.

General Problems in the Camps

All respondents indicated that malaria was the most urgent problem in the camps. Three men reported that they had contracted the disease during their stay in the camps. All men said that for health-related problems they had to travel either to Paramaribo or to the nearest health post of the Medical Mis-sion. In and around most of the gold-mining camps, no medical facilities were available. The Surinamese gold miners also complained about the vi-olence and unsafe conditions in which they had to work. They would like to see some form of regulation of the gold sector and more involvement of the police. They blamed the Brazilians for the dangerous situation because of the Brazilian hot-tempered nature.

Safer Sex Practices

One of the respondents realized during the interview that he had an active STD. The nine remaining respondents claimed never to have contracted an STD. They all admitted that their knowledge about conventional STDs was poor and that they did not consider it to be a serious problem. HIV/AIDS, on the other hand, had their attention. Five of the ten had taken an HIV antibody test because of unprotected sex and because they had seen people with AIDS in the interior and were afraid of this disease. In spite of their expressed fear for HIV/AIDS, condom use was low. Five men indicated that they never used them, two men used them sometimes, and three men claimed to use them regularly. The two main reasons for not using condoms were the unavailability of condoms in the interior and the reduced pleasure due to decreased sensitivity.

The following safer sex measures were reportedly practiced by the respondents:

- Screening of women ("I only go with beautiful, healthy looking, and nice-smelling women")
- Taking bush medicine or using a *tapu*[10] for protection
- Taking antibiotics after sex
- Trusting in God
- Never having sex with a women during her period
- Only having vaginal sex
- Only having sex with women who practice safer sex themselves

Three respondents reported personal marihuana use and eight men reported regular alcohol use. One respondent used local herbs to stimulate his sexual potency.

Specific Needs

When asked about specific needs, three main areas were mentioned. Firstly, improvement of the general health and sanitary situation in the camps, specifically the malaria problem. It was suggested that encouraging cooperation between traditional healers and the formal health sector might address the problem. Secondly, the men expressed the need for more education on HIV/AIDS and other STDs. Finally, the Surinamese gold miners mentioned regulation of the gold sector as a specific need, including controlling or expelling illegal Brazilians, because they were seen as the main troublemakers.

FINAL THOUGHTS

This study indicates that the gold business and the sex business in the interior of Suriname are associated. The high demand for sexual services among gold miners with gold and money to spend in combination with the scarceness of women in most gold-mining areas creates ideal conditions for a thriving sex business. In spite of the inhospitable environment of the rain-forested interior, for gold miners as well as for sex workers, the earnings seem to outweigh the hardships and dangers of the work. Four topics emerge from the study as areas for future attention.

First, the developments in the gold-mining sector will, in the long run, undoubtedly have a devastating impact on the local environment as a whole, including the effects of the use of large amounts of mercury on public health. With gold miners and sex workers constantly on the move, traveling from one gold-mining area to the other, different health concerns are becoming apparent, such as malaria and STDs/HIV. According to the 1997 annual report of the Medical Mission, the malaria belt has moved 100 km northward in the last two years (Medische Zending 1998:2). The social environment of the local communities is also being affected. More and more men are attracted by the gold and leave their villages. Young boys quit school in favor of the search for gold. The women and girls stay behind in the villages and have to find ways to survive. The presence of groups of single men with a demand for sex creates opportunities for local women and girls to earn a living through sex work. The results of this study have provided the researchers with indications of a shift in mores and mentality in the local communities. In some areas, sex work has become the major option for survival. It has become acceptable and is being passed on to the next generations. Still recovering from the damages caused by the insurgency, the new economic development projects seem to add to the further disruption of community and family life in the eastern part of the interior of Suriname. Gold mining may bring material progress, but at what price?

The second topic for possible study concerns teenage sex workers. For most of girls interviewed, sex work offered a solution to overcome poverty. In this study, mothers who had been driven into the sex business by poverty had often introduced their daughters to the same lifestyle. This was the case with three of the teenage respondents, all of them Maroons, who had been forced by their mothers to perform sexual services to gold miners who had come to the village, looking for sex. These girls had learned, at a very young age, how their bodies can provide a livelihood, or "make things happen." For these three girls, sex work was no longer a choice but had become a way of life. As they became older, they grew accustomed to this life, and they had never really considered other options. All three of them acknowledged the fact that they had become professional sex workers. Although they preferred to do something else, they realized that their choices were limited. They dreamed about meeting the right man who would save them from the sex business.

The majority of teenage respondents, however, described sex work as an easy way of making extra money. At the age of fourteen or fifteen they had started to grant sexual favors in return for money, gold, or other luxurious commodities. The interviewers had a hard time recruiting this group of teenage sex workers because they denied selling commercial sex. For them, having sex for extras in order to be able to buy luxuries was not considered sex work. In general, these teenagers demonstrated a laissez faire attitude. According to them, what they were doing was not such a "big deal" and they did not seem to have any major objections to it. Most of them showed ignorance and naivety in their general conduct, especially in their sexual behavior. With regard to their health, they felt like most teenagers do: invulnerable. STD/HIV knowledge among this group was extremely low, as was their knowledge on prevention and safer sex practices. They consequently demonstrated high risk behavior, in most cases not even aware of the dangers.

A third topic to be considered is HIV/AIDS, which, in 1998, was very apparent in the interior of Suriname. Both female and male respondents knew that HIV is not simply an issue debated at a distant, national level. They were aware that a number of people in the interior were living with or had died of AIDS. One sex worker mentioned that she had been personally affected by AIDS through her sister, who had died of the disease. And still they continued to reportedly take risks. As was explained by the respondents in this study, their concerns about HIV were less severe and urgent than issues of poverty, violence, and other health issues they face on a daily basis.

For HIV/STD prevention among sex workers, the SMLA uses a harm-reduction approach.[11] This approach attempts to reach sex workers through their own social networks and to offer them the opportunity to participate in a process of self-directed behavior change in close cooperation with peer educators. Until now, this approach has worked for the club and street workers. The results of this study provide the SMLA with the challenge of reaching out to new target groups who have, for the most part, been invisible, as well as non-self-identifying sex workers.

Finally, in Suriname, the promotion of commercial sex is prohibited by law. Club-based sex work, however, is unofficially recognized and regulated through registration and licencing of nightclubs. Rules and agreements regarding visas, work permits, and biweekly STD checkups are in place for foreign female club workers. From a public-health standpoint, the conditions in which the (foreign) women operate are reasonably safe and healthy. The working and living conditions of street workers, on the other hand, are less favorable. Street work is not organized through red-light areas or tolerance zones. There are some streets in Paramaribo known for sex work, but police and community-authority actions in the last two years have closed down the most popular areas. The women were forced to move their business downtown, making themselves more visible and vulnerable for police actions. The Stichting Maxi Linder Associatie has organized street workers to defend their rights and improve their working and living conditions. Together with the sex workers, the SMLA crusades for recognition and regulation of the sex business, the recognition of commercial sex as an option for people to make a living, and regulation by the state in order to grant sex workers access to state benefits and pensions and to protect them from violence and abuse. Internal regulation is also advocated through, for example, setting a fixed price for different sexual practices and making condom use and regular STD checkups mandatory. The SMLA hopes that regulation will decrease competition, increase empowerment, and stimulate solidarity among colleagues. In addition, the respondents, both female and male, also argued for regulation of the gold sector in order to make their working environment a safer place.

NOTES

1. Estimated at the end of 1996 (Source: Algemeen Bureau Statistiek)
2. HIV: Human Immunodeficiency Virus.
3. SMLA: Stichting Maxi Linder Associatie (Maxi Linder Foundation), a non-governmental organization for female commercial sex workers.
4. Global HIV/AIDS surveillance data (Geneva, July 1998).
5. HIV/AIDS surveillance data from the National STD/HIV Prevention and Control Program.
6. HIV seroprevalance study conducted by the SMLA for the STD/HIV task force among 189 female sex workes, street based, in Paramaribo, in January and February 1996.
7. *Sranan Tongo* serves as the unofficial lingua franca by which most ethnic groups in Suriname communicate.
8. *Back poen:* Sexual practice whereby the man enters the woman's vagina from behind.
9. Medical Mission (*Medische Zending*): Non-governmental organization, responsible for the delivery of primary health care in the interior of Suriname.
10. *Tapu:* Maroon word for charm. This may be an amulet, talisman, or herbal potion with magic powers to help or protect the individual against evil and disease.
11. "Harm reduction supports a continuum of change that supplants an all-or-nothing approach and acknowledges that small incremental steps are still progress and necessary to longer-term change. Whether dealing with alcohol use, drug use, or sex, a harm-reduction approach identifies a range of risk; encourages people to start where they are able in order to protect themselves or their partners, to set their own realistic targets, and to move at their own pace" (Elovich 1996:1).

Part 4

Strategies for the Twenty-first Century

12

"Givin' Lil' Bit fuh Lil' Bit"

Women and Sex Work in Guyana

RED THREAD WOMEN'S DEVELOPMENT PROGRAMME

The current period of global restructuring is reconfiguring the position of the Caribbean in relation to international flows of labor and capital. One outcome of this is the marketing of the region as a provider of services, of which tourism—and prostitution as an associated hospitality industry and foreign exchange earner—is a prime example. However, the situation in Guyana is different from that in the island states of the Caribbean. First, not only is tourism in Guyana much less developed, but the particular form that recent initiatives have taken is ecotourism. While this involves a clientele that participates in tourism as an item of conspicuous consumption, the consumption of the "Other" that takes place is more ethereal than corporeal. Secondly, while even in those Caribbean territories with a more traditional form of tourism, prostitution is not always linked to tourism; in Guyana it is even less so.

In Guyana the sex industry is not highly organized, there is little reliance on women from other countries (although this may be slowly changing as exotic dancers are recruited from abroad), and there are no organized brothels. If tourism and prostitution are not so clearly related in Guyana, sex work is linked to and profoundly affected by the restructuring of the Guyanese economy during the 1990s. The flurry of economic activities resulting from the implementation of structural adjustment policies in the 1980s has opened up the country to foreign investment (now slowed by the current political impasse[1]), which in turn has served to produce a relatively new clientele (businessmen) and business-related activities in a context of economic immiseration and highly restricted and low-paying jobs for women.

Even prior to structural adjustment, women traders engaged in prostitution as a means of procuring goods and evading customs restrictions.[2] Today, increasing numbers of women appear to be engaging in sex work (some more obviously than others), and some groups—Amerindians and schoolgirls — appear to be especially vulnerable to deception and coercion.[3]

This chapter attempts to provide a framework for discussing some aspects of sex work in Guyana. Our focus is on women engaging in heterosexual encounters for pay, largely because women are predominantly workers and men clients.[4] Given the paucity of baseline data on sex workers in Guyana, this study is a preliminary one. Its aims are twofold: to examine the nature and context of sex work in Guyana; and to explore a number of themes that arose from our data. We commence by outlining the methodology and the legal framework, then go on to consider the factors behind the entry of women into sex work and the working conditions among the women interviewed. We move on to look at the blurring of boundaries between family life and sex work and the opportunities and barriers through which women negotiate their sexual agency. We close by considering strategies for change, as well as the implications for outsider involvement, based on a recognition of our own positionality as non-sex workers.

METHODOLOGY

Our methods involved both primary and secondary data collection. Primary data were collected using nonprobability samples. While this makes it more difficult to generalize from the results of the study, we felt the need to address specific groups of women was best served by this approach. Additionally, given the level of social opprobrium attached to sex work, it may have been difficult to gain the consent of large numbers of women to being interviewed.

A workshop was held in July 1997 with Red Thread members who formed the research team.[5] The ideas and draft in-depth interview schedule that came out of these sessions were discussed and modified at the first meeting of researchers and coordinators of the overall project held in Trinidad and Tobago in August 1997. Formal interviewing did not, however, start until January 1998 because of the tensions and then violence leading up to and following the December 1997 national elections in Guyana (see endnote 1). A further set of workshops was conducted with the research team once the first interviews had been completed to discuss some of the problems and gaps in the responses. All interviews were completed between January and April 1998.

With our focus on qualitative data gained through interviews with small samples of women, and an emphasis on the diversity of forms of prostitution, we also focused on an ethnically diverse sample. The majority of the women were from the country's two major ethnic groups of Indo- and Afro-Guyanese (hereto referred to as Indian and black), although a number were identified as mixed. Given the disproportionate representation of Amerindian women among sex workers (Danns 1996, Branche 1998) we also ensured their representation in the sample. Moreover, in light of recent concerns over the entry of schoolgirls into the sex trade (Danns 1996, Branche 1998), we specifically targeted them. The women were working in four different locations: clubs, hotels, and bars in the capital city, Georgetown; Georgetown streets; guest house-bars in settlements along the coast, including Georgetown; and mining camps in the country's interior. Some of the women had worked in neighboring Suriname, while a few also worked on the cargo ships docked at various wharves in Georgetown.[6]

Some of the women were interviewed during the day as well as at night at their places of work, which enabled the research team to acquire a glimpse into some of the conditions and the women and men involved. Women from the mining camps were interviewed at Bartica and Linden, two towns that serve as stopping points for persons coming out of the interior.[7] Interviews were also conducted at the Red Thread office. All interviews were carried out by groups of at least two Red Thread members.[8] In all we spoke with twenty-three sex workers.

Research team members also met with a number of other persons involved in organizations that directly or indirectly had a bearing on the issues with which we were concerned. These were: a project officer at the National AIDS Program Secretariat; a doctor from the Genito-Urinary Medicinal (GUM) clinic at the Georgetown Hospital, which treats sexually transmitted diseases (STDs); a lawyer working with Legal Aid and a board member of Help and Shelter, a service offering counseling and legal advice for women who have suffered domestic violence; a guest-house owner; and the Police Commissioner, in a telephone interview. Karen de Souza of Red Thread was interviewed about a trip she made in August 1997 to investigate allegations of young Amerindian girls working as prostitutes in liquor bars on the Essequibo Coast. A debriefing session was also held with the research team to discuss the interviews as well as other information relating to sex work in Guyana.

Finally, secondary data relating to sex work in Guyana were collected, including laws relating to prostitution; occasional newspaper articles; the results of a seroprevalence study among sex workers in Georgetown conducted in 1993 (Carter et al. 1997); an extended report on prostitution in a locally produced journal, the *Guyana Review*; and a recent study by George Danns (1996) on child prostitution in Guyana.

PROSTITUTION AND THE LAW IN GUYANA

The law on prostitution in Guyana is antiquated. Dating from the colonial era, it has yet to be revised. Based on the Criminal Law (Offenses) Act (Cap 8:01), a conviction for keeping a brothel results in two years' imprisonment. Prostitution-related activities are also indictable under the more recent Summary Jurisdiction (Offenses) Act (Cap 8:02). This provides for offenses triable in a Magistrates' Court and makes it illegal for a man to keep a brothel (defined as a "common ill-governed or disorderly house") or to earn a livelihood off the earnings of prostitutes. Also illegal are soliciting in a public place and loitering or importuning others for the purpose of prostitution. The fines imposed by this legislation are not only minimal—up to G$1,000 (approximately U.S.$7) and six months' imprisonment in the case of brothel owners (increasing to a maximum of G$2,000 or around U.S.$14, and twelve months' imprisonment for subsequent convictions), and up to twelve months and whipping or flogging for other offenses—but are also rarely applied.

WOMEN: THE WORKING SEX

> Most girls run away from home because they don't want to do work home. They don't want wash they plate, they don't want make up the bed. Those are people who would want to go into prostitution.... They don't want to take on responsibility, they are going to end up in prostitution.

The opinion above, expressed by a guest-house owner in Georgetown, echoes popular stereotypes regarding women's involvement in prostitution in Guyana. Yet, far from the image of the feckless young woman portrayed in these depictions, economic hardship was the single most important reason given for entering the sex trade among the vast majority of the women interviewed in our survey. Crisis and structural adjustment over the last two and a half decades have resulted in a dramatic rise in the number of women seeking work, but this increase has not been matched by a growth in female labor market opportunities (twenty-one of the women had been born and raised outside of Georgetown, where the bulk of the formal and informal service sector jobs for women are concentrated; see Peake and Trotz 1999). Becoming a sex worker, then, is for most a decision made against a backdrop of limited, highly exploitative, and poorly paid employment:

> I was comin' from wuk one day and a friend know me, she is from the West Bank too, but [she] move out and come to Georgetown, [she seh] wha' you doin' guard wuk in dis hot sun, girl, yuh ent see me, I does go in the bush. Hear

she, how much money yuh does wuk fuh? I seh twelve thousand a month, sometimes when I wuk overtime I does reach a lil fourteen, but the wuk on the overtime is very hard.... [She seh] suh hear wha' ah tellin' yuh, ah have a shop in the bush, is not my shop is my boy shop at Fourteen Mile.... She seh you could get a pennyweight [in gold] a short-time and two pennyweight a sleep [long-time].... She seh what would happen, you bring yuh gold to me and I will burn it and mek sure is gold and not bronze—you will tell me, well you goin' and do a business and how long you spend in dat room, so that within a certain time I ent see you, I'll come rap at the room or send my gentleman to rap up the room. She seh I'll give you X amount of advance right... like to carry you up in the bush.

Just over a quarter of the women cited sex work as their first income-earning activity. The remainder had previously worked as domestics, waitresses, petty vendors, craft makers and security guards. One woman had been a junior officer in the army. Another, who had previously earned G$6,000 a month as a domestic, was making G$2,000 per client as a sex worker in an out-of-town guest house. Faced with restricted income-earning opportunities, the women in our survey are further disadvantaged in their search for a livelihood by their limited formal qualifications. While many had gone on to secondary or community school, none had been able to finish, only three had received any additional training (typing and in the military), and two women had received no formal education. Sex work, notwithstanding the immense stigma attached to it and the dangers for unprotected workers, easily remains among the most economically viable options for poor women with limited education. The vast majority of the women had been introduced to the trade through friends and informal contacts, some taking them as far as Paramaribo (Suriname) to work. In one case the woman's partner was the instigating factor.

At the same time, economic factors cannot be divorced from other considerations. The gendered obligation of women to provide for their children against a backdrop of unremitting hardship has led to more women entering the labor force, as well as the increasing visibility of women in nontraditional sectors of the economy (Peake and Trotz 1999, Trotz 1998). The importance and responsibilities of motherhood clearly emerged as well from the interviews with sex workers. Just under 80 percent of the women had started sex work in the last six years, and only two women had started over twelve years ago. The average age was twenty years, ranging from sixteen to thirty-eight years (the high numbers of recent entrants might also be suggestive of the fact that women largely tend not to remain in the trade beyond a certain age range). Fifteen of the women had children (of whom three, at the most, had children only *after* they started working). In all cases, some—if not all—were preschoolers or in primary school. As one woman stated simply, "I did it for the sake of my children."

Sex work additionally served as an escape route from physical or sexual abuse by a partner or family member; for other women, it was abandonment by a partner or migration of family members that was the precipitating factor. Routine police harassment had contributed to one trader's decision to find another job. For some, migration to Suriname had provided the introduction to sex work (although it was not always their original intention). In five instances women had not initially realized what was expected of them—three had applied for jobs as waitresses, one woman had been taken into the interior by her boyfriend, while another said simply that she had been "tricked" into the business:

> [A woman] seh she want a girl fuh wuk with her and when I reach up in the bush right, now it was a Friday afternoon when I reach up with her, the Saturday she tell me look a room and mek heights [organize oneself to go about one's business]. Dey get some people does carry yuh in the bush and dey don't tell yuh the truth why dey carrying yuh in the bush.... So I go to dem girls and I ask, what is dis mek heights? What yuh got fuh do in dis room? And dem girls start explaining to me, I start to collect [understand].

For some of the younger women, sex work appeared to be a lifestyle: one sixteen-year-old Indian girl only worked Saturday and Sunday evenings, giving a regular G$2,000 per week to her aunt to bank for her, the rest going on fancy clothes and alcohol.

The wide range of responses from this small sample demonstrates that not only do different women offer varying reasons, but a number of factors (including coercion) may influence each woman. Economic factors are thus mediated by multiple issues, all of which must be taken into account in any attempt to fully understand the specific contexts that frame women's entry into the sex trade.

WORKING THE DAY AND NIGHT SHIFT: THE WOMEN'S WORKING CONDITIONS

One of the most important distinctions was the geographical location in which the women were working, one differentiation being between working in the densely populated coastal zone versus the interior (variously referred to as the bush or rainforest), where the mining camps are located. A further distinction on the coast relates to working in the city of Georgetown versus the small villages dotted along the coast. Perhaps the most visible sex workers are women who work on the streets in Georgetown. They begin in the evening and continue through the night in downtown business areas, on certain streets and around the main—Stabroek—market, where there are a number of small liquor stores and restaurants. The clientele is diverse, but these women, the oldest of the general sample, are least paid (see later discussion).

There are also guest house-bars well known for their reliance on sex workers to attract paying customers who will patronize the bar and pay for a short-time room. At one establishment, only alcohol was served. The majority of the men who frequent the guest houses are locals, and in Georgetown they include those who live elsewhere but come to the city to conduct business. Men come for a drink and to meet women during the day or straight after work. Guest house workers meet clients during the day, starting around nine or ten o'clock in the morning and finishing around midday or mid-afternoon. Some may also be long-term boarders whose living quarters double as their workplace.

At the other end of the spectrum are the women who work at popular nightclubs and upscale hotels and bars (Palm Court, Pegasus, Tower, Woodbine), as well as on a strip of road known locally as "the boulevard," a popular entertainment spot dotted with small Chinese restaurants, sound systems blaring the latest tunes, and drinking and karaoke bars that open from late afternoon until the early hours of the morning. Clients take women—or are taken—to a nearby hotel or guest house. Sex workers are predominantly young women, and it was here that the research team noticed a lot of teenagers. They dress "in the latest fashion, these close-fitted dresses like halter backs, short pants in the latest style you can think about" (research team interview). Many of the clients are gold miners (commonly referred to as porknokkers) flush with money and out for a night of "fun." There are also foreigners and middle-class men. The cargo ships (carrying imported goods or bauxite) that line the harbors and also lie out in the Atlantic Ocean house men that are almost entirely foreigners. Women meet them in local clubs or go to the wharves and gain permission (or bribe an officer or wharf guard) to board the freighters where they spend the night with one of the sailors.

Gold and diamond mining in Guyana's interior have in turn given rise to a number of support industries such as shops, bars, and airstrips. Prostitution is a critical feature of the interior mining economy; mining is a male-dominated activity and coastlanders leave their families at home. Sex workers come primarily from the coast as well, often recruited by shop proprietors to work in their bars and attract business. Everyone—sex workers included—hopes to profit from the spin-offs generated by mining. One study noted that a windfall find (referred to as a "lash" or a "shout") generated expansive outlays of money. One such shout yielding around fifty carats of diamonds led to a celebration that cost around U.S.$400, U.S.$80 of which was spent on procuring the services of prostitutes (Roopnaraine 1997). Women try to "mek heights" in good times and may try to move to other base camps around the area during the slack periods. Clients include Amerindians but are predominantly black and Indian coastlanders as well as Brazilians from across the border. (Brazilian sex workers are also present in some of the camps close to the border.)

In terms of ethnicity, we did not discern any differences insofar as reasons for entering sex work were concerned (although job options do vary, with Amerindian women experiencing the highest rates of unemployment). However, there were some variations in terms of location. One study has noted that Amerindian sex workers in the hinterland are rare (and they certainly do not operate within their home communities) and that women instead tend to establish long-term relationships, primarily with non-Guyanese gold and diamond seekers (Roopnaraine 1997). Amerindian women, then, work mainly in the city and in bars and guest houses on the coast. Many are recruited to work as waitresses and domestics and are informed only when they arrive at their place of employment that they are expected to provide sexual services. The four Amerindian women in our survey worked in guest houses and on the ships, with one woman working at various mining camps outside of her community of origin; none worked at the upscale end of the market. The Indian women we interviewed worked in all locations except the mining camps and in general seem to have a less visible presence in the interior. Only the black and mixed women worked across all categories. Most women were unconcerned about the ethnicity of the men they slept with. Some, however, expressed a distinct preference.[9] In one case an Indian woman's partner permitted her to have only Indian and white, but not black, clients.

Among sex workers there is short-time and long-time work, the former ranging in time from ten minutes to one and a half hours, while long-time sex involves a "sleepout." Prices for short-time sex ranged on average from G$500 to $5,000; a "sleep" could earn a woman up to G$10,000.[10] These prices, however, are not independent of context or place: for street workers, short-time prices ranged from G$500 to $1,000; in guest houses, prices ranged from G$700 to $2,000; in bars and hotels the range was G$3,000 to $5,000; and in the mining camps the average payment was one pennyweight of gold, i.e., G$1,600. There were also differences among the women's prices, which might be increased if they had access to wealthy or foreign clients.[11]

Thus, street workers tend to earn the least, followed by women who live or work out of the guest houses that offer rooms for them and their clients. Women who worked in Georgetown on the ships or out of prominent hotels, bars, and nightclubs earned the highest amounts. Given their clientele, payments are often in foreign (U.S.) currency, and generous tips and gifts are an expected part of the trade.

Age was found to be an important differentiating factor in terms of earnings. For example, none of the schoolgirls we interviewed worked on the street. (Their average earnings for a short-time ranged from G$1,600 to $5,000 or approximately U.S.$11 to $36). For all the women, the average age of the highest earners was twenty years, compared with twenty-four years for women in mining camps, thirty-one years for street workers, and thirty-two years for women working in guest houses.

To be sure, these divisions are neither clear-cut nor absolute, as most of the women had worked at more than one location (only three of the women had not worked at more than one place). This fluidity also extended across national borders. Three of the women had started working in Suriname (in bars and occasionally on ships) before shifting to Guyana, while one continued to move back and forth across the border. While our interviews focused only on Guyanese women, migration also works in the other direction. Sex workers from Brazil have had a long presence in the mining camps along the southern border (Roopnaraine 1996). Other reports indicate that an increasing demand from the local entertainment industry in recent years has given rise to the recruitment of women from Brazil, Trinidad, and elsewhere in the Caribbean as go-go dancers, lap dancers, and exotic dancers in bars and at private shows along the coast. These women work in the city during the week and out of town on weekends (*Guyana Chronicle*, April 14, 1998; *Stabroek News*, April 18, 1998).

At the same time, not all women's sex work histories suggested easy movement from one sector to another. For example, women located in the higher ranks of sex work appeared to migrate only between locations that are similarly placed on the earnings scale. In response to the question "Where do you work?" one woman identified the ships, two nightclubs and four prominent hotels, depending on where business was best. On the other hand, very few of the women interviewed in the lowest earning categories worked in the more lucrative sectors of the business: significantly, one who did was relatively young—nineteen years old. More work is required to determine the extent to which a clear hierarchy exists and to analyze some of the barriers to entry into the higher paying sectors of sex work.

BLURRING BOUNDARIES
(OR, THE GAINS OF MAINTAINING DIFFERENCE)

As long as you are exchanging sex for something material...you're doing sex work right.... You even play the sex workers with your own husband, because woman say she's all weak and you see he has some money and you need a new dress, so today you going to roast a piece of beef and some chicken and you put up candles and you got to be nice because you got your eyes on the man's money. You're being a sex worker, you're playing a sex worker, is sex work, and there's a lot of it, because of economic situation. I mean a lot of women in

Ministries, various places. Because people don't go to bed for nothing, but because they are out on the street and they go to South Central [one of the guest houses], they say well I'm on to the sex work. And I am more afraid of them or afraid for them where transmission of STDs or HIV or AIDS [is concerned] because [I would think] I am not a sex worker and this guy is working at the Ministry and I don't have to use a condom. The women on the street, they know what they are doing, so when a man come to them, they say you have to use a condom because they know to themselves that they wouldn't accept, OK (Dusilley Cannings, National AIDS Program Secretariat).

Guyana, as elsewhere in the Caribbean, operates on a double standard insofar as sexuality and sexual relations are concerned. From an early age it is young girls whose mobility is likely to be constrained and it is women who are always in danger of being labeled loose or slack, whereas similar activities are more likely to earn men the reputation of being a stud. Sex workers are "different" from other women in their obvious refusal of gendered interpretation of the spaces they should and should not be occupying. If their selling of (hetero) sexual labor confirms them as women, they resemble men in their occupation of public spaces at night and their engagement in a series of casual encounters. Through their transgressions, they show up the unnaturalness of taken-for-granted gendered divisions of spaces and activities. The disjuncture is "managed" by defining them as inferior, immoral, and lacking the values of family life.[12] Yet, as the quotation above clearly suggests, sex acts that involve material exchanges are the defining features of many marriages and relationships as well as prostitution. Moreover, as our interviews clearly showed, there is no clear boundary between prostitution and "normal" family life.

In the first place, the sex work of the women surveyed and family life are closely intertwined. As we have already noted, support of the family, and in particular younger children, is the most critical reason for women to enter the sex trade. Moreover, while they are careful to distinguish between "sexing for work" and "sexing with your man" (see later discussion), sex workers may enter into longer-term relationships with preferred clients. In fact, one-third of the women were currently in relationships at the time of the interviews, many with ex-clients whom they had met while working.

One case study vividly highlights this issue. Jennifer is a twenty-six-year-old woman who has been a sex worker for six years. She has worked primarily in the mining camps and has five children, all under ten years of age. The father of at least one was someone she met on the job. At present Jennifer has three "regulars" in addition to her other clients (most of whom tend to be married men). Expectations differ little from the way in which other women not involved in sex work describe their relationships with men (Peake and Trotz 1999). As she says,

Yuh wash dey clothes, sometime yuh prepare lil food fuh dem and so, and yuh tek it down to the work ground and so, and dem does seh ha, dis girl interested in me and so, and all like dat well I does get anything from dem and so.... All like if yuh know dey working late, yuh mek lil snack and yuh carry it fuh dem, yuh treat dem nice like if is yuh husband yuh living wid, right... because if yuh don't treat dem good, dey wouldn't treat you good.

In response Jennifer gets extra tips, occasional gold, clothes and transportation "fare" when she needs to go to the coast to see her children. On one or two occasions she stopped working after taking a "regular," but reentered the business when support was not forthcoming. (One man refused to acknowledge paternity of a child because he said Jennifer was "picking fare" [having sex with paying clients] and the father could be anyone.)

As Jennifer's experiences show us, while it is the regular payment of money for sex that is seen as degrading by outsiders, in fact the material exchanges that underwrite sexual relations are not confined to prostitution. In somewhat similar fashion and based on his research in Trinidad, Daniel Miller has argued that within the cultural logic of nonmarital unions in the Caribbean, money signifies and affirms the existence and value of a relationship. Miller specifically makes a distinction between marriage and other unions (common-law, visiting), although we would maintain that in fact such exchanges are crucial to all types of relationship in the Caribbean, despite representations to the contrary (Miller 1994:194–195).[13] The blurring of the lines is becoming even more apparent in the current economic climate, which is increasing the material imperative for women to enter into relationships with others who can become providers (or important contributors).[14] Perhaps the only significant difference between sex workers and "other" women is that the former are openly having multiple sexual relationships with men at one time, rather than subscribing (or pretending to subscribe) to monogamous unions or serial monogamy.

However, the discouragement of autonomous expressions of female sexuality as transgressing gender ideals in Guyanese society[15] results in the maintenance of a discursive distinction between prostitution and family life that denies any correspondence between the two realms.[16] Moreover, we should not underestimate the power of representation and the reality of its consequences for women defined as transgressing familial boundaries and labeled with what Gail Pheterson (1996) refers to as the "whore stigma."

Indeed, all of the women agreed that they were seen as lesser persons by virtue of being sex workers: "Guyanese people are most irrespectful, dey don't really look at prostitutes, dey would say dey is whores and dey would look at dem, yuh know, try to keep far and don't even want talk to dem, even like dey are in the way too." Interestingly, those who had worked in Suriname were of the view that there was a far less moralistic attitude to sex work—at least where foreigners were concerned—that made it easier to work.[17]

> [People] view it bad because they curse people, tell yuh how you is a whore and yuh does pick fare on the street.... But in foreign country nobody looks, nobody cares what yuh do, what yuh do dat's your business, nobody has no saying in yuh life, but in Guyana people always look to see what yuh do, when yuh go in, when yuh come out, and in foreign yuh don't get none of those problems, yuh stand up in the streets, the boys dem would pass, dey wouldn't even tell yuh nothing, just the men dat coming to like do business wid you would come....

Families could also be condemnatory (although far less than we had expected). For some of the women, family members, including current partners, knew how they were earning an income and there appeared to be no negative consequences, especially where financial support was forthcoming. (One woman, for instance, had built a house for her mother and siblings on the proceeds from sex work.) Others experienced regular verbal abuse. In a number of instances family members believed that the women were doing other things (such as being unemployed, working as traders and waitresses, or visiting friends in the city). Some women chose work in the interior or in Suriname, not simply on account of prospective earnings, but also out of a desire to keep their source of livelihood hidden from their family (one woman had a small cigarette and sweet stall in Guyana that was financed through the money she continued to make as an occasional sex worker in Suriname). A few believed that their families would have nothing to do with them if they found out. However, the majority of the women pointed out that what they did was their own business and they did not care what their families or communities thought, once they were able to earn a living and support their children (although this may well have been a defensive stance, taken for the benefit of the interviewers): "[The community] see me as a whore, but I tell meself me ent no whore, is just survival fuh my children, [they call me] satan, the big whore, the big pokey bitch...."

Women were also highly scathing of what they described as hypocritical mores:

> When dey go fuh stone da woman down, she was a prostitute, yuh hear what God turn and tell dem, who don't have no sin cast the first stone, none a dem coulda cast the stone because all a dem had sin, so nobody can't cast no stone on me out here, all a dem got sin.

Other women also came in for specific criticism. Sex workers insisted that by acknowledging what they did, they were far better off than women who condemned them while engaging in unsafe sex with unfaithful partners:

When me and dem get story, the first ting dey say is you are a prostitute, you are a whore bugger [engaging in anal sex for money], you do dis, you do dat.... Dat don't bother me 'cause dey get nuff women living in dey house and dey don't know what dey man going and do behind dey back, and...dem is the one that does dead wid AIDS, 'cause a man does go wid other woman and dey does carry it home...but yuh see the prostitute out deh does protect dem self wid a condom, yuh does hardly find prostitute dying wid AIDS.

As one woman summed up:

No, no listen, I am not doing anything wrong to my body, if yuh deh living home, yuh ent coming on the street and yuh living with a man, the first ting he don't have money to give you or he got other women wid you. So I come out here, use a condom, get my money, go home and sleep, the only thing is that I losing me night sleep, and it don't bother me.

The implicit contrast in this statement is striking indeed; it is the prostitute, who openly acknowledges her work and the unreliability of men and takes steps to protect herself and not be fooled, who is most comfortable and whose losses are least.

CREATING SPACES: MORAL ECONOMIES OF SEX WORK IN GUYANA

Stereotypical representations of sex workers not only deny the blurring of boundaries that exist in Guyanese society, but by denying sex work any legitimacy (in common parlance it is seen as "slackness" or "wutlessness," implying an absence of or disregard for rules), they also overlook the social mores through which sex work is given meaning for those involved. The moral economy (Scott 1976) of sex work elaborated in the interviews differentiated with the group of women we spoke with as well as set out certain codes of conduct for sex work itself.[18] Nor was this found to be exactly the same for all women. In the following paragraph one woman explains the protocol involved in getting business in a bar in the interior:

Where dey does sit down and drink, yuh does go up there and have game which we does play, dominoes and draught; sometimes yuh sit down playing there, somebody choose you, whichin it have some girls does run up to men. I don't like dat run up way because dey does seh, she too brazen with she self.... But you see when you sit down, play yuh little domino and ting...hear what does happen now, you sit down playing and somebody choose you, they don't come and say well a choose you, dey does bring a juice, cause remember dey don't know what you drinking, and they now speak to you, they does say goodnight, they point to you, you say goodnight, how are you, you answer back, at least me, I answer back in a courteous way.... Some of them say take this, and I would say thanks, from the time I get that juice I done know what it is, that I get, I get pick, whichin sometimes a man would come and give you a juice, and he don't have no intention, but he spirit go out for you, he ent got no intention because he ent got no gold, but he would leave you for a next night, and he would return.

The excerpt above shows us how some women may use dominant notions in Guyanese society in order to distinguish themselves from and situate themselves above other sex workers. In the previous example, the sex worker differentiated herself from more "brazen" and less "respectable" advances. Other women also talked about dressing appropriately as important to ensure respect from clients ("If yuh dress loose off, den yuh ent looking good"). That sex workers are not and do not see themselves as a homogeneous group has critical implications for organizational strategies, a point to which we return later.

Far from being passive women who men can simply pick up and have their way with, the sex workers we spoke with were actively involved in negotiating the terms of the exchange and some rules of the game. Money is handed over in advance. In the interior if payment is to be made in gold, the metal is burned to test its authenticity and then weighed to guarantee against short-changing. It is bad practice to provide services with the promise of future payment, unless the client is a regular and is known for being reliable. In addition to probably never getting paid, the sex worker could stand to lose respect among clients:

It would bring problem, like yuh know they would get disrespect fuh you, it would bring eye pass. Now let we say...you trust [credit] somebody tonight right, [and] he ent turn up to pay [later], you keep yuh mouth shut 'cause you goin' [be] shame. He gone tell he friend dem and he gone mek laugh off of you. I see it happen to people, so I wouldn't do that.

Another would not have sex with any of the men from her community, only with "dead stranger," because as she said, "I want when I walk pon de road, nobody mustn't diss [insult] me, dey mustn't get disrespectful."

Women charge for straight sex, and should they agree to anything more, a higher price is usually demanded: "[I have] straight sex, no position if yuh didn't pay me fuh dat, yuh pay me fuh break [ejaculate]." A number of the women said they would only undress or vary their routine with established clients. A short-time session ends with the sexual release of the client, but if he is taking too long, women may ask for more money. Several sex workers had strategies to "speed up" a session, and women also did not like clients to become inebriated ("You won't make a man drink too much, so you will get him to break fast, but if he drinks a lot then he won't"). Significantly all the women, with one exception, initially denied performing oral or anal sex (in two cases women were forced), although they said these services were frequently asked for.[19] In Guyana such subjects are highly taboo and not readily (if at all) admitted to or discussed openly. In fact the easiest way to "shame" a woman in public is to accuse her of engaging in oral or anal sex. Indeed all the women said that these were things that foreigners, homosexuals, or dirty women engaged in. In this respect distancing is important in Guyanese society and possibly even more so for the sex workers being interviewed by outsiders, all too aware of their reputations as being sexually loose.

In conducting business, it is also important to create emotional spaces of one's own: "Is just the money yuh want mek yuh see, yuh doing this business, is not really yuh desire to do it." Several of the women were very clear that the selling of one's body did not imply that one was selling one's self: "I will say is a job I doing.... I don't go fuh feelings, I does just go fuh me money." Another reiterated: "Like when yuh going picking fare...like yuh mustn't kiss, yuh mustn't romance and dem thing dat." Several of the women did not undress fully, some taking off only their shoes and underwear. Nor were clients given complete access to women's bodies. Some women, for example, did not kiss, and we repeatedly found that women's breasts were off-limits ("Some a dem [men] does want suck yuh bubby, some does want you kiss dem, I does tell dem no, no I ent deh suh, you not me husband, yuh come fuh have an affair and we finish wid dat"). Occasional exceptions were made for regular clients. In short, as one woman succinctly noted, "[When I have sex with a client] I be like a log."

Finally, sex work was identified by all the women as a job, but not all of the women saw their work as a permanent occupation. Those who did were predominantly older women, for whom sex work is perhaps best described as a survival strategy. For younger women and those at the higher end of the market, it was hopefully a means to an end. Among this group, a successful sex worker was not someone who could get the best clients and call the highest prices (for it is understood that this situation will not last forever and that one's "sexual capital" is likely to decrease the older one gets) but someone with a good business head, who would have something to show for her involvement in sex work. Over three-quarters of the women we interviewed tried to save.[20] Women used both formal (bank) as well as informal (penny bank, boxhand, puzzle box, burying money) saving and credit mechanisms. Not surprisingly, women working in the higher-paying areas, who charged more and were often paid in foreign (U.S.) currency, had been able to accumulate quite large sums of money in the bank (for example, G$90,000, G$350,000, and U.S.$1,600). Two younger girls had an older family member open a bank account for them. Among the plans outlined were to purchase a minibus or truck; to start a fish business; to build a house and open a shop;

and to run a cigarette stand. A few women also articulated their desire to finish school or take private lessons (mainly to acquire secretarial skills). Not surprisingly, making a better life for one's children was a paramount concern in women's plans for the future. As one woman explained:

> I'll try to advise younger women dan meself, also older ones who discontinue, 'cause I would say like dey don't know what dey doing, you do dis thing, because you [in] need and when yuh get the money yuh switch, yuh try to do something else, yuh don't do dis thing all the days of yuh life, try to finish, yuh have children. Whilst dey small yuh do it, when dey get big yuh stop. That's why yuh save, yuh get 50 U.S. a night yuh try to save, yuh spend half yuh save half, yuh try to save, if I never use to save a coulda never get me house in one year and I build a house, a two-bedroom house.

She continued:

> I'll advise that you would get dis money yuh must save it, put it to uses so when yuh get older yuh won't have to still doing this, because it have old people still on the street doing prostitution, and I feel they doing prostitution fuh like 20 years and still dey have nothing.... Some of dem have children [and] dey have nothing to show dey children; well dey children find out dey doing prostitution and still dey have nothing to say, "Well when a was doing prostitution dis is what I did."

The interviews were a testimony to the aspirations and hopes of sex workers and further showed the potential of sex work to provide an avenue for personal financial savings. Its importance is further underscored in a context in which women generally have far less access to capital and credit and are less likely or able than men to obtain loans to set up small businesses (Mondesire and Dunn 1995).

CONSTRAINTS AND LIMITS

Undoubtedly, foregrounding the spaces that sex workers create for themselves enables us to avoid a perspective, however well-meaning, that depicts such women as victims. At the same time, an emphasis on the sexual agency of women should not lead to a prematurely romanticized portrayal of resistance and in the process foreclose a discussion of the very real constraints that sex workers face in their daily lives, both on as well as off the job. It is important to explore how women negotiate limits and challenge their ongoing marginalization in Guyanese society and to acknowledge that many simply may not succeed.

For a start, the plans women outlined to save regularly, invest in businesses, return to school, or migrate are frequently thwarted by the high cost of living, particularly where the woman is a major or single contributor to her household, as the following description starkly reveals:

> Sometime yuh want lil sugar, yuh might not even got lil milk fuh yuh children and yuh ent got money fuh cook fuh yuh children, and yuh go wid dis person, accepting so yuh will get the money fuh come and give yuh children something next morning, [but] next morning yuh children just watchin' yuh and you watchin' dem, eye water [tears] come to my eyes, yuh talkin' but yuh ent got nothin' to give dem and yuh go wid persons to get a raise to give them ting or to buy tings fuh dem.

Income fluctuations are a common occurrence. Some women may be on the road for the greater part of the night, but not every day or night is likely to produce business. A number of the women worked seven days a week, the length of time depending on whether they were able to get any business: "Sometimes me ent get money, me does stay till dayclean [daybreak]." Women frequently buy "rations" [bulk buy] to tide them over. Sex workers living permanently in guest houses may also face high daily rents, while those working in mining camps must not only provide childcare on the coast while they are away but additionally worry about the debts they owe and face prohibitive prices for food, clothing, housing, transportation, and beverages. In one case a worker in a mining camp was charged G$1,000 a day for the room if she did not have a client and G$500 if she used the room for sex.[21] In the interior as well, men are always on the lookout for a "fresh" [a new arrival], which can threaten business prospects for already established workers, particularly if they are older:

> Like when yuh deh too long in a shop and dem [men] ent reach [meet] yuh, yuh know dem meet fresh dey call it fresh, like people heard a boatload full a girls come in, so yuh have to mek heights fast, soon as yuh go in the bush yuh have to start mekkin' yuh heights and come out so dat yuh wouldn't be too long at the shop, or else dey back yuh out and collect the fresh.

Even one sixteen-year-old complained of men in the bush moving onto new partners.

Like other self-employed women (and indeed several in the private sector), sex workers have no right to pensions (although current pensions are patently inadequate even for those entitled to them) and no source of income if they get pregnant, and only one woman contributed to the National Insurance Scheme. Getting out is difficult in the absence of viable employment alternatives. We have no information on ex–sex workers, but the example of two women—one in the business for nineteen years and another for eleven years and both working at the lower ends of the market—suggests that women may exit the trade as a result of age, health, or if they are able to depend on older children for financial support, as job opportunities for older women are even more precarious (Peake and Trotz 1999). In short, the dream to eventually open a business may remain just that for most. It is also important to note that where one works may differentiate one's chances of accumulating enough capital to leave, and in this regard the women working out of hotels and bars in Georgetown and those on ships are likely to have the greatest chances.

Moreover, the nature of women's involvement in the sex trade is akin to their secondary position in other sectors of the labor market and their subordination to men. None of the women we interviewed admitted to giving money to a "pimp," but as we have seen, several women who were supporting households were in relationships with men who knew exactly what they were doing. Given the stigma attached to a woman who is known to "mind a man" in Guyanese culture, denial on the part of sex workers when faced with such a question by outsiders is perhaps to be expected ("I don't have no pimps, I don't wuk wid no pimps, I ent fucking my soul case out, fuh go and pay no man, dat is bare nonsense, is best I mind a man dan pay a pimp"), although it was acknowledged that for other women (never those interviewed), paying relationships with men other than clients do exist. Dusilley Cannings, of the National AIDS Program Secretariat in Guyana, also noted the presence of men. Unlike pimps elsewhere who actively recruit women and control their earnings and movement, in Guyana men are more likely to be paid to "protect" sex workers from possible violence by clients. In clubs and guest houses the "chucker outers" [bouncers] are employed by managers, but along the boulevard they are paid by the women and also help a sex worker to get clients in exchange for a fee of G$500.

The absence of regulation in the sex trade industry in Guyana combines with an apparently growing demand for commercial sexual services to create exploitative working conditions for sex workers with no avenue for redress. We have already referred to the growing entertainment industry, its control by men, and the use of schoolgirls in the making of videos for distribution locally and overseas. Guest-house, bar, and club owners are also predominantly men who exert considerable control over sex workers. Perhaps the most vulnerable in this regard are younger and Amerindian women in rural and hinterland areas who are frequently enticed—and often coerced—into the sex trade through the promise of a well-paying waitressing or domestic job, who never receive their payment directly from the clients, and who are paid poor wages, which are more often than not withheld. There appears to be an organized ring involved in procuring young Amerindian women seeking employment (unemployment rates are highest in hinterland areas, where the vast majority of the Amerindian population resides). While there is widespread knowledge on the coast of this state of affairs, very little is done to protect the women. Gaining their trust and overcoming their fear and suspicion is a difficult if critical task, made even more daunting by the paucity of viable employment alternatives for Amerindian women. One investigation into working conditions in the Barima-Waini and Pomeroon-Supenaam Region in Essequibo, found that Amerindian women—many under eighteen years old—were being hired as waitresses, cleaners and domestics, but none would admit to providing sexual services for men (interview with Karen de Souza; see also Branche 1998).

In the mining camps, shopkeepers are important persons in a sex worker's life, often responsible for her being there in the first place. Figures of protection against clients who are violent or refusing to pay, they may also themselves exploit women in the interior: "Some people would go in the interior to pick fare, they would get malaria, sometime if dem ent really get somebody to tek care [of dem], like certain shop people to tek care of dem, certain shop people would just left dem pon dey own and dey will just pine away till dey dead, and just bury in the bush."[22] Sex workers may hand over part or all their earnings to the shopkeeper for safekeeping (a few experienced workers dig a hole in the ground and bury the money or gold at night), but many are often given back "short money." To complain or to allege dishonesty is to risk being put off the landing and having one's debts called in. Less experienced and particularly younger women may also be forced to give a dredge owner or other "big man" [a person in authority] a "piece," i.e., sex, by a shopkeeper, who is not unknown to request sexual favors himself. Women sometimes—but far less frequently—procure workers for prospective clients. Instances of women running bars in rural areas and in the interior and exploiting and physically abusing younger (and, in the interior, frequently Amerindian) women have also been noted (Branche 1998). One example cited in the interviews concerned a former sex worker who had opened her own bar in the interior but whose practices differed little from the male proprietors.

The marginalization of sex workers, and the proscribed nature of the work they engage in, make it extremely difficult for them to seek protection from physically abusive clients, pimps, and guest-house owners. Moreover, where women are ostensibly being hired as waitresses, cleaners, and domestics, there may be reluctance, shame or fear to come forward and disclose the actual nature of their work. There exists no agency that can deal specifically with sexual and physical abuse of sex workers, like Help and Shelter, which was set up to provide counseling, legal, and other services for women who have experienced domestic violence from partners.[23] The Domestic Violence Act did not envisage a situation of abuse of a sex worker by her client, where the relationship is one of "employer–employee or prostitute–client" (unless the offender is a pimp who may also be in a relationship with the woman). The only available recourse at the moment, then, is to make a report at the police station and to seek normal remedies under the law for assault and battery (interview with lawyer, Legal Aid). Here, however, sex workers are likely to encounter extreme discrimination and disrespect: they are not credible because they are, by virtue of their occupation, immoral and untrustworthy; it is impossible to rape a woman who offers her sexual services for sale; and in any case such women not only ask for but fully deserve what they get. In this regard, even violence from a partner which is dealt with under the Domestic Violence Act, becomes difficult to report when the victim is a sex worker. As one woman commented, "If a man bully me, don't give me money and dey [the police] get to hear that I am a prostitute, do you think dey goin' to look into dat? I can't go and say he try to rape me, dey wouldn't look into it, that is the police force." Another noted wryly that if a client said that he had been robbed, the sex worker would be the first to be picked up.

The general distrust of the police is also related to the experiences (and expectations) of the sex workers. It is widely believed that the police force is often inclined to "turn a blind eye" to prostitution. Greater tolerance, however, is less likely to be official or unofficial policy than it is a matter of the prerogative of individual officers in a context in which the sex worker is always in a position of subordination to the law. None of the women we interviewed had ever been formally charged or fined, but the general tendency to "stay out of police way" indicates that law enforcement officials are by no means absent from the lives and minds of sex workers.[24] In this regard, it appears to be the women working on city streets who are most vulnerable to being stopped and picked up for loitering by the authorities: "The other night a police vehicle pass and the police say don't let him pass back and see us there liming, and I explain that a have children and I got to hussle a dollar fuh dem and he seh he ent business wid dat, we gat to come off the road." Women could be picked up and locked up overnight for loitering, and the demand of sexual favors did occur. One woman had been given a choice of sex or payment of a G$1,000 bribe, while another from a mining camp had been told by a police officer that unless she had sex with him, she would be put off the landing. Women working in Suriname also alleged harassment from police (Scouties); in one case a sex worker had been robbed at gunpoint. It is important to investigate the implications of women working overseas without relevant documents and in constant fear of being caught without papers and deported. Are these women likely to be targeted more?

Marginalized by the stigma attached to sex work that leaves women potentially open to verbal and physical abuse by clients and in the absence of adequate protection from the police (who may themselves be perpetrators of crimes against sex workers), a number of the women arm themselves with knives. On the boulevard some recalled an incident in which a sex worker was taken out of town, beaten, robbed, and raped before being dumped, as proof that they were all potential victims and needed to protect themselves. All the women also preferred to conduct their business in hotels where they could call for help if needed, as cars, alleyways, and the seawall were dangerous places. One or two—who worked the more profitable areas—also had designated taxi drivers whom they would rely on to collect them after they had finished. These measures are not always sufficient. Eight of the women had been robbed or had experienced some form of violence (in two cases women were forced to have anal and oral sex), and we have reason to believe that the figure is much higher.[25]

Health issues are another critical factor for sex workers (and although there are a number of other occupation-related health concerns—malaria in mining camps, for example—that warrant consideration, we confine our discussion here to STDs). Over 70 percent of the women visited the government health clinic, while two women utilized the services of private doctors.[26] However, women working out of Georgetown—in the mining camps—were less likely to have regular access to health provision (at present there are only two GUM clinics that deal specifically with STDs, and both are located in urban centers—in Georgetown and New Amsterdam), and only one Amerindian woman visited a clinic. One schoolgirl was also ashamed to go for checkups, while another claimed to have malaria yet was hospitalized shortly after the interview with AIDS. Over-the-counter drugs—including antibiotics—are used (interview with Dusilley Cannings, National AIDS Center). One woman stated, for example, that "if yuh don't have a condom, yuh would tek a try and then drink two antibiotic [procured from a friend] after."

Condom use in Guyana continues to be seen as largely a woman's responsibility. Although clients engaging in multiple sexual encounters without using condoms place sex workers at considerable risk, it is the prostitute who in fact ends up taking the rap for the spread of STDs, as popular representations depict them as engaging indiscriminately and wilfully in unsafe sex (also see Kempadoo 1996). In fact one report noted that among sex workers, "safe sex is the first law of survival" (Branche 1998:9). In our survey as well, all but three of the women said that they used condoms and never had sex "bareback." Most bought condoms, as women claimed that the ones that are provided free of charge from health clinics are expired or ineffective.[27] Given that a study in 1993 found very little knowledge of HIV transmission among sex workers in Georgetown (Carter et al. 1997), these findings are positive evidence of heightened awareness relating to bodily practices and health and sexually transmitted diseases. In large part this is due to workshops sponsored by the National AIDS Program Secretariat and the efforts of individuals like Cannings to engage the concerns of sex workers. At the same time, we must consider the extent to which women feel comfortable talking openly about such issues with others whom they have just met and who are not involved in the trade, especially in a climate in which the words prostitute and AIDS go hand-in-hand in the popular imagination (we have already seen in the previous section how women distanced themselves from engaging in sexual acts that in Guyana are associated with "dirtiness"). "Slippages" in the interview transcripts led us to this conclusion, as a few of the women had become pregnant and had abortions on the job, while some had contracted STDs. Moreover, a seroprevalence study conducted in Georgetown by the Pan American Health Organization (PAHO) in 1993 found that 25 percent of a sample of 108 sex workers was HIV positive (Carter et al. 1997) and it is possible that this estimate is on the conservative side (especially given that Guyana is now estimated to have the highest rate of HIV infection in the region after Haiti). Cannings recalled that in one session on STDs, seven out of twelve sex workers had contracted syphilis. While sex workers are self-aware and conscious of the risks involved (and this came across clearly in the interviews), whether they were always able to enforce condom use or safe sex practices was another matter. There are no programs targeted at clients, and men prefer not to use condoms. In a difficult economic situation one of the problems is that refusing to have "bareback" sex may result in the loss of a client, where there are other women who will agree to forsake a condom for more money. Sexual violence is another problem that women may encounter. These factors highlight the need for organizing initiatives that come from sex workers themselves; a point to which we return in the final section of this chapter.

Another—somewhat related—issue is the use of alcohol and drugs. Nineteen of the women used alcohol with clients, with several women saying that it was easier to go with a client when they drank. Drug use has been identified as an increasing problem among younger sex workers in particular, in a country where there are few treatment and counseling programs. While all of the women denied using drugs (given the illegal nature of such activities, affirmation would be highly surprising!), many knew someone who was addicted, and further pointed out that clients frequently tried to get them to share cocaine or cocaine-based drugs with them. Guyana is now a major transhipment point for drugs coming out of Latin America and this has contributed greatly to the easier availability of street drugs, including for sex workers, putting paid to several of the women's aspirations to save and get out of the business with their savings going instead to purchase cocaine. As Cannings of the National AIDS Program Secretariat noted:

> I think women before in the sex work had one aim...[to save and invest].... I think now what the cocaine has done is...the first smoke you smoke, the high you experience, you never get it again. That is the reason why they have to keep smoking, as to try to get the first high. Okay. How we know that [is] because it get them broke, it get them sick.

Drug dependency places sex workers in a particularly vulnerable position, as an addict in need of a regular fix is in danger of "agreeing" to unprotected sex and is less likely to be able to set the financial terms of the sexual exchange. In one workshop organized by the National AIDS Program Secretariat, for instance, role-playing involving a client and a drug-dependent sex worker ended with the latter agreeing to unprotected oral sex.

ORGANIZING FOR CHANGE

We close by reflecting on some of the implications of our findings for articulating and implementing strategies for change.[28] The diversity that we have seen militates against any approach that sees sex workers as a homogeneous category. While sex workers share a number of experiences, there are also differences—of age, ethnicity, and location—which must be taken into consideration. In some areas questions of coercion are clearly paramount and require steps to be taken to prevent deception and exploitation of Amerindian women. The issue of schoolgirls also requires separate consideration, and here it is, moreover, a question of accessibility and disclosure.[29]

At present the only initiative with and for sex workers in Guyana started in the early 1990s and involved a PAHO-sponsored seroprevalence survey among Georgetown sex workers. Out of this has come a sex workers' project under the auspices of the National AIDS Program Secretariat, sponsored by CAREC (Caribbean Epidemiology Centre), and located in the Ministry of Health. Its resources are limited. The office is open during the week only during the daytime and there are only two persons on the project, the program manager and the project officer (Cannings). A third person was recently hired to train voluntary counselors in the various regions of the country. Workshops have been held with sex workers to discuss such issues as STDs, condom use and safer sex, and alcohol and drug abuse (interview with Cannings).[30] Steps are now being taken to train sex workers as peer educators, and plans are also afoot to organize (with the GUM clinic) regular health checks and (with the Guyana Responsible Parenthood Association) pap smears for women (interview with Cannings). Although the program office is based in Georgetown, visits have been made to Linden, Mahdia, and other communities in the Essequibo.

Most of the women agreed that there should be an organization for sex workers. Some proffered the view that sex workers should be helped to find alternative opportunities to earn a living: "OK, like I would say...like form something that prostitutes I would say could like do something else, even like do some trading like yuh know, learn something or make something and dey could even sell or something, and mek their own business." Others saw the need for organizing in order to legalize sex work and end the discrimination women currently faced: "If it was legal we woulda got to get some paper or something, I glad if dey could get serious and leh we get some kind of paper, so we could go in dem disco and hussle, not pun the street, like yuh know, police can come and raid we off, I glad if dey can do dem ting." The protection of sex workers was also identified as a possible role: "[The organization could] just to look into our problems, well like if we go wid a guy and he don't want to pay us, just look into the matter for us...that they won't bully yuh know, nuff young men like to bully." One woman from the mining camps made a similar observation: "Like get an out-station right, like is somebody let we say sex you and dey don't want to pay, dey would got somebody to arrest dem and say no man, yuh have to pay dis girl and so." The diversity of responses underscores the need not only for flexibility and openness, but most importantly for the initiative and the driving and organizing force to come from sex workers themselves: "Well, yes, it all depends like if they come together and say they want something to be done, then I think that something should be done."[31]

This brings us, finally, to the role Red Thread (and similar "sister outsiders" [Lorde 1984]) can play in this regard, based on our involvement in the research process over the past year. Certainly our access to information was somewhat limited by the fact of our noninvolvement in sex work and thus our implication in the wider societal norms that would stereotype prostitutes as deviant. However, this situation was ameliorated by the research team members, who were able to talk to the sex workers because of their commonality of trying to make a living in a tough economic climate. Nor would we want to suggest that barriers between women are permanent, or that relationships based on trust and mutual respect are impossible. They are not, but they take a great deal of work and time. We do believe, however, that Red Thread's role can only be supportive (for example, providing spaces for women to meet, helping to break down barriers between sex workers and non-sex workers, helping with the organization of workshops) and that the agenda must be defined primarily (although not necessarily exclusively) by sex workers themselves. Where Red Thread can possibly take a more proactive role is in challenging the silences around sexuality that exist in Guyanese society and institutions (in our schools, our places of worship, our homes) and the discriminations upon which they are based, which result, yet again, in the devaluation of women and women's labor.

NOTES

1. The nonacceptance by the major opposition party—the People's National Congress (PNC)—of the December 1997 election results, in which the People's Progres-

sive Party (PPP)/Civic was reelected, led to a tense situation in which the PNC refused to take their seats in parliament. Street demonstrations in January and again in June led to Caricom intervention in an attempt to shore up the political crisis, which had spilled over into the economic arena and was severely affecting any gains made under structural adjustment.

2. Having sex with customs officers was an activity that was engaged in as a form of bribery, allowing women traders to avoid paying taxes on goods they were importing.

3. There are reports of schoolgirls involved in the making of pornographic videos (frequently without their knowledge or consent) for distribution locally and overseas (see Danns 1996), and also entering into sexual relations with minibus drivers for money. The minibus drivers pick the girls up from school and take them to places where they can have sex, for which the girls are given gifts or cash (interview with Red Thread research team).

4. Given the taboo nature of homosexuality, discussing such matters would also have been difficult in light of the short timescale of our research.

5. These included Cora Belle, Shirley Goodman, Halima Khan, Linda Peake, Chandra Persaud, Vanessa Ross, Karen de Souza, and Alissa Trotz.

6. The general breakdown of all interviews was as follows: seven worked in hotels, clubs, and bars; six worked in mining camps; four worked on the streets; and six worked in guest houses. Amerindian women were represented in all categories except the street and clubs (one woman worked exclusively on ships), while the schoolgirls worked in the first two categories. In all, four of the women were Amerindian, six Indian, five black, and six mixed.

7. Linden is located on the upper Demerara River, about sixty miles inland, while Bartica is positioned at the confluence of three rivers, the Essequibo, Cuyuni, and Mazaruni Rivers, approximately 40 miles inland.

8. The interviews lasted one hour on average and were taped, transcribed, and checked. Follow-up interviews were carried out where questions were missed or clarification was needed. Generally, one woman was approached, who then acted as the contact person, finding other sex workers who were willing to talk with us about their experiences and perceptions. Interviewees were paid G$2,000 for their time (at the time of the interviews U.S.$1 = G$140). There were no refusals, the result, we believe, of the financial incentive (especially among those at the lower-paying ends of the business) combined with the fact that sex workers themselves mediated our initial meetings with other women.

9. One Amerindian woman stated that she did not have sex with Amerindian men because they insulted her. Another Indian woman preferred to sleep with black men only. The other women who had views on the subject expressed a preference for "their own kind." It would appear that "ethnic sameness" may lead to a situation in which the woman is treated derogatorily, but it may also be opted for given negative stereotypes of "ethnic others" (a few of the non-black women, for example, said that they did not sleep with black men because they had heard that they beat and robbed women). Undoubtedly clients also "desire" certain types of women more than others, based on stereotypes associating gender, ethnicity, and sexuality (Kempadoo 1996). Sometimes preferences may not run along any of these expected lines. One Indian woman was turned down by a "Negro boy" because, she reported, he said he

didn't deal with Civic (a reference to the current PPP/Civic Government, seen as representing the interests of Indians in Guyana). As we have not interviewed any of the men, we do not have any information to pursue these issues.

10. These prices are for "straight sex" only; if a woman agreed to "pose" in various positions, prices would be raised accordingly.

11. Our findings thus lead us to question a recent classification suggested in the *Guyana Review* (Vol. 63, 1998) that suggests zoning sex workers in Guyana into three categories, one of which is identified as "streetwalkers" located on the street, ships, and entertainment spots. The other two categories are mature call girls, with a clientele of rich men and foreigners, and "brothel girls" based at guest houses. As we have seen, there is a substantial difference in the anticipated earnings of street workers based on location.

12. We would thus expect a different set of questions to be raised by male sex workers in Guyana, who are largely street workers and appear predominantly to conduct their business with men. We did not find any evidence in the interviews that any of the prostitutes engaged in homosexual sex for pay, although a few of the women said that there were prostitutes who were lesbians outside of work. (The—derogatory—terms used to describe homosexuality locally are *sodomite, cockson, buller.*)

13. Miller also posits that the reaffirmation—through exchanges of money and services—has to be ongoing, which is what supposedly distinguishes it from prostitution. In Jennifer's case, though, the boundaries are even more blurred than this.

14. Some examples are schoolgirls having relationships with much older men—and sometimes with their parent's knowledge—in order to get money for uniforms, books, clothes, and other items that they could not otherwise afford, or women entering into relationships with men in the hope of getting a visa to "go outside" and do better, again with familial consent. At the same time, we do not want to suggest that sex work is an available option for low-income women only. It is, however, far more hidden and denied among middle and upper sections of society, making it more difficult to detect (see the quotation that opens this section).

15. At the same time, sex work in the context of Guyana does not necessarily signify female sexual autonomy or exist completely outside of the dominant sphere of sexual relations; witness the intense homophobia we encountered, for example, and the nature of women's interactions with men on the job.

16. This is not perhaps surprising, for Caribbean society continues to uphold marriage as the superior familial arrangement and consistently denies equal validity to common-law and visiting relationships. The distinction made between prostitution and family life is thus implicitly talking about a certain type of "normal" familial arrangement. As researchers have noted, this differentiation is an expression of class, gender, sexual, and racial power (Alexander 1997, Lazarus-Black 1994, Smith 1996).

17. In the interior as well, where almost all the women are prostitutes and virtually everyone except Amerindians is working away from home, there does not seem to be much in the way of moral reproach of the kind found on the coast.

18. This was found to be the case across all categories of sex workers interviewed, including the mining camps where one may argue that women are far less constrained than in their home communities.

19. These responses foreground the limits of disclosure when the interviewers are not sex workers themselves or have not been in the field for a sufficiently long time to build up a relationship of trust.

20. All the women who worked in guest houses and in hotels/bars/nightclubs tried to save; this was not the case for women working on the streets and in mining camps. Only one Amerindian woman was able to save.

21. In the interior it has been noted that the moral economy of gold and diamond mining requires coastlander men to engage in ostentatious displays and to demonstrate their generosity through profligate spending when they make a profitable finding (Roopnaraine 1997). The question here is whether there is any gendered difference insofar as sex workers are concerned. Four of the women were mothers of young children living on the coast (in one case the child had migrated) and in three cases were their main sources of support. Only two of the women were able to save occasionally. The information we collected suggests that none of the women was making a windfall from their jobs. However, one of the women was unable to save due to the temptation to spend one's money out (on clothes, for example), suggesting a possible parallel in some respects with the way in which the miner's money is viewed (the money, like the "shout" which makes it possible, is here today and gone tomorrow). However, further research is needed on this issue.

22. Moreover, the identity of the dead woman may never be known, as many sex workers use false names and addresses while working in the interior and their families may not even know where they are located.

23. And at any rate most of these services are based in Georgetown.

24. Indeed, a seroprevalence study carried out among sex workers in 1993 noted that female sex workers in Georgetown had recently been the target of police efforts to "clean up the streets" (Carter et al. 1997:452).

25. The vast majority of the women knew someone who had been the victim of violence, but it was never themselves. Moreover, Karen de Souza, who made initial acquaintances with women in the boulevard, notes that the stories she was told were slightly different and included far more violence when tapes were not being used to record sex workers' conversations.

26. The guest-house manager we interviewed said that regular checkups at the hospital were a prerequisite for women who worked out of his location.

27. Nor are free condoms always available. During the survey, a local newspaper carried a report that the Ministry of Health had run out of condom supplies and was unsure when it would receive new stocks.

28. We note again that this is a small study and that not all groups of women and men involved in the sex trade in Guyana have been included. The paucity of information hinders efforts to understand the complexity of the sex trade. Further research is needed, for example, on clients as well as the involvement of schoolgirls and men as sex workers.

29. Schoolgirls are reluctant to be identified, knowing that they more than anyone else are not "supposed" to be involved in sex work. One workshop for sex workers was unable to attract any schoolgirls: "I don't think they had the nerves to come to the workshops" (interview with Cannings), most likely for the same reason.

30. The workshops had a snowball effect. Cannings noted that when they first started, twelve women came out, then thirty. By the time she organized a workshop for street workers, more than 100 women came.

31. Nor do we think that this is a straightforward task. While we did find examples of women relying on each other for support, cooperation was more the exception than the rule. Instead women spoke of competition from other women (including telling clients that other sex workers had AIDS or were dirty) or said they fended for themselves. As we have also seen, there is a hierarchy within sex work that suggests that interests may not be similar and that women may see themselves as different. These are all issues that have to be worked out in process; we raise them here only to draw attention to the factors that militate against any easy or simplistic conclusion.

13

For the Children

Trends in International Policies and Law on Sex Tourism

KAMALA KEMPADOO AND RANYA GHUMA

The long-standing relationship between sex, prostitution, and tourism have been widely recognized by scholars in Third World and tourism studies (Fanon 1963, Turner and Ash 1976, Press 1978, ECTWT 1983, Cohen 1984, Crick 1989, Hobson and Dietrich 1994, Harrison 1994). It was, however, due to feminist research and action around prostitution in Southeast Asia in the 1980s that "sex tourism" was identified as a concept to refer to practices structured in the tourism industry that involve the exchange of material goods or money for sexual labor (Matsui 1989, Mies 1989, Enloe 1989, Truong 1990, Isis-wicce 1990). The concept has since become common currency among academics and journalists to denote practices that range from highly organized tours for sexual pleasure to incidental "romantic" encounters between the tourist and "native," and which incorporate men and women as both tourists or clients and sex workers (Urry 1990, Hall 1992, el-Gawhary 1995, Leheny 1995, O'Connell Davidson 1996, Pattullo 1996, Pettman 1997, Oppermann 1998). There is, however, little formal recognition of sex tourism by international authorities and nothing to date that reviews current global polices on the issue. In this chapter we examine dominant trends in the international discourse on sex tourism, as refracted through policies and laws of international agencies, governments and nongovernmental organizations (NGOs), which aim to control and regulate the global tourism industry or seek to address the social impacts of tourism.

Attention to sex tourism by international agencies is of very recent origin, and thus the initiatives taken so far are still to unfold into clear policies and

291

concrete actions. Nevertheless, our research shows that the discourse focuses little on sex tourism in general but almost exclusively on "child prostitution." This focus can in part be attributed to the immense amount of pressure that has been exerted through the ECPAT (End Child Prostitution in
Asian Tourism) campaign and the ease with which the subject of sex between adults and children evokes widespread condemnation. It is indeed far
easier to mobilize or gather consensus around something so evidently "evil"
as pedophilia than it is around issues that concern sex between adults. It
would appear, however, that this focus not only serves to obscure the working conditions for adult women and men in the sex sector by ignoring the
population completely (and hence denying it legitimacy, visibility, agency,
and human rights) but, equally as important, to deflect attention away from
the complicity of the broader tourism industry, government, and international agencies in sustaining activities that are in most countries defined by
law as criminal. That is, the emphasis on child prostitution as the main problem in sex tourism can be seen to quietly allow other forms of prostitution
to continue to take place without hindrance, scrutiny, or attention to the
human rights of women and men who provide sexual services in the
tourism industry.

THE UNITED NATIONS

The United Nations, as one of the influential bodies on international relations, has not developed any specific conventions to address sex tourism.
Prostitution—a constitutive element of sex tourism—is, however, explicitly
dealt with in the 1949 UN Convention for the Suppression of Traffic in Persons and the Exploitation of Prostitution of Others, the 1979 Convention for
the Elimination of All Forms of Discrimination Against Women (CEDAW),
and the 1989 Convention of the Rights of the Child (Wijers and Lap-Chew
1997, Bindman 1997). A Program of Action for the Prevention of the Sale of
Children, Child Prostitution and Child Pornography was also adopted in
1992 by the UN Commission on Human Rights (Lim 1998). Many other conventions on social, political, civil, cultural, workers and human rights are
also indirectly applicable (Bindman 1997).

The main thrust of UN conventions since 1949 has been to suppress the
trafficking of women, brothel keeping, pimping, and procuring for the purposes of prostitution and to prevent the exploitative use of children in prostitution. Analyses of these instruments shows that although the conventions
have been framed within a discourse that appears to support a complete
abolition of prostitution, they do not unequivocally call for the complete
eradication of all forms of prostitution. Laura Reanda (1991), for example,
contends that the 1949 convention regards prostitution as a human rights vi-

olation only if it involves overt coercion, leaving untouched the issue of voluntary prostitution and the violation of human rights of those who "choose" prostitution as a form of work. Jo Doezema (1998), on the other hand, argues that there is little doubt that the 1949 convention was developed within a context dominated by movements and ideologies that sought to completely eradicate prostitution—at a historical moment when the notion of prostitution as a matter of personal choice and a form of work did not exist — and thus is for all intents and purpose an abolitionist instrument. Such ambiguity in the earlier documents has, however, been somewhat addressed through the international women's movement, particularly in the form of the CEDAW convention. While on the surface this convention can be easily interpreted as a treatise to abolish all forms of prostitution, a careful examination of the document and developments around the convention allows for a more qualified understanding. In the first place, an early attempt by Morocco to amend the convention to include a call for the suppression of all prostitution and not just of the "exploitation of prostitution" was rejected, indicating that the designers of the convention explicitly allowed for a distinction to be made between notions of coerced and noncoerced forms of prostitution (Doezema 1998, Wijers 1997). The convention thus seeks to abolish forced prostitution and allows for the recognition of voluntary prostitution.[1] Second, in 1992, a general recommendation by CEDAW was made to include prostitutes among those who needed to be offered equal protection under the law (Doezema 1998). Prostitutes were recognized in the convention as deserving of rights that others in society enjoy. In addition to this move away from the idea of completely abolishing prostitution to one that recognized the human and civil rights of sex workers, in 1996 the UN special rapporteur on violence against women commissioned an international research project on the trafficking of women that was designed and implemented from a perspective that recognized prostitution as a form of labor (see Wijers and Lap-Chew 1997). This trend within the UN would seem to open possibilities for a recognition of prostitution as the employment of sexual labor and of prostitutes as sex workers, raising questions about how the human, labor, social, cultural, and civil rights of those who purposefully sell sex in the tourism industry could be protected.

Nevertheless, within the UN it seems that the right hand does not always know what the left is doing. While heading in the direction of defining prostitution as sexual labor that is not always coerced or seen as an expression of violence to women, and of recognizing prostitutes as persons deserving of legal protections, another element has crept into the discourse. In December 1996, the UN General Assembly passed a resolution on "The Traffic of Women" that was reaffirmed in December 1997, in which states and international organizations were urged not only to prevent trafficking, but also to consider enacting legislation "to prevent sex tourism."[2] The issue of prostitution within the tourism industry—"sex tourism"—explicitly made its way into the UN discourse under the rubric of "trafficking," equated with coercive and oppressive practices. The suppression of sex tourism is a necessary corollary in this approach. The recent nuanced definition regarding prostitution and respect for sex workers and their rights articulated through the CEDAW convention is thus contradicted by the representation of sex tourism as a form of coerced prostitution that requires abolition.

THE INTERNATIONAL LABOR ORGANIZATION

As a UN specialized agency that promotes concepts of human rights and labor rights, the Conventions of the International Labor Organization (ILO) are considered (like Conventions of the United Nations) to be international treaties and thus binding on those states who ratify them. From these conventions, minimum labor standards of freedom of association, the right to organize, abolition of forced labor, equality of opportunity and treatment, and other standards regulating work conditions are enumerated. However, to date the ILO has not developed any specific convention regarding the position on sex workers but prefers to leave this to existing national or local laws on prostitution, only indirectly addressing sex worker rights through existing labor conventions: "Where prostitutes are considered as workers with rights under standard labor legislation, the concern would be to ensure that they, like other legitimate workers, are entitled to proper working conditions and protection from exploitation and discrimination" (Lim 1998:v). The ILO does, however, deal with the issue of child labor in tourism, which, to the extent that child labor includes child prostitution, can be interpreted to address child sex tourism. Convention 138 of 1973 prohibits the admission of people under the age of eighteen to dangerous employment and mentions "moral hazards" as one such danger (Bindman 1997; Belau, personal communication April 24, 1998). Furthermore, in 1997, the ILO Tripartite Meeting on the Effects of New Technologies on Employment and Working Conditions in the Hotel, Catering, and Tourism Sector (Geneva, May 12–16, 1997) adopted a "resolution concerning the sexual exploitation of children and child labor," suggesting that the ILO is taking increasing steps toward addressing sex tourism in the framework of labor rights (Belau, personal communication, April 24, 1998).

Maggie Black, in the ILO-commissioned report *In the Twilight Zones: Child Workers in the Hotel, Tourism and Catering Industry* (1995), adds a significant contribution to the definition of child labor and child sexual exploitation by arguing that sexual exploitation of children employed in travel and entertainment industries is an occupational hazard (6). She further argues that much of the media coverage of "sex tourism" and "child sexual exploitation" is hyperbolic and misinformed. Her ground breaking research in Kenya, Mexico, the Philippines, and Sri Lanka shows that many child prostitutes provide services to local customers above and beyond those provided to sex tourists, thus stressing the need to examine child labor in all its dimensions rather than just in the narrow arena of the tourism industry.

The 1998 ILO report by Lin Leam Lim on prostitution in Southeast Asia, sheds further light on the direction that the organization is taking. From the extensive data and information that is presented on Indonesia, Malaysia, the Philippines and Thailand, Lim argues for a two-pronged approach, where adult prostitution would "be viewed as a matter of personal choice and as a form of work" and child prostitution as "a form of coercion and violence against children...forced labor and a contemporary form of slavery" (2). With the understanding that "working conditions of prostitutes vary greatly," she insists that legislation, policies, and programs need to take the differences between groups of workers in the sex sector into account and that the official stance "cannot be one of neglect or nonrecognition" of the issue (213). Indeed, Lim recommends that a clear position be taken that supports careful decriminalization or legalization of prostitution rather than its abolition or prohibition. The latter situation, she states "would mean banning the sector," consequently pushing prostitutes into criminality, leaving them even more vulnerable to marginalization, exploitation, and abuse (214). In order to protect sex worker rights, she argues, the existing prostitution laws require reform or review, and special measures need to be put into place (214). It is a clear call to the ILO to take further steps regarding the situations of sex workers internationally and to go beyond a reliance on existing laws.

Lim, however, does not completely escape the trend that has already been established by the UN: of associating sex tourism with the exploitation of children. She argues: "Sex tourism tends to be an important source of commercial sexual exploitation of children," and recommends more stringent measures to be adopted for the tourism sector.

THE GLOBAL TOURISM INDUSTRY

Most of the initiatives to address sex tourism within the tourism industry are predicated on the position of the World Tourism Organization (WTO), an organization that traces its origins to a 1925 non-governmental organization, the International Union of Official Tourist Publicity Organizations, and which by 1997 had entered into a formal agreement with the United Nations as a UN executing agency (WTO 1998a). As the only large-scale intergovernmental organization representing various actors of the tourism industry, the WTO serves as a key player in international discussions of tourism policies and their implications. It extends membership not only to sovereign states but also to members of the public and private sector, hence industries in sectors that are either directly or indirectly involved in the tourism industry carry great influence. The organization derives much of its support from 138 member states and territories that are classified as "full members" of the WTO. Approximately 350 nonterritorial entities representing industry and non-governmental organizations take part in the WTO as "affiliate members," including airlines, hotels, restaurants, tour operators, travel agents, and educational and research staff. Finally, "associate membership" is extended to those territories that are not responsible for their own foreign relations, provided that the government that oversees those policies agrees to membership. WTO associate members are currently represented by Aruba, Macau, Madeira, and the Netherlands Antilles (WTO 1998b). Full members, associate members, and affiliate members are further divided into six regional commissions: Africa, the Americas, East Asia and the Pacific, Europe, the Middle East, and South Asia. Currently Argentina, Bolivia, Brazil, Chile, Colombia, Costa Rica, Cuba, the Dominican Republic, Ecuador, El Salvador, Grenada, Guatemala, Haiti, Jamaica, Mexico, Nicaragua, Panama, Paraguay, Peru, Uruguay, and Venezuela comprise the Regional Commission for the Americas (WTO 1998c). Because of a lack of funding support from the United States Department of State, the United States withdrew as a member of the WTO in December 1996. Canada also withdrew its membership from the WTO. However, both countries may attend WTO functions as observers.

In October 1995, the WTO adopted a "Declaration on the Prevention of Organized Sex Tourism," which was developed at a two-day consultation meeting in Saint-Vincent, Italy (*WTO News* 1995). It requested governments represented in the WTO to act through the implementation of national laws and bilateral agreements in order to eradicate organized sex tourism. It further asked donor countries and aid agencies to undertake initiatives that would help to develop more sustainable forms of tourism development in areas where sex tourism is prevalent. Representatives from the Universal Federation of Travel Agents Association (UFTAA), International Hotel Association (IHRA), International Association of Tour Managers (IATM), the United Nations, the World Health Organization (WHO), and the United Nations Educational, Scientific and Cultural Organization (UNESCO) also attended the meeting, along with non-governmental organizations such as ECPAT (End Child Prostitution in Asian Tourism). Following from this statement, the WTO sent a delegation, in 1996, to Brasilia to attend the International Seminar on the Sexual Exploitation of Children and Adolescents in the Americas, which was organized by Brazil's national tourism administration. The Chief of the WTO Committee on Quality of Tourism and Development, Henryk Handszuh, led a workshop on sex tourism during this seminar. Many of the tools mentioned in the Declaration on the Prevention of Organized Sex Tourism were incorporated in the Brasilia Charter, which was adopted by delegates to the conference (*WTO News* 1996).

From these measures the WTO has taken increasingly active and vocal steps to extend the discussion of sex tourism. Working in close cooperation with ECPAT, the WTO was instrumental in facilitating the convening of the Stockholm Congress Against the Commercial Sexual Exploitation of Children, held in August of 1996. Heads of state of many UN countries as well as international agencies attended the congress, which intended to build upon the work of the UN Convention on the Rights of the Child in order to facilitate the eradication of child sexual exploitation in tourism (WTO 1995). This congress appears to represent a major turning point in how the WTO addresses the issue of sex tourism on an international level, shifting the focus to the child victim of sexual exploitation. A key entity emerging from this conference was the Child Prostitution and Tourism Watch, a task force comprised of tourism industry groups, governments, and NGOs. As stated by the WTO, the aims of the international campaign are to "prevent, uncover, isolate, and eradicate the exploitation of children in sex tourism" (WTO 1998d). By 1997, the focus of the WTO's concern about sex tourism was almost exclusively defined in terms of child prostitution.

Other key groups within the tourism industry have also turned their attention to the issue of sex tourism and, like the WTO, stress the situation of children. ECTAA (Group of National Travel Agents and Tour Operations Association within the European Union) and FIYTO (Federation of International Youth Travel Organizations) have, for example, both issued condemnations of "child sex tourism" and suggest to members to support efforts to eradicate child sexual exploitation in tourism. ECTAA's analysis is that sex tourism in developing countries is the primary cause of child sex abuse, a very different situation, it claims, to that in "industrialized societies" where "child abuse often involves close relatives or acquaintances of the victims" (ECTAA 1996). The IUF/UITA/IUL (International Union of Food Agriculture, Hotel, Restaurant, Catering, Tobacco and Allied Workers Associations) attempts to take a broader outlook and recognizes both "prostitution tourism" and "child prostitution" as problematic for the tourism industry. However, the statement that "any lasting solution to the problem of prostitution, in particular child prostitution, requires that progressive social and economic reforms provide the objective conditions for children to cease being treated as commodities" clearly points to children as the primary group warranting attention (IUF/UITA/IUL 1996).

That the issue of sex tourism is an uncomfortable one for tourism industry groups is evident from the position taken by other groups, such as IFTO (the International Federation of Tour Operators) and IATA (International Air Transport Association). These avoid associating "sex" with "tourism" altogether and instead establish resolutions against the "sexual exploitation of children" and "commercial sexual exploitation of children" (IFTO 1998, IATA 1996). This position denies the existence of organized sex tourism and instead attributes the incidences of prostitution to the actions of individual tourists. The IH&RA (International Hotel and Restaurant Association) maintains a similar focus on the sexual exploitation of children, in the absence of an image of the tourism industry as an active agent in this exploitation, arguing that "unfortunately, some child sex abusers may attempt to use hotels as the location where they commit their crimes" (IH&RA 1996). UFTAA similarly pledges "to combat the prostitution related to so-called 'sex tourism' and to protect the child victims of such tourists..." (UFTAA 1998). HOTREC (the Confederation of National Associations of Hotels, Restaurants, Cafes and Similar Establishments in the European Union and the European Economic Area), in its attempt to delink the tourism industry from child sex tourism, states:

> HOTREC and its member associations, however, very much regret the frequent use of precisely the latter expression "child sex tourism." The association of the three words "child, "*sex*" and "tourism" is highly damaging to the image of the tourism industry. Such crimes occur because of child sex abusers and, unfortunately, they occur in all sorts of circumstances which are not related to tourism activities (HOTREC 1997).

In this discourse the object of sex tourism is constructed as a "child victim," while the perpetrator of the exploitation is a "child abuser," with the situations of organized sex tourism and prostitution practices between adults being completely ignored. Thus not only has the focus on sex tourism become even further diluted, but several of the tourism industry groups actively attempt to deny any form of responsibility for sex tourism, fingering individual pedophiles as the problem.

Within the tourism industry, the IFWTO (International Federation of Women Travel Operators) is one of the few that maintains a focus on *both* child sex tourism and organized sex tourism. IFWTO members and associates pledged in 1997 "never to promote or assist in the promotion of travel, tours, or programs designed for sexual exploitation and to encourage local, regional, and national measures to prevent and eradicate 'sex tourism,'" explicitly acknowledging the role that the tourism industry itself holds in sustaining a sex tourism sector (IFWTO 1998). The IFWTO takes the original WTO position seriously, for it calls not only for the recognition of the culpability of the tourism industry in promoting and organizing sex tourism but also for the abolition of all prostitution practices within the tourism industry. It is a position that echoes the recent UN resolution on the trafficking of women as well as a radical feminist position concerning prostitution (Chapkis 1997). It also carries an abolitionist implication, leaving little space for the recognition of adult sex workers or for the protection of sex-worker rights within the tourism industry. It is a position that supports the campaign against the exploitation of children in sex tourism yet which contradicts the CEDAW convention.

In contrast to the earlier mentioned tourism industry associations that have in various ways attempted to address the issue of sex tourism, the Caribbean Tourism Organization (CTO) has made no statements or resolutions on either sex tourism or the sexual exploitation of children. Although claiming to be aware of the WTO work on the issue and the resolution of 1995, the CTO remains silent on the subject, giving little leadership or direction for states or tourism boards in the Caribbean region.

NATIONAL GOVERNMENTS

The implementation of national laws concerning sex tourism from major tourist-sending countries has exclusively dealt with the punishment of any involvement of a national in child prostitution while abroad. Extraterritorial child sex tourism legislation has been passed in a number of major tourist-sending countries such as Australia, Belgium, France, Germany, Japan, New Zealand, Norway, Sweden, the United States, Canada, and the United Kingdom (*WTO News* 1997). Most of these extraterritorial laws define the obtaining of sexual services from children as well as the promotion of child sex tours as a crime. Therefore, both procurers of child prostitution and tour agents and operators who facilitate child sex tourism are included under the scope of these laws. Because of the difficulty in prosecuting extraterritorial cases (gathering evidence, etc.), countries such as the UK have stated that, if possible, the criminal (a national of the UK) should be extradited from the home country to the place where the offensive act took place for trial (One World 1996). Bilateral agreements between states would facilitate such extradition. Other countries such as Australia have heard cases of violations of the extraterritorial child sex tourism laws in magistrate courts at home.

The case of Australian initiatives to combat child sex tourism provides an example of how international conventions, non-governmental groups, and domestic pressure interact in the formation of laws combating child sex tourism, and the scope of this legislation in the prosecution of violators of the law. Michael Hall (1998) explains how media attention promoted by increasing lobbying attempts of groups such as ECPAT in the late 1980s led to efforts to implement national legislation controlling aspects of sex tourism. Significantly, as ECPAT has limited its scope to dealing with children in sex tourism, national legislation has only defined legal accountability if the sex worker involved is a child. The emphasis on child sex tourism as opposed to sex tourism in general is characteristic of the majority of extraterritorial sex tourism legislation.

Under increasing pressure from NGO groups such as ECPAT and international organizations such as the United Nations Children's Fund (UNICEF), the Australian government ratified the Convention on the Rights of the Child in 1990. Article 34 of the convention, which calls for states to undertake the protection of children from sexual exploitation, was a critical component in facilitating future legal initiatives, as were recommendations by the Special Rapporteur on the UN Commission on the Program for the Prevention of the Sale of Children, Child Prostitution and Child Pornography (Hall 1998). In 1993, federal officials agreed to enact laws enabling prosecution of Australian nationals engaged in sex tourism, as well as Australian nationals involved in arranging or promoting child sex tours. The resulting Crimes (Child Sex Tourism) Amendment Act of 1994 expanded on the Crimes Act of 1914 to include activities of Australians engaging in, promoting, or profiting from child sexual exploitation (Hall 1998). With the amendment, Australia has had more arrests using extraterritorial sex tourism laws than any other country with similar laws (*Fiji Times*, August 28, 1997). Significantly, in October 1996, Melbourne magistrate courts undertook the prosecution of an Australian man accused of promoting sex tourism—a milestone in enforcement of Child Sex Tourism legislation.

However, events surrounding the creation and implementation of this legislation are under criticism. The House of Representatives Standing Committee on Legal and Constitutional Affairs (HRSCLCA), in an advisory report to the House of Representatives, expressed strong concern about the lack of consultation and constructive evaluation of the extraterritorial laws before their adoption (Hall 1998). ECPAT's role in the passing of the law also cannot be understated. Hall points out that ECPAT was referenced in over two-thirds of the parliamentary speeches supporting the passage of the amendment. Also, largely due to the intense lobbying efforts of ECPAT, the Australian government has established a new "National Council for the Prevention of Child Abuse" to oversee implementation of the Stockholm Congress Agenda for Action (ECPAT 1997). Furthermore, ECPAT has undertaken a campaign to pressure the Australian Federal Immigration Minister to implement mandatory police checks for sponsors of unaccompanied children who enter Australia (ECPAT 1997). While the organization has proven to be a valuable source of information regarding child sex tourism, it appears to have, in many ways, monopolized the debate in Australia concerning sex tourism. As a result, no substantial laws hold the tourism industry accountable for the exploitation of sex workers unless it is in connection with a child.

In the Caribbean, no explicit laws, policies, or programs have been put in place to explicitly address sex tourism, although many countries formally criminalize and prohibit prostitution as described elsewhere in this book. Even so, in Curaçao, a brothel was licensed by the colonial government in 1949 and by 1998 was being converted into a site that would appeal to tourists and other foreign visitors to the island.[3] In Jamaica in 1998 the Minister of Commerce proposed the creation of red-light districts in tourism-dominated towns (see chapter 6 by Campbell et al.). Furthermore, in both Jamaica and the Dominican Republic, laws to prevent "harassment of tourists" have been put in place. To date, however, these efforts have been exclusively articulated through the interests of governments and the formal business sector, who are eager to maintain the flow of visitors—and hence foreign exchange—to the country. Within these efforts, little attention is given to the rights or needs of those who work in prostitution. In such a scenario, the government simply takes on the role of "pimp," becoming the third party that exploits the prostitution of others, placing itself in the position of violating international conventions. "State pimpage" could become the norm if this trajectory were to be followed by other Caribbean nations.[4]

NON-GOVERNMENTAL ORGANIZATIONS

Several NGOs have been active in addressing the issue of sex tourism over the past two decades. The Ecumenical Coalition on Third World Tourism (ECTWT) and the Filipina feminist organization GABRIELA were among the first to become internationally visible for their work in the area during the 1980s (ECTWT 1983, Matsui 1989). However, any discussion attempting to evaluate how sex tourism and the sex worker are discussed in international debates would be incomplete if it did not include a detailed description of the non-governmental organization ECPAT and the enormous role it has assumed in directing national and international endeavors focusing on sex tourism. Later in the chapter we also examine the very recent initiative of the U.S.-based organization, Equality Now.

ECPAT, as a non-governmental charitable association, was established in 1990, with its headquarters in Bangkok, Thailand. Its international campaign was established in 1991, with the goal of working to end child prostitution in Asian tourism through "political action, changes in law, education, and media coverage" (ECPAT 1996:46). While the organization's original concern was Asian tourism, it now aims to target child prostitution, child pornography, and trafficking of children for sexual exploitation by both local populations and foreign populations involved in the international tourism trade.

The "ECPAT network" includes a mix of groups and organizations from over twenty-five countries. Various national groups have been established in the United States, Belgium, Bangladesh, Brazil, Cambodia, Canada, Denmark, France, Finland, Germany, India, Italy, Japan, the Netherlands, New Zealand, Norway, the Philippines, Sri Lanka, Sweden, Switzerland, Taiwan, Thailand, the United Kingdom, and Vietnam. An "executive committee" with representatives from the different national groups and organizations serves as a "policy-making body," directing programs, organization, staff, financial supervision, and management. Finally, ECPAT includes as part of its organizational structure a working committee, which convenes at least once a year to discuss the implementation of executive policies (ECPAT 1998a).

ECPAT's aim of achieving media coverage and influencing laws has been accomplished in the majority of countries that have passed substantial legislation dealing with child sex tourism. The organization claims the international recognition of the "reality and extent of commercial sexual exploitation of children" as one of its major achievements (ECPAT 1996). As part of its original area of focus, the organization also claims a primary role in the movement for legal change in the Philippines, Sri Lanka, Taiwan, and Thailand. As it moved to influence child sex tourism discussions internationally, the influence of ECPAT is very evident in the formation of extraterritorial laws punishing the sexual exploitation of children through tourism, particularly in Germany, France, Australia, the United States, Belgium, New Zealand, Canada, and Ireland (ECPAT 1998a). With offices in more than thirty countries, ECPAT's international presence cannot be understated. The organization played a significant role in convening the First World Congress against the Sexual Exploitation of Children in Sweden in 1996, bringing together representatives from UN states and international agencies to discuss the issue of commercial sexual exploitation of children, particularly as it relates to tourism. Finally, ECPAT's "legal campaign" has been defined as the main focus of its network efforts. Through developing an "international legal monitoring program" with Asian countries, the organization hopes to follow up cases and study laws concerning child sex tourism and to facilitate networking with government agencies and lawyers who are willing to offer free legal services for children and witnesses to a crime. As a result, ECPAT has helped bring to court many cases of violations of child sexual exploitation laws in Asian courts (ECPAT 1998a).

Considering the extent to which ECPAT has influenced various international and national movements dealing with the issue of sex tourism, how it frames this debate within its own literature and ideology is of paramount significance in understanding the information from which national laws and other legal endeavors are constructed. ECPAT explicitly states that its purpose is protecting children and makes no claims of advocating the rights of all people involved in sex tourism. Nor is there a mention of adult prostitutes or sex workers in ECPAT's mission statements. Such a neglect of the dimensions of sex tourism is further evident in the "Country Reports," which provide information on the state of child sex tourism in various tourist destinations (ECPAT 1996b). Child sex tourism is seen as a developing evil in the tourism industry, while exploitation of workers in the sex tourism industry is virtually ignored. However, it is ECPAT's underlying abolitionist ideology about prostitution in general that is the most damning for the situations of adult sex workers. In a document entitled "Client, Customer, Exploiter: The Users of Child Prostitutes," ECPAT writes:

> Child abusers come from all walks of life and social backgrounds. The majority of these men become child abusers through their use of prostitutes. Children constitute a larger proportion of workers in the sex trade and are often found in the lower end of the market, where the prices are cheap and the conditions are worst. For those who deliberately seek sex with children law and social conventions make it difficult and dangerous to satisfy their interests. Prostitution enables them to have instant access to children. Prostitution is especially attractive to pedophiles and child preferential abusers (1998c:1).

The implication presented here is that prostitution can be generally blamed for the sexual exploitation of children, and that by eradicating prostitution, child sex tourism would disappear. It further does what abolitionist parties are renowned for: in order to "prove" the oppressive nature of prostitution, statistics about prostitution are provided for which the source is not given (Murray 1998). ECPAT thus highlights that "85 percent of prostitutes report being sexually abused as children," and further, that "90 percent of the prostitutes are being coerced into prostitution by pimps, etc." (1998c). These "key facts" are presented without any reference or contexualization and serve to condemn all forms of prostitution as inherently oppressive and abusive phenomena. The significance of its abolitionist phraseology and the absence of the image of a prostitute as a worker deserving of rights and advocacy is very relevant, as ECPAT remains the leading voice in international movements dealing with sex tourism.

Since 1996, the women's rights group Equality Now has engaged in a campaign against U.S.-based sex tour operators and to raise public awareness of the problem of organized sex tourism from the United States. It is one of the few NGOs in a tourist-sending country that is concerned with the eradication of organized sex tourism for and between adults. Writes Ken Franzblau of Equality Now: "The campaign was launched in response to the concerns expressed by women's groups in Asia that U.S.-based human rights groups and women's organizations could best address the exploitation of Asian women by focusing on the demand created by sex tourists" (personal communication, August 18, 1998). Equality Now has targeted specific companies that organize sex tours to Southeast Asia, estimating that there are at least twenty-five such agencies in the U.S. (Budhos 1997). The campaign launched by Equality Now does not stop at public exposure but rather seeks to prosecute companies that are found to be organizing the tours. This strategy is, in the context of legislation applicable in the U.S., not a straightforward matter. While the Violent Crime Control and Law Enforcement Act of 1994 "makes travel with intent to engage in any sexual act with a juvenile punishable by up to ten years imprisonment," the organization of prostitution between adults outside the U.S. falls under an array of local laws that deal with the organization of prostitution by a third party and that are subject to a variety of interpretations. Equality Now has, however, been advised that the Racketeer Influenced and Corrupt Organizations (RICO) Act and the Travel Act provide some tools at the national level for obtaining a conviction of sex-tour operators, although the terms are so very precise that unless all are met, the Acts cannot be enforced (T. Davis 1998). To add to this dilemma, after four years of being in force, not a single person had been prosecuted under the national Acts which prohibit child prostitution (Frantzblau, personal communication, August 18, 1998).

Equality Now's campaign is focused on ending organized sex tourism and is premised on a broader abolitionist perspective on prostitution. Citing the 1949 UN convention on the trafficking in persons, the organization insists that prostitution is "incompatible with the dignity and worth of a human person" and it is convinced that the practice of sex tourism is "degrading and exploitative...destroying the lives of so many girls and women" (*Women's Action* 1996).

A ONE-SIDED DEBATE

In this review of policies, resolutions, conventions, and intentions around sex tourism, it is easily discernible that child prostitution is the primary concern. This focus, while important, also manages to trouble the larger debate in several ways. First, in the campaign against child prostitution, an assumption, articulated most clearly by ECPAT, is that the entire sex trade needs to be eradicated. Sex tourism is unequivocally equated with coercive practices, and it is this perspective that informs the work being undertaken on the subject by the UN, the tourism industry, and various national governments. This abolitionist or, as some term it, "anti-prostitution" position on prostitution, however, not only contradicts the CEDAW convention that acknowledges the rights of prostitutes but also contests the "pro-sex work" trend in the ILO that recognizes prostitution as a form of labor subject to regulation and protection under labor laws. Two distinctly opposing ideological positions are thus in operation within the international discussion on prostitution in the tourism industry.

Second, in the dominant abolitionist perspective, sex tourism in developing countries is represented as the main cause of child prostitution. Such a claim can be misleading, constituting a partial representation of global realities. Situations for young people in countries in Asia where the tourism industry is barely involved, such as in India, the Ivory Coast or Senegal in Africa (Sleightholme and Sinha 1997, Tandia 1998, Anarfi 1998), as well as in Guyana, Colombia and Suriname in South America (see chapters 7, 11, and

12) indicate that the sexual exploitation of children takes place in many other arenas than the tourism industry. This information is easily glossed over or dismissed as inconsequential, and, instead, global generalizations are drawn from a few, highly focused studies. Furthermore it is not always clear that the tourism industry is where child prostitution starts. Rather, multiple causes for children to enter into sex work have been identified. One branch in the tourism industry maintains, for example, that it is due to the presence of pedophiles who entice children to have sex; others contend that the reason young people enter into prostitution is because of abuse in the home. Underdevelopment or maldevelopment of Third World areas continues to be viewed as a major factor. The reduction of causes of child prostitution so that the tourism industry alone is blamed creates a highly biased interpretation.

Third, in the international debates, sex tourism is separated from other forms of prostitution and is singled out as a form that deserves to be eradicated. The underlying assumption is that because large numbers of children are involved in sex tourism, the kind of prostitution that occurs in that particular sector is far more destructive and damaging than prostitution elsewhere. Nevertheless, this line of argument is predicated upon weak empirical evidence, indicating a fracture between social practices and the kind of knowledge that is being constructed about sex tourism. The relationship that is assumed between numbers of children relies on anecdotal information and locally specific research. Prostitution researchers themselves repeatedly point out that numbers of people who are involved in prostitution, including children, are extremely inaccurate. Sittirak, for example, points to the great variability in estimates about the number of prostitutes in Thailand, explaining that the estimate of the numbers "remains under constant debate, with a 'reliable' estimate not having been agreed upon yet" (1998:81). In her report for the ILO, Lim also underlines this point, stating: "It is not always possible to have precise figures on the extent of child prostitution" (1998:171). She severely criticizes ECPAT for using statistics that appear to her to be an exaggeration of the problem (172). In short, the number of children in sex tourism worldwide is unknown, as is the number of adults, and hence the overrepresentation of child sex workers in the tourism industry cannot be stated with certainty. The claims and generalizations about child prostitution in the tourism industry and, by extension, about the exceedingly harmful effects of sex tourism require far more substantiation and careful documentation than presently exists.

If one were to embark on a global survey of child prostitutes, one would run up against a problem that is far more fundamental than those mentioned above, namely the distinction between a child and an adult prostitute. While under some laws and conventions a person under the age of eighteen who works in prostitution is labeled a "child," under others she or he is often defined as an adult for purposes of sexual consent, marriage, and work (Black 1994, Lim 1998, Hanson 1998). To Douglas Hodgson (1995) the discrepancy in international conventions about the age when childhood ends and adulthood begins is one of the greatest limitations to discussing child prostitution. Given that laws allow young people to legally work, marry, and engage in sex in their early teen years in many countries, the young person is simultaneously deemed adult enough to consent to sexual intercourse and paid employment yet too young to be involved in a combination of the two. Demands by children to be acknowledged as independent earners and providers compound the issue and serve to blur the boundaries between child and adulthood even further (Swift 1997). The case study in Cartagena, Colombia, in chapter 7, and the situation for young male sex workers in Rio de Janeiro, Brazil, and in Thailand (Montgomery 1998, Longo 1998), illustrate this complexity fully, bringing into question whether these young people should be banned from selling sex or instead be protected and empowered by laws pertaining to child labor, marriage, and sexual consent.

Finally, the continual association of sex tourism with children obscures the realities for sex-working adults in the tourism industry. As this research on the Caribbean demonstrates, the situation for adult sex workers is very complex, with the majority working quite independently, within the broader context of uneven global development and racialized, gendered definitions of Third World sexuality. The intricate and challenging discussion around the issues of prostitution as legitimate work and not only as coercion is conveniently avoided in the dominant discourse on sex tourism, and with this goes the neglect of issues such as working conditions, safe sex practices, and the strategies that sex workers employ for self-empowerment. Adult prostitutes who strive to take control of the conditions and terms under which they provide sexual labor are consequently left vulnerable to criminalization, police harassment, extortion, and physical violence by clients and with very few avenues to seek protection of their human rights. The imbalance of power between sex worker and clients within the context of labor and civil and human rights is neither the focus of attention nor of concern to the international community.

By turning a blind eye to adult participation in sex tourism, the door also remains open for governments and the tourism industry to inadvertently violate local and international laws and conventions that criminalize prostitution and outlaw forced prostitution. Silence, in this instance, signals complicity with existing practices, which in many cases contradict the law. The focus on child prostitution also relieves the tourism industry itself from having to take any further actions, and provides an avenue for hoteliers, government tourism boards, restaurateurs, travel agents, tour operators, and other agencies that shape the broader tourism sector to continue to extract profit from sexual labor without the cost of maintaining the working force. In the name of "eradicating the sexual exploitation of children," the tourism industry can bow out of its responsibility of contributing to global development that supports human development and emancipation in the long term. It offers the industry a convenient way of appearing to do the right thing without having to reconfigure itself drastically or having to invest much in the human capital on which it is predicated.

CONCLUSION

Sex tourism as a particular form of prostitution is of concern to many international and national agencies, yet there appears to be little international consensus and many contradictory positions on the subject. Ideas about the suppression and abolition of sex tourism cohabit with notions of supporting prostitutes' rights. The gaps that are evident in the discourse provide space for not only oppositional and confused perspectives, but also for a privileging of some issues and a moratorium on others. The subject of child prostitution within the tourism industry is of paramount concern and dominates the international discourse on sex tourism. This particular emphasis clouds the broader picture, obscuring adult relations in the tourism industry, stimulating unsubstantiated resolutions and policies, as well as promoting an anti-prostitution stance. The discursive erasure of whole sectors of the population that work within the tourism industry, along with a lack of acknowledgment of lived realities, denies independent teenager and adult sex workers a place and voice in the tourism industry.

Policies and laws addressing sex tourism require careful development and information about everyday practices before they can be effective in addressing the complexity of sex tourism. The solutions, however, are also not simple and require time. Investment, sound research, and a full commitment by the international community to a development process that is grounded in notions of sustainability and human rights would seem desirable and, in the light of realities such as presented in these case studies in the Caribbean, a necessary way forward.

NOTES

1. The distinction between forced and voluntary prostitution is, however, also problematic. As I have argued elsewhere, it obscures the complexity and the range of situations that are evident in the sex trade (Kempadoo 1998). Doezema (1998) also points out how the distinction is used to distinguish prostitution in "developing" countries from that in North America and Western Europe with the consequence that

Third World sex workers are discursively located as victims and denied a sense of agency and subjectivity.

2. See the United Nations General Assembly Resolutions A/RES/51/66 of December 1996 and A/RES/52/98 of December 1997.

3. As Jacqueline Martis explained in her report on her fieldwork during the project conference held in Jamaica on July 16–17, 1998. See also chapter 9 on the Netherlands Antilles.

4. I have argued elsewhere that this is a concept that can be applied to the situation in Curaçao, where the government has suspended its own laws outlawing third-party organization of the sex trade in order to legalize a brothel (Kempadoo 1995). The complicity of the state in countries such as Cuba and the Dominican Republic in facilitating prostitution also suggests that this dimension of the Caribbean sex trade requires much more consideration.

14

A Human Rights Perspective on the Sex Trade in the Caribbean and Beyond

CYNTHIA MELLON

When we examine the social and economic situation that sex workers face throughout the Caribbean and Latin America from a human rights perspective, it becomes clear that women and men involved in the sex trade—along with much of the rest of the population—lack access to rights that are enshrined in the conventions of the United Nations along with the basic tenets of labor rights covered by the conventions and recommendations of the International Labor Organization (ILO). Research into the lives of sex workers has also brought forth evidence that many people lack access to basic rights before and during their participation in the sex trade as well as after they leave it for other activities. These particularly include rights contained in the International Convention on Economic, Social and Cultural Rights along with some aspects of the Convention on Civil and Political Rights and cover such basic aspects as access to a reasonable level of health care and to primary education.

All the studies included in this book describe the economic situation of the countries in which research was carried out. In many cases, neoliberal restructuring policies and World Bank programs have taken their toll on already precarious economies in such a way that large sectors of the population find themselves with little access to formal economic activities. Some of the studies in this book (Cabezas, chapter 5; Phillips, chapter 8; Campbell et al., chapter 6) describe essentially skewed development strategies in which dollars entering the country through tourism are available only through formal means to a very limited sector of the population. While this unequal access to the tourist dollar is perhaps most apparent in the "all-inclusive" tourist enclaves, for which Jamaica is especially noted, all the countries in which tourism is prevalent are characterized by low wages within the sector and few opportunities for employing local people in viable long-term jobs. Given this situation, people have little choice but to seek access to some of the income arising from tourism through informal economic activities—one of which is sex work.

While the links between sex work and tourism are important social and economic issues for the region, a better understanding is needed about the extent to which other, non-tourism types of prostitution take place in some countries, along with their links to the prevailing economic patterns and which sectors are benefitting from them. The studies from Suriname and Guyana contained in this book examine non-tourism economies that offer women few employment opportunities at decent wages. The case of Suriname exemplifies a situation in which the current unregulated boom in gold mining is being carried out at a low-technology level which offers few jobs for women, with the exception of cooking and camp maintenance work or sex work, all of which are characterized by unsafe and substandard conditions. In some cases, mining foremen have even managed to profit directly from sex work by providing miners with a "sex-on-credit" system in which they receive a healthy percentage of the money earned through sex workers' labor (Antonius-Smits et al., chapter 11).

The study on Guyana illustrates the way in which the economic restructuring that has taken place in the country throughout the 1990s—which followed in the wake of the structural adjustment policies imposed by the International Monetary Fund in the 1980s—has opened up the country to foreign investment while leaving women with access to only a limited range of low-paying jobs. Given these conditions, it is little wonder that many women have turned to sex work. Their clients range from foreigners who come to do business in the country to miners in the bush and sailors on the cargo ships that dock at Georgetown, the capital city. The studies on Belize and Colombia present examples of countries that do have tourism but in which a substantial sector of the sex workers' clients is comprised of local men, thus presenting yet another variant on the political economy of sex work.

A number of authors have recently provided excellent analyses on the reasons why it is essential that sexual labor be viewed as an economic activity—often used in combination with other types of work—that some women and young men utilize as part of their economic strategy for supporting themselves and their families, for "getting by" in lean economic times, or for realizing goals (Kempadoo 1996 and 1998, Bindman 1997). In contrast to this position, the perspective that views prostitution as a totalizing activity by which the sex worker is defined or which characterizes prostitution as an immoral activity that must be abolished serves to marginalize and further isolate people in the sex trade. This view reenforces the already clandestine nature of sex work and adds to the difficulties sex workers face by making it harder for them to demand and defend their rights (Kempadoo 1998, Bindman 1997, Lim 1998, Mellon 1998).

It should be recognized that in some countries that are heavily dependent on tourism, the sex trade plays a considerable role in the national economy. Sex work is classified as an informal activity and, in spite of the fact that several studies show that linkages exist between sex work and tourism, no exact figures are available for the Caribbean. Studies carried out in some Asian countries have provided information on the ways the sex trade is linked into other areas of the economy, along with estimates of the number of people involved in secondary activities that support the trade, including taxi drivers, hotel personnel, and purveyors of food and drink to clients and sex workers (Boonchalaksi and Guest 1998). Similar linkages exist for the region, particularly in high tourism countries like Jamaica and the Dominican Republic.

When sex workers are characterized as immoral persons engaged in illegal and unacceptable behavior or as victims acting against their will and controlled by others, they become invisible as workers to which rights apply. Where prostitution is illegal, it goes underground, causing those working in the sector to become vulnerable to abuse for which they cannot seek protection from the police or other representatives of the state. Even where sex work is not technically illegal, the social stigma frequently placed on sex workers tends to have a similar invisibilizing effect.

When looked at from a labor rights perspective, however, it becomes clear that sex workers frequently experience conditions similar to those found in other low-status jobs in the informal sector, including long hours, lack of job security, low wages, and unsafe working conditions (Bindman 1997:6). Where sex work is illegal, sex workers may be arrested or harassed by the police without having access to basic human rights or protection under their own national laws. Where sex work is legal but not viewed as a labor activity, it remains difficult for sex workers to achieve minimum standards and personal safety in their work, especially in an atmosphere where the labor rights of other workers are also potentially being violated (Bindman 1997).

Increasingly, sex workers are forming their own organizations, which are characterized by varying degrees of militancy (Kempadoo 1998). For some, the focus has been mainly on assuring personal safety and dignity for sex workers, along with strengthening strategies for lowering the health risks connected with the sex trade. Other groups have formed in order to deal with specific issues, such as abuse by the police or by club or brothel owners. With some exceptions, most have yet to work toward adequate labor standards for sex workers. However, as this approach begins to be taken, it is possible that sex workers may find allies in the established labor movement who are willing to support campaigns in this area (Lim 1998).

Two of the strongest sex worker groups in the region are the Maxi Linder Association of Suriname and the Movimiento de Mujeres Unidas (MODEMU) group in the Dominican Republic. Both are examples of sex workers' organizations that take an integral approach to improving the lives of sex workers, working to provide health education and AIDS prevention information while, at the same time, increasing women's awareness of the issues of wages, work conditions, equality, and health and safety (Antonius-Smits et al., chapter 11; Cabezas, chapter 5; Kempadoo and Doezema 1998). Both groups interact with different levels of government and are vocal in demanding that sex workers have access to labor rights and fair working conditions. Other groups throughout the region, many of which are located in Latin America, are at different stages of consolidating themselves, and new groups continue to be formed.

It has been pointed out that the rights that sex workers need to access can be addressed in the already existing human rights conventions and that most issues related to working conditions could be made subject to ILO standards (Bindman 1997:8).[1] However, it remains clear that sex workers must not be restricted from organizing and seeking allies in other sectors if these rights are to be achieved. And while it may be difficult to define and regulate labor that takes place in the informal sector (an increasingly common reality in these neoliberal times), it should be remembered that human rights are universal and apply to all and that national legislation may not legitimately contravene the standards set down in the Universal Declaration of Human Rights (Bindman 1997:6-7).

All the studies presented here make ample reference to the types of problems that sex workers in the region face. While a few of these problems may be country specific, most are common across the region. Arising from this attempt to catalogue the difficulties and abuses sex workers experience is a series of policy recommendations that could be made to governments and to agencies that advocate for social justice, including sex workers' own organizations. Inherent in this attempt to pinpoint what may be needed to improve the situation of sex workers is an exploratory discussion that is taking place among the different organizations and individuals seeking change in this area. An effort is being made to understand some of the differing positions within the sector itself with regard to possible ways of improving the situation for sex workers and their families. However, consensus has yet to be reached among sex workers and their allies on the best course to take in certain areas, especially with regard to the possible role of government. There are differing opinions as to whether the sex trade should be legalized, regulated, or allowed to remain the same. In general, however, it would seem that a human- and labor-rights approach, together with one that advocates for the collective economic rights of entire communities, may best serve to guide policy aimed at improving the situation for people in the sex trade.

Beyond that, however, and most importantly of all, is the need to listen to the voices of people in the sex trade, since they are the ones best able to judge what their needs are and assess the merits and results of any policies that may be put in place.

THE SEX TRADE FROM A RIGHTS PERSPECTIVE

When looked at from a human rights perspective, some of the issues and abuses that have been identified become framed within commitments the states have made that require them to maintain certain minimum standards. There are obvious limitations to this approach. UN and ILO standards generally lack enforcement mechanisms, and it is widely recognized that all states violate or ignore important aspects of the conventions. However, the rights framework does provide goals within international law toward which to aspire, along with some standards by which to measure the legitimacy of national legislation and local practice (Bindman 1997:6–7).

Of particular interest at this time is the International Convention on Economic, Social and Cultural Rights (ICESCR), which most countries have signed. Under the convention, subscribing countries are required to report periodically to a UN committee on the progress that is being made in the realm of economic justice. While governments naturally tend to present themselves in the best possible light, people's organizations are also expected to present parallel or "shadow" reports, which often present quite a different picture from the official submission. As grassroots and local organizations (including sex workers' groups) become familiar with how to use the UN system, pressure can be brought to bear on governments to answer to documented discrepancies.

In the South, there is increasing discussion of ways to make compliance with the ICESCR justiciable through the use of legal mechanisms. Importantly, the convention requires states to provide free and mandatory education, at least at the primary level. This in itself could have a noticeable effect for many poor families for which school fees are impossible. (In the set of studies presented here, women interviewed about their reasons for doing sex work frequently mentioned the need to raise money to pay their children's school costs. Others have identified that they cannot aspire to other types of work, since they spent only a few years in school because of their parents' poverty.) (See Red Thread, chapter 12; and Campbell et al., chapter 6.) It may also be worthwhile to analyze national development policies that are discriminatory toward the development of some sectors in society in the light of the ICESCR.

Both the Convention on the Elimination of All Forms of Discrimination Against Women (CEDAW) and the Universal Declaration of Human Rights contain articles on the inalienable right of all human beings to work and to freely choose their job or profession. Discrimination against sex workers is clearly in violation of this right.

Sex workers also experience discrimination in society in ways that are in violation of the International Covenant on Civil and Political Rights (ICCPR). These problems are often connected with the discriminatory and abusive treatment they experience as migrant workers and the general lack of protection they experience in society as sex workers. Sex workers report that they know they cannot rely on help from the police in cases where they experience rape or sexual violence or when clients rob them or refuse to pay, since they are often characterized as immoral people who are somehow outside of society and thus not eligible to partake in rights guaranteed to other citizens.

With regard to labor practices and standards, numerous clauses contained in ILO conventions and recommendations are applicable to workers in the sex trade. A move toward fully recognizing sex work as labor would make it possible for workers in the industry to seek compliance with such standards.

The suggestions presented here with regard to the applicability of international human rights standards in the sex trade are by no means exhaustive but represent an attempt to locate policy recommendations for the region within the international human rights framework. While there are those who express frustration with the slowness and lack of enforcement available to the UN system, resorting to and seeking compliance with the international standards as set out in the human rights conventions that most of the world's countries have signed is one of the possible strategies for drawing attention to and seeking remedy for the human rights abuses many people in the sex trade experience. To the extent that bodies such as the ILO begin to include sex work in the realm of their jurisdiction, the international conventions may become an important avenue for ultimately improving conditions for people in the sex industry.

SEX WORK IN THE CARIBBEAN: PROBLEMS SEX WORKERS FACE

As outlined above, an attempt at listing and defining some of the most pressing problems sex workers in the region have identified reveals a pattern of economic and social discrimination that affects different aspects of their lives. While some situations are specific to certain countries, in many cases the problems sex workers identified appeared to be generalized across the region.

Of particular note is the problematic relationship sex workers in many countries face with the police. This situation is directly linked to the fact that sex work remains in a sort of limbo with regard to its legal status. While in some countries the actual practice of sex work is not illegal, a number of activities or situations that are connected with it are. These may include living off the earnings of a sex worker, soliciting clients for sex workers, and sex workers living together, whether they are operating a business or not. The laws may be sufficiently ambiguous or complicated so that neither sex workers nor the police really understand their application. However, in many of the countries that formed part of this study, police are using the supposed rigidity of the law in matters regarding sex work to carry out ongoing discrimination against sex workers. This type of police harassment may include jailing, physical abuse, and fines. In order to try to save themselves from these experiences, sex workers are sometimes expected to pay bribes to the police in the form of money or free sexual services. While police harassment against sex workers is a problem in many countries, it is particularly acute in the Dominican Republic, where it is taking the form of mass arrests of sex workers, many of whom have their rights further violated while in jail. Women caught in the police sweeps that frequently take place in the tourism area have been tortured and raped while in jail (Cabezas, chapter 5). Colombian sex workers have reported similarly abusive situations (Mayorga and Velásquez, chapter 7).

Despite the supposedly good intentions of their creators, laws that require sex workers to undergo mandatory periodic checkups for STDs may also violate prostitutes' rights and leave them open to further abuse by the police. In Colombia and the Dominican Republic, police sometimes use the inability to produce health certificates as an excuse to arrest sex workers, despite the fact that, in some cases, the health certificate requirement may have been declared unconstitutional.

The situation of minor or very young sex workers must also be taken into account. In Cartagena, Colombia, for example, underage sex workers can receive treatment for STDs at a municipal clinic only if they can prove they are involved in a "rehabilitation" program. This type of discrimination is not only dangerous for the sex workers but is a violation of their human rights (Mayorga and Velásquez, chapter 7).

Age affects sex workers in other ways as well. In nearly every country under study, it was reported that a sex worker can expect her earnings to go down as her age goes up (Mayorga and Velásquez, chapter 7; Red Thread, chapter 12). Thus, older women (in some cases, those over the age of twenty-five) may find themselves forced to the sidelines of the trade without having found a suitable income-earning substitute (and without access to anything like a pension), as the market demands and attracts younger and younger women. Looked at in this light, cases like that cited in chapter 11 on Suriname, which present the Maroon community as turning its young teenage girls to prostitution, could be viewed as a logical (though unfortu-

nate) response to this particular market demand in light of the serious economic disadvantages the communities are facing.

In the larger context, the entire question of child and youth prostitution
needs to be reexamined in ways that go beyond the sensationalist treatment
the issue has received in recent years (Kempadoo and Ghuma, chapter 13).
Minimally, it would appear that analysis dealing with young people involved in prostitution cannot be delinked from a recognition of the unacceptable economic realities in which they and their families are living. While
children working in prostitution is neither an acceptable nor a justifiable solution, studies like those contained in this book show prostitution to be one
of a number of limited, hazardous, and difficult economic options young
people must deal with in societies that are unwilling or unable to provide
any type of social or economic safety net to families and communities. Nor
can it be delinked from other issues related to the most exploitative aspects
of child labor.[2]

The cases cited in this publication in which Amerindian women involved
in sex work are being abused and exploited by those who hold economic
power over them, or had entered the sex trade as a result of deceptive tactics by would-be employers, come under a special category (Red Thread,
chapter 12). Under ILO Convention 169, indigenous and tribal peoples are
entitled to special protections with regard to recruitment and conditions of
employment.[3] Cases in which Surinamese Maroon communities are destabi-
lized by gold-mining activities are also in violation of this particular ILO convention, which includes an article that requires governments to seek community consultation with indigenous or tribal peoples on development
activities in their regions.[4]

An example of questionable and irresponsible legislation is a law currently being proposed for the Dominican Republic that is aimed at making
it illegal to live off the earnings of a sex worker. If passed, such a law could
make sex workers' immediate family members whom they are supporting
(including their mothers and their children) vulnerable to arrest. It is important to note that anecdotal evidence suggests it is not uncommon for sex
workers' incomes to be the only source of household income for some families (Mullings, chapter 3). Thus, a law that on the surface may appear to be
aimed at limiting the activities of pimps in fact may be very damaging to sex
workers and their families.

Migrating in order to increase one's economic possibilities is a fact of life
for sex workers, as it is for many other people in the region. There are indications that sex workers may face considerable police harassment when
they are in places other than their country of origin, regardless of whether
they are documented or not. Some of the examples cited in the studies are
the treatment of Guyanese, Dominican, and Colombian women working in
Suriname and Haitian women working in the Dominican Republic. Being in

a technically illegal immigration position makes women particularly vulnerable, since they are unlikely to report any sort of crime or abuse they experience, as this could lead to their arrest and deportation.

Finally, as mentioned earlier, the way tourism is structured in many countries results in problems not only for sex workers but for the larger population of poor and working-class people who remain unable to partake in development and economic plans that do not include them. Any attempt to better the situation of sex workers in tourism countries must take into account the economic rights and needs of the entire communities to which they are linked, and seek to include them in development plans (Mullings, chapter 3).

A summary of the principal problems identified by sex workers in the region might look like this:

1. A lack of economic and job opportunities in all the countries under study. Tourism as well as other development strategies frequently benefits multinational and overseas corporations rather than local people and communities.
2. The need for people to migrate from their country of origin or from one part of the country to another in order to find work.
3. Lack of protection for immigrant sex workers from abuse by the authorities and others regardless of the legal status of their situation in the host country. In some cases, non-national sex workers, especially, experience discrimination and harassment by the police.
4. Vulnerability to physical and psychological abuse from clients and police due to the clandestine or illegal status of sex work.
5. Exploitative and insecure working conditions.
6. Problems related to health and health care for sex workers and their families. These include lack of access to adequate and affordable health care as well as preventative health care information and materials (including condoms). There are also problems with attitudes and practices among public health officials who do not respect the human rights and dignity of sex workers.
7. People who work in the sex trade experience discrimination in their societies because they are sex workers.
8. Lack of access to full participation in civil society due to educational disadvantages and societal discrimination toward sex workers.

RECOMMENDATIONS

The following are some recommendations for addressing problems sex workers face in the region. They have grown out of issues identified in the

regional research project and from discussion that took place at the conference "The Working Sex: Caribbean Development, Tourism, Sex and Work,"
in Kingston, Jamaica, July 1998. Some of the recommendations presented
here were identified for use in the specific context of particular countries in
which studies were carried out, while others seem to be applicable to the
entire region.

1. States should seek to clarify the legal situation of sex work without
   criminalizing sex workers and without putting more power into the
   hands of brothel owners and others who are in a position to exert economic pressure on sex workers. As long as sex work remains a clandestine activity, workers in the industry will continue to be vulnerable
   to abuse, with limited possibilities for taking open and organized action toward accessing and ensuring their rights. Due to the ambiguous
   nature of their legal status, sex workers are vulnerable to abuse by authorities, clients, and others for which they cannot seek protection and
   redress from the state.
2. Sex work must be recognized as a labor activity to which both national
   labor legislation and ILO standards apply. Labor rights are never
   achieved easily. However, having access to the necessary legal instruments is an essential element for improving working conditions.
   Where national labor legislation and practice is not in line with ILO
   standards or is weak and incomplete, it must be strengthened.
3. Work must be done to counter the social discrimination sex workers
   face in society. Although changes in the way people think require
   long-term effort, making sure sex workers are protected under law as
   members of society with rights and as workers is an essential step toward countering at least the more visible effects of discrimination.
4. Sex workers who migrate to work in other countries must have access
   to state protection from both the host country and their country of origin. Regardless of the "legality" of a person's presence in a country, all
   people should have access to human rights and protection from abuse.
   The concept of "labor migration" and national boundaries needs to be
   revised in the light of the current global situation.
5. Access to health care is a right contained in the International Convention on Economic, Social and Cultural Rights. While this is still far from
   being a reality in most countries, it is a standard toward which to aspire. Sex workers need access to health care and to health education
   and preventative programs around AIDS/HIV and sexually transmitted
   diseases (STDs). However, the elements of coercion present in many
   of the existing state-run programs constitute a violation of sex workers'
   human rights and dignity. No programs should be put in place without
   consultation with sex workers, and their scope should include clients

as well. Minors must not be denied access to curative and preventive measures for STDs. The ongoing work of sex workers' organizations in the area of AIDS/HIV education and prevention should be recognized, encouraged and supported.

6. The situation of children and adolescents involved in prostitution should be given special and separate consideration, since their needs and realities are frequently different from those of adults. Child prostitution must be examined in the context of the general economic injustice which puts people in the position of having to work for their survival before they have achieved physical and intellectual maturity. Attempts at assisting child sex workers should not lead to further abuse of their rights and should be congruent with the legal age of sexual consent in the country.

7. The situation of indigenous and Maroon women and their communities should be given special attention. Compliance with ILO Convention 169 on the Rights of Indigenous and Tribal Peoples should be sought and policies should be put in place to guarantee that the women of these communities will gain knowledge of and access to their rights as well as opportunities for education and economic advancement that are in keeping with the goals they themselves identify.

8. The lack of real development strategies that include the majority of the population of countries (as opposed to a small economic elite) is a serious problem. Job training programs must be put in place, and these should be made especially available to women and youth. If such programs are to be truly accessible, they should be held at hours during which women can attend, and include the possibility of child care. However, job training should be seen as a complement to job development programs and not the other way around. Training people for jobs that do not exist is a dead-end effort.

9. While tourism is currently one of the few economic avenues open to many Caribbean countries, the current structure whereby multinational companies hold a monopoly on tourism profits is untenable for local populations. Action must be taken so that local people can have some influence over tourism policy. Community-based tourism, as is beginning to be practiced in some regions, should be explored as an option.

DISCUSSION AND FINAL REMARKS

The implementation of recommendations like those outlined above will require much work and concentration of efforts by sex workers and their organizations and by the larger society of which they form a part. In the case of Jamaica, for example, it has been suggested that dialogue among representatives

of the state, the private sector, and sex workers will be necessary if the society is to break through the problems surrounding legislation that is discriminatory to sex workers and through problems caused by police abuse
(see Kempadoo and Mellon 1998). This model of broad-based societal dialogue may be relevant for other countries as well. Similar dialogue will also
be necessary if we are to move beyond the existing contradictions between
public and private morality that are manifested in the discrimination sex
workers face in society. It has been suggested that in order to confront the
problem of police abuse it will be necessary to develop a structure that centers on advocacy and mediation on behalf of the sex workers. This will likely
require the participation of both sex workers' organizations and members of
the legal profession who are committed to working in collaboration with
them.

The establishment and management of health services for STDs and
HIV/AIDS should also be undertaken with the involvement of sex workers if
these programs are to truly serve their needs in a nondiscriminatory manner.

The recognition of sex work as a labor activity will require much input
and commitment from such international bodies as the ILO in conjunction
with dialogue and awareness campaigns aimed at national and local unions
and community organizations. Some of this work is now beginning to take
place within the ILO, which has produced several publications that deal
with labor issues related to sex work (Lim 1998, Black 1995). Cases such as
Suriname, where women are living and working in very unsafe and substandard conditions in the gold fields, should be given special and immediate attention as should those involving indigenous and Maroon women.

In addition to the recommendations outlined here, it has been pointed out
that there is a need for further research in a number of areas if we are to gain
an understanding of sex work today in order to support the needs and rights
of sex workers. These include coordinated research on existing programs in
countries where an innovative approach has been taken with an eye toward
incorporating relevant aspects of such programs into local initiatives. Research into the demand side of sex work, as represented by clients, is also
needed. It is also essential that research be carried out that seeks to understand the increasing involvement of youth in sex work and that the situation
of male sex workers be systematically explored as well.

The area of job training aimed at helping people make a transition from
sex work to other types of jobs needs to be given special attention. It is important to recognize that many people engage in sex work because of a lack
of other economic options in their region or because sex work simply pays
more than other jobs that may be available to them. In the case of child and
youth prostitution, where extreme poverty is nearly always present as a mo-
tivating factor, a look at the options the entire society offers to poor people
must be examined in light of the International Convention on Economic, So-

cial and Cultural Rights (ICESCR). Job training programs, especially those whose stated aim is that of "rehabilitating" young sex workers, may not necessarily reflect the context and the real economic situation in which people have to survive. Sex workers cannot realistically switch to jobs that may pay up to two or three times less than what they are making at the present time and training programs that expect them to do so cannot possibly be adequate for addressing the situation. For the case of Colombia, it has been suggested that young sex workers might be more productively trained for job placements that would help them find work in existing local industries. In any event, job training is not a viable alternative for sex workers of any country unless it is carried out in conjunction with programs for developing employment and improving the economy in general (Kempadoo and Mellon 1998).

Finally, the question of economic development in the region, and specifically the heavy dependence on tourism as the only viable option for many of the region's countries, needs to be re-examined. In the case studies presented in this collection, it has been shown repeatedly that the "all-inclusive" model of packaged mass tourism benefits only a few people in Caribbean societies, with the bulk of the profits being siphoned off by multinational owners. A real push toward options of community-based tourism activities could provide a more just distribution of the tourism dollar in a way that would benefit more people. A shift to this type of model will not be easy since it means going against current economic trends and powerful economic interests. However, experiments with such models are currently underway in a number of countries and may be worth exploring in the Caribbean context. Mullings (chapter 3) has suggested an innovative approach that would recognize the contribution sex workers are making to the tourism economy and seek to both utilize their skills in other tourism areas and bring sex work into the realm of community-based tourism, thereby ridding the trade of many of the negative aspects that result from clandestinity and marginalization.

The situation of economic development in general presents a huge challenge for communities and small nations, especially in light of the types of free trade and investment agreements that are currently being promoted for the hemisphere (Klak 1998). It should be recognized that local and national development programs, along with support for local industries and initiatives, could become extremely difficult to implement once these types of agreements come into effect. The clauses defining "national treatment" contained in such agreements as the proposed Free Trade Agreement for the Americas and the Multilateral Agreement on Investment (MAI) essentially prohibit states from taking measures to protect or promote local industries and economic initiatives without extending the same level of protection to foreign investors within their national boundaries. Thus, despite good intentions and innovative planning, countries may soon find that their options are limited. Attempts to regain control of their economies and to empower local populations as essential participants in economic endeavors may be ruled to be in violation of investment and trade agreements national leaders have signed. This poses a problem for achieving the type of people-centered economic development that represents the only truly sustainable alternative for the future. The intention behind saying this is not to discourage much-needed efforts for countries to regain control of their economic agendas. It is essential, however, that local populations and governments gain an understanding of the real content of multilateral agreements, which could present limitations for future attempts to improve economic options for the region.[5] At the same time, however, it is essential that new approaches to development be tenaciously sought if the goal of improving the economic situation for all members of society, sex workers included, is ultimately to be met.

NOTES

I am grateful to the researchers in the project "Tourism and the Sex Trade in the Caribbean" who helped shape this section on policy recommendations through very concrete contributions based on the findings of their fieldwork.

1. For an in-depth examination of sex work in relation to existing UN Human Rights and ILO standards, see Bindman 1997.
2. For an in-depth discussion of child prostitution from a perspective within the ILO, see Lim 1998.
3. Article 20, ILO Convention 169 on the Rights of Indigenous and Tribal Peoples.
4. See Article 20, ILO Convention 169 on the Rights of Indigenous and Tribal Peoples. It should be noted that working groups of indigenous people at the United Nations Human Rights Commission are in the process of amending and improving this and other international conventions, in an effort to make them enforceable.
5. At the time of this writing, negotiations for the MAI, after a period of intense international promotion, have been suspended due to strong objections from some countries, notably France. Popular education and public rejection of the agreement seem to have played a role in this unprecedented turn of events. However, the global tendency toward the promotion of supranational pacts of this type has not yet run its course, and the long-term nature of such interstate commitments makes them particularly problematic for countries in development.

Bibliography

Abraham–van der Mark, Eva. "Marriage and Concubinage among the Sephardic Merchant Elite of Curaçao." *Women and Change in the Caribbean*, ed. Janet Momsen, 38–50. London: James Currey, Kingston: Ian Randle, Bloomington: Indiana University Press, 1993.

Abrahams, Roger. *The Man-of-Words in the West Indies*. Baltimore: Johns Hopkins University Press, 1983.

Acevedo, J., personal interview, Cartagena, October 1997.

Ahumada, Consuelo. *El Modelo Neoliberal y su Impacto en la Sociedad Colombiana*. Santafé de Bogotá: El Áncora Editores, 1996.

Alberts, Tineke. *Je Lust en Je Leven: Een inventariserend Onderzoek naar Relatievorming, Sexueel Gedrag en de Preventie van AIDS op Curaçao*. Curaçao: Nationale AIDScommissie van de Nederlandse Antillen en de Geneeskundige-en Gezondheidsdienst van het Eilandgebied Curaçao, 1992.

Alegría, Margarita, Mildred Vera, Daniel Freeman, Rafaela Robles, María del C. Santos, and Carmen L. Rivera. "HIV Infection, Risk Behaviors and Depressive Symptoms among Puerto Rican Sex Workers." *American Journal of Public Health* 84.12 (December 1994): 2000–2002.

Alegría, Margarita, Mildred Vera, Carmen Rivera, Margarita Burgos, Ann Finlinson, and María del C. Santos. "Puerto Rican Sex Workers: HIV Risk Behaviors and Policy Implications." New York: Centro de Estudios Puertoriqueños, 1994.

Alexander, Jacqui. "Erotic Autonomy as a Politics of Decolonization: An Anatomy of Feminist and State Practice in the Bahamas Tourist Economy." *Feminist Genealogies, Colonial Legacies, Democratic Futures,* ed. Jacqui Alexander and Chandra Talpade Mohanty, 63–100. London: Routledge, 1997.

Allen, Rose Mary. "Curaçaoan Women's Role in the Migration to Cuba." *Mundu Yama Sinta Mira: Womanhood in Curaçao,* ed. Richenel Ansano, Joceline Clemencia, Jeanette Cook, and Eithel Martis, 59–78. Curaçao: Fundasho Publikashon, 1992.

Anarfi, John K. "Ghanaian Women and Prostitution in Cote d'Ivoire." *Global Sex Workers,* ed. Kamala Kempadoo and Jo Doezema, 104–113. New York: Routledge, 1998.

Anderson, Patricia, and Michael Witter. "Crisis, Adjustment and Social Change: A Case Study of Jamaica." *The Consequences of Structural Adjustment: A Review of the Jamaican Experience,* ed. Elsie LeFranc, 1–55. Kingston: Canoe Press, 1994.

Angueira, Luisa Hernández. "Across the Mona Strait: Dominican Boat Women in Puerto Rico." *Daughters of Caliban: Caribbean Women in the Twentieth Century*, ed. Consuelo López Springfield, 96–111. Bloomington: Indiana University Press, London: Latin America Bureau, 1997.

Antonius-Smits, Christel, Henna Malmberg-Geuicherit, and Ruben Del Prado. *Situation Analysis of Children and Women in Suriname*. Paramaribo: UNICEF, 1994.

Arber, Sarah. "Designing Samples." *Researching Social Life,* ed. Nigel Gilbert, 68–92. London: Sage, 1993.

ASONAHORES. (Asociación Nacional de Hoteles y Restaurantes, Inc.). *Estadísticas Seleccionadas del Sector Turístico*. Santo Domingo, 1995.

Aymer, Paula L. *Uprooted Women: Migrant Domestics in the Caribbean*. Westport, Conn.: Praeger, 1997.

Azize Vargas, Yamila, and Kamala Kempadoo. "Tráfico de Mujers para Prostitución, Trabajo Doméstico y Matrimonio." 1996.

Báez, Clara, and Ginny Taulé, ed. *Género y Sociedad* 1.2 (September–December 1993).

Bailey, Beth, and David Farber. *The First Strange Place: Race and Sex in World War II Hawaii*. Baltimore: Johns Hopkins University Press, 1992.

Banco de la República. *Compendio Estadístico de Bolívar y Cartagena*. Cartagena: Banco de la República, 1992.

Barrow, Christine. "Finding the Support: Strategies for Survival." *Social and Economic Studies* 35.2 (1996): 131–176.

Barry, Kathleen. *Female Sexual Slavery*. New York: New York University Press, 1984.

Barry, Tom, Beth Wood, and Deb Preusch. *The Other Side of Paradise*. New York: Grove Press, 1984.

Batista, Ramón. Interview conducted at COVICOSIDA. Puerto Plata, July 1997.

Beckles, Hilary. *Natural Rebels: A Social History of Enslaved Black Woman in Barbados*. London: Zed Books, 1989.

Bell, Gustavo. *Cartagena de Indias de la Colonia a la República: Colección de Historia No. 3*. Santafé de Bogotá: Fundación Simón y Lola Guberek, 1991.

Bergés de Farray, Arita. "Aspectos Legales de la Prostitución en la República Dominicana. "*Seminario sobre la Prostitución*, 53–66. Dominican Republic: Asociación Dominicana Pro Bienestar de la Familia, 1983.

Bernstein, Laurie. *Sonia's Daughters: Prostitutes and Their Regulation in Imperial Russia*. Berkeley: University of California Press, 1995.

Biersteker, Susan. "Promoting Safer Sex in Prostitution: Impediments and Opportunities." *Promoting Safer Sex*, ed. Maria Paalman, 143–152. Amsterdam: Swets and Seitlinger B.V., 1990.

Bindman, Jo. "An International Perspective on Slavery in the Sex Industry." *Global Sex Workers: Rights, Resistance and Redefinition* ed. Kamala Kempadoo and Jo Doezema, 65–68. New York: Routledge, 1998.

_____. *Redefining Prostitution as Sex Work on the International Agenda*. London: Anti-Slavery International, 1997.

Bishop, Ryan, and Lillian S. Robinson. *Night Market: Sexual Cultures and the Thai Economic Miracle*. New York: Routledge, 1998.

Black, Maggie. *In the Twilight Zone: Child Workers in the Hotel, Tourism and Catering Industry*. Geneva: International Labour Office, 1995.

Block, Alan A., and Patricia Klausner. "Masters of Paradise Island: Organized Crime: Neo-Liberalism and the Bahamas," *Dialectical Anthropology* 12 (1987): 85–102.

Boletín Informativo Cotelco, Bogota (May 1997).

Bolles, A. Lynn. "Economic Crisis and Female-headed Households in Kingston, Jamaica." *Women and Change in Latin America*, ed. June Nash and Helen Safa. Albany: SUNY Press, 1985.

_____. "Sand, Sea, and the Forbidden." *Transforming Anthropology* 3.1 (1992): 30–34.

Bonetti, Mario. "Causas Culturales de la Prostitución en Santo Domingo." *Seminario sobre la Prostitución*, 39–52. Dominican Republic: Asociación Dominicana Pro Bienestar de la Familia, 1983.

Boonchalaksi, Wathinee, and Philip Guest. "Prostitution in Thailand." *The Sex Sector: The Economic and Social Bases of Prostitution in Southeast Asia*, ed. Lin Lean Lim, 130–169. Geneva: International Labour Office, 1998.

Bourdieu, Pierre. *Distinction: A Critique of the Judgement of Taste*. London: Routledge and Kegan Paul, 1984.

Brace, Laura, and Julia O'Connell Davidson. "Desperate Debtors and Counterfeit Love: The Hobbesian World of the Sex Tourist." *Contemporary Politics* 2.3 (1996): 55–78.

Branche, Jennifer. "Sex Work in Guyana." *Guyana Review* 6.63 (April 1998).

Brathwaite, Farley. *Unemployment and Social Life: A Sociological Study of the Unemployed in Trinidad*. Bridgetown: Antilles Publications, 1983.

Brennan, Denise E. *Everything Is for Sale Here: Sex Tourism in Sosúa, the Dominican Republic*. Ph.D. Diss. Yale University, 1998.

Britton, Samuel G. "Tourism, Capital and Place: Towards a Critical Geography of Tourism." *Environment and Planning D. Society and Space* 9.4 (1991): 451–478.

Brussa, Licia. "Migrant Prostitutes in the Netherlands." *Vindication of the Rights of Whores*, ed. Gail Pheterson, 227–240. Seattle, Wash.: Seal Press, 1989.

Budhos, Marina. "Putting the Heat on Sex Tourism." *Ms.* (March/April 1997).

Bush, Barbara. *Slave Women in Caribbean Society: 1650–1838*. Bloomington: Indiana University Press, 1990.

Cabezas, Amalia Lucía. "Discourses of Prostitution: The Case of Cuba." *Global Sex Workers: Rights, Resistance and Redefinition*, ed. Kamala Kempadoo and Jo Doezema, 79–86. New York: Routledge, 1998.

_____. *Pleasure and Its Pain: Sex Tourism in Sosúa, the Dominican Republic*. Ph.D. Diss. University of California, 1998b.

Campani, Giovanna. "Women Migrants: From Marginal Subjects to Social Actors." *Cambridge Survey of World Migrations*, ed. Robin Cohen, 546–550. Cambridge: Cambridge University Press, 1995.

Cannings, Dusilley, and Jennifer Rosenweig. *Female Commercial Sex Worker's Project: Final Report*. Georgetown, Guyana: National AIDS Programme Secretariat, 1997.

Caribbean Tourism Organization (CTO). *Statistical Report*. 1996.

Caribbean Week, 14–27 February 1998.

Carter, Keith. "Female Sex Workers' Seroprevalence Survey, Georgetown, Guyana." Preliminary Report. 1993.

Carter, Keith, B. Harry, M. Jeune, and D. Nicholson. "HIV Risk Perception, Risk Behavior, and Seroprevalence among Female Commercial Sex Workers in Georgetown, Guyana." *Public Health* 1.6 (1997): 451–459.

Carty, Linda. "Women in Caribbean Tourism: The 'Unlabeled' Commodities." Paper presented at the 5th conference of North American and Cuban Philosophers, Havana, Cuba, July 1994. Photocopied.

Cassirer, Bruce, 1997, http://www.travelxn.com/features/negril/

Castañeda, Digna. "The Female Slave in Cuba during the First Half of the Nineteenth Century." *Engendering History: Caribbean Women in Historical Perspective*, ed. Verene Shepherd, Bridget Brereton, and Barbara Bailey, 141–154. New York: St. Martins Press, 1995.

Caulfield, Sueann. "The Birth of Mangue: Race, Nation, and the Politics of Prostitution in Rio De Janeiro, 1850–1942." *Sex and Sexuality in Latin America*, ed. Daniel Balderston and Donna J. Guy, 86–100. New York: New York University Press, 1997.

Cavalcanti, C., C. Imbert, and M. Cordero. *Prostitución, Esclavitud Sexual Feminina.* Santo Domingo, Dominican Republic: CIPAF, 1986.

CBS (Central Bureau for Statistics). Statistical Yearbook for the Netherlands Antilles, 1997.

Centro de Estudios Sociales y Demográficos (CESDEM). "Encuesta sobre Conocimientos, Creencias, Actitudes y Prácticas acerca del SIDA/ETS en Trabajadoras Sexuales y Hombres Involucrados en la Industria del Sexo en las Localidades de Puerto Plata, Sosúa y Monte Llano." Mimeo. Puerto Plata: COVICOSIDA, 1996.

Centro de Orientación e Investigación Integral (COIN). *Juntarnos: Memorias Primer Congreso Dominicano de Trabajadoras Sexuales.* Santo Domingo, Dominican Republic, 1996.

_____. *Infosida* [newsletter], July 1996.

_____. *La Industria del Sexo Por Dentro.* Santo Domingo, Dominican Republic, 1994.

Centro de Promoción y Solidaridad Humana (CEPROSH). *Proyecto Hotelero.* Puerto Plata, 1997.

CEPAL. *Panorama Social de América Latina 1996.* Santiago: Naciones Unidas, 1997.

Cepeda, Fernando. *Dirección Política de la Reforma en Colombia.* Santafé de Bogotá: FONADE/Departamento Nacional de Planeación, 1994.

Chapkis, Wendy. *Live Sex Acts: Women Performing Erotic Labor.* New York: Routledge, 1997.

Chatterjee, Pratap. "Cyanide Spill Could Be Long Term Disaster." IPS News Service. Washington, D.C., 30 August 1995.

Chevannes, Barry. "Sexual Behaviour of Jamaicans: A Literature Review." *Social and Economic Studies* 42.1 (1993).

Clarke, Edith. *My Mother Who Fathered Me: A Study of the Family in Three Selected Communities in Jamaica.* London: Allen & Unwin, 1957.

Codrescu, Andre. "Picking the Flowers of the Revolution." *New York Times Magazine*, 1 February 1998, 32–35.

Cohen, Erik. "Lovelorn Farangs: The Correspondence between Foreign Men and Thai Girls." *Anthropological Quarterly* 59.3 (1986): 115–127.

_____. "The Sociology of Tourism: Approaches, Issues and Findings," *Annual Review of Sociology* 10 (1984): 373–92.

_____. "Thai Girls and Farang Men: The Edge of Ambiguity." *Thai Tourism: Hill Tribes, Islands and Open-Ended Prostitution*, 249–268. Studies in Contemporary Thailand, No. 4. Bangkok: White Lotus Press, 1996. First published in 1982.

Colchester, Marcus. *Guyana Fragile Frontier: Loggers, Miners and Forest Peoples.* London and Kingston: Latin America Bureau, World Rainforest Movement and Ian Randle Publishers, 1997.

Conferencia Episcopal de Colombia. *Desplazados por Violencia en Colombia.* Santafé de Bogotá: Conferencia Episcopal de Colombia, 1995.

Congreso Mundial contra la Explotación Sexual de los Niños. *Nota Informativa y Reseñas Regionales.* Stockholm: Congreso Mundial contra la Explotación Sexual de los Niños, 1996.

Consejería Presidencial para la Política Social, Departamento de Planeación Nacional. *Plan Nacional de Acción en Favor de la Infancia: Situación en 1996 y Perspectivas para 1998–2000.* Santafé de Bogotá, July 1996.

Conway, Dennis. "The New Tourism in the Caribbean: Reappraising Market Segmentation." *Tourism Marketing and Management in the Caribbean,* ed. Dennis Gayle and Jonathan Goodrich, 167–173. London: Routledge, 1993.

Cooper, Carolyn. *Noises in the Blood: Orality, Gender and the 'Vulgar' Body of Jamaican Popular Culture.* London: Macmillan Caribbean, 1993.

Cooper, Marc. "For Sale: Used Marxism." *Harpers Magazine,* March 1995: 54–66.

Corbin, Alain. *Women for Hire: Prostitution and Sexuality in France after 1850.* Trans. by Alan Sheridan. Cambridge, Mass.: Harvard University Press, 1990.

Cornwall, Andrea, and Nancy Lindisfarne, ed. *Dislocating Masculinity.* London: Routledge, 1994.

Corte Constitucional. *Sentencia No. SU–476.* Santafé de Bogotá, 1997.

_____. *Sentencia No. T–620.* Santafé de Bogotá, 1995.

Crick, Malcolm. "Representations of International Tourism in the Social Sciences: Sun, Sex, Sights, Savings, and Servility." *Annual Review of Anthropology* 18 (1989): 307–344.

Dann, Graham. *The Barbadian Male: Sexual Attitudes and Practice.* London: Macmillan, 1987.

_____. "'de Higher de Monkey climb, de More 'e Show 'e Tail: Tourists' Knowledge of Barbadian Culture." *Journal of International Consumer Marketing* 6 (3/4) 1994: 181–204.

Danns, George K. *Child Prostitution and Child Sexual Exploitation in Guyana: A Study of Children in Especially Difficult Circumstances.* Georgetown: UNICEF, 1998.

Davis, Nanette J. *Prostitution: An International Handbook on Trends, Problems and Policies.* Westport, Conn.: Greenwood Press, 1993.

Davis, Tania. Memorandum to Ken Franzblau, Equality Now, 5 May 1998.

de Alburquerque, Klaus. "Sex, Beach Boys and Female Tourists in the Caribbean." *Journal of Sexuality and Culture* 2 (1999):87–112.

de la Soledad Valdéz, Iris A. "Leyes y Prostitución en Republica Dominicana." *Juntarnos: Primer Encuentro Dominicano de Trabajadoras Sexual,* 96–101. Santo Domingo: Imprenta "La Unión," 1996.

de Moya, E. Antonio, and Rafael García. "AIDS and the Enigma of Bisexuality in the Dominican Republic." *Bisexuality and AIDS in International Perspective,* ed. Peter Aggleton, 21–35. London: Taylor & Francis, 1996.

de Moya, E. A., Rafael García, Rosario Fadul, and Edward Herold. "Sosúa Sanky-Pankies and Female Sex Workers." Santo Domingo: Instituto de Sexualidad Humana, Universidad Autónoma de Santo Domingo, 1992.

De Ware Tijd, "Na Diep Dal Lichte Stijging Goudprijs," 14 March 1998.

de Zalduondo, Barbara O., and Jean Maxius Bernard. "Meanings and Consequences of Sexual-Economic Exchange: Gender, Poverty and Sexual Risk Behavior in Urban Haiti." *Conceiving Sexuality: Approaches to Sex Research in a Postmodern World,* ed. Richard. G. Parker and John H. Gagnon, 157–180. New York: Routledge, 1995.

Deere, Carmen Diana, Peggy Antrobus, Lynn Bolles, Edwin Melendez, Peter Phillips, Marcia Rivera, and Helen Safa. *In the Shadows of the Sun: Caribbean Development Alternatives and U.S. Policy.* Boulder, Colo.: Westview, 1990.

del Omo, Rosa. "The Cuban Revolution and the Struggle against Prostitution." *Crime and Social Justice* 12 (1979): 34–40.

Departamento Administrativo de Planeación, Departamento de Bolívar. *Plan de Desarollo 1995–1997: Dimensionando el Desarrollo de Bolívar.* Cartagena: Departamento Administrativo de Planeación, Departamento de Bolívar, 1995.

Departamento de Planeación Nacional. *Documento Conpes. Sistema Nacional de Atención Integral a la Población Desplazada por la Violencia* No. 2924. Santafé de Bogotá: Departamento de Planeación Nacional, 1997.

Díaz González, Elena. "The Quality of Life in Cuba's Special Period." *Carta Cuba: Lessons from Cuba's Special Period,* 12–23. Havana: Facultad Latinoamericana de Ciencias Sociales, 1995.

Díaz, Elena, Esperanza Fernández, and Tania Caram. "Turismo y Prostitución en Cuba." Paper presented at the 21st annual conference of the Caribbean Studies Association, San Juan, Puerto Rico, May 1996. Havana: Facultad Latinoamericana de Ciencias Sociales.

Doezema, Jo. "Forced to Choose: Beyond the Voluntary v. Forced Prostitution Dichotomy." *Global Sex Workers,* ed. Kamala Kempadoo and Jo Doezema, 34–50. New York: Routledge, 1998.

Domínguez, María Isabel. La Mujer Joven en los '90. Havana: CIPS, 1998, Unpublished.

Duarte, Isis. "Household Workers in the Dominican Republic: A Question for the Feminist Movement." *Muchachas No More,* ed. Elsa M. Chaney and Mary Garcia Castro, 197–220. Philadelphia: Temple University Press, 1989.

ECPAT, "Client, Customer, Exploiter," 30 January 1998c, http://www.rb.se/ecpat/exploit.htm

ECPAT, "Country Reports," 30 January 1998b, http://www.rb.se/ecpat/country.htm

ECPAT, "The ECPAT Campaign," 30 January 1998a, http://www.rb.se/ecpat/on_us.htm

ECPAT. *End Child Prostitution, Child Pornography and the Trafficking of Children for Sexual Purposes: An Information Booklet.* Bangkok: ECPAT International and ECPAT Australia, 1996.

ECPAT Bulletin, 1997.

ECTAA, "Declaration against Child Sex Tourism," November 1996, http://www.world-tourism/org/sextouri/ectaa-a.htm

ECTWT. *Tourism, Prostitution, Development.* Ecumenical Coalition on Third World Tourism in cooperation with the Center for Development Education (Zentrum für Entwicklungsbezogene Bildung-ZEB), 1983.

Elder, Glen. "The Life Course and Human Development." *Handbook of Child Psychology* Vol 1. *Theoretical Models of Human Development.* 5th ed., ed. R.M. Lerner and W. Damon. New York: Wiley, 1998.

Elder, G., J. Mondell, and R. Parke, ed. *Children in Time and Place: Developmental and Historical Insights.* New York: Cambridge University Press, 1993.

el-Gawhary, Karim. "Sex Tourism in Cairo." *Middle East Report* (September–October 1995): 26–28.

Elovich, Richard. "Staying Negative—It's Not Automatic: A Harm Reduction Approach to Substance Use and Sex." New York: *Gay Men's Health Crisis AIDS and Public Policy Journal* (summer/fall 1996).

Emeagwali, Gloria. "Introductory Perspectives: Monetarists, Liberals and Radicals: Contrasting Perspectives on Gender and Structural Adjustment." *Women Pay the Price: Structural Adjustment in African and the Caribbean,* ed. Gloria Emeagwali, 1–12. Trenton, N.J.: Africa World Press, 1995.

Empresa Promotora de Turismo. *Informes de Estadísticas de Turistas en Cartagena 1994–1997.* Cartagena, 1997.

Endoe, Corey Makira. *The Reproductive Health of Prostitutes in Negril.* Kingston, 1994. Unpublished.

Enloe, Cynthia. *Bananas, Beaches and Bases: Making Feminist Sense of International Politics.* Berkeley: University of California Press, 1989.

Esnal, Luis. "Racismo, Lado Oscuro de Brasil." *El Tiempo,* 6 September 1998.

Espino, María Dolores. "Tourism in Cuba: A Development Strategy for the 1990s?" *Cuba at the Crossroads: Politics and Economics after the Fourth Party Congress,* ed. Jorge F. Peres-López, 147–165. Gainesville: University of Florida Press, 1994.

Espino, María Dolores. "Tourism in Cuba: A Development Strategy for the 1990's?" *Cuban Studies,* 23 (1993): 49–69.

Fanon, Franz. *Black Skin, White Masks.* London: Paladin, 1970 (originally published in 1952).

———. *The Wretched of the Earth.* New York: Grove Press, 1963. Originally published in French in 1961.

Fantasy Getaway Guide Service. http://www.fantasytours.com.

Featherstone, Mike, ed. *Consumer Culture and Postmodernism.* London: Sage, 1991.

Fernandez, Nadine. "Race Re-emerges in the Cuban Public Domain." Conference Paper. American Anthropology Association Meetings. Philadelphia, 1998.

Ferreira, Francisca. "Prostitución y Tráfico de Mujeres en República Dominicana." Paper presented at the Latin American and Caribbean Regional Meeting on the Trafficking of Women. Puerto Rico, May 1996. Photocopied.

Ferrer, Pedro Luis. "100% Cubano." Miami: Carapacho Productions compact disc #CP–100101, 1994.

Figueroa, Peter, et al. "Is HIV/STD Control in Jamaica Making a Difference?" Unpublished paper, n.d.

Fiji Times, "International Tribunal Reviews Australian Child Sex Laws," 28 August 1997.

Findlay, Eileen J. "Decency and Democracy: The Politics of Prostitution in Ponce, Puerto Rico, 1890–1900." *Feminist Studies* 23.3 (fall 1997): 471–499.

FIYTO. "Resolution to Combat Child Sex Tourism." 47th Annual Conference, Paris, September 1997. Online. Available: http://www.world-tourism-org/sextouri/fiyto-a

Flair Magazine. "The Changing Face of Prostitution," 5 November 1987.

Flórez, Carmen, and María G. Cano. *Mujeres Latinoamericanas en Cifras Colombia.* Santiago, Chile: Instituto de la Mujer/Ministerio de Asuntos Sociales de España/ Facultad Latinoamericana de Ciencias Sociales FLACSO, 1993.

Forte, Janet. "Amerindians and Poverty." *Transition* 20–21 (1993): 53–74.

Freeman, Carla. "Reinventing Higglering across Transnational Zones." *Daughters of Caliban: Caribbean Women in the Twentieth Century*, ed. Consuelo López Springfield, 68–95. Bloomington: Indiana University Press, London: Latin America Bureau, 1997.

French, Joan. "Hitting Where It Hurts Most: Jamaican Women's Livelihoods in Crisis." *Mortgaging Women's Lives: Feminist Critiques of Structural Adjustment*, ed. Pamela Sparr, 165–179. London: Zed Books, 1994.

Fundación Renacer. *Programa de Rehabilitación y Reinserción Social dirigido a menores vinculados a la prostitución*. Cartagena, 1997.

Fusco, Coco. "Hustling for Dollars." *Ms.* Magazine, September/October 1996, 62–70.

_____. "Hustling for Dollars: Jineterismo in Cuba." *Global Sex Workers: Rights, Resistance and Redefinition*, ed. Kamala Kempadoo and Jo Doezema, 151–166. New York: Routledge, 1998.

Gabriel, Yiannis, and Tim Lang. *The Unmanageable Consumer: Contemporary Consumption and Its Fragmentations*. Thousand Oaks, Calif.: Sage Publications, 1995.

Gallardo Rivas, Gina. *Buscando la Vida: Dominicanas en el Servicio Doméstico en Madrid*. Santo Domingo: Centro de Investigación para la Acción Femenina, 1995.

Garay, Luis. "En Torno a las Relaciones Internacionales y la Globalización: Una Síntesis Analítica Reflexiva." *Análisis Político* 31: 24–41.

Gayle, Dennis. "The Jamaican Tourist Industry: Domestic Economic Growth and Development." *Tourism Marketing and Management in the Caribbean*, ed. Dennis Gayle and Jonathan Goodrich, 41–57. London: Routledge, 1993.

Geggus, David P. "Slave and Free Colored Women in Saint Domingue." *More Than Chattel: Black Women and Slavery in the Americas*, ed. David Barry Gaspar and Darlene Clark Hine, 259–278. Bloomington: Indiana University Press, 1996.

Gibson, Mary. *Prostitution and the State in Italy, 1860–1915*. New Brunswick: Rutgers University Press, 1986.

Giddens, Anthony. *Sociology*. Cambridge: Polity Press, 1989.

Gil, Rosa M., and Carmen I. Vazquez. *The María Paradox: How Latinas Can Merge Old World Traditions with New World Self-Esteem*. New York: G.P. Putnam's Sons, 1996.

Gil, Vincent E., M. Wang, A. Anderson, G. Lin, and Z. Wu. "Prostitutes, Prostitution and STD/HIV Transmission in Mainland China," *Social Science Medicine* 42.1 (1996): 141–152.

Gleaner. "Another Wooden Shoe Awardee?" 21 June 1998.

_____."Minimum Wage Cannot Mask Economic Problems," 6 July 1998.

_____. "Only 'Big Man' Benefitting from Tourists' Safety," 26 January 1998.

_____. "Poverty Alleviation," 4 November 1997.

_____. "Sex Shops Don't Have a Prayer with the Church," 25 June 1998.

_____. "Threat to Tourism," 16 June 1997, http://www.jamaica-gleaner.com/gleaner/19770616/cleisure/c1.html.

Government of Belize. *Belize Report for the Fourth World Conference on Women: Action for Equality, Development and Peace*. Belize City: Angelus Press, 1995.

_____. *From Girls to Women: Growing Up Healthy in Belize*. Benque Viejo del Carmen: Cubola Productions, 1997.

_____. *1991 Belize Family Health Survey Final Report*. Atlanta: U.S. Department of Health & Human Services, 1992.

Government of Jamaica. "Honourable Francis Tulloch's Contribution to the Budget Debate," 5 May 1998. Unpublished.

_____. *National Industrial Policy—Growth and Prosperity: The Way Forward.* Kingston: Jamaica Information Service, 1996.

Graaf, Ron de, Ine Vanwesenbeek, Gertjan van Zessen, Straver Visser, and Jan Visser. "Prostitution and the Spread of HIV." *Safe Sex in Prostitution in The Netherlands,* 2–24. Amsterdam: Mr A. de Graaf Institute, 1992.

Grasmuck, Sherri, and Rosario Espinal. "Market Success or Female Autonomy? Income, Gender and Household Decision-Making among Microentrepreneurs in the Dominican Republic." Presented at the conference *La República Dominicana en el Umbral del Siglo XXI, Pontificia Universidad Católica Madre y Maestro.* Santo Domingo, 24–26 July 1997.

Green, Cecilia. "Historical and Contemporary Restructuring and Women in Production in the Caribbean." *The Caribbean in the Global Political Economy,* ed. Hilbourne A. Watson, 149–172. Boulder, Colo.: Lynne Rienner, 1994.

Grewal, Inderpal. *Home and Harem: Nation, Gender, Empire and the Cultures of Travel.* London: Leicester University Press, 1996.

Grittner, Frederick K. *White Slavery: Myth, Ideology and American Law.* New York: Garland Publishing, 1990.

Günther, Armin. "Sex Tourism without Sex Tourists." *Sex Tourism and Prostitution: Aspects of Leisure, Recreation and Work,* ed. Martin Oppermann, 71–80. New York: Cognizant Communications, 1998.

Guy, Donna J. *Sex and Danger in Buenos Aires: Prostitution, Family, and Nation in Argentina.* Lincoln: University of Nebraska Press, 1991.

Hall, C. Michael. "Gender and Economic Interests in Tourism Prostitution: The Nature Development and Implications of Sex Tourism in South-East Asia." *Tourism: A Gender Perspective,* ed. Vivien Kinnaird and D. Hall. London: Routledge, 1994.

_____. "The Legal and Political Dimensions of Sex Tourism: The Case of Australia's Child Sex Tourism Legislation." *Sex Tourism and Prostitution,* ed. Martin Oppermann, 87–96. Elmsford, N.Y.: Cognizant Communications, 1998.

_____. "Sex Tourism in South-East Asia." *Tourism and the Less Developed Countries,* ed. David Harrison, 64–74. London: Belhaven Press, 1992.

Hall, Stuart. "The Question of Cultural Identity." *Modernity and its Future,* ed. S. Hall, D. Held, and T. McGrew. Oxford: Polity Press, 1992.

Hanson, Jody. "Child Prostitution in South–East Asia: White Slavery Revisted?" *Sex Tourism and Prostitution,* ed. Martin Oppermann, 51–59. Elmsford, N.Y.: Cognizant Communications, 1998.

Harrison, David, ed. "Tourism and Prostitution: Sleeping with the Enemy? The Case of Swaziland." *Tourism Management* 15.6 (1994): 435–443.

_____. *Tourism and the Less Developed Countries.* London: Belhaven Press, 1992.

Harrison, Faye V. "Women in Jamaica's Urban Informal Economy: Insights from a Jamaican Slum." *Third World Women and the Politics of Feminism,* ed. Chandra Talpade Mohanty, Ann Russo, and Lourdes Torres, 173–196. Bloomington: Indiana University Press, 1991.

Hart, Angie. "Missing Masculinity? Prostitutes' Clients in Alicante, Spain." *Dislocating Masculinity: Comparative Ethnographies,* ed. Andrea Cornwall and Nancy Lindisfarne, 48–65. London: Routledge, 1994.

Hartsock, Nancy. *Money, Sex, and Power.* Boston: Northeastern University Press, 1985.

Haynes, Lila. "Cuba." *International Tourism Reports* 3 (1996): 4–23.

Hegstrom, Edward, and Geoffrey Mohan. "Urge to Close Belize's Door: Historically Diverse Nation Skeptical of Latest Immigrants." *Newsday*, 11 October 1998.

Helg, Aline. "Race in Argentina and Cuba, 1880–1930: Theory, Policies and Popular Reaction." *The Idea of Race in Latin America*, ed. Richard Graham, 37–70. Austin: University of Texas Press, 1990.

Henriot, Christian. "From a Throne of Glory to a Seat of Ignominy: Shanghai Prostitution Revisited (1849–1949)." *Modern China* 22.2 (1996): 132–163.

Henriques, Fernando. *Prostitution and Society: Europe and the New World.* Vol. 2. London: Macgibbon & Kee, 1993.

_____. *Prostitution in Europe and the Americas.* New York: Citadel Press, 1965.

Hernández, Javier, personal interview. Cartagena, October 1997.

Hershatter, Gail. "The Hierarchy of Shanghai Prostitution, 1870–1949." *Modern China* 15.4 (1989): 463–498.

Hirst, Paul, and Grahame Thompson. *Globalization in Question: The International Economy and the Possibilities of Governance.* Cambridge: Polity Press, 1997.

Hobson, J., S. Perry, and Uta C. Dietrich. "Tourism, Health and Quality of Life: Challenging the Responsibility of Using the Traditional Tenets of Sun, Sea, Sand and Sex in Tourism Marketing." *Journal of Travel and Tourism Marketing* 3.4 (1994): 21–38.

Hodgson, Douglas. "Combating the Organized Sexual Exploitation of Asian Children: Recent Development and Prospects." *International Journal of Law and the Family* 9.1 (1995): 23–53.

Høigård, Cecilie, and Liv Finstad. *Backstreets: Prostitution, Money and Love.* University Park: Pennsylvania State University Press, 1986.

hooks, bell. *Black Looks: Race and Representation.* London: Turnaround, Boston: South End Press, 1992.

_____. *Outlaw Culture: Resisting Representations.* London: Routledge, 1994.

HOTREC, "Declaration against the Sexual Exploitation of Children," 27 April 1997, http://www.world-tourism-org/sextouri/hotrec-a.htm

Howell, Ron. "Cuba '92: Desperate for Cash." *New York Newsday*, 27 September 1992.

Hunt, Lynn, ed. *The Invention of Pornography: Obscenity and the Origins of Modernity, 1500–1800.* New York: Zone Books, 1996.

IATA, "Final Resolution Condemning Commercial Sexual Exploitation of Children," Geneva, November 1996, http://www.world-tourism-org/sextouri/iata-a.htm

IFTO, "Code of Conduct against the Sexual Exploitation of Children," 2 February 1998, http://www.world-tourism-org/sextouri/ifto-a.htm

IFWTO, "Resolution against Sex Tourism," 2 February 1998, http://www.world-tourism-org/sextouri/ifwto-a.htm

Igbinovia, Patrick Edobor. "Prostitution in Black Africa." *International Journal of Women's Studies* 7.5: 430–449.

IH&RA. "IHA and Its Member Associations against the Sexual Exploitation of Children," adopted in Mexico City, 30 October 1996, http://www.world-tourism-org/sextouri/iha-a.htm

Imbert Brugal, Carmen. *Tráfico de Mujeres: Visión de una Nación Exportadora.* Santo Domingo: CE-Mujer, 1991.

International Organization for Migration (IOM). "Trafficking in Women from the Dominican Republic for Sexual Exploitation." Budapest, 1996.

Ioannides, D., and K. Dabbage. *The Economic Geography of the Tourist Industry.* New York: Routledge, 1998.

Isis-wicce. *Women's World* 24 (winter 1990/1).

IUF/UITA/UIL, "Resolution on Prostitution Tourism," adopted by the IUF HRC Trade group Board, Budapest, December 1995, and endorsed by the IUF EC, Geneva, April 1996, http://www.world-tourism-org/sextouri/iuf-a.htm

Jeffreys, Shiela. *The Idea of Prostitution.* Melbourne: Spinifex, 1997.

Jodah, Desiree Kissoon. "Courting Disaster in Guyana." *Multinational Monitor* 16. 11 (November 1995).

Kalm, Florence. "The Two 'Faces' of Antillean Prostitution." Photocopied. 1985.

Kane, Stephanie C. *AIDS Alibis: Sex, Drugs and Crime in the Americas.* Philadelphia: Temple University Press, 1998.

_____. "Prostitution and the Military: Planning AIDS Intervention in Belize." *Social Science Medicine* 36.7 (1993): 965–979.

Karch, Cecilia A., and G. H. S. Dann. "Close Encounters of the Third Kind." *Human Relations* 34 (1981): 249–268.

Kempadoo, Kamala. "COIN and MODEMU in the Dominican Republic." *Global Sex Workers: Rights, Resistance, and Redefinition,* ed. Kamala Kempadoo and Jo Doezema, 260–266. New York: Routledge, 1998.

_____. "Dominicanas en Curaçao: Mitos y Realidades." *Género y Sociedad* 4.1 (May–August 1996): 102–130.

_____. *Exotic Colonies: Caribbean Women in the Dutch Sex Trade.* Ph.D. Diss. University of Colorado, 1994.

_____. "Globalizing Sex Workers' Rights." *Global Sex Workers,* ed. Kamala Kempadoo and Jo Doezema, 2–28. New York: Routledge, 1998.

_____. "The Migrant Tightrope: Experiences from the Caribbean." *Global Sex Workers,* ed. Kamala Kempadoo and Jo Doezema, 124–138. New York: Routledge, 1998.

_____. "Prostitution, Marginality, and Empowerment: Caribbean Women in the Sex Trade." *Beyond Law* 5.14 (1994): 69–84.

_____. "Regulating Prostitution in the Dutch Caribbean." Paper presented at the 20th annual conference of the Caribbean Studies Association, Curaçao, Netherlands Antilles, May 1995.

_____. 'Sandoms' and Other Exotic Women: Prostitution and Race in the Caribbean." *Race and Reason* 1.3 (1996): 48–53.

Kempadoo, Kamala, and Jo Doezema, ed. *Global Sex Workers: Rights, Resistance, and Redefinition.* New York: Routledge, 1998.

Kempadoo, Kamala, and Cynthia Mellon, ed. *The Sex Trade in the Caribbean.* Boulder: University of Colorado/CAFRA/ILSA, 1998.

Kerr, Paulett A. "Victims or Strategists: Female Lodging Housekeepers in Jamaica." *Engendering History: Caribbean Women in Historical Perspective,* ed. Verene Shepherd, Bridget Brereton, and Barbara Bailey, 197–212. New York: St. Martins Press, 1995.

Kinnaird, Vivian, and Derek Hall. *Tourism: A Gender Analysis.* Chichester, N.Y.: John Wiley and Sons, 1994.

Kinnaird, Vivian, Uma Kothari, and Derek Hall. "Tourism: Gender Perspectives." *Tourism: A Gendered Analysis,* ed. Vivian Kinnaird and Derek Hall, 1–34. Chichester, N.Y.: John Wiley and Sons, 1994.

Klak, Thomas. "Thirteen Theses on Globalization and Neoliberalism." *Globalization and Neoliberalism: The Caribbean Context,* ed. Thomas Klak, 3–23. Boulder, Colo.: Rowman and Littlefield, 1998.

Klein, Herbert S. *African Slavery in Latin America and the Caribbean.* New York: Oxford University Press, 1986.

Kovaleski, Serge. "Cash-Strapped Cuba Courting Tourists," *Washington Post,* 15 January 1999.

Kreniske, John. "AIDS in the Dominican Republic: Anthropological Reflections on the Social Nature of Disease." *AIDS in Africa and the Caribbean,* ed. George C. Bond, John Kreniske, Ida Susser, and Joan Vincent, 33–50. Boulder, Colo.: Westview Press, 1997.

Kruhse–Mount Burton, Suzy. "Sex Tourism and Traditional Australian Male Identity." *International Tourism: Identity and Change,* ed. Marie-Francoise Lanfant, John Allcock, and Edward Bruner, 192–204. London: Sage, 1995.

Kutzinski, Vera M. *Sugar's Secrets: Race and the Erotics of Cuban Nationalism.* Charlottesville: University Press of Virginia, 1993.

Lagro, Monique, and Donna Plotkin. "The Suitcase Traders in the Free Zone of Curaçao." Port of Spain: Caribbean Development and Co-operation Committee, Economic Commission for Latin America and the Caribbean, 1990.

Lamur, Humphrey, and Julia Terborg. *Risicoperceptie en Preventiestrategieen—Creools—Surinaamse Bezoekers van een Rotterdamse SOA-Poli.* Delft: Eburon, 1994.

Lancaster, Roger Nelson. *Life Is Hard: Machismo, Danger and Intimacy of Power in Nicaragua.* Berkeley: University of California Press, 1992.

"Lap Dancing and Facials." *Stabroek News,* 17 April 1998.

Lastra Torres, Teresa. "Vulnerability and Social Risk: Women in the Sex Trade." *Women's Health Journal,* January 1998.

Laurie, Nina. "Negotiating Femininity: Women and Representation in Emergency Employment in Peru." *Gender, Place and Culture* 4.2 (1997): 235–251.

Laws of Barbados, Minor Offences Act, The Government of Barbados, 1998.

_____. The Sexual Offences Act, The Government of Barbados, 1993.

Lazarus-Black, Mindie. *Legitimate Acts and Illegal Encounters: Law and Society in Antigua and Barbuda.* Washington: Smithsonian Institution Press, 1991.

Lee, Wendy. "Prostitution and Tourism in South-East Asia." *Working Women: International Perspectives on Labour and Gender Ideology,* ed. N. Redclift and M. Thea Sinclair, 79–103. London: Routledge, 1991.

LEFÖ (Lateinamerikanische Emigrierte Frauen in Österreich). *Traffick in Women,* ed. Ilse König. Vienna, 1998.

Leheny, David. "A Political Economy of Asian Sex Tourism." *Annals of Tourism Research* 22.2 (1995): 367–384.

Levine, Phillippa. "Venereal Disease, Prostitution and the Politics of Empire: The Case of British India." *The Journal of the History of Sexuality* 4.4 (1994): 579–602.

Levy, Carl. *Emancipation, Sugar and Federalism: Barbados and the West Indies, 1833–1876.* Gainesville: University of Florida Press, 1980.

Levy, Diane E., and Patricia B. Lerch. "Tourism as a Factor in Development: Implications for Gender and Work in Barbados." *Gender and Society* 5.1 (March 1991): 67–85.

Lewis, Linden. "Masculinity and the Dance of the Dragon: Reading Lovelace Discursively." *Feminist Review* 59 (summer 1998): 164–185.

Ley No. 24–97. *Contra la Violencia Intrafamiliar.* Santo Domingo, Dominican Republic: Editorial Taller, 1997.

Lim, Lin Lean, ed. "Child Prostitution." *The Sex Sector*, 170–205. Geneva: International Labour Office, 1998.

_____. "The Economic and Social Bases of Prostitution in Southeast Asia." *The Sex Sector*, 1–28. Geneva: International Labour Office, 1998.

_____. *The Sex Sector: The Economic and Social Bases of Prostitution in Southeast Asia.* Geneva: International Labour Office, 1998.

Listín Diario, "Organización Denuncia el Turismo-Sexo Dominicano," 28 August 1996.

Lladó, Juan. "El Plan Nacional de Desarrollo Turístico." Presented at the *Conference X Convención Nacional y Exposición Comercial,* Santo Domingo, 25–28 September 1996.

Longo, Paulo Henrique. "The Pegação Program: Information, Prevention and Empowerment of Young Male Sex Workers." *Global Sex Workers*, ed. Kamala Kempadoo and Jo Doezema, 231–239. New York: Routledge, 1998.

López, Cecilia, and Abello, Alberto. *El Caribe Colombiano: Realidad Regional a Final del Siglo XX.* Santafé de Bogotá: Departamento Nacional de Planeación/Observatorio del Caribe Colombiano/Tercer Mundo Editores, 1998.

Lorde, Audre. *Sister Outsider: Essays and Speeches.* Trumansburg, N.Y.: Crossing Press, 1984.

Lowenthal, David. "Race and Colour in the West Indies." *Daedalus* 1.2 (1967): 580–626.

MacCannell, Dean. *The Tourist: A New Theory of the Leisure Class.* 2nd ed. New York: Shocken Books, 1989.

Macklin, C. L. "Global Garifuna: Negotiating Belizean-Garifuna Identity at Home and Abroad." *SPEAReports*, Vol. 9, 162–173. Belize City: SPEAR, 1993.

Macmillan, Terry. *How Stella Got Her Groove Back.* New York: Penguin, 1996.

Maingot, Anthony P. "The Offshore Caribbean." *Modern Caribbean Politics,* ed. Anthony Payne and Paul Sutton, 259–276. Kingston, Jamaica: Ian Randle Publishers, 1993.

Majors, Richard. "Cool Pose: The Proud Signature of Black Survival." *Changing Men: Issues in Gender, Sex, and Politics* 17 (1986): 5–16.

Manderson, Lenore, and Margaret Jolly. "Sites of Desire/Economies of Pleasure in Asia and the Pacific." *Sites of Desire, Economies of Pleasure: Sexualities in Asia and the Pacific,* 1–26. Chicago: University of Chicago Press, 1997.

Manier, Benedicta. "RD está entre Países de Turismo Sexual." *El Nacional,* 31 August 1996.

Margolis, Maxine. *Little Brazil: An Ethnography of Brazilian Immigrants in New York City.* Princeton: Princeton University Press, 1994.

Martin, U. C. H. "Hoe 'Campo Alegre' Ontstond." *Koperen Polyfonie* 24 (1984): 30–42.

Martin de Holan, Pablo, and Nelson Phillips. "Sun, Sand, and Hard Currency: Tourism in Cuba." *Annals of Tourism Research.* 2.4 (1997): 777–795.

Marx, Karl. *Grundrisse.* Harmondworth Eng.: Penguin, 1973.

Massiah, Joyceline. "Women's Lives and Livelihoods: A View from the Commonwealth Caribbean." *World Development* 17.7 (1989): 965–977.

_____. "Women in the Caribbean." Special issue of *Social and Economic Studies* 35 (1986): 2–3.

Maticka-Tyndale, E., D. Elkins, M. Haswell-Elkins, D. Rujkarakorn, T. Kuyyakanond, and K. Stam. "Contexts and Patterns of Men's Commercial Sexual Partnerships in Northeastern Thailand: Implications for AIDS Prevention." *Social Science Medicine* 44.2 (1997): 199–213.

Matos-Rodriguez, Felix V. "Street Vendors, Pedlars, Shop-Owners and Domestics: Some Aspects of Women's Economic Roles in Nineteenth-Century San Juan, Puerto Rico, 1820–1870." *Engendering History: Caribbean Women in Historical Perspective*, ed. Verene Shepherd, Bridget Brereton, and Barbara Bailey, 176–193. New York: St. Martins Press, 1995.

Matsui, Yayori. *Women's Asia.* London: Zed Press, 1989.

Matthews, Harry G. *International Tourism: A Political and Social Analysis.* Cambridge, Mass.: Schenkman Publishing Company, 1978.

Mayorga, Laura. "Life History Interviews of People Living in a Poor Urban Community in Santafé de Bogotá, 1996–1998." Unpublished paper, 1998.

McAfee, Kathy. *Storm Signals: Structural Adjustment and Development Alternatives in the Caribbean.* Boston: South End Press, 1991.

McClaurin, Irma. *Women of Belize: Gender and Change in Central America.* New Brunswick: Rutgers University Press, 1996.

McClintock, Anne. *Imperial Leather: Race, Gender and Sexuality in the Colonial Contest.* New York: Routledge, 1995.

McClintock, John M. "Sex and Tourism in Cuba." *Hemisphere* 5.1 (fall 1992): 27–28. Originally published in the *Baltimore Sun*, 12 July 1992.

Medische Zending. *Jaarverslag 1997.* Paramaribo: Medische Zending, 1998.

Mellon, Cynthia. "El sexo que trabaja...." *Utopías* 5 (August 1998): 41–43.

Mies, Maria. *Patriarchy and Accumulation on a World Scale: Women in the International Division of Labour.* London: Zed Books, 1986.

Miller, Daniel. *Modernity, An Ethnographic Approach: Dualism and Mass Consumption in Trinidad.* Oxford: Berg Publishers, 1994.

_____, ed. *Acknowledging Consumption: A Review of New Studies.* New York: Routledge, 1995

Ministry of Health. *Report of a Knowledge, Attitude, Behaviour and Practices Study among Female Commercial Sex Workers.* Unpublished report conducted as part of the evaluation of the USAID/AIDSCAP/Jamaica Project. Kingston, Jamaica, 1996.

Miolan, Angel. *Turismo: Nuestra Industria sin Chimeneas.* Santo Domingo: Editorial Letras de Quisqueya, 1994.

Moberg, Mark. *Myths of Ethnicity and Nation: Immigration, Work, and Identity in the Belize Banana Industry.* Knoxville: University of Tennessee Press, 1997.

Moitt, Bernard. "Slave Women and Resistance in the French Caribbean." *More Than Chattel: Black Women and Slavery in the Americas*, ed. David Barry Gaspar and Darlene Clark Hine, 239–258. Bloomington: Indiana University Press, 1996.

Momsen, Janet. "Tourism, Gender and Development in the Caribbean." *Tourism: A Gender Analysis*, ed. Vivian Kinnaird and Derek Hall, 106–120. New York: John Wiley & Sons, 1994.

Mondesire, Alicia, and Leith Dunn. *Towards Equity in Development: A Report on the Status of Women in Sixteen Commonwealth Caribbean Countries.* Georgetown, Guyana: Caribbean Community Secretariat, 1995.

Montgomery, Heather. "Children, Prostitution and Identity: A Case Study from a Tourist Resort in Thailand." *Global Sex Workers,* ed. Kamala Kempadoo and Jo Doezema, 139–150. New York: Routledge, 1998.

Morris-Jarra, Monica. "No Such Thing as a Cheap Holiday." *Tourism in Focus* 26 (autumn 1996): 6–7.

Morrissey, Marietta. *Slave Women in the New World: Gender Stratification in the Caribbean.* Lawrence: University Press of Kansas, 1989.

Mosquera, Claudia. *Estrategias de Inserción de la Población Negra en Santafé de Bogotá: Aca antes no se Veían Negros.* Bogotá: Observatorio de Cultura Urbana/Instituto Distrital de Cultura y Turismo, 1998.

_____. "Familias de Sectores Populares Cartageneros: Elementos para su Comprensión." *Las Familias de Hoy en Colombia,* ed. Presidencia de la República and Consejería Presidencial para la Política Social and Instituto Colombiano de Bienestar Familiar, 79–161. Bogotá: Presidencia de la República y Consejería Presidencial para la Política Social/Instituto Colombiano de Bienestar Familiar/Fondo de las Naciones Unidas para la Infancia, 1994.

Mowforth, Martin, and Ian Munt. *Tourism and Sustainability.* New York: Routledge, 1997.

Murray, Alison. "Debt-Bondage and Trafficking: Don't Believe the Hype." *Global Sex Workers,* ed. Kamala Kempadoo and Jo Doezema, 51–64. New York: Routledge, 1998.

Narváez, Farid, personal interview, Cartagena, October 1997.

Neal, Rodney H. "Globalization and Development: Challenges and Prospects for Agriculture." *SPEAReports,* Vol. 9, 32–40. Belize City: SPEAR, 1993.

OAS. *Economic Analysis of Tourism in Jamaica.* Unpublished technical report of the OAS in co-operation with the Jamaica Tourist Board and the Ministry of Industry, Tourism and Commerce. Washington, D.C.: Organization of American States, 1994.

Observer. "Hamilton Wants Formal Red Light Districts," 13 June 1998.

O'Carroll-Barahona, Claris, Juanita Altenberg, Dusilley Cannings, Christel Antonius-Smits, and Ruben Del Prado. *Needs Assessment Study among Street-Based Female Commercial Sex Workers in Paramaribo, Suriname.* Paramaribo: National AIDS Programme, Ministerie can Volksgezondheid, 1994.

O'Connell Davidson, Julia. *Prostitution, Power and Freedom.* Cambridge: Polity Press, 1998.

_____. "Sex Tourism in Cuba," *Race & Class* 38 (July/September 1996): 39–48.

O'Connell Davidson, Julia, and Jacqueline Sanchez Taylor. "Child Prostitution and Sex Tourism: Cuba." Bangkok: ECPAT, 1996.

_____. "Child Prostitution and Sex Tourism: The Dominican Republic." Bangkok: ECPAT, 1996.

One World News Service, "Britain Joins the Campaign against Child Sex Tourism," 25 July 1996, http://www.oneworld.org/newws/reports/jul96-children.html

Ong, Aihwa. "The Gender and Labor Politics of Postmodernity." *Annual Review of Anthropology* 20 (1991): 279–309.

Oppermann, Martin, ed. *Sex Tourism and Prostitution: Aspects of Leisure, Recreation and Work.* Elmsford, N.Y.: Cognizant Communications, 1998.

Orozco, Iván, and Gómez Juan Gabriel. *Los Peligros del Nuevo Constitucionalismo en Materia Criminal.* Santafé de Bogotá: Ministerio de Justicia/Instituto de Estudios Políticos y Relaciones Internacionales, 1997.

Padilla, Nelson, and Andrea Varela. "Nuestra Ruanda." *Cambio* 16. 12 May 1997: 204.

Paez, Sandra. "Busca Cuba Atraer Capitales Extranjeros e Incentuar su Comercio." Panamá: NTX, 31 January 1999.

Palacio, Joseph. "What Rural People Are Saying about Rural Community Development" *SPEAReports* Vol. 8. Mexico: Cubola Productions, 1992.

Palacio, Myrtle. "A Social Profile of Belize City." *SPEAReports* Vol. 6. Mexico: Cubola Productions, 1990.

Palmer, Catherine A. "Tourism and Colonialism: The Experience of the Bahamas." *Annals of Tourism Research* 21.4 (1994): 792–811.

Pareja, Reynaldo, and Santo Rosario. *Sexo, Trabajo, Sida, y Sociedad.* Santo Domingo: Imprenta "La Unión," 1992.

Passell, Peter. "Forbidden Sun and Sin, Communist Style." *New York Times Magazine,* 7 November 1993, 66–67.

Pattullo, Polly. *Last Resorts: The Cost of Tourism in the Caribbean.* Kingston, Jamaica: Ian Randle, 1996.

Paul, Amy Raquel. *"It Isn't Love, It's Business": Prostitution as Entrepreneurship and the Implications for Barbados.* Ph.D. Diss. University of California, Los Angeles, 1997.

Peake, Linda, and Alissa D. Trotz. *Gender, Place and Ethnicity: Women and Identities in Guyana.* London: Routledge, 1999.

Pérez Duval, Marisela, and Carmen Julia Gómez. "La Desigualadad de Género en la República Dominicana." Paper presented at the conference *La República Dominicana en el Umbral del Siglo XXI, Pontificia Universidad Católica Madre y Maestro,* Santo Domingo, 24–26 July 1997.

Perio, Gaelle, and Dominique Thierry. *Tourisme Sexuel au Bresil et en Colombie.* Rapport D'Enquete. TOURCOING, 1996.

Pettman, Jan Jindy. "Body Politics: International Sex Tourism" *Third World Quarterly* 18.1 (1997): 93–108.

Pheterson, Gail. *The Prostitution Prism.* Amsterdam: Amsterdam University Press, 1996.

_____. "The Whore Stigma: Female Dishonour and Male Unworthiness." *The Prostitution Prism,* 37–64. Amsterdam: Amsterdam University Press, 1996.

Phillips, Joan, and Graham Dann. "Bar Girls in Central Bangkok: Prostitution as Entrepreneurship." *Sex Tourism and Prostitution: Aspects of Leisure, Recreation, and Work,* ed. Martin Oppermann, 60–70. New York: Cognizant Communications, 1998.

PIOJ. *Economic and Social Survey of Jamaica 1993.* Kingston: Planning Institute of Jamaica, 1994.

_____. *Economic and Social Survey of Jamaica 1995.* Kingston: Planning Institute of Jamaica, 1996.

Pivar, David J. "The Military, Prostitution and Colonial Peoples: India and the Philippines, 1885–1917." *The Journal of Sex Research* 17.3 (1981): 256–267.

Plachy, Sylvia, and James Ridgeway. *Red Light: Inside the Sex Industry.* New York: PowerHouse Books, 1996.

Plumridge, Elizabeth, and Jane Chetwynd. "Discourses of Emotionality in Commercial Sex." *Feminism & Psychology* 7.2 (1997): 165–181.

Policía Nacional. *Instrucciones para Educar y Prevenir la Prostitución Infantil.* Santafé de Bogotá, 1996.

Policía Nacional, Departamento de Bolívar. *Reportes de abril, junio y julio de 1996.* Cartagena, 1996.

Poon, Auliana. "Competitive Strategies for a 'New Tourism.'" *Progress in Tourism, Recreation and Hospitality Management*, ed. C. Cooper, 91–102. London: Belhaven Press, 1989.

_____. "Flexible Specialization and Small Size: The Case of Caribbean Tourism." *World Development* 18.1 (1990): 109–123.

Press, Clayton M., Jr. "Reputation and Respectability Reconsidered: Hustling in a Tourist Setting." *Caribbean Issues* 4 (1978): 109–119.

Previda, Eduardo Klinger. "El Impacto Económico del Turismo en República Dominicana." Paper presented at the conference *X Convención Nacional y Exposición Comercial*, Santo Domingo, 25–28 September 1996.

"Prostitutie op Aruba." Paper presented to the Bonaire conference on prostitution, 1978. Photocopied.

Pruitt, Deborah J. "'Foreign Mind': Tourism, Identity and Development in Jamaica." Ph.D. Diss. University of California, Berkeley. 1993.

Pruitt, Deborah, and Suzanne LaFont. "For Love and Money: Romance Tourism in Jamaica." *Annals of Tourism Research* 22.2 (1995): 422–440.

Pryce, Ken. *Endless Pressure.* Harmondsworth: Penguin, 1979.

Raffaelli, M., R. Campos, A. Merritt, E. Siqueira, C. Antunes, R. Parker, M. Greco, D. Greco, N. Halsey, and the Street Youth Study Group. "Sexual Practices and Attitudes of Street Youth in Belo Horizonte, Brazil." *Social Science Medicine* 37.5 (1993): 661–670.

Ramírez, Sergio. "Dónde están los Pobres?" *Cambio* 16. 27 July 1998.

Reanda, Laura. "Prostitution as a Human Rights Question, Problems and Prospects of United Nations Action." *Human Rights Quarterly* 13 (1991): 209–211

Reddock, Rhoda. *Women, Labour and Politics in Trinidad and Tobago.* London: Zed Press, 1994.

Renacer. *Programa de Rehabilitación y Reinserción Social Dirigido a Menores Vinculados a la Prostitución.* Cartagena, 1997.

Report by the Steering Committee of St. Maarten to the Bonaire conference on prostitution, 1978. Photocopied.

Reuters, "Cuba Sees 1.7 Million Tourists in '99, a 21% Rise," 13 January 1999, http://www.cubanet.org/CNews/y99/jan99/13el.htm

Richardson, Bonham C. *The Caribbean in the Wider World, 1492–1992.* Cambridge: Cambridge University Press, 1992.

Richter, Linda. *The Politics of Tourism in Asia.* Honolulu: University of Hawaii Press, 1989.

Riley, Ingrid. "Prostitutes Raking in Big Bucks," *The Jamaica Observer*, 21–23 January 1994.

Roberston, Claire. "Africa into the Americas? Slavery and Women, the Family and the Gender Division of Labor." *More Than Chattel: Black Women and Slavery in the Americas*, ed. David Barry Gaspar and Darlene Clark Hine, 3–42. Bloomington: Indiana University Press, 1996.

Rodríguez, Iraida Calzadilla. "Turismo Crecio," *Granma*, 5 January 1999.

Rodríguez, Kelly, personal interview, Cartagena, October 1997.

Roopnaraine, Terence. "Freighted Fortunes." Ph.D. Diss. University of Cambridge, 1997.

Rousseau, G. S., and Roy Porter, eds. *Exoticism in the Enlightenment.* Manchester: Manchester University Press, 1990.

Sacks, Valerie. "Women and AIDS: An Analysis of Media Representations." *Social Science Medicine* 42.1 (1996): 59–75.

Safa, Helen I. *The Myth of the Male Breadwinner: Women and Industrialization in the Caribbean.* Boulder, Colo.: Westview Press, 1995.

Said, Edward. *Orientalism.* New York: Vintage Books, 1979.

Sanchez Taylor, Jacqueline. "Marking the Margins: Research in the Informal Economy in Cuba and the Dominican Republic." Discussion Paper No. S97/1, Department of Sociology, University of Leicester, 1997.

Saunders, Alphea. "Should J'ca Decriminalise Prostitution?... Local Leaders Respond," *The Herald*, 21 June 1998.

Schalkwijk, Martin. *De Situatie in de Dorpen aan de Boven-Suriname Rivier.* Paramaribo: De Surinaamse Zendings Vliegdienst, 1996.

Schwartz, Rosalie. *Pleasure Island: Tourism and Temptation in Cuba.* Lincoln: University of Nebraska Press, 1997.

Scott, James. *The Moral Economy of the Peasant: Rebellion and Subsistence in South-East Asia.* New Haven, Conn.: Yale University Press, 1976.

Seabrook, Jeremy. *Travels in the Skin Trade: Tourism and the Sex Industry.* London: Pluto Press, 1997.

Secretaría de Estado de Turismo. *Turismo en Cifras, 1980–1996.* Santo Domingo, 1996.

Segal, Danial A. "'Race' and 'Colour' in Pre-Independence Trinidad and Tobago." *Trinidad Ethnicity,* ed. Kevin Yelvington. Knoxville: University of Tennessee Press, 1993.

Senior, Olive. *Working Miracles: Women's Lives in the English-Speaking Caribbean,* London: James Currey, Bloomington: Indiana University Press, 1991.

Señor, Luis. *Código Penal Dominicano Anotado 1865–1985.* Empresión Editoria Unión, 1989.

Shoman, Assad. *Thirteen Chapters of a History of Belize.* Belize City: Angelus Press, 1994.

Shrage, Laurie. *Moral Dilemmas of Feminism.* London: Routledge, 1994.

Silié, Rubén, and Manuel Colón. "Ajuste Estructural y Modelo Neoliberal en República Dominicana." *Los Pequeños Países de América Latina en la Hora Neoliberal,* ed. Gerónimo de Sierra. Mexico: Editorial Nueva Sociedad, 1994.

Silvestre, Emmanuel, Jaime Rijo, and Humberto Bogaert. *La Neoprostitución Infantil en República Dominicana.* Dominican Republic: UNICEF, 1994.

Simmons, Alan B., and Jean Pierre Guengant. "Caribbean Exodus and the World System." *International Migrations Systems: A Global Perspective,* ed. M. Kritz et al., 94–114. Oxford: Clarendon Press, 1992.

Simon, Francoise. "Tourism Development in Transition Economies: The Cuba Case." *Columbia Journal of World Business* 30.1 (1995): 26–39.

Sittirak, Sinith. *Daughters of Development: Women in a Changing Environment.* London: Zed Books, 1998.

Smith, Raymond T. "Hierarchy and the Dual Marriage System in West Indian Society." *The Matrifocal Family: Power, Pluralism and Politics,* Raymond T. Smith, 59–80. New York: Routledge, 1996. First published in 1987.

_____. *The Matrifocal Family: Power, Pluralism and Politics.* ed. London: Routledge, 1996.

SMLA/NAP. *Het Leven Van Maxi Linder, Suriname's Meest Gevierde Commerciele Sexworker in de 20ste Eeuw.* Paramaribo: Stichting Maxi Linder Associatie in Samenwerking met het Nationaal AIDS Programma, 1994.

Sparr, Pamela, ed. *Mortgaging Women's Lives: Feminist Critiques of Structural Adjustment.* London: Zed Books, 1994.

_____. "What Is Structural Adjustment?" *Mortgaging Women's Lives: Feminist Critiques of Structural Adjustment,* ed. Pamela Sparr, 1–12. London: Zed Books, 1994.

SPEAR. *SPEAReports.* Vol. 9, *Globalization and Development: Challenges and Prospects for Belize.* Belize: SPEAR, 1993.

STATIN: *Jamaica Labour Force Survey 1992.* The Statistical Institute of Jamaica, 1993.

_____. *The Labour Force 1996.* Kingston: The Statistical Institute of Jamaica, 1997.

Stoller, Robert. *Perversion: The Erotic Form of Hatred.* London: Karnac, 1986.

Streicker, Joel. "Remaking Race, Class, and Region in Tourist Town." *Identities* 3–4 (1997): 523–555.

_____. *Sentiment and Self-Interest: Constructing Class and Gender Identities in Cartagena.* Ph.D. Diss. Stanford University, 1992.

_____. "Sexuality, Power and Social Order in Cartagena." *Ethnology* 32 (1993): 359–374.

_____. "Spatial Reconfigurations, Imagined Geographies, and Social Conflicts in Cartagena." *Cultural Anthropology* 12 (1997): 109–128.

Strout, Jan. "Women, the Politics of Sexuality, and Cuba's Economic Crisis." *Cuba Update* (April/June 1995): 15–18. Also published in *Socialist Review* 25.1 (1995): 5–15.

Sturdevant, Saundra, and Brenda Stolzfus. *Let the Good Times Roll: Prostitution and the U.S. Military in Asia.* New York: The New Press, 1992.

Sunday Observer, "A Teenage Prostitute Tells Her Story," 24 March 1996.

Superclubs, "Hedonism II Promotional Brochure," n.d.

Swift, Anthony. "Let Us Work!" *New Internationalist.* July 1997.

Tadiar, Neferti Xina M. "Sexual Economies in the Asia-Pacific Community." *What Is in a Rim? Critical Perspectives on the Pacific Region Idea,* ed. Arif Dirlik, 183–210. Boulder, Colo.: Westview Press, 1993.

Tannahill, Ray. *Sex in History.* New York: Scarborough House, 1992.

Tauli-Corpuz, Victoria. "The Globalisation of Mining and Its Impact and Challenges for Women." *Third World Resurgence* 93 (January 1997).

Taveras, Luis L. "Desarrollo y Perspectivas del Turismo Dominicano." Discurso pronunciado por el Secretario de Estado de Turismo, Santo Domingo, 21 July 1993.

Tena, Gerardo. "Turismo: Un Arma de Doble Filo para la Cuba Comunista." Havana: AFP. 6 November 1998

Terborg, Julia. *AIDS en Prostitutie: Deelonderzoek I: Geregistreerde Prostituees.* Paramaribo: National AIDS Program, Ministerie Van Volsgezondheid, 1990.

_____. *AIDS en Prostitutie: Deelonderzoek I: Onderzoek onder geregistreerd prostituees.* Report. Paramaribo: National AIDS Program, 1990a.

_____. *AIDS en Prostitutie: Deelonderzoek II: Onderzoek onder mannelijke klanten van de dermatologische dienst.* Report. Paramaribo: Nationala AIDS Programma, Report, 1990.

Tour and Travel News, "New CRC Gives Hoteliers Choice of Res Systems," T6–7 (1990).

Travel Industry World Yearbook 40, 1996–7, New York: Child and Waters Inc. 1997: 76–86.

Trotz, Alissa D. "Guardians of Our Homes, Guards of Yours? Economic Crisis, Gender Stereotyping and the Restructuring of the Private Security Industry in Georgetown, Guyana." *Caribbean Portraits: Essays on Gender Ideologies and Identities,* ed. Christine Barrow, 28–54. Kingston: Ian Randle Publishers, 1998.

Truong, Than Dam. "Serving the Tourist Market: Female Labor in International Tourism." *Feminism and Sexuality: A Reader,* ed. S. Jackson and S. Scott, 373–378. New York: Columbia University Press, 1996.

_____. *Sex, Money and Morality: The Political Economy of Prostitution and Tourism in South East Asia.* London: Zed Books, 1990.

Turner, Louis, and John Ash. *The Golden Hordes: International Tourism and the Pleasure Periphery.* New York: St. Martin's Press, 1976.

UFTAA, "Child and Travel Agents Charter," 2 February 1998, http://www.world-tourism-org/sextouri/uftaa-a.htm

Urry, John. *Consuming Places.* New York: Routledge, 1995.

_____. *The Tourist Gaze: Leisure and Travel in Contemporary Societies.* London: Sage, 1990.

Valentino, Margaret, and Mavis Johnson. "On the Game and on the Move." *Prostitutes, Our Life,* ed. Claude Jaget. Bristol, U.K.: Falling Wall Press, 1980.

Valiente, Carmen, personal interview, Cartagena, October 1997.

van Ammelrooy, Anneke. *Vrouwenhandel: De Internationale Seksslavinnenmarkt.* s'Gravenhage: BZZTôH, 1989.

Van Wijk, Karina, and Isabel G. Barboza. "Costa Rica: Sharing the Health Concerns of Women Working in Prostitution." *Women at Risk: Revealing the Hidden Health Burden of Women Workers.* Santiago, Chile: LACWHN, 1990.

Vanwesenbeeck, Ine. *Prostitutes' Well-Being and Risk.* Amsterdam: VU University Press, 1994.

Varela, Carlos. *Carlos Varela en Vivo,* Artex CD #074, Canada: Artex S.A., 1993.

Velandia, Manuel. *En la Jugada: Una Experiencia del Consumo de Sustancias Psicoactivas y de la Infección por HIV/SIDA, a Partir de la Construcción de la Identidad Particular y del Redescubrimiento del Propio Cuerpo, en Menores Vinculados a la Prostitución.* Santafé de Bogotá: Naciones Unidas/Programa Japonés de Prevención de la Drogadicción/Fundación Apoyémonos, 1996.

Vélez, Carlos. *Gasto Social y Desigualdad: Logros y Extravíos.* Santafé de Bogotá: Departamento Nacional de Planeación, 1995.

Vélez, Jaime, personal interview, Cartagena, October 1997.

Villamizar, Carlos, personal interview, Cartagena, October 1997.

Wade, Peter. *Gente Negra: Nación Mestiza: Dinámicas de las Identidades Raciales en Colombia.* Santafé de Bogotá: Universidad de Antioquía/Instituto Colombiano de Antropología/Siglo del Hombre Editores/Ediciones Uniandes, 1997.

Wagner, Ulla. "Out of Time and Place: Mass Tourism and Charter." *Ethnos* 42 (1977): 38–52.

Walkowitz, Judith R. *Prostitution and Victorian Society: Women, Class and the State.* Cambridge: Cambridge University Press, 1980.

Walvin, James. "Selling the Sun: Tourism and Material Consumption." *Revista/Review Interamericana* 22.1–1 (summer 1992): 208–225.

Watson, Hilbourne A., ed. *The Caribbean in the Global Political Economy.* Boulder, Colo.: Lynne Rienner Publishers, 1994.

———. "Caribbean Options under Global Neoliberalism." *The Caribbean: New Dynamics in Trade and Political Economy,* ed. A. T. Bryan, 165–206. Boulder, Colo.: Lynne Rienner Publishers, 1995.

———. "Recent Attempts at Industrial Restructuring in Barbados." *Latin American Perspectives* 17.1 (1990): 10–32.

Wekker, Gloria. *Ik Ben Een Gouden Munt: Subjectiviteit en Seksualiteit van Creoolse Volksklasse Vrouwen in Paramaribo.* Amsterdam: VITA, 1994.

WHO. *AIDS—Images of the Epidemic.* Geneva: World Health Organization, 1994.

Wignall, Mark, "Prostitution: Whose Pleasure, Whose Purgatory?" *Daily Observer,* 22 June 1998, 8.

Wijers, Marjan, and Lin Lap-Chew. *Trafficking in Women, Forced Labor and Slavery-like Practices in Marriage, Domestic Labor and Prostitution.* Utrecht: STV, 1997.

Wilkinson, Bert. "Guyana-Environment: Cyanide Leak Is Country's Worst Disaster," IPS New Service, 25 August 1995.

Wilkinson, Paul F. *Tourism Policy and Planning: Case Studies from the Commonwealth Caribbean.* Elmsford, N.Y.: Cognizant Communications, 1997.

Wilson, Peter. "Reputation and Respectability: A Suggestion for Caribbean Ethnology." *Man* 4.1 (1969): 70–84.

Witter, Michael, ed. "Higglering/Sidewalk Vending/Informal Commercial Trading in the Jamaican Economy: Proceedings of a Symposium." Mona, Jamaica: University of the West Indies, Department of Economics. Occasional Paper No.4, 1989.

Wolf, Diane L. 'Situating Feminist Dilemmas in Fieldwork." *Feminist Dilemmas in Fieldwork,* ed. Diane L. Wolf, 1–55. Boulder, Colo.: Westview Press, 1996.

Wolf, Naomi. "The Making of a Slut." *Ms.,* March/April 1997, 44–48.

Women's Action 12.1, December 1996.

World Bank. *Jamaica: A Strategy for Growth and Poverty Reduction,* Country Economic Memorandum. Washingtonm D.C.: The World Bank, 1994.

World Nightlife Guide for Women, "Sex Travel Information Service: A Travel Guide for Men," http://www.sex-adventures.com/world.htm

World Sex Guide, Information on Jamaica, 6 May 1997, http://www.paranoia.com/faq/prostitution/Negril.txt.html.

WTO News, "Child Prostitution and Tourism Watch," 2 February 1998d, http://www.world-tourism-org/tourism.org/sextouri/intro.htm#purpose

———, "Campaign Launched against Child Sex Tourism," May 1997.

———, "Frequently Asked Questions," 20 March 1998b, http://www.world-tourism-org/faq/faq.htm

———, WTO, "What We Offer." 11 October 1998a, http://www.world-tourism-org/offer.htm#Mission

———, "WTO Commission for America (CAM)," 20 March 1998c, http://www.world-tourism-org/memstate/americas.htm

———, November–December 1995.

_____, "Brasilia Charter Condemns Sex Tourism," May–June 1996.

WTTC Travel and Tourism Research Report 1996/1997, http://www.wttc.org/WTTC-GATE.NSF/965b67eb651768af002564df003be712/6f9dbfb1ca173e8b002565ef004231b2?OpenDocument

Young, Lola. *Fear of the Dark: 'Race,' Gender and Sexuality in the Cinema*. London: Routledge, 1996.

Young, Robert. *Colonial Desire: Hybridity in Theory, Culture and Race*. New York: Routledge, 1995.

Index

About the Editor and Contributors

Christel Antonius-Smits is assistant head of the department of public health of the Faculty of Medical Sciences at the Anton de Kom University of Suriname.

Amalia L. Cabezas obtained a Ph.D in ethnic studies from the University of California, Berkeley. She is author of "Discourses of Prostitution: The Case of Cuba" in *Global Sex Workers*.

Shirley Campbell is academic director of the Jamaica College Semester Abroad Program: Gender and Development, which is sponsored by the School for International Training, Vermont.

Nadine Fernandez is an assistant professor of anthropology in the sociology/anthropology department at Florida International University, Miami. Her research on Cuba addresses issues of race, gender, interracial couples, and the social impact of tourism.

Ranya Ghuma is a master of arts candidate in the arab studies program at the Center for Contemporary Arab Studies, Georgetown University, Washington, D.C. Her research interests include human rights, refugee rights, and women and minority issues in the countries of the Middle East and North Africa.

Kamala Kempadoo is a sociologist and assistant professor in the Women's Studies Program at the University of Colorado, Boulder. She started research on sexual labor and the global sex trade in the late 1980s. She is also editor and co-author of *Global Sex Workers: Rights, Resistance and Redefinition*.

Jacqueline Martis is a sociologist and works for the Central Bureau of Statistics for the Netherlands Antilles as senior health statistician. She has also done research on violence against women and drug-related issues. She is a member of CAFRA (the Caribbean Association for Feminist Research and Action).

Laura Mayorga is a Ph.D. candidate in psychology at the University of California, Berkeley. Her dissertation is about how poor parents in Bogotá, Colombia, raise their children in the context of economic strain.

Cynthia Mellon was coordinator of the Gender and Power program at the Instituto Latinoamericano de Servicios Legales Alternativos (ILSA) in Bogotá, Colombia, during the time these studies took place. She is a member of the steering committee of the Working Group on Women and the Economy and is dedicated to achieving women's economic rights.

Patricia Mohammed is head of the Gender and Development Studies department, University of the West Indies, Mona, Jamaica. She has published extensively in the field of gender studies and is editor of the special issue of *Feminist Review*, "Rethinking Caribbean Difference."

Beverley Mullings is assistant professor in the department of geography at Syracuse University. She has published a number of articles on the gender impacts of industrial restructuring in the Caribbean.

Julia O'Connell Davidson is a reader in sociology at the University of Leicester. She started research on prostitution in Britain in 1993. She is author of *Prostitution, Power and Freedom*.

Althea Perkins worked as a research assistant in Gender and Development Studies at the University of the West Indies, Mona, Jamaica. At present she is a lecturer at Browns Town Community College, Jamaica.

Joan Phillips is a Ph.D. candidate at the University of Luton, England. Her main research interest is sex tourism in Southeast Asia and the Caribbean. She is co-author of "Bar-Girls in Central Bangkok: Prostitution as Entrepreneurship," in *Sex Tourism and Prostitution*.

A. Kathleen Ragsdale is a Ph.D. candidate with the department of anthropology, University of Florida, Gainesville. Her research interests incorporate principles of applied and visual anthropology to focus on issues of gender relations that impact women's lives in an increasingly globalized world system.

Red Thread Women's Development Programme, in existence for over ten years, is a Guyanese women's organization engaged in community education, research, and other activities, aimed at improving the material well-being of women.

Jacqueline Sanchez Taylor has been researching sex tourism since 1995 and is currently working on an Economic and Social Research Council–funded project on prostitution in the Dominican Republic and Jamaica. She is a research associate in the department of sociology, University of Leicester, England.

Jessica Tomiko Anders is a master's candidate with the department of anthropology, University of Florida, Gainesville. She specializes in the study of identity formation as it relates to the creation of sociopolitical movements.

Pilar Velásquez is currently completing research for a project on political culture and voting behavior in Bogotá, Colombia, at the Luis Carlos Galán Institute for the Development of Democracy. Her scholarly interests include women's political participation and political parties.